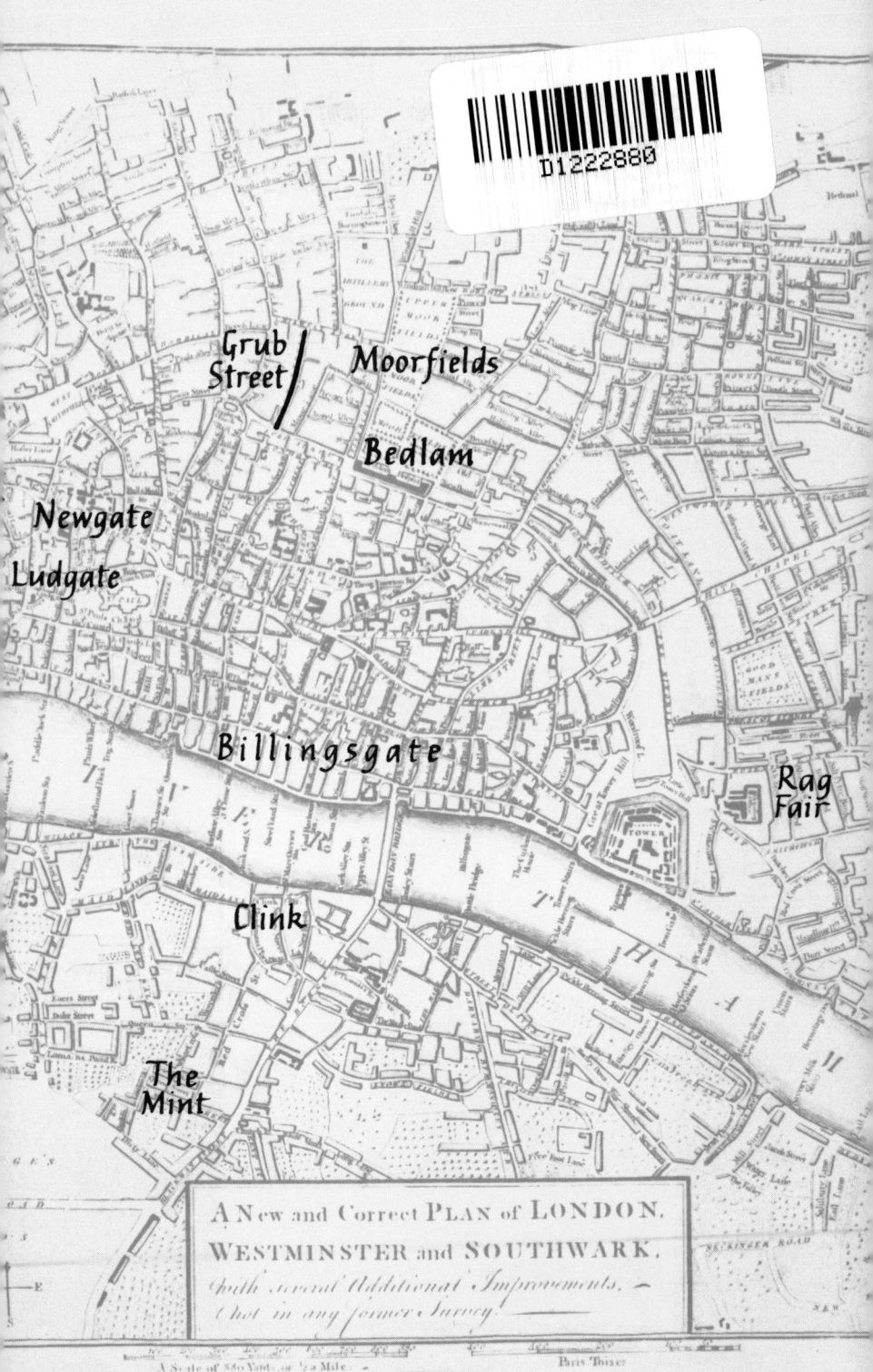

Grub
Street

Moorfields

Bedlam

Newgate

Ludgate

Billingsgate

Rag
Fair

Clink

The
Mint

A New and Correct PLAN of LONDON,
WESTMINSTER and SOUTHWARK,
With several Additional Improvements,
Not in any former Survey.

A Scale of 880 Yards, or ½ a Mile

GRUB STREET

Studies in a Subculture

Drawn and Etched by J.T.Smith.   Drawn in July 1791.

DOMESTIC ARCHITECTURE.
NORTH EAST VIEW OF AN OLD HOUSE LATELY STANDING IN SWEEDON'S PASSAGE, GRUB STREET.

GRUB STREET

Studies in a Subculture

PAT ROGERS

'Grubstreet, the name of a street in London, once
inhabited by persons who wrote for hire,
hence used for a paltry composition.'

Nathaniel Bailey and others,
A Universal Etymological Dictionary

METHUEN & CO LTD

London

First published in 1972 by
Methuen & Co Ltd
11 New Fetter Lane, London EC4
© 1972 Pat Rogers
Printed in Great Britain
by W & J Mackay Limited, Chatham
SBN 416 11690 6

Distributed in the USA by
HARPER & ROW PUBLISHERS, INC.
BARNES & NOBLE IMPORT DIVISION

Contents

CONTENTS

Illustrations

'Domestic Architecture. North east view of an old house lately standing in Sweedon's Passage, Grub Street'. Drawn and etched by J. T. Smith, July 1791.   *frontispiece*

'A New and Correct Plan of London, Westminster and Southwark'. Made for J and R Dodsley between 1756 and 1761 and included in *London and Its Environs Described*, 1761.

front endpaper

Map of 'Creplegate Ward'. From p. 70 of John Strype's edition of Stow's *Survey of London*, 1720.   *back endpaper*

Preface

This book is an expanded version of an essay which was awarded the Le Bas Prize at Cambridge University in 1969. To that composition, which was entitled 'Grub Street: an historical essay', I have added a good deal of supplementary evidence and documentation. However, its gravamen survives intact. In both cases I have sought to show how the Augustan satirists built upon the facts of contemporary life. Their metaphors, their narrative ploys, their *mise-en-scène*, their casting procedure, can all be related to particular social circumstance – for example, the choice of Moorfields as a venue for duncely exploits brings with it quite explicit associations of crime, poverty, martial ardour, sexual misbehaviour, low literary commerce and much else. This general case is, I hope, confirmed by the reading of *The Dunciad* in its revised form as an epic of Grub Street *eo nomine*, the contention of my first chapter (although it is not *dependent* on the rightness of that conjecture, for any cogency it may have).

The process of transformation has proved long and laborious. It could not have been achieved without the patience and support of Methuen & Co, and especially Patrick Taylor. Publishers are inured to waiting, and academic authors prone to make them wait. None the less, my gratitude is more than token.

In view of the contemporary fashion for 'environmental' studies, it may be worth recording that the section on the ecology of Dulness in the Introduction was written at the end of 1967 and beginning of 1968. I had considered omitting the section; but on second thoughts, this seemed an undue deference to modishness. I have therefore let it stand.

Stock, Essex   P.R.

Acknowledgements

Most of the work for this book has been undertaken in the Guildhall Library, the Corporation of London Records Office, the Greater London Council Records Office, Westminster Library, the Public Record Office, the British Museum Library and Cambridge University Library. I am grateful to archivists and librarians who have allowed me access to their collections.

The best way to understand an age, of course, is to read its own books and journals, to look at its own paintings and engravings. But to limit oneself to contemporary sources, when modern scholarship can add so much by way of instruction and delight, is to eat acorn with the swine. Among published writings, the work of these authorities has left me hugely in their debt: Dorothy George, Dorothy Marshall, J. H. Plumb, Sir Leon Radzinowicz, George Rudé, James Sutherland and the late Sir William Holdsworth. Earlier generations of topographical writers, ranging from Strype, Maitland and Malcolm to H. B. Wheatley and Sir Walter Besant, have provided indispensable aid. Nor have I disdained the vast library of popular books on London: the works of E. B. Chancellor furnished a range of usually reliable (if not precisely scholarly) information. Like other commentators on the Plague and the Great Fire, I have found the studies of W. G. Bell still unsupplanted as comprehensive accounts of their subject. Finally, I have relied heavily on the mapmakers of London, especially those of the late seventeenth and early eighteenth centuries. The modern *Survey of London* is alas uncompleted, but the extant volumes in this series, along with certain publications of the London Topographical Society, have always been at hand to consult as informants of the last resort. For a general presentation of the city at the time, Ogilby, Morden and Lea, and Rocque survive without serious challenge from any modern reconstructions.

ACKNOWLEDGEMENTS

When I began on this book, I was lucky to receive the encouragement of Ian Jack, Denis Donoghue and George Watson, whose own distinguished achievements were a stimulus in themselves. Ian Watt kindly read an early draft of the opening sections and made shrewd but charitable criticisms. None of these gentlemen is to be held accountable for the errors and imperfections of the book which has actually emerged.

I have indicated my indebtedness by a specific reference in the footnotes wherever possible. But my enthusiasm for the world delineated in this book was a contagion early succumbed to; and I cannot be sure that I have not on occasions borrowed ideas or emphases unwittingly from previous students of the age.

Abbreviations

Short forms and cue titles are employed for the most frequently consulted printed sources, as follows:

Arbuthnot.   G. A. Aitken, *The Life and Works of John Arbuthnot* (Oxford, 1892).

Baddeley.   J. J. Baddeley, *An Account of the Church and Parish of St Giles, without Cripplegate* (London, 1888).

Bayne-Powell.   Rosamond Bayne-Powell, *Eighteenth-Century London Life* (London, 1937).

Besant.   Sir Walter Besant, *London in the Eighteenth Century* (London, ed. 1925).

Butt.   *The Poems of Alexander Pope*, ed. J. Butt (London, 1963).

Calendar.   *The Newgate Calendar*, ed. G. T. Wilkinson (London, ed. 1963).

Clifford.   J. L. Clifford, *Young Samuel Johnson* (London, 1962).

Cross.   W. L. Cross, *The History of Henry Fielding* (New Haven, 1918).

Defoe, *Letters.*   *The Letters of Daniel Defoe*, ed. G. H. Healey (Oxford, 1955).

Defoe, *Tour.*   Daniel Defoe, *A Tour thro' the Whole Island of Great Britain*, ed. G. D. H. Cole (London, 1927).

Denton.   W. Denton, *Records of St Giles' Cripplegate* (London, 1883).

E/C.   *The Works of Alexander Pope*, ed. W. Elwin, W. J. Courthope (London, 1872–89).

Ehrenpreis.   Irvin Ehrenpreis, *Swift: The Man, the Works and the Age* (London, 1962–).

Faber.	*The Poetical Works of John Gay*, ed. G. C. Faber (London, 1926).
Fielding.	*The Complete Works of Henry Fielding*, ed. W. E. Henley (New York, ed. 1967).
George.	M. Dorothy George, *London Life in the Eighteenth Century* (Harmondsworth, 1966).
Gomme.	*Topographic History of London*, ed. G. L. Gomme (London, 1904).
Harben.	Henry Harben, *A Dictionary of London* (London, 1918).
Holdsworth.	Sir William Holdsworth, *A History of English Law* (London, 1922–38).
Irving.	W. H. Irving, *John Gay's London* (Cambridge, Mass., 1928).
Journal.	Jonathan Swift, *Journal to Stella*, ed. H. Williams (Oxford, 1948).
Lee.	William Lee, *Daniel Defoe : His Life and Recently Discovered Writings* (London, 1869).
London Past & Present.	H. B. Wheatley, P. Cunningham, *London Past and Present* (London, 1891).
Maitland.	William Maitland, *The History and Survey of London* (London, 1756).
Malcolm.	J. P. Malcolm, *Anecdotes of London, during the Eighteenth Century* (London, 1810).
Marshall.	Dorothy Marshall, *Dr Johnson's London* (New York, 1968).
Moore, *Checklist.*	J. R. Moore, *A Checklist of the Writings of Daniel Defoe* (Bloomington, 1960).
Moore, *Citizen.*	J. R. Moore, *Daniel Defoe Citizen of the Modern World* (Chicago, 1958).
New Remarks.	*New Remarks of London . . . Collected by the Company of Parish-Clerks* (London, 1732).
Oldmixon.	John Oldmixon, *The History of England* (London, 1735).
Paulson.	*Hogarth's Graphic Works*, ed. R. Paulson (New Haven, 1965).

Pope, *Correspondence.*	*The Correspondence of Alexander Pope*, ed. G. Sherburn (Oxford, 1956).
Pope, *Prose Works.*	*The Prose Works of Alexander Pope*, ed. N. Ault (Oxford, 1936), Vol. I (all published).
Radzinowicz.	Leon Radzinowicz, *A History of English Criminal Law* (London, 1948–).
Romances and Narratives.	*Romances and Narratives by Daniel Defoe*, ed. G. A. Aitken (London, 1895).
Sherburn.	George Sherburn, *The Early Career of Alexander Pope* (Oxford, 1934).
Society.	*Memoirs of the Society of Grub-Street* (London, 1737).
Steeves.	Pope, *The Art of Sinking in Poetry*, ed. E. L. Steeves (New York, 1952).
State Trials.	*State Trials*, ed. T. B. Howell (London, 1812).
Stow.	John Stow, *The Survey of London* (London, ed. 1633).
Straus.	Ralph Straus, *The Unspeakable Curll* (London, 1927).
Strype.	John Strype's edn of Stow's *Survey of London* (London, 1720).
Sutherland.	James Sutherland, *Defoe* (London, ed. 1950).
Swift, *Prose Works.*	*The Prose Works of Jonathan Swift*, ed. H. Davis et. al. (Oxford, 1939–68).
Swift, *Correspondence.*	*The Correspondence of Jonathan Swift*, ed. H. Williams (Oxford, 1963–5).
Swift, *Poems.*	Swift, *Poetical Works*, ed. H. Davis (London, 1967).
Tale.	Swift, *A Tale of a Tub* [etc.], ed. A. C. Guthkelch, D. Nichol Smith (Oxford, ed. 1958).
Thornbury.	Walter Thornbury, *Old and New London* (London, nd.).
TE.	The Twickenham edition of *The Poems of Alexander Pope*, ed. J. Butt (London, 1939–69). *The Dunciad*, ed. J. Sutherland, is quoted from

	the third edition (1963). For the one-volume text, see Butt.
Trevelyan.	G. M. Trevelyan, *England under Queen Anne* (London, ed. 1965).
Turberville.	*Johnson's England*, ed. A. S. Turberville (Oxford, 1933).
Watt.	Ian Watt, *The Rise of the Novel* (Harmondsworth, 1963).
Webb.	Sidney and Beatrice Webb, *English Local Government* (London, ed. 1963).
Wheatley.	H. B. Wheatley, *Hogarth's London* (London, 1909).
Williams.	Aubrey Williams, *Pope's Dunciad* (London, 1955).

In Memory of my Mother

Introduction

The Topography of Dulness

Thus, *Wit* has its Walks and Purlieus, out of which it may not stray the breadth of an Hair, upon peril of being lost. The *Moderns* have artfully fixed this *Mercury*, and reduced it to the Circumstances of Time, Place and Person. Such a Jest there is, that will not pass out of *Covent-Garden*; and such a one, that is nowhere intelligible but at *Hide-Park* Corner.

Swift, A Tale of a Tub

———————◆◆◆◆◆———————

'Grub Street' entered the language in the seventeenth century, became almost a household phrase in Hanoverian England, and survives in modern parlance with a rather diminished identity. Its metaphorical sense lives on, although the road itself was renamed Milton Street in 1830 and has now been swallowed virtually whole in the immense Barbican building scheme. This loss of physical presence is a shame. For we can hardly grasp the full force of the metaphor unless we know something of the literal existence of the place. The geographical environs of Grub Street were noisy, squalid and crowded; the moral overtones which the phrase carried in its transferred sense came initially from this fact, and were heightened for contemporaries by the social character which the district continued to bear. Hack writers actually did live in Cripplegate Ward Without, in and around Grub Street. This fact, I believe, gives an added dimension to the many opprobious references to denizens of the place which we find in Augustan literature – satire especially.

Yet very little is known about the sociology of the region. The milieu of Duncehood was, first and foremost, the parish of St Giles', Cripplegate, in the liberties of the City of London. Now it is not hard to find out much solid fact concerning the ecology of this parish and its environs in the early eighteenth century. Surprisingly, no one has ever troubled to do this. The card catalogue of the Guildhall Library, which is perhaps the most compendious reference tool we have to London topography, contains only two entries under the heading 'Grub Street'. In one case, the connection with the street is fortuitous. In the other, we are led to a privately printed monograph of mid-Victorian origin – an amiable and rather desultory work by an antiquarian, very much characteristic of its period, and not very full or rigorous in its scholarship. And that is about all.[1] More recent students have rarely bothered to note, even in passing, the existence of a real place called Grub Street, even though they use the name as a chapter heading and liberally besprinkle their pages with the phrase in its figurative application.[2] One aim of this book is to show that the social conditions in which the hacks lived and worked are not beyond research. Another is to establish the fact that this material, once assembled, can fill out our understanding of eighteenth-century literature at a level deeper than that of mere 'topographic' reference.

If tragedy concerns itself with the insupportable, then satire takes as its province what may just be borne. Augustan satire is peculiarly occupied by that harsh, fetid, oppressively physical world of pain and pestilence which dominates the landscape of Pope, Swift and Hogarth. All satirists need to have enemies. But not all have found it necessary to name names so insistently, to enrol their victims in a society of folly, to stick so closely to topical reality. For these men, the characteristic butt is not a generalised Maevius but an individualised Thomas Wharton. The typical setting is not a vague infernal region but a particular locality such as Covent Garden market or Temple Bar.[3] London, indeed, becomes a central symbol of their work. The city serves as a type of Pandemonium. Its streets, courts and alleys constitute a new map of hell. Its markets, theatres, prisons, hospitals and ditches make up a gazetteer of folly and iniquity. Many critics have supposed that the density of topographic reference in all these artists is a mere trick in the fingers. I think it is less superficial than that. The Augustans use the physical detail of contemporary London to support their fictions, much as Dante used the theological scheme of St Thomas as a poetic framework, or as Blake and Yeats employed an invented mythology. The difference is that Pope did not contrive his own moral universe. His satiric cosmology is based on the geography of the London of his day. He makes topography serve as moral symbolism.

A number of influential recent commentators have argued that we need not concern ourselves unduly with the victims of Augustan satire. No: more than that, they have asserted that it is positively distracting to do so. This book has been actuated by a radically different belief. I shall contend that it *is* profitable to adopt, at least for a moment, the Dunce's eye view.[4] By studying the victim in his natural habitat, we do gain considerable insight into the procedures and motivation of the satirist. By taking seriously the replies which the hack made to Swift, for instance, we may often find out more about the Dean's intentions than if we restricted ourselves to the presuppositions of Renaissance humanism, or the *données* of Anglican rationalism. It is, apart from anything else, a favourite device of the Scriblerian party to beat down an opponent with his own weapon. Footling writers the Dunces may have been – many certainly were – but their existence was no footling thing for the course of English satire.

Bad writing has often been the occasion, or proximate cause, of good – witness *Northanger Abbey*. The great stroke of the Augustan satirists was to make the world of low literature serve as subject and setting of their works. Both Swift's *Tale* and *The Dunciad* reflect in their narrative the buffeting, combative existence of the hacks; their imagery is filled with disease and disaster, as were the seamier parts of London familiar to the hack. This means that the scribbler's environment is as much the satiric target as the writers themselves. Grub Street is the Dunces' milieu; but it is also the expression of their corporate identity. Like so many Scriblerian inventions, it has one foot in the real world, the other in an imaginative realm.

As everybody knows, the subject-matter of Pope, Swift and Hogarth is replete with obnoxious detail. Their recurrent motifs are squalor, pestilence, ordure, poverty: their mode is one of physicality, their tone is often that of outrage or disgust. (Sometimes a hyberbolic outrage for comic ends, but that makes little difference.) I do not think it has been sufficiently realised that this reflects not only a general inheritance, from Juvenal or Bosch, but also a particular response to the conditions of the time. Climatic events of recent history, such as the Plague and the Great Fire, suffuse their imagery and hang over their drama. Once again, we can only come to grips with their richest artistic statements if we desert the overcrowded consulting room of the private pathologist, and follow the satirists to the seething crowd outside Newgate or to the public spectacle which was Bedlam. Theirs was a clamorous, savage, often brutal world. In Professor Plumb's words, it was filled 'with violence and aggression, with coarse language and gross manners, with dirt, disease and lust.'[5] London, especially, was in many parts overcrowded, malodorous, tumultuous: an insecure, neurotic city where King Mob might at any time resume his reign after the briefest interregnum. (Sacheverell, Ormonde, the gin act, the excise crisis – almost anything might be the occasion.) Small wonder that the art of satirist fixes, with hallucinatory clarity, on the here and now. As for the 'now', we may recall how many of the figures portrayed by Hogarth are identifiable individuals, compared with those of Rowlandson. And as for the 'here', there is a further consideration we should keep in mind.

London was then a much smaller place than it is today. The population of the combined metropolis, including Westminster, Southwark and the out-parishes, fell short of 700,000 at the start of the eighteenth century; moreover, these people were herded together appallingly closely in many districts. Most inhabitants of the capital lived near their work. Merchants were beginning to acquire country-boxes at Clapham or Hampstead, but the City was never the ghost-town at the weekends which it is today. Again travel was slow, virtually always on the surface of the earth (rarely subterranean and never superterrene), and often dangerous – it demanded one's full attentiveness. One was, besides, longer about a given journey: 'This Town is grown to such an enormous size,' wrote Mrs Pendarves to Swift in 1736, 'that above half the day must be spent in the streets in going from one place to another.'[6] Places only a few miles distant from the city were regarded as remote: Ward of Hackney could be so identified – as opposed to Ned Ward of Moorfields, say – almost as though he were an ancestral laird. Defoe in Stoke Newington was an early

4

exurbanite. Moreover, it was not yet customary to give numbers to houses, so that a particular coffee-house or bookseller's shop would be located by a physical description, even on the cover of a letter – 'over against Catharine Street' or 'two doors from the Exchange'. Finally, really large buildings were comparatively rare. There were no vast offices, no blocks of flats, no railway termini. Thus, apart from the occasional private mansion such as Montagu House or Marlborough House (and they were mostly on the outskirts), the main public edifices stood out stark and unmistakable. Churches, prisons, hospitals, mercantile centres – this was the kind of landmark which any Londoner would know from childhood. It takes an imaginative effort to put oneself into this visual setting, with its primary horizontal emphasis: but that is the world into which the hacks were born.

It is interesting to note that, at a climatic moment in *Clarissa*, a novel now somewhat overburdened with moral-cum-metaphysical readings, the same particularity reasserts itself. When Clarissa is arrested as she leaves St Paul's, Covent Garden ('at the door fronting Bedford Street'), she is told by the sheriff's officer that she must accompany him to High Holborn. 'I know not where High Holborn is,' is her bewildered response – geographical innocence of the city's thoroughfares portending, of course, much more. Then, 'looking about her, and seeing the three passages, to wit, that leading to Henrietta Street, that to King Street, and the fore-right one, to Bedford Street, crowded, she started. Anywhere – anywhere, said she, but to the woman's!' (Letter CV.) This passage has something of the flavour of a tableau in classical history painting – Hercules at the fork in the road. Something but not all: for the mythological suggestions are severely qualified by the explicitness with which the streets are named. Even at such a fateful moment for the heroine, Richardson keeps his eye on the imaginative geography of the scene. Clarissa's reluctance to go back to Mrs Sinclair's is conveyed by a sort of vertiginous befuddlement, in which the streets appear before her distracted gaze as alarming moral alternatives.[7]

It follows from all these facts, that to contemporaries, the social mode of the satirists was all the more comprehensible because of its ready dependence on topography. In 1730 one navigated not by tube stations or bus routes, but by given features of the landscape, most of which played an obvious part in the religious, legal or commercial life of the city, and dominated a little hinterland of their own. Smithfield, St Paul's and the Fleet River are straightforward examples. Similarly, one navigates the satire of Pope, Gay or Swift with the help of these conspicuous directional aids: now become moral landmarks, they carry special associations – broadly sociological or historical – which help to underpin the satire. In this book I try to provide a sort of gazetteer, to assist the modern reader to pick up these associations with something of the fluency and delight with which men and women of the eighteenth century seized on them. This is a route-map to explore the comedy of Grub Street. For the *zest* with which Pope and Swift, especially, responded to the facts of life around them is not always fully appreciated. In an age when the life of the streets was a standard theme, Swift stands out for the vivid and graphic immediacy of his handling of this topic. The sense of fascinated outrage which penetrates the satire of both men appears with notable force in this area of their response. I shall try in this book to convey something of this energy: an energy often of rejection and contumely, yet an indispensable factor in the concentrated power of their satire. In the imaginatively charted streets of London, Blake – the Londoner born and bred – hears the youthful harlot's curse as a kind of universal malediction. With the Scriblerians, fixing on an external reality somehow alien yet deeply compelling, the harlot becomes a character in a localised drama: her utterance is specified, as it is registered on the mind of the author and reader with the sharpness of outline that belongs to idyll and to nightmare. It is exactly the distinction of Pope and Swift that they are *not* transcendental in Blake's way.

*　　　*　　　*

It has, of course, long been recognised that satire in this age is rich in topographic allusion. But this has nearly always been dismissed as a sort of local colour, and not much has been made of this recognition in the service of worthwhile critical ends. In most cases, a little inert social history is dredged out of *Trivia* and poems of that kind, for a section entitled 'The Life of the Streets'.[8] That is, the movement is from literature towards documentation. The author combs satiric literature in order to tell us something about early eighteenth-century life in the capital. This book proceeds in an opposite direction. I hope to show how a knowledge of London topography can inform and enrich a reading of the greatest satire of the period. That is another distinction in passing. Usually critics have found it necessary to engage in London espionage with Ned Ward, and to bring in Pope or Gay only as incidental witnesses from outside, literary daytrippers rather than residents. Here the great writers will be allotted a more central place.

The only serious study of the topography of *The Dunciad*, for example, is that of Aubrey Williams. Excellent as this is, it concentrates entirely on the itinerary of the Dunces' 'progress', and the relation of that to the course followed by the official party on the real-life Lord Mayor's Day.[9] In the context of Williams' immediate purposes, this was an unimpeachable procedure on his part. But there remains a great deal else. For the effective geography of the poem is not confined to the carnival procession of folly to St Mary le Strand and back again. It includes a much denser review of the city, its inhabitants and its institutions; and likewise relies on a far more inward acquaintance with London topography than most of us can hope to possess today. This, of course, is not in order merely to make out the external action of the poem, or the siting of any particular episode. Rather, it is so if we are to understand the imaginative workings of Pope's fiction, and to respond to its underlying human and social implications. On one level, the poem is about the onset/ spread/contagious power/epidemic character/low associations of evil. This pestilence may be described as folly, Dulness, modernism, the uncreating word – what you will. About the *content* of Pope's views, if we may distinguish such a thing, I am in almost total agreement with the splendid and authoritative reading provided by Professor Williams. But the *method* of the poem is perhaps even more complex, more fully orchestrated and more effective than he allows. My view of *The Dunciad*, briefly, is that it is a work where human geography becomes symbolism.

The image of the City, in Augustan satire, is a sombre one. Pope, impelled by his 'rage for order', fixes again and again on the thorough-fares of London in order to image disorder. Swift reverts to the dirt and rubble of the streets; his is a world of garrets, night-cellars, prostitutes. John Gay devotes an entire poem to the effective refutation of an ironic thesis:

Happy *Augusta*! law-defended town![10]

Elsewhere Gay composes town eclogues and Newgate pastoral. In each case the point is the same. The unpleasant physical facts of the contemporary town serve as a negative image: an actuality of poverty, confusion and immorality to set against the dream of learning, the vision of heroism, or the pastoral idyll. London, failing to be an Augustan metropolis of epic stature, exposes – as it literally contains – the sordid reality which is the empire of Dulness.

There is a good reason why the satirists should have used geography to make their point. At this time spatial arrangement was still regarded as in some manner symbolic. The self-evident mode of revelation found in a Gothic cathedral was no longer imitated. But the lay-out of a Georgian country-house does, more subtly, affirm a whole hierarchical system of values. To move through such a house is to enact a declaration of assent to the Augustan notions of social living. As one traverses the ground floor, from the imposing central salon, through formal reception-rooms into the library and private apartments, one experiences a sense of public dignity melting into personal amenity. (Sometimes the separation of the parts is more clearcut: but the basic point still holds. At Blenheim, the great hall and the saloon are flanked, in the central block, by state apartments: the private quarters are set at right-angles, in each wing, though this is disguised on the main North front by the curving arcade. But then Blenheim was a monument to official virtue. A house like Stowe is more typical; as well as patriotic zeal, the mansion testifies to the moral value of 'retirement'.)

On occasions, this sense of material symbolism was taken to excess. It was certainly very strong in Horace Walpole, who actually slept with a copy of Magna Carta on one side of his bed and the

warrant for the execution of Charles I on the other.[11] Walpole carefully compiled *A Description of . . . Strawberry Hill* (1774), and
laid out its separate parts with deliberate artifice: much as he would
have adjusted the *disponsibles* of a literary composition. Not all the
arrangements were, perhaps, ideal: the pantry was next to the oratory,
and the kitchen seems to have been in the opposite corner of the villa
from the refectory – which cannot have pleased the servants.[12] But,
all in all, it is plain that Walpole did wish to make definite statements
about himself and his own mode of living by the way space was
allocated. Pope's rhetorical point derives from a similar insight. The
way London is laid out testifies to the life which is led there.

The density of topographic allusion, then, in Pope's work is no
accident. Places and poems are capable of every kind of mutual relationship. In this case, the social background of a living London goes
to inform the whole imaginative construct which Pope has fabricated.
A number of factors which contribute to that process are worth brief
examination.

Initially, we should remember that on one level *The Dunciad* is a
poem about civil dudgeon. From the Restoration onwards an important strand of polite literature takes its origin from what we might
call, following the title of a play by John Crowne (1683), city politics.
The fervour with which issues were fought out in London a little
later has been described by two recent historians: 'A political ther-
mometer would have recorded a constant high temperature in the
capital during the reigns of William and Anne . . . Party politics
mixed with both the business and pleasure of Londoners. . . . The
spirit of party . . . penetrated into the leisure haunts of the capital.'
Now, it is true of course that Pope does not directly take up these
squabbles in his work: his comments on the attempts to annex *Cato*
by the two parties, on its opening night, are detached and amused.
But he was after all the son of a London merchant, even though one
who had retired to the seclusion of Windsor Forest. He grew up
during the time of ferment described in the last quotation. As a result,
his work is stuffed with references to aldermen and City magnates –
his Horatian poems, perhaps most conspicuously. Just as Swift
brought in the famous episode involving Sir Humphrey Edwin into

9

his *Tale*, so Pope never transferred his imaginative gaze from London
for very long. Macaulay once observed that in this age 'the influence
of the City of London was felt to the remotest corner of the realm.'
This is true artistically, as well as politically.[13] The reasons for that
lie partly in the sociological character of the place around 1700.

London was then by far the biggest town in the land. The metropolitan area contained about one eighth of the entire population of
England and Wales.[14] For this reason alone, civil broils took on
microcosmic significance, at the same time as they constituted in
sober reality macrocosmic facts. The city as a whole covered a relatively small space by modern standards. Yet within a few square
miles there were marked disparities in living standards, whether we
interpret that phrase to connote economic levels or *mores*. Restoration
London was not much more than a congeries of villages. Hence the
readiness with which men and women of the time distinguished
between the separate zones of the town, physically adjacent as they
were. Steele – to take one example among many – has a character in
The Tender Husband remark: 'You are so public an envoy, or rather
plenipotentiary, from the very different nations of Cheapside, Covent
Garden, and St James's: you have, too, the mien and language of
each place so naturally . . .' Addison was to use exactly the same
significant image ('an aggregate of several nations, distinguished from
each other by their respective customs, manners and interests . . .')[15]
It was in this way there grew up the situation described by Ian Watt
as a typical feature of the new urbanised landscape: 'this combination
of physical proximity and vast social distance.'[16] Grub Street was
within comfortable walking distance of, say, the new Bank of England.
But it was not a very well worn path, for a great dividing line (symbolised neatly by the old walls of the City) stood between the two.
Similarly, the slums of St Giles' ran almost up against the opulent
new developments to the north of what was beginning to be called
Oxford Street: yet their interaction was minimal. In a less sophisti-
cated society, it would seem that visible barriers such as a ditch or a
bastion count for more in psychological terms; remarkably often, the
parish and ward divisions follow some such obvious feature. The
social contours are mapped out by the geographical terrain.

There is an important reason why place names crop up with such remarkable frequency. To the modern city-dweller, the title bestowed on a road or a district is a historical accident – a dead metaphor. To the Augustans, the metaphor was still living, at least in part. If one looks at a contemporary map of London, this becomes clear. Take as a convenient instance the map published by Dodsley in 1761, used for the endpapers of Boswell's *London Journal*.[17] In the borough of Southwark, the following is a complete list of the streets named: The Broad Wall, Angel Street, Melancholy Walk, Gravel Lane, Love Lane, Bankside, Bear Garden, Maid Lane, Clink Street, Dead Man's Place, Red Cross Street, Dirty Lane (twice), Foul Lane. I have set down these names as they came: it would be possible to rearrange them in a more striking, quasi-narrative order. It must be apparent that such titles fulfil more than a narrow attributive role. They are descriptive labels. People of the age still saw symbolic meanings in a name, which in any case was held to be of divine origin and hence magical in quality. A clear case of what happened is provided by the widespread view that the Great Fire was a visitation from the Almighty: a view sanctioned by the erroneous belief that the fire had started in Pudding Lane and ended at Pie Corner – and must consequently have been designed as a warning against gluttony. The same literal-minded concern with nomenclature emerges from one of the many poems written just after the fire, 'London's Remains' (1667):

> *PHYSICIANS COLLEDG* next, its *Seat* did *Fit*,
> Whether by Chance there plac'd or *Wit*.
> It stood at *Amen*, *Paternoster's* close;
> For he needs pray that takes a *Dose*.

The punning only works because people still took place names seriously, as an indication of what you might expect to find there.[18]

Pope capitalises on this situation, which provided him with a readymade symbolic framework, in a variety of ways. One of his concerns is to suggest that a certain kind of soil breeds and nurtures a certain kind of plant. That is, he takes over from the second *Georgic* the idea that there is a proper habitat for each created thing:

> Nunc locus arvorum ingeniis . . .

It is a long way, perhaps, from willows and vines to starveling writers (that is part of the joke.)[19] But 'the genius of soils' can be applied to human ecology, as well as that of plants. This is one reason why Pope takes such pains to describe 'The cave of Poverty and Poetry' at the outset. 'Th' imperial seat of Fools', whether Rag Fair or Grub Street, is the nerve-centre for Dulness; but in addition it is a type of the social degradation that waits on Dulness ('Emblem of music caus'd by Emptiness . . . The cave of Poverty and Poetry.') Moreover, Pope deliberately selects an image which relates the spiritual squalor of his victims to the actual squalor which he had set out in his 'Further Account of . . . Curll':

> Here in one bed two shiv'ring sisters lye.

In this, they are but avatars of the scapegrace life led by professional hacks: the two translators in bed together in Moorfields, the other pair in the flock-bed at Cursitor's Alley. Both unions, needless to say, are sterile.

Another rhetorical stratagem is to insinuate that literary vice, because it is practised in the same dingy quarters as social wrong-doing, is directly equivalent. Everyone knows the famous couplet about Lady Mary, in the Horatian satire addressed to Fortescue:

> From furious *Sappho* scarce a milder Fate,
> P-x'd by her Love, or libell'd by her Hate . . .[20]

What *The Dunciad* shows is that you got yourself libelled in just the same districts as you got yourself poxed. A topographic identity becomes a moral equivalence. Again, a third device is to deflate grandiose pretensions by reminding the Dunce that his epic ambitions are acted out in downtown slums and suburban alleys. Blackmore's claims as a heroic poet have to withstand a succession of blows in the poem, but few more cutting than the reminder that his effective audience does not extend beyond Tottenham and Hungerford. Pope has dramatised in spatial terms an evaluative critical judgement. We cannot move far in *The Dunciad* without finding this kind of technique. It is an almost topological poem: space and distance are part of its essential mechanics.

The propositions outlined so far may perhaps be corroborated by the insights of the modern study of human ecology. A standard text on *Urban Society*, for instance, described how residential zones follow 'differences of social class, religion, ethnic origin, and race.' And, arguing that 'the division of labour and social differences often reinforce one another', the authors state:

> Social isolationism is reinforced by spatial isolationism; the more people are spatially segregated, the less likely are they to come into intimate contact with each other. At least the possibilities of close relationships on the basis of social equality are greatly reduced. Instead, contacts tend to be formalized, confined principally to the market place or the work situation. People who . . . have contacts of a strictly economic character, may live in entirely different social and ecological worlds.

This is surely apposite to the relations of Pope and his book-sellers. Tonson, alone, had purchased enough respectability at Barn Elms to acquire something approaching friendship, though not equality. Lintot may be used as a subscription agent, but will still be a Dunce. It is much the same with Swift and men like Motte, Barber and Faulkner, whom he genuinely liked (though here London's remoteness from Dublin is a factor). The ease with which the major writers kept themselves at a distance from the trade, except in the purely mercantile role, is symbolised by the fact that Pope scarcely ever went into the City, if his correspondence is any guide, although the trade was increasingly centred there. Nor, of course, did he make many excursions into St Giles' or Cripplegate. His contacts with Drury Lane seem remarkably few, for one who was connected quite closely with the theatre for a number of years. Pope's rejection of the way of life of the city is fitly represented by his withdrawal to Twickenham, whatever the legal basis of that move. Yet he did spend a great deal of time in London, and as we have seen displayed abundant knowledge of the town. It remains true that his first-hand dealings with the enclaves of Dulness must have been fleeting and lacking in intimacy.

The same textbook contains this passage:

> Human ecology goes farther than merely determining where designated groups are localized or where particular functions of these groups are performed. It is also concerned with interactive relationships between individuals and groups and the way these relationships influence, or are influenced by, particular spatial patterns and processes.[21]

Now, Pope's treatment of social reality as he saw it makes clear how 'particular spatial patterns and processes' (such as the westward march of the trading class) influences relationships. Augustan society superimposed a spatial segregation on a vertical social hierarchy, and amongst other things *The Dunciad* gives us an imaginative vision of the moral entity which was the city, imaged by its topographic and ecological indentity. The 'map' is finally only a palimpsest. For the Grub Street which shows up there as an outlying enclave is no more than a shadow on the wall of the cave. The real Grub Street is elsewhere: an outlying enclave in the metropolis of letters.

*   *   *

The argument of this book is laid out on a simple plan. Chapter I describes the main centres of Dulness, notably the history and character of Grub Street proper, and locates the Dunces themselves in their particular haunt. The second chapter examines some of the ways in which the 'real life' of London affect Augustan writing. By this I mean not simply the literal occurrence of fire, disease and rioting within eighteenth-century works, but also the imaginative resonance of these motifs in the idiom of satire. After this comes a section of the 'criteria' for admission to Duncehood: that is, the social and literary characteristics of a hack. The fourth chapter considers Swift's dealings with Grub Street. The fifth is concerned with what might be called the existential state of Dulness: the psychology, rather than the social condition, of professional writers. Defoe's career is reviewed, as it is both typical and wildly aberrant for authors in this period. In addition, there is a brief survey of Fielding's use of Grub Street themes and terminology. This leads on to the final chapter, describing the gradual blurring of the Grub Street idea, as it loses contact with its original topographic base.

Throughout the book, I have attempted to present a world and not merely to juggle with ideas. First and foremost, this is a history – of words, of places, of feelings. The overriding intent is that of describing how things were, or seemed to people, at a specific moment of time. I do not assert that there is a necessary connection between Grub Street and squalid social conditions: rather, that there was an observable link at this period. It may be that in other ages the hack would stand in a different relationship to the major artist. I have not considered the question, for I am not engaging in the theory of literature. How permanent the conditions that I describe were, is a question which must be left to scholars of other periods, or of all periods, if such there be. In other words, this book starts from and returns to the concrete eighteenth-century setting. It attempts to show what one literary form, satire, took from contemporary life: and how that 'real' world is transfigured by art. It is a study of one aspect of the eighteenth-century mind: its curious loyalty to the actual.

Epigraph. *Tale*, p. 43.

1. See Ch. VI. After the first draft of this book had been substantially completed, a work by Philip Pinkus was published under the title *Grub Street Laid Bare* (London, 1968). This contains a pleasing fund of anecdote. But it must be stated that the book adds further impetus to what I have called the Grub Street Myth. Its subtitle, 'The scandalous lives and pornographic works of the Original Grub St. writers, together with the bottle songs which led to their drunkenness, the shameless pamphleteering which led them to Newgate Prison, and the continual pandering to public taste which put them among the first almost to earn a fitful living from their writing alone', does no disservice to the contents. More to the present point, Mr Pinkus writes blandly, 'Grub Street itself is a metaphor', (p. xi) without enquiring any further into the basis of this imaginative transference. And his first chapter begins: 'There was an actual Grub Street once. According to the *New English Dictionary*, it is now called Milton Street, near Moorfields in London – which may or may not be relevant. But the Grub Street we know is an eternal spirit that dwells in the heart of every author whose belly is at odds with his principles. . . . Today . . . we call it Fleet Street or Madison Avenue . . .' (p. 13). As this book will show, it is highly relevant that Grub Street, for instance, lay near Moorfields – the present tense is hardly appropriate, since Moorfields as such no longer exists and Milton Street, too, was effectively gone by 1968. Furthermore, we can hardly understand the derived meaning of Grub Street, in the metaphorical and almost metaphysical sense to which Mr Pinkus alludes, if like him we dismiss the vehicle of the metaphor at the very outset. Mr Pinkus's book, one might say, is really about hacks at large; whereas this study is concerned with the genesis of the metaphor, the interaction of tenor and vehicle, the name and nature of Grub Street in general and – crucially – in particular.

2. A number of examples are given in Ch. VI. An interesting case in point is that of Sir Ivor Jennings' section on Grub Street in his *Party Politics*, vol i *The Appeal to the People* (Cambridge, 1960), pp. 134–53. The original Grub Street was more than a publicity machine: its associations were quite different from those of modern Fleet Street.

3. It should never be forgotten that early editions of *A Tale of a Tub* were garnished with a cut of a wholly unmistakable Bedlam, those of *The Dunciad* with a scene at Bridewell Bridge depicted by no less a hand than Francis Hayman. There is really no possible ambiguity in these cases. Whatever general or symbolic reference we give to these vignettes, it remains a fact that the narrative prescribes a definite locality which the illustrator has no qualms in setting down with the careless fidelity that goes with utter familiarity. It has been pointed out that T. S. Eliot used as the basis of a scene in the *Four Quartets* a recollection of Gloucester Road underground station; and it is argued that in a novel he would probably have named the location quite openly. I am not entirely sure about this; but that the Augustan satirists would have done as much, I am quite certain. See Graham Hough, *An Essay in Criticism* (London, 1966), p. 117. The fact is that most present-day critics are insufficiently literal-minded when it comes to Scriblerian comedy.

4. By this I do not mean that we should take the hacks' word for everything. Pinkus's intention to present 'the story of the Grub Street hacks through their own writings' seems a curious undertaking. 'What evolves from this,' he says, 'will not be pure, laboratory-tested historical truth, but the usual amalgam of fact and fiction that contemporary writers create of their own world. Where it is not history it becomes legend, and legend has its own validity. Surely the legend that the hack writers created of themselves is as much a picture of Grub Street as any so-called objective study.' Yes; but a different kind of picture. The validity of legend is one thing, the rejection of historical evidence quite another. Pinkus concludes, 'The final effect, at least, is immediate, and what the reader cannot see he should be able to smell' (pp. xi–xii). We may hope to achieve this immediacy without sacrificing objectivity quite so shamelessly.

5. For the views of J. H. Plumb on violence and aggression in the eighteenth century, cf. the following: *England in the Eighteenth Century* (Harmondsworth, 1950), pp. 2–4; *The First Four Georges* (London, 1956), pp. 14–20; *Sir Robert Walpole: The Making of a Statesman* (London, 1956), pp. 30–4; *Men and Places* (Harmondsworth, 1966), pp. 19–21.

6. Swift, *Correspondence*, IV, 475.

7. Incidentally, we know a good deal about Clarissa's movements around London – which churches she attended on which occasion, the address of Lovelace's wigmaker, and so on. One recalls that another cockney, Defoe, built up his plague-ravaged London from contemporary observation and

from childhood memories, notably of St Botolph's, Aldgate and St Stephen's, Coleman Street. See an excellent article by Manuel Schonhorn, 'Defoe's *Journal of the Plague Year:* Topography and Intention', *RES* XIX (1968), 387–402.

8. Irving, pp. 150–222. It should be added that Irving's book is well written and makes no bones about its real aims. There are other less distinguished examples in this genre.

9. See Williams, esp. pp. 29–41.

10. Faber, p. 81.

11. W. S. Lewis, *Horace Walpole* (London, 1961), p. 73.

12. See Austin Dobson, *Horace Walpole: A Memoir* (London, 1910), map opp. p. 212.

13. G. S. Holmes and W. A. Speck, *The Divided Society* (London, 1967), pp. 40–1, 132: cf. Macaulay, I, 274.

14. George, p. 319: cf. Watt, p. 184, and authorities cited there.

15. *The Tender Husband*, ed. C. Winton (London, 1967), p. 14: Watt, p. 184, citing *Spectator*, no. 403. See also George, p. 91, for Jack Ketch's Warren as constituting 'a separate town.'

16. Watt, p. 185.

17. I refer to the Yale edition, ed. F. A. Pottle (London, 1950).

18. *London in Flames, London in Glory*, ed. R. A. Aubin (New York, 1943), p. 97.

19. *Georgics*, II. 177: translated by Dryden, 'The nature of the several soils now see . . .'

20. *Imitations of Horace*, Sat II. i. 83–4 (Butt, p. 616).

21. N. P. Gist and Silvia F. Fara, *Urban Society* (New York, 5th edn, 1964), pp. 96, 118–46. See also sections on 'City versus the Country', pp. 528–30: 'The City in Literature', pp. 530–1: and Ch. XXIII, 'The Image of the City'. Relevant to any consideration of eighteenth-century London, as regards the siting of various political, cultural, religious, recreational and other socially important localities, is Robert E. Dickenson, *The West European City* (London, 1951), pp. 254–8.

In emphasising the spatial drama which underlines the moral dialectic of Pope's poem, I do not wish to suggest a one-for-one correspondence between the two. It is of course true that the broad social character of a given area might be qualified by a number of factors, which could affect its imaginative availability for Pope. None the less, one would be hard put to if one were to seek a Dunce resident in Cavendish Square (erected in the early 1720's) or, a member of the literary aristocracy who openly frequented Jack Ketch's Warren.

I

The Suburban Muse

But as it is fatall to the Suburbs of every great Citie, to be infected with some foule and unclean Birds, that there build their nests, although not with professed and ignominious staine of lewd life; because (within the limits of *Houns-ditch*) dwell many a good and honest Citizen, that will never endure such scandalous neighbourhood: yet there are crept in among them a base kinde of vermine, wel-deserving to bee ranked and numbred with them, who, our old Prophet and Countryman *Gyldas*, called *Aetatis atramentum*, the black discredit of the Age, and of place where they are suffered to live.

Stow, Survey of London

O Grub Street! thou fruitful Nursery of tow'ring Genius's! How do I lament thy downfal? Thy Ruin could never be meditated by any who meant well to *English Liberty*: No modern *Lycaeum* will ever equal thy Glory . . .

Arbuthnot, Preface to John Bull

━━━◆◆◆◆━━━

Where was Grub Street? The question is not just rhetorical. I have borrowed the formula from B. H. Bronson, whose essay 'When was Neo-classicism?' offers a new perspective on the eighteenth century by regarding the age 'as if it were a spatial rather than a temporal panorama.'[1] My intention is broadly analogous. I wish to consider the lexical space occupied by the term 'Grub Street', along with its derivatives: and to do that, I shall start from geography. The panorama we shall be looking at is that of the real city of London.

A recent work on the politics of the age of Anne suggests that party writing occupied 'most of the rank and file of what came to be known, half-affectionately, half-contemptuously as "Grub Street" '. It is not beyond argument that a hack author would have readily detected any affection in the way this expression was used. Still, the more interesting point is the way in which Grub Street is safely distanced by the quotation marks that encompass it. So it is no surprise to find the same distinguished historian (this time as co-author) writing elsewhere:

> For politics as for journalism, the end of the Stuart censorship of the press, with the lapse of the Licensing Act in 1695, proved a seminal event. To it can be traced the spectacular rise of 'Grub Street', that fictitious abode of a new generation of political writers whose many different talents . . . were recruited by the Whig and Tory parties.[2]

Now the truth is that the phrase we are considering incorporates not a fiction, but synecdoche. And contemporary usage – as opposed to subsequent misapplication of the term (Ch. VI) – reflects more than a fabulous existence. Grub Street was, as Ian Watt accurately describes it, a legend.[3] That is to say, the figurative meaning was based on a vestigial historical truth. This germ of reality became increasingly remote and spectral, but it was there all the same.

The clue to this situation was provided forty years ago by A. S. Turberville, though no one seems to have taken the hint:

> The original and actual Grub Street, as distinct from the Grub Street of metaphor, acquired its notoriety in the seventeenth century and is thus described in Johnson's *Dictionary* – 'a street near Moorfields, much inhabited by writers of small histories, dictionaries, and temporary poems.' Hence the term Grub Street came to be used in reference to the essentially ephemeral production of the literary hack.

Perhaps this is to imply a readier distinction between tenor and vehicle of the metaphor than can always be made; but otherwise it is an excellent statement of the position. Turberville does two things. He lends the expression a historical dimension and makes it clear that the figurative sense postdated a specific and literal usage. Secondly, he quotes Johnson's significant definition virtually in full (barring the examples provided). Now the first few words of that entry are usually slid over without much thought. In fact, the propinquity to Moorfields which Johnson remarks on at the outset was of the utmost significance in the development of the term and the concept, 'Grub Street'. On his own admission Johnson did not frequent the street – he had perhaps never been there as late as 1783, when he facetiously suggested dining there with the miscellaneous writer Hoole, who had been brought up in Grub Street. But everyone knew the whereabouts of the street; and Johnson not the least, as St John's Gate was a bare half-mile away (Ch. II).

Presently, Turberville supplies another pointer. He writes:

> Defoe is indeed the great exemplar of the literary Jack of all Trades, and as such he is one of the greatest citizens in the Grub Street republic. The author of Robinson Crusoe came of humble parentage, his father being a butcher in the parish of St Giles, Cripplegate . . .

Later on, I shall set out Defoe's credentials for recognition as a Dunce, and assess his place in the 'Grub Street republic' (as Turberville, with an unconscious Augustanism, puts it). Here it is enough to note that the truth extends well beyond the facts mentioned. For instance, James Foe was a resident of Fore Street – the very centre of the duncely parish of St Giles', on one side of which the church itself stood, whose eastern end adjoined Moorfields, and into which debouched a road of moderate size called – Grub Street! Moreover, Defoe died in an alley a matter of yards away from this same street.[4]

The essence of the matter is there. Grub Street acquired its notoriety for a combination of reasons. These included the fact that it lay at the heart of a district long in ill repute on account of its poverty and unhealthy character. In addition, there were specific places in its immediate vicinity, such as Moorfields and Bedlam, with which Grub Street could easily be connected: a circumstance which played straight into the hands of those consummate allegorisers, Pope and Swift. Again, it was the case that writers actually were domiciled in this region; and there were further historical links (Cromwell, Milton and John Foxe were all associated with the church of St Giles'). Moreover, looking at the relation of the district to the City and other wards such as Farringdon Without, we can see that the parish occupied a special position in the overall geography of London. In particular, St Giles' figured itself to Pope as one of the 'liberties' of the City – the twilight areas surrounding the rich and powerful centre administered by the ancient corporation. In other words, the region was uniquely suited to the symbolic role cast for it by the satirists. It was the earlier practitioners of this genre, Marvell and Oldham for example, who had established the usage. But it was the great Augustan satirists who first saw the moral, comic and artistic possibilities offered up to them by the accidents of urban ecology.

The rest of this chapter takes the form of a review of these factors. I shall consider first the physical location of Grub Street, its history, its social character, and its environmental status. It is not necessary to show that all the facts mentioned would be known to Pope and his friends. The broad picture was assuredly available to them. They could gauge both the 'physical proximity' and the 'vast social distance' noted by Watt as endemic to the city, so conspicuous were these in early eighteenth-century London.[5] The ward and parish of Cripplegate (their boundaries were coextensive) provide a remarkably good case in point. Grub Street was a mere stone's throw from the City within the walls: but in sociological terms it was light-years distant.

Meridian of Grub Street

The district had enjoyed what is usually called a chequered history. That means, as it usually does, a history of pretty well unmixed gloom and murk. The tenebrosity of the place started generations before the obscure writers came to hide there from the ravages of bailiffs, creditors, and better poets – all of whom located their quarry without difficulty. The rise in the currency of 'Grub Street', as a literary expression, came at a time when hackney authors inhabited the region. But it was not these men who gave the street its bad name. *That* it had from the start.

I know of only one, very brief, attempt to relate the social history of Grub Street to the acceptation of this term in literary usage. Ronald Paulson writes in his study of *A Tale of a Tub*:

> The Hack's milieu, Grub Street, would have had certain connotations for a contemporary. The street, whose name came from a refuse ditch (grub) which ran alongside it, lay outside the old walls, in Cripplegate, and like other of the areas lying outside the immediate jurisdiction of

the city became a haven for wanted men. Through the seventeenth century it carried a reputation for harbouring dissenters, who took their printing presses there to escape more active surveillance; and, in fact, both Cromwell and Milton lived there. All sorts of scurrilous writing, pornographic as well as seditious, was spawned in Cripplegate and along its main street. It had already passed its peak of prosperity by 1700, and by the time Pope attacked it, and the *Grub Street Journal* flourished, and Samuel Johnson lived there, its population of hacks had dwindled to only a fraction of its former size. Thus, to a Londoner, Grub Street would have suggested dissenting and scurrilous literature; and the word Grub might have further suggested a refuse ditch and a verb meaning 'to dig up, to destroy by digging', as well as 'a small worm that eats holes in bodies' (Johnson) – all connotations which Swift exploits in the course of the *Tale*.[6]

Taken as a whole, this is a most valuable lead: though there is a nice symbolism in the fact that it occurs in a foot-note! Nevertheless, many reservations have to be made as to detail. I shall list these as briefly as possible.

(1) Paulson does not seem clear as to whether he is talking about the literal street itself, the ward of Cripplegate or indeed that gateway, so called. This leads to confusion in places. (2) The liberties of the City were *not* 'outside the immediate jurisdiction' of the city courts. They were physically a little removed, and so 'active' surveillance may have been harder. It is certainly true that the wards surrounding the city, outside the walls, did become known as refuges for the outcast: but from a judicial and administrative standpoint they were part of the City. (3) There is no evidence that Cromwell lived in the ward, so far as I am aware, although he married at St Giles'. Milton did live in the parish but not (as Paulson's phrasing might suggest) in Grub Street. (4) Grub Street had been the main street in earlier centuries. By the time we are considering it was possibly less important than Fore Street, and certainly less imposing socially than White Cross Street and other parts of the ward. (5) Paulson cites no evidence for his statement that the street 'had passed its peak of prosperity' by 1700; and I believe this would be hard to come by. It can be shown that Grub Street had not been a prosperous place in the early part of the seventeenth century. (6) Similarly,

Paulson provides no backing for his very strange assertion regarding the 'population of hacks'. Since no-one has ever actually *named* a scribbler living there, and since the primitive population returns of the age do not recognise the sociological category 'Hack', it is difficult to imagine on what Paulson has based his statement. One of my aims, indeed, is to indicate some of the evidence which might affect the contentions discussed under this and the previous heading. (7) Johnson is not known to have lived in the ward at all, let alone the literal Grub Street. It is possible that Paulson is shifting into the metaphoric application here (as with the title of Bloom's book, *Samuel Johnson in Grub Street*).[7] In the context, such a procedure on his part is either unguarded or disingenuous.

Grub Street had to overcome the initial handicap of a poor site. Originally an extensive marsh occupied the land eastward from the Fleet Ditch as far as Bishopsgate. On the eastern side of this tract lay Moorfields, 'the great fen', of which more presently. The ground to the west of Moorfields was scarcely less swampy, though it did not function as a refuse-tip. The proximity of so much by way of 'noisesome waters' inevitably had its effect.[8] Cripplegate parish became notorious for the ague in winter and fever or the black death in the summer. The land commanded a poor price and by course of nature the inhabitants of the ward tended to be paupers or little better. In 1635 the Lord Mayor and Council appointed the Commissioners of Sewers, along with Inigo Jones (then Surveyor-General), to look into the annoyance caused by the over-charging of the main sewer, which had been flooded out by the unspeakable Moorditch. As one might expect, infection had been rife in the area. The plague raged there the following year too. When the Great Plague was at its height, thirty years later, nearly eight thousand people of the parish were buried, most of these as a result of the disease. By the early eighteenth century, the region was overburdened with poor people once more. In addition, Cripplegate had for some time been known as a haunt of counterfeiters, receivers, beggars, foreigners and houses of ill repute. As the historian of St Giles' parish says, the poor were always in evidence: but so, too, were the idle and feckless.[9] Stow is clear on the point. It is possible also to trace in extant parish records the social disrepute into which Cripplegate fell. For example, a list of tithes and rentals in 1638, covering the whole city, makes dispiriting reading when we get to St Giles'.[10] Here the average valuations were notably low. One or two streets are not too bad. But for the most part we read of tenements rated at no more than 30s. or £1, and properties at £3 or £4, especially in the side-alleys. (In the West End, valuations of £20 and more were commonplace.) It can be said with certainty that it was not the influx of hack writers later in the century which induced a loss of caste in Grub Street. It was already a depressed area.

The etymology of the name accords with this picture. As Paulson suggests, the most widely accepted view is that the derivation is from 'grube', a drain or ditch. Forms which are found in early records are 'Grobstrat' and 'Grubbestrate' (twelfth century).[11] The name therefore carried overtones of refuse-disposal; and suited the satirists' rhetorical aim of connecting vice and squalor with the sewerage of the town. From this point of view Grub Street conveniently linked up with Fleet Ditch, the main artery of disease and Dulness (Ch. II). 'Grub' was also defined by Nathan Bailey as a maggot and as 'a dwarf or short fellow' – the puny stature of a mediocre writer.

As regards nomenclature, there was an appropriate irony, too, in the fact that the parish church should have been dedicated to St Giles, in Cripplegate. Modern scholars doubt whether cripples really did congregate around the postern at this point,[12] but to Pope or Swift that would not reduce the availability of the notion. Equally, St Giles was peculiarly well cast as the special protector of Dunces. As Thomas Fuller had written, in his *Worthies of London*:

> St Giles is accompted the patron of creeples; and whereas churches dedicated to other saints of better footmanship get the speed of him and come into the city, generally lame St Giles *laggeth* behind in the suburbs, as in London, Cambridge, &c.[13]

This, then, was the saint of the halt and the lame, the feeble and those with impaired faculties. He was the protector of beggars, as well as cripples. Pope's victims bear the mark of Cain – Dulness, a sort of hereditary and quasi-syphilitic condition – and their proper place of sojourn is the precincts of St Giles' church. They belong to the suburbs: and this connotes, in 1720, not the comfortable place of retirement, but the 'scandalous neighbourhood[s]' to which Stow had referred.[14] A Dunce is a pariah who has been driven outside the City walls. St Giles' is thus a refuge in more than a literal sense. It serves as a topographic metaphor, to suggest the outcast and enfeebled state of Duncehood.

The population supported in these areas is hard to assess accurately. Hatton in 1708 gives a figure of four thousand houses (this includes both the London liberty and the Middlesex portion).[15] Demographers are not entirely agreed on the population which this would indicate when applied to individual residents. It seems reasonable, however, to take the mean figure which obtained at the 1801 census, i.e. six to seven persons per dwelling.[16] This would yield a total of about twenty-five thousand. The parish clerks' survey of 1732 yields a gross figure of 4910 houses, of which 1800 only lay in the London segment.[17] Clearly it was the Middlesex part which was developing most quickly at this period, a fact recognised by the creation of the parish of St Luke's, Old Street in 1733 (6 Geo.II.c. 28).[18] Maitland's figures confirm the accuracy of this assessment. By the end of the century St Giles' alone was shrinking; St Luke's continued to grow but not at the spectacular rate of parishes farther out from the city. Not long afterwards Grub Street itself lost its identity; but we know that Milton Street quite failed to change its black spots. A writer of the 1850's remarks that the street is 'noted for its great number of alleys, courts, and back-ways, and old inn-yards'.[19] If the density of population had declined, that was partly a matter of residential property giving way to commercial buildings, partly the disappearance of the worst of the rickety seventeenth-century housing – but scarcely at all an index of a better social character for the area. The old City chapel, briefly a theatre, had however become a bath-house, which suggests some amelioration in living conditions.

By far the fullest account of Cripplegate is to be found in the nineteenth-century history by Rev. W. Denton, incumbent of St Bartholomew's, Moor Lane (erected in 1850).[20] This is reliable on most points of fact, amply documented, and forms an unpretentious but worthy monument to the historical zeal which augmented local piety in so many Victorian clerics. Nor is his social and economic history altogether betrayed by a picturesque style:

> Gradually there grew up in the early part of the middle ages a population of tanners and skinners, catgut makers, tallow melters, dealers in old clothes, receivers of stolen goods, charcoal sellers, makers of sham jewellery, coiners, clippers of coin and silver refiners, who kept their melting-pot ready day and night for any silver plate that might come to hand, toilers in noisesome trades and dishonest dealers. Down to later times ale and beer houses of the worst reputation, and yet even worse than such reputation, stood at the edge of the moor, where, despite the City authorities, gambling was always going on. . . . Even murder was not infrequent, and was seldom enquired into and punished. Forgers of seals, of bills, of writs, professional pick-purses, sharpers and other thieves, conjurors, wizards and fortune tellers, beggars and harlots found a refuge here.

Sharpers, thieves, beggars and harlots – it sounds like a recipe for the hack author, as the Scriblerians present that class. Denton goes on to describe various forging offences. He points out, too, that 'perhaps because of the lawless character of the moor outside Cripplegate . . . executions frequently took place there,' with thieves and murderers left dangling in their chains on Moorfields. He then refers to the dismal housing conditions prevailing in this kind of area: an aspect of the Middle Ages which waned all too slowly in Cripplegate.[21]

As Denton's study brings out, the area remained a blighted one. The parish was forced to maintain at least four 'cages' for the purpose of housing two main groups: the unfortunate poor and idle imposters. Such places were also the refuge for destitute women at the time of lying-in, and for homeless persons generally. One such cage stood 'at Grub Street end'. Quackery continued to hold Cripplegate dear: 'it was the outskirts of the town', Denton writes, 'and . . . a favourite retreat for fortune-tellers, astrologers, coiners, pick-pockets, *et hoc genus omne* . . . The gibbets on the moor and the grave yards near, the memorials of times of pestilence, yielded a supply of the horrid materials popularly supposed to be used by these diviners.' To the pagan imagination, Cripplegate Without was a locality instinct with memories from its troubled past. As for the burial grounds, there were six at least: St Giles' own churchyard, the so-called Upper

Churchyard in White Cross Street, the Pesthouse ground, Tindal's (in Bunhill Fields), the Quaker cemetery and the Bedlam ground. The poor, as well as suicides, were buried near the Pest House in the north-eastern corner of the parish. At times of plague these places came into special prominence; but their presence was always felt. Apt, then, that the first book of *The Dunciad* should fashion a grave-yard for obscure literary names.

All the hereditary taints of Dulness were thickly in evidence here during the seventeenth century. The quarrels of the age were acted out in the forty-three acres of St Giles' as warmly as anywhere. Religious dispute, inevitably, headed the list; and equally inevitably, politics followed on that. So we find Ned Ward writing:

> O bury not my peaceful corpse
> In Cripplegate, where discord dwells
> And wrangling parties jangle worse,
> Than alley's scolds or Sunday's bell.

There is nice irony that Ward, Dunce and alley-cat of the literary world, should offer up this cry. Cripplegate knew more of corpses than peace. At the time of the Civil War, a large section of the population were zealous Parliamentarians. The Vicar of St Giles' was a strong loyalist. He was eventually deprived, despoiled of his goods and imprisoned: an item in the loyalist martyrology that befitted such a parish. Subsequently, a Presbyterian lectureship was instituted during the 1640's and 1650's; four volumes of sermons delivered on the foundation were published (1661–90) by Samuel Annesley. Annesley had been presented to the living by Richard Cromwell in 1659; he was predictably ejected soon after the Restoration. He is most relevant to this history, perhaps, as an early mentor of Defoe; but any such unquenchably dissident spirit would be typical of Cripplegate at this period.

Parliamentarians or independents were one thing: anabaptists or fifth-monarchy men a different proposition. Fanatical republicans were believed to have made the parish their sheltering-place after Charles II had returned: but this may only be rumour. More firmly established is an affray of January 1661, when the Saints rose and began rioting through the city. The hard core of fanatics ultimately

entrenched themselves in the Blue Anchor alehouse near Moorfields, and set up a protracted defence. At least twenty men were
killed before the fifth-monarchist leader, Venner, and nine other
survivors could be captured. All were executed: one in White Cross
Street, one in Red Cross Street. The head of every rioter was set up
on London Bridge. Then, a generation later, popular discontent
again inflamed the brittle emotions of the inhabitants. In 1695 the
gaol of Finsbury Manor (near modern Finsbury Pavement, at its
junction with Chiswell Street) was burnt to the ground. The mob
had been incensed by alleged corruption in official places, as well as
by a periodic fit of xenophobia against the Huguenot refugees. The
militia was called into service to quell the disturbance. As we shall
see, destructive rioting was a hallmark of Dulness in action. And the
mode of demolition is just as indicative. Fire had long ravaged
Cripplegate, along with other rickety and densely-peopled quarters
of London. In FitzStephen's time drunkenness and frequent fires
had been accounted the two chief inconveniences; with the Dunces,
inebriation and incendiary urges came together. In fact St Giles'
church itself had been partially destroyed by fire in 1545, when most
of the tower perished: a calamity rather greater than that suffered in
the bombing of 1940, so far as one can judge. Likewise the Fortune
Theatre, between Golden Lane and White Cross Street was burnt
down one Sunday in 1621. It was rebuilt in brick, but the interior
was once again ravaged in 1649 – not through divine visitation, some
thought, or even through common arson: the intervention of the
puritan conscience was suspected. Whatever the cause, fire was a
constant threat in the parish. The bonfires set up in White Street
and in Moorfields during the Gordon riots serve as a convenient
emblem of the destructive energy common to Duncehood and to fire
(see Ch. II).

Another of the plagues of Dulness, as I have called them, was the
pestilential fever itself. As indicated, the parish was particularly
badly hit. In 1603, that onset of the disease which used to be put
among the contributory causes of Jacobean melancholy (when *that*
ailment was recognised) coursed through St Giles'. Not far short of
three thousand people died that year from plague. And of course in

1665 the district again suffered appallingly – part of Moorfields was still a city laystall and refuse tip. Tillotson wrote to Sancroft, 'I am sure that the miserable condition of St Giles' Cripplegate is more to be pitied than any other parish in or about London, where all have liberty, the parish not being able to relieve their necessities.' Burial places understandably grew hard to come by; as early as June 1664, a year before, the White Cross Street graveyard had been closed for fresh burials by order of the vestry. The most famous cemetery, however, was the 'Parish Field' up against Old Street – the Pest-house Burying Ground. Here the destitute were brought to be interred. During the Great Plague it became hopelessly over-subscribed, if one may put it that way: large numbers of victims had been removed to the pest house, as Defoe's *Journal* tells us,[22] and inevitably many of them died in a short space of time. As a result the burial ground was closed for seven years.[23] When it reopened, the northern part of the parish was once again provided with its most fitting emblem: the resting-place of those hapless men and women who were the incurable victims of contagious disease. It should be added that in 1699 proposals were made to make a burial place in some waste ground at Butler's Alley, off Grub Street itself. Nothing came of the suggestion, but it indicates the status of the neighbour-hood. Incidentally, the 'Parish Field' should not be confused with Bunhill Fields. The latter, originally known as Tindall's, was the place of burial for Defoe, Bunyan and many other dissenters. St Giles' parish was indeed a harbinger of mortality – its very name must have served as a *memento mori* to contemporary Londoners.[24] The most symptomatic of all the observations which Denton makes regarding this parish of misfortune is the following:

> The mental strain and terror which people were under in this dreadful time were evinced in the numbers who are recorded to have lost their reason during this visitation of the plague. In parish account-books side by side are notices of sums paid for the removal of the plague-stricken to the Pest House, and of moneys given for the conveyance of the insane to Bedlam.

The felicitous, if cruel, touch by which Pope places the breeding ground of Dulness, with all its spawning 'nameless Somethings', its

maggots and its 'craw[ing] . . . feet' (B.I.56ff), close to the walls of
Folly, stands revealed and explained. Each onslaught of the plague
brings new inmates to Bedlam; and each fit of Dulness does the
same.

From the 1720s there was, too, a workhouse in Sugar Loaf Court,
off Moor Lane (next adjoining Grub Street). This was additional to
that founded in Beech Lane around 1700, the first in the City. As
befitted a parish named after the patron saint of cripples and beggars,
a notable mental hospital was later sited there: St Luke's, in Old
Street, on the west side of City Road. In 1733 a church was erected
in the same street and a separate parish formed, also dedicated to
St Luke. Both survived into the nineteenth century. For the rest,
Cripplegate Ward was chiefly noteworthy for its complement of
breweries, taverns, almshouses and Jewish enclaves. The northern
part of the ward, outside the liberties of the City, was no better. The
1638 assessment recorded the fact that this region 'consist[ed] of a
multitude of poor people'. For the parish as a whole there are references such as, 'Lost per annum in tithes by reason of the extreme
poverty of the place, £100.' Let no one suppose that it was the
literary imagination which brought disgrace to Grub Street.[25] The
historian Oldmixon (himself a Dunce) records a Tory riot, set up by
the rabble of Cripplegate in 1723.[26] Dissenting houses and conventicles abounded in this vicinity. There had long been trouble with
the municipal plumbing: apart from the episode of the sewers in
1635 the water-course of the Company of Barber-Surgeons ran into
St Giles' churchyard, with baneful results, and had to be diverted.
Plague, as we have seen, was rife; and fire almost as destructive. The
parish church just escaped in 1666, though some of its windows appear to have been damaged; later on, the primitive fire-fighting
equipment which the ward possessed became a cause for concern.
There was a high concentration of foreigners in the population. Even
in Elizabethan times, a perceptible number of aliens were recorded
in the region of Grub Street and Golden Lane. After the revocation
of the Edict of Nantes, in 1685, a flood of French protestants took
refuge in Cripplegate. The Irish also settled in large numbers. Not
surprisingly, Grub Street, Golden Lane and Moor Lane headed the

list of the 'dirtiest and meanest parts of the town' where cheap lodgings were to be had.[27]

What of Grub Street *per se*? In the seventeenth century, Denton states, it was 'going down in the world'. Surrounded by conventicles, and housing the single openly proclaimed popish meeting house in London,[28] its condition was assuredly no better in the early years of the next century. One or two 'spacious or handsome houses', such as those known – however unreliably – as Dick Whittington's and as General Monk's, did survive:[29] it was Victorian commerce, rather than the disgrace suffered at the wits' hands, which killed these places. But there were exceptions in the street. Denton relates this loss of caste to its environs, and cites a seventeenth-century writer: 'a nasty stinking lodging in jayle is sweeter land than any garden-house about Bunhill.'[30] Yet the truth is that Grub Street contaminated its surroundings quite as much as the reverse; and the residents who thought that things would get better if the name were changed were not altogether naïve. Grub Street had been picked out for notoriety among a score of such extramural blackspots. The choice was arbitrary but it was not unfair.

Denton writes of the old walled city:

> The suburbs of London – and when this term suburb is used in old writers, the city parishes immediately lying without the gates were meant – abounded with the most lawless classes of the community. Little Moorfields was dangerous to the unwary, with its small low alehouses and tenements of a still more disreputable kind. Grub Street, which at best was never a safe place, had become in the time of the Tudors . . . in a great measure deserted except for low gambling houses and bowling alleys . . . The 'Harrow' in Moorfields was well-known to the City authorities as one of the 'harbouring houses for masterless men, and for such as live by theft and other such like shifts.'

The historical associations remain encrusted on to the name. Grub Street in Pope's poem is a harbouring house for those who live by literary theft and other such shifts. It is the proper home, topographically and morally, of the suburban muse.

This, then, is the typical pattern of a twilight zone. Contemporary descriptions provide further evidence of the social character of Grub

Street proper. Stow has little to say of the street itself, but he does describe the shortcomings of the parts about Moorfields, and mentions the ditches and lay-stalls scattered about the parish. (He also alludes with some misdirection to the prostitutes around Wood Street, in the ward of Cripplegate Within.)[31] It has been stated that, in the sixteenth century, Grub Street was full of 'small and mean domiciles, good enough for beggars and literary men, but too bad for any more self-respecting class.'[32] Certainly, when Lancelot Andrewes was incumbent of St Giles', from 1589 to 1604, and Thomas Morley served as church organist, the parish had names on which to pride itself: John Foxe, the Martyrologist, Martin Frobisher and John Speed were buried here between 1587 and 1629. It was at the church that Oliver Cromwell married Elizabeth Bourchier on 22 August 1620. Then, later in the century, Milton was to occupy various addresses in this part of London: Jewen Street and Artillery Walk, off Bunhill Row, and was to be buried at St Giles' in 1674. But these substantial men are the exception. It was chiefly the submerged elements of the population that came to Cripplegate. The most notable literary men to emerge from the region in later years were Defoe (the son of a butcher and presbyterian) and Bernard Mandeville, who was domiciled there in 1700 along with many other emigrés.[33] A few years later the parish received a less welcome immigrant.

Around 1713–14 Jonathan Wild, recently of the Wood Street Compter in Cripplegate Within, took a house in Cock Alley, right up against St Giles', on the corner of Fore Street and White Cross Street. Here Wild and Mary Milliner set up their first thriving establishment. The house became a favourite haunt of thieves, prostitutes, highwaymen and gamblers; more importantly, it was the centre of Wild's initial ventures as a receiver of stolen property and 'thief catcher'. Pope seems to have known about Wild's association with Lewkner's Lane; it is possible that he was also aware of the fact that Wild had started off in the immediate environs of Grub Street. Incidentally, Wild himself referred in a published pamphlet to 'a bucklemaker near Cripplegate': this might mean himself, but more likely it is Edward Burnworth, alias 'Young Frazier', a notorious rogue who ended up in Newgate.[34] Once again we find that poverty and disease anticipate a more serious charge – that association with crime which pervades so much of the topography of Duncehood.

The best contemporary account is that of Strype, in his re-scension of Stow's *Survey of London* (1720). The maps prepared for this edition, incidentally, are of great independent interest;[35] and Strype's descriptions are exceedingly valuable, not least the follow-ing:

> *Grubstreet*, very long, coming out of *Forestreet*, and running North-wards, into *Chiswell Street*; but some small part, to wit, from *Sun Alley* to *Chiswell Street* is not in the Ward, but in the Liberty of *Fins-bury*. This *Street*, taking in the whole, is but indifferent, as to its Houses and Inhabitants; and sufficiently pestered with Courts and Alleys, the Names of which are as follows . . .

This might serve as an epigraph to *The Dunciad*. The haunts of Dul-ness, taking them in the whole, are distinctly indifferent as to locale and personal composition. *Their* quarters of London are pestered with courts and alleys. Translating this ecological metaphor, we may say that morally, for Pope, contemporary culture is riddled with the mean, the devious, the soiled, the gimcrack constructions of Dulness. Eighteenth-century writers, as Paul Fussell has shown, often use the image of a stately mansion or keep to body forth their sense of achieved stability (Burke's use of Windsor Castle is the most famous example). The flimsy, verminous structures of Grub Street were therefore fit emblems to convey an antithetical order of things.[36]

Strype then goes on to describe certain of these side-alleys. It is enough to mention these in summary form. Lund Alley is 'long and ordinary' (the sense of the latter word, in Strype's usage, is roughly that of 'mediocre'). Honeysuckle Court is, surprisingly, 'pretty good, with new built Houses'. But Flower de Lis Court is 'very small and ordinary'; Flying Horse Court, 'long, but ordinary built; and by consequence, the Inhabitants answerable'. Likewise for Pope, the inhabitants of a district are 'answerable' to the character of that dis-trict in terms of housing, social standards, occupational structure, and so on. The Nags Head Inn has been recently rebuilt 'out of a Place called *Soldiers Court*, which was before old and decayed'. Next comes Oakley Court, 'large and open; the greatest part, at present, unbuilt and lying wast'. Butlers Alley is 'narrow and ordinary'; whilst Cross Keys Court is 'indifferent large, and old built'. Maidenhead Court and Great Bell Alley are little better. Uniquely, Haberdashers Court, at the upper end of the street, is 'very genteel, with new well built Houses . . . This Court was made out of two old ones, *viz. Paviers Court and Robin Hood Court.*' Next to it, Sun Court is 'but small'. How long this privileged enclave of Grub Street survived, I do not know. Assuredly the street as a whole was anything but genteel. In another passage Strype follows Stow's account:

> . . . *Grub Street*, of late Years inhabited (for the most part) by Bowyers, Fletchers, Bowstring Makers and such like Occupations; now little occupied; Archery gives place to a Number of Bowling Allies, and Dicing Houses, which in all Places are increased, and too much frequented.

Both the vices and the homily look more Elizabethan than Georgian; but at all events Grub Street had been known as a place of idleness long before Queen Dulness let out her infectious yawn over it.[37] Maitland a few years later was to elaborate on this description in certain particulars. He glosses the ward of Cripplegate Without in these terms:

> A large Tract of Ground, containing several Streets, and all crowded with Courts and Alleys; the chief are *Fore-street*, the *Postern-street*, *Back-street* in *Little-Moorfields*, *Moor-lane*, *Grub-street*, *Whitecross-Street*, *Redcross-street*, *Beech-Lane*, *Golden-lane*, *Barbican*, and *Jewen-Street*. . . .

This is a veritable gazetteer of duncely localities. Fore Street, the birthplace of Defoe, is described as 'broad, and inhabited by Butchers, Smiths, Turners, &c. runs from the North End of *St Giles's Cripplegate* Church to *Moor-Lane*, Eastward, and then falls into *Postern street*, which leads to *Little Moorfields*, against *New Bethlehem* . . .' The propinquity of Bedlam is thus stressed yet again. Maitland speaks of the many courts and alleys around St Giles's, and lists both Little Cock Alley ('ordinary') and Great Cock Alley, which is Jonathan Wild's ('a large Place, indifferently built, and has a passage into *Whitecross-street* . . .'). The words 'indifferent, mean, narrow' recur in these descriptions. For instance, Moor Lane, directly along-side Grub Street, is termed 'for the Generality, but meanly built and inhabited, especially the upper End, which is narrow', and which leads incidentally through Ropemakers Alley (where Defoe died) and Butlers Alley to Grub Street. Maitland's description of Grub Street and its 'mean, small and ordinary' courts (excepting Haberdashers Square) is taken from Strype more or less verbatim. White Cross Street and Red Cross Street come off a little better, but Golden Lane is 'of no great Account either for Buildings or In-habitants'. The Barbican is notable chiefly because old clothes are sold there, a doubtful distinction when one thinks of Rag Fair.[38]

To the west of Cripplegate lay Jewen or Jewin Street, which en-tered Red Cross Street just beyond the churchyard of St Giles's. This was the route to Aldersgate, and beyond that to Smithfield – a district abutting on the westernmost fringe of the parish, so that the 'Smithfield Muses' might almost be said to occupy the next 'apartment' (Swift's word) to those of Grub Street. Jewen Street was situated on the site of the former Jews' Garden, which according to Stow was at first the only place in England appointed for the burial of Jewish citizens. It later became a pleasure garden, and ac-quired a cockpit.[39] However, this indignity did not last – the cockpit disappeared, only to be replaced by a conventicle, which would hardly have raised the street in Pope's estimation.[40] Contemporary descriptions of the district are usually quite favourable: the street is said to be 'well built and inhabited, except at the West End, of some Trade for *Button-Mould-Makers*'.[41] But it had certain disagreeable connotations, cockpit and conventicle apart, and leaving aside the brewhouse which had been set up in the sixteenth century.[42] The first prominent literary resident was John Milton, from 1661–2. Here a good part of *Paradise Lost* was written, and Marvell visited the poet. But the standard was not maintained. John Dunton, eccentric pub-lisher and author, who duly achieved a niche in *The Dunciad* ('a broken Bookseller and abusive scribler' – note to A.II.136), sent out his works to the world from this address at one period. Again, that archetypal Dunce Charles Gildon was lodged there shortly before his death. We learn this from two rather pathetic letters he wrote to

Matthew Prior in 1721. Blind and feeble, he had evidently left his garret in Chancery Lane, and moved into the purlieus of Grub Street. His letters are headed 'Bull Head Court', which Maitland describes as 'old Buildings, but well inhabited'. Prior died a matter of weeks later, and there is no more extant correspondence between Pope and himself – but it is quite likely that Pope would have known, by one means or another, where his favourite victim spent his latter days. Another connection with the book trade was provided by John Leake, father-in-law of Samuel Richardson, who was a printer in Jewen Street following his move from Aldersgate. Subsequently Leake went the way of several other members of his profession and took up business in the vicinity of St Paul's.[43] Incidentally, Jewen Street has suffered the same fate as Grub Street itself: the Barbican project has swallowed it without trace.

By 1867 the formerly genteel Haberdashers Square had become 'a squalid quadrangle'. Houses on both sides of Grub Street had been levelled during construction work for the Metropolitan Railway. Today the line from Moorgate to Aldersgate station runs under what was Grub Street and became in 1830 Milton Street[44] (commemorating, most probably, not the poet, but a builder who owned the lease).[45] However, there is scarcely any of Milton Street surviving. The upper stretch of about eighty yards, near the junction with Chiswell Street, alone remains. Whitbread's brewery is all that has managed to resist the huge Barbican development. Fore Street now contains, not butchers and turners, but the National Telephone Exchange. One can walk on a raised pedestrian footway above the street, and gaze down on Defoe's (probable) birthplace and Milton's place of rest from a modernistic complex of shops, restaurants and offices. Destruction continues to attend the region, centuries after the Plague. It was in Fore Street that the first bombs fell during the blitz, in August 1940. There is an irony, too, in the fact that eschatology continues a visible presence with the London Mortuary, on the junction of Ropemaker Street and Moor Lane. But finally the impression left by the redevelopment programme is more positive than that. Stage 3 of the Barbican scheme is without doubt the most imaginative and happy transformation the region has ever known. It is interesting that as late as 1953 the Cripplegate region was described by a land economist as 'a muddled area', with depressed hinterland areas, 'some of them around Jewen Street'. From the 'value contour map' appended, it emerges that troughs of low-valuation in market terms existed on the west side of Milton Street and in the vicinity of a goods station between White Cross Street and Red Cross Street. The new pattern, as determined by the Barbican scheme, shows a quite different set of 'value contours'. Incidentally, the district was chosen for study as 'the largest single devastated area in the City of London' after the war.[46] But at long last the Cripplegate region has outlived its poverty and ugliness. It has taken a couple of centuries longer to do so, than Grub Street did to lay its own, metaphoric, ghost.

The Caves of Poverty and Poetry

Dulness is specifically linked with a number of parts of London. These include references to 'the Smithfield Muses'; the 'bleak recess' of the Goddess, at first Rag Fair and then near Bedlam; and the area around the Strand. I shall consider each of these, not just as a 'venue' of *The Dunciad*, but as poetic and dramatic counters: they operate much as do the sustained patterns of imagery in Shakespeare, or the symbolic figures in the Jamesian carpet.

Take the relatively simple case of Smithfield. As all commentators have noted, from Martinus Scriblerus onwards, this was the scene of Bartholomew Fair. It was a district thereby associated with raree-shows and low farces. Williams is accordingly justified in seeing its presence as connoting a degree of theatricality – a low pantomimic quality in Dulness.[47] But there is more to it than that. In the first place, as Swift's 'City Shower' reminds us, a tributary stream ran from Smithfield to the Fleet Ditch near Holborn Bridge, adding its quota of dogs, cats, 'Dung, Guts, and Blood' to the foul drain as it crept sluggishly to the Thames. As a matter of fact, the bed of such a stream was found by archaeologists in 1924, running along what is now Cowcross Street – a matter of fifty yards north of the modern

Smithfield market, near Farringdon tube station. The district thus contributed its own share of pollution to the City, and indeed was responsible for some of that oozing, evil-smelling water in which the Dunces were pleased to hold their high heroic games of mud-diving. The area drained by this stream, in addition, would include the notorious bog of Moorfield, the pleasure-ground for the stately residences of Grub Street.

Secondly, the area immediately surrounding Smithfield had an infamous reputation as a haunt of the dissolute. The *Newgate Calendar* reported the existence of a house here which sheltered 'all sorts of burglars, footpads, fences and other villains'. It is said that this house 'stood alongside the brook, whose rapid torrent was well adapted to convey away everything that might be evidence of crime . . . Once a sailor was decoyed there, robbed and thrown naked out of a window into the stream, and was taken up at Blackfriars Bridge a corpse.' This account dates from later in the century, when Robert Mylne (despite Dr Johnson's efforts) had been allowed to site his bridge almost at the precise venue of the Dunces' acquatic sports. Nevertheless it indicates the general notoriety of the Smithfield area. Even before the Restoration 'every street between Golden Lane [in Cripplegate] and Smithfield' was regarded as a place of ill fame. Early in the nineteenth century, this was one of the districts where typhus raged most strongly. The historical reasons for this state of affairs have been explained by Dorothy George, who notes that the liberty of West Smithfield, just outside the walls to the north-west of the City, was soon inhabited by a depressed population, forbidden by guild regulations to exercise their trade within the City itself.[48] When, therefore, Pope conjured up the name at the very start of his poem:

> Books and the Man I sing, the first who brings
> The Smithfield Muses to the Ear of Kings . . . (A.I.i)

and moreover kept the basic reference in his revised *Dunciad*,[49] a whole constellation of associations was set twinkling. As early as this, the notions of plague, poverty and pollution, which are to serve as a leitmotif throughout, are called up .

Consider another example. In the first version, at A.I.27, Pope names for the headquarters of Dulness, the honour he subsequently transfers to the neighbourhood of Bedlam, a locality known as 'Rag Fair'. He supplies the curt note, '*Rag-fair* is a place near the *Tower of London*, where old cloaths and frippery are sold .'⁵⁰ The text itself is a little more communicative:

> Where wave the tatter'd ensigns of Rag-Fair,
> A yawning ruin hangs and nods in air;
> Keen, hollow winds howl thro' the bleak recess,
> Emblem of Music caus'd by Emptiness:
> Here in one bed two shiv'ring sisters lye,
> The cave of Poverty and Poetry.
> This, the Great Mother dearer held than all
> The clubs of Quidnunc's, or her own Guild-hall.
> Here stood her Opium, here she nurs'd her Owls,
> And destin'd here th' imperial seat of Fools.
> Hence springs each weekly Muse, the living boast
> Of Curll's chaste press, and Lintot's rubric post,
> Hence hymning Tyburn's elegiac lay,
> Hence the soft sing-song on Cecilia's day,
> Sepulcral lyes our holy walls to grace,
> And New-year Odes, and all the Grubstreet race.
>
> (A.I.27–42)

One might assume that Pope is invoking the propinquity of the Tower so that it may serve as a symbol of historic endurance, as (just off-stage) the Castle had done in *Windsor Forest*. The truth is almost the opposite. The Tower provides an ironic contrast to the squalid neighbourhood surroundings; the main point of the note is to localise Dulness. 'Th' imperial seat of Fools' is set up, in fact, at the heart of a notorious hotbed of vice and penury. The wider poetic purpose which sustains the joke here is a familiar one in Pope. He wishes (and this is what *The Dunciad* is largely about) to associate his literary victims with *acknowledged* lowlife haunts. In this passage Pope explicitly states that the City connections of which Aubrey Williams makes so much ('her own Guildhall') are secondary. Dulness is identified by the range of its productions (cheap weekly journalism; the dying confessions of highwaymen; annual poems to order, beautifully caught in a line of clashing sibilants and dribbling expectoration;

commissioned epitaphs; celebratory odes by the Laureate, and so
on.) The last line quoted draws these ideas together and links them
firmly with Grub Street. Hardly anyone seems to have thought it
worthy of notice that the venue of the poem should have been shifted
across London between the two versions. This radical change was
made easier for Pope because he had already identified Grub Street –
the 'Cell' of B.I.33, as I shall argue – with the cave of poverty and
poetry. Some of the work had already been done for him, in fact.
Hard actuality once again came to the rescue of poetic invention.

In order to understand this point, we shall have to look briefly
at the known facts with regard to Rag Fair. The fair itself is best
known to us through eighteenth-century prints. One, called 'High
Change, or Rag Fair', was published by Thomas Bowles (1795). It
shows the eastern part of Rosemary Lane near Well Close Square on
the edge of Stepney. More familiar is Rowlandson's water-colour of
the same scene, 'The Rag Fair'. Both these views show a teeming,
pullulating world full of sharpers and hucksters. They portray, in
fact, what is now the inmost part of Cable Street: that is, the City
end. But Rag Fair took place all down the middle of Rosemary Lane;
it extended the length of modern Royal Mint Street to the very edge
of the Tower itself. In this respect Pope's note is not at all misleading.

Nor, granted his disparaging intent, is the phrase concerning
'old cloaths and frippery'. A modern writer has stated that Rag Fair
was more squalid even than Petticoat Lane. 'Much of the clothing
that was sold there was stolen; the market was also the final destination of all cast-off rags, in an epoch notorious for its careless habits
and for seldom or never changing its linen.'[51] If one substitutes
'poems' for 'clothes' here, one can see what Pope is implying. The
sale of old clothes, incidentally, went on here until the second quarter
of the nineteenth century. At this time the region was transformed,
successively by the moving of the Mint from the precincts of the
Tower to the new building in Royal Mint Street (as Rosemary Lane
became in due course), and by the carving out of St Katharine's
Docks just to the south, with attendant work on rail depots.[52] It was
only at this time that 'Rag Fair' lost its strong pejorative overtones.

In any list of black spots drawn up from the seventeenth to the nineteenth century, the name of Rosemary Lane, with its environs, is sure to figure. Strype, in 1720, describes the mean alleys in the district, as well as the 'small, nasty and beggarly' streets around the Minories, just to the north. He tells of the fair held on Little Tower Hill.[53] Goodman's Fields, whose insalubrious reputation was not improved by the coming of the theatre in 1728, lay immediately adjacent. Sir John Hawkins was particularly severe on the matter:

> . . . What was apprehended from the advertisement of plays to be exhibited in that quarter of the town, soon followed: the adjacent houses became taverns in name, but in truth they were houses of lewd resort; and the former occupiers of them, useful manufacturers and industrious artificers, were driven to seek elsewhere for a residence.[54]

This process was beginning, we should note, in the very year during which the first version of *The Dunciad* appeared. But it is doubtful if Rosemary Lane itself had ever harboured many 'useful manufacturers and industrious artificers.' As late as Mayhew, indeed, we find the Irish community singled out for comment in this locality – always the sign of a depressed area. For the earlier period, however, Mrs George provides abundant evidence of the standing of this quarter. Rosemary Lane is named along with East Smithfield, Hounsditch, Petticoat Lane and Goodman's Fields as 'a deplorable district', and a 'dangerous neighbourhood'. In the late eighteenth century, we find an account isolating the most unhealthy regions of London. The writer speaks of

> the wretched inhabitants of some streets in St Giles' [in the Fields] parish, of the courts and alleys adjoining to Liquor Pond Street, Hog Island, Turnmill Street, Old Street, Whitecross Street, Grub Street, Golden Lane, the two Brook Lanes, Rosemary Lane, Petticoat Lane, Lower East Smithfield, some parts of upper Westminster, and several streets of Rotherhithe, etc.

These are the districts we shall come on repeatedly, the purlieus of Dulness. The high concentration of streets listed in and around Cripplegate Ward will be apparent.[55] Nor is this the only occasion on which Rag Fair is aligned with the Grub Street area – most conveniently, from the point of view of Pope. A seventeenth-century source names as centres of prostitution

> St Giles [in the Fields], Turnbul Street . . . Long Acre near the Mews, Drury Lane, Sodom and all her painted drabs, . . . Ratclife Highway, Rosemary-lane, Shore-ditch, Morefields, White-crosse-street, Golden-lane, every street twixt that and Clarken-well, Cow-crosse, Smith-field . . . and all the country girls.[56]

Even more apposite is a pamphlet of 1767, which refers to the 'cheap lodging' (only, at present, not so cheap) to be found in the 'dirtiest and meanest parts of the town'. These latter are, predictably, named as 'Grub Street, Golden Lane, Moor Lane, Fee Lane, Rag Fair or the Mint'.[57] Three of these are Cripplegate addresses: one is the refuge in Southwark to which a recent poet laureate, Nahum Tate, had been obliged to flee, and where Pope locates one of Curll's authors in 1716: and another is Rag Fair. The associations which the place would call up in the mind of a reader, when *The Dunciad* first came before the public, can scarcely be doubted.

Only six years before, Defoe, who must have known the district well, had brought out *Colonel Jack*. In the first two pages Jack tells us that he 'had [his] Breeding, *viz.* near *Goodman's-fields*'. His youth was spent in such activities as 'rambling about' Rosemary Lane and Ratcliff. After his nurse died, Jack and his companions lived for some years each winter in the glasshouse near Rosemary Lane. On one occasion he went to Rag Fair and bought two pairs of shoes and stockings there for fivepence. He then visited a 'boiling Cook's in *Rosemary-Lane*' and found almost equally cheap fare.[58]

In 1724, two years later, a book came out under the title of *The History of the Remarkable Life of John Sheppard*. This has been reprinted as Defoe's, and may well be his. But the point is immaterial. There are several references to Rosemary Lane in this short essay in the rogue's biography. Together with *A Narrative of all the Robberies, Escapes, &c. of John Sheppard*, another work attributed to Defoe, it provides further revidence of the social image which Rag Fair had acquired. On one occasion Sheppard was taken, following a tip-off by his mistress Edgworth Bess, in Rosemary Lane itself. He had been lodging there with the mother of his associate, Joseph Blake or 'Blueskin' – a highwayman almost as well-known at the time as Sheppard himself. Perhaps more interesting is a passage in the *History*, describing the reactions of the populace after Sheppard had been caught for the last time: 'Newgate night and day [was] surrounded with the curious from St Giles's and Rag-Fair, and Tyburn Road daily lined with women and children, and the gallows as carefully watched by night lest he should be hanged incog., for a report of that nature obtained much upon the rabble.'[59] Rag Fair, it is safe to conclude, was peopled by 'the rabble'. Its links with the criminal class made it the more suitable for Pope's purposes. (Incidentally the hangman who had executed both Strafford and Charles I lived and died in the street, a further blemish on its name.)

It is not only chapbooks and popular novels which supply testimony to the standing of Rag Fair. Sober annals of criminal justice show us a murderer pursued by the mob to the Fair (that was in 1760). Sir Alan Herbert's researches have dredged up the story of a draper in Great Turnstile, Holborn, who lost forty-three pairs of stockings in the year 1733; he instantly (as the court deposition reveals) sent a boy to look for them in Mr Hancock's, of Rosemary Lane, opposite the Chequer alehouse. The eighteenth-century idea of the place is well conveyed in an account which mentions 'lawless Petticoat Lane and Rosemary Lane', where 'thieves run from side to side eluding officers'. And as always prostitution went along with crime, indicated by Tom Durfey's reference to the 'sisterhood of Nightingale Lane', adjoining the Fair, and a long list of other quarters of London including Rosemary Lane, Saffron Hill, Whetstone Park and Lutenor's Lane. There was one fairly pleasant residential district in the vicinity, near Well Close Square; but even this had been less salubrious at one time, as a paragraph in Defoe's *Tour* makes apparent:

On the more *Eastern* Part, the same Increase [in building] goes on in Proportion, namely, all *Goodman's Fields* . . . and the many Streets between *White-Chapel* and *Rosemary Lane*, all built since the Year 1678. *Well Close*, now called *Marine Square*, was so remote from Houses, that it used to be a very dangerous Place to go over after it was dark, and many People have been robbed and abused in passing it; a Well standing in the middle, just where the *Danish* Church is now built, there the Mischief was generally done.

It had been, in short, a Moorfields of the East End. The 'many streets' which had been developed now constituted a different sort of blot on the landscape. In the words of a modern historian, the region – which made up the northern fringe of Wapping – contained 'small houses, chandler's shops, brothels, cheap lodging houses, alehouses, taverns . . .' Grub Street itself had nothing more to offer. A final link was with Execution Dock, 'so call'd, because it is the only Place where Pirates and Sea-robbers are executed'.[60] This Tyburn of the river lay at the southernmost extent of East Smithfield, a region which Rag Fair typified.

It can be seen, then, that it was no casual or arbitrary choice by which Pope first assigned 'th' imperial seat of Fools' to Rosemary Lane. Economic and social history had already underwritten this imaginative stroke. Rag Fair, a place infamous for crime, prostitution, poverty and cheap secondhand trading, makes an exact emblem for Pope's artistic point. Grub Street, likewise, is a place notable for literary crime, for poverty of invention, for the prostitution of poetry, and for the retailing of shoddy stolen goods. It was perhaps chance that the literal Grub Street had often been linked with Rosemary Lane under the first set of headings. It was no accident that Pope introduced Grub Street into his own description of Rag Fair. With a kind of prevenient grace, the instincts of a great artist led Pope to incorporate in his first version of *The Dunciad* the hint of his recast poem. What had been simile, then evolved into metaphor. *The Dunciad* of 1743 has become, quite openly, the epic of Grub Street; the cave of poverty and poetry has moved from the neighbourhood of the Tower to the neighbourhood of Bedlam. Cripplegate replaces Port-soken Ward: but the character of the district is changed not a whit.

I turn now to this second home of Queen Dulness, set in the vicinity of Bedlam. The meridian of Grub Street (as Dr Arbuthnot called it),[61] was not a state of mind but an actuality. By a species of metonymy, the literal environment of the street came to colour the figurative sense of the term. In the work of Pope and Swift, above all, Grub Street is regularly associated with Moorfields, and implicitly or explicitly with Bedlam. Indeed the entire *Dunciad* serves to enforce this connection: that is, to show Grub Street and Bedlam as coeval 'colleges' in the vicinity of Moorfields. Now the latter district had long enjoyed an unhealthy reputation on several accounts: while Bedlam – as is well known – had served writers for some time as a type of frenzied or deluded behaviour. The manner in which the Augustan satirists develop this connection will repay study.

As often, Dr Johnson gives us the clue: or at least Boswell. In 1783 the biographer reports the following conversation:

> Mrs. Burney wondered that some very beautiful new buildings should be erected in Moorfields, in so shocking a situation as between Bedlam and St Luke's Hospital; and she said she could not live there.
> JOHNSON. 'Nay, Madam, you see nothing there to hurt you. You no more think of madness by having windows that look to Bedlam, than you think of death by having windows that look to a church-yard.'[62]

Grub Street, to the eighteenth-century observer, had windows that looked out both on Bedlam and on to a churchyard – on a madhouse and a burial ground. As it happened, no beautiful buildings *were* erected in Moorfields in the first half of the century.[63] The only important construction (after Hooke's new hospital) was the imaginary college set up on the spot in the revised *Dunciad*. Nevertheless, the associations were the same.

The clearest instance of the mental trick to which I have alluded comes in a letter from Pope to Broome of 16 February 1719. The poet looks forward to the 'day of [his] deliverance' when the *Iliad* should be off his hands. He writes:

> I shall retire a *miles emeritus*, and pity the poets militant who are to succeed me. I really wish them so well, that if my gains by Homer were sufficient, I would gladly found an hospital, like that of Chelsea, for such of my tribe as are disabled in the muses' service, or whose years require a dismissal from the unnatural task of rhyming themselves, and others, to death. Poor Gildon should have his itch and – cured together, and old Dennis not want good looking after, and better accommodation than poets usually meet with in Moorfields.[64]

George Sherburn glosses the last word 'the site of Bedlam'. Yes: that is the main point; but there is a submerged joke in the fact that the natural habitat of the active 'poets militant' was just over the way, the other end of Fore Street. The kind office referred to – that of setting up a hospital for incurable hacks – was ironically carried out by Pope and Swift more than once; again, *The Dunciad in Four Books* may be seen as the execution of this early hint. It should also be re-called that Swift speaks of '*Moor-Fields*', i.e. Bedlam, as one of the institutions to which the author of the *Tale of a Tub* is most indebted for assistance. Swift's *Serious and Useful Scheme, to make an Hospital for Incurables* is headed 'from my garret in Moorfields'. Nor was this collocation made only by the major satirists. Henry Carey, who often employs such Swiftian themes as the Smithfield shows and the juggler Fawkes, tells the story of an apprentice who treated his girl 'with a sight of Bedlam, the puppet-shews, the flying chairs, and all the elegancies of Moorfields'.[65] The irony of this latter phrase may require some elucidation .

As a historian of London writes, 'This "Moorfields" was orig-inally a swamp into which much of the City refuse was thrown. Little by little it was raised and attempts made to drain it . . .' The place became in time the first of London's recreation grounds, much fav-oured by the beau monde and frequented by Pepys among others. Stow was lyrical about the improvement which had been effected: at the start of his chapter on Cripplegate, he described Fore Street and the Postern, and then proceeded:

> Of these More-fields you have formerly read, what a moorish rotten ground they were, unpassable, but for Cawswaies purposely made to that intent; what they were also in our owne neerer times of memory, even till Sir *Leonard Hallyday* was Lord Maior of *London* . . . And what they are now at this instant, by the honourable cost and care of this City . . . For the Walkes themselves, and continual care of the City, to have them in that comely and worthy maner maintained: I am certainly perswaded, that our thankfulnesse to God being first truely performed, they are no meane cause of preserving health and whole-some ayre to the City, and such an eternal honour thereto, as no iniquity of time shall ever be able to deface.

Thus complacently Stow moves on in his next sentence to Moor

Lane and Grub Street. Later on, in treating of the suburbs without the walls, he includes a fuller description of the fen, 'a waste and unprofitable ground a long time', and the ditching operations carried out there to make it more habitable (and, doubtless, profitable).[66] Such pious genuflexions before the idol of civic thrift would have greatly amused Pope. He had, however, a better reason for his scepticism.

The point is that Moorfields served as something more than a pleasure ground, or than a site for military exercises. The 'walks' were, quite simply, the haunts of prostitutes of either sex. A pamphlet by Jonathan Wild, in reply to one by Charles Hitchen, appearing in 1718, contains the following:

> Not long after this a gentleman in liquor, dropping into the Blew Boar near Morefields with a woman of the town immediate lost his watch. He applied himself to the M[arshal] [Hitchen], desiring his assistance, but the man being well acquainted with the walk between Cripplegate and Morefields had the good fortune to find out the women.[67]

There is other evidence that the walk dividing upper and lower Moorfields was traditionally allocated to homosexuals. Add to these the fact that the games played on Moorfields were not always innocent (we find contemporary references to such 'Moorfield exercises as qualify a man first for the road and then for the gallows'); that suicides were buried in the ditches there; that the homeless fled to the spot and camped there after the Great Fire; that the function of a refuse tip did not entirely die out even when the district had become 'a patchwork of haphazard new building';[68] that dissenters and later Wesleyan preachers set up their pulpit in this locality; that neighbouring parishes sent their dead to the new burial ground at Moorfields when the Plague had overtaxed their own facilities for interment; add all these, and it is not surprising that Moorfields should have held on to its former reputation long after Stow had rhapsodised over its transformation. Defoe knew the district well: as his biographer has said, if he had run hard from his father's house in Fore Street he could have reached Moorfields in less than five minutes.[69] So could any child brought up in Grub Street: comfortably so. We find that Colonel Jack in making his escape from a robbery in the City went 'down old *Bedlam*, into *Moorfields*', where it was at last safe to pause for breath. On a second occasion, after a daylight raid in the region of Smithfield, Jack and his accomplice Will meet up at their 'old agreed Rendezvous' in Moorfields. To get there, Jack has to run like the wind 'thro' innumerable Alleys' and 'cross all the streets' – and that includes Grub Street.[70]

The delinquency sheet for Moorfields is a long one, and it will be enough to mention a few representative items in a broadly chronological order. The historian of St Giles' parish has described the general trend:

> For a century and a half these fields presented a scene of great liveliness, and became a proverb for a riotous assemblage. Instead of roundabout phrases about 'hubbub and confusion,' men said of any great tumult, 'It's as bad as Moorfields.' Thus a royalist writer, speaking of the Parliament, in King Charles I's time, says, 'By the noise they made at every factious resolve, you would take it to be a Moorfields tumult at a wrestling, rather than a sober council at a debate'.

The implications of this for *The Dunciad* are obvious. A Grub Street tumult, one might say, was a Moorfields tumult in its hack-literary aspect. As for particular affrays, one can point to an affair in 1664 (of which more in a moment), an occasion around 1720 when the watch-house was attacked by forty toughs, and an episode in 1764 when a sodomite arrested in the Mall (a gravel walk running east-west across the fields) was snatched away by a large gang who beat off the constables.[71]

Denton goes on to observe that

> The fields were the meeting ground of the apprentices, the place where workmen met to discuss the fall of wages and the rise in price[s] . . . the spot used for political gatherings of all kinds when folk-motes had ceased, and discontent or patriotism could find no sufficient outlet in the Common Hall.

The first function was illustrated by the 'great tumult' in 1664, when two apprentices had been put in the pillory. Their fellows took a number of retaliatory measures, including breaking the pillory to pieces and 'deforcing' the house of the apprentices' master. On the

Sunday following some four or five thousand apprentices met together, with the largest gathering in Moorfields.[72] Later in the eighteenth century the venue for such gatherings was more often St
George's Fields in Southwark – perhaps because building was going
on steadily in the parish of St Luke's (formerly the northern part of
St Giles'), and only the Fields themselves remained unoccupied. As
to the other gatherings, we find records of the Spitalfields weavers
assembling in Moorfields in 1765. They were 'accompanied by drums'
and arrayed in a kind of symbolic uniform. In this manner they
marched to St James's and Westminster Hall, which they surrounded:
a ritual progress the Dunces had enacted a generation earlier. In
1773 the same body of men again used Moorfields as a setting to vent
industrial grievances. The Spitalfields Act (13 Geo.III.c.68) was
a direct outcome of the discontent expressed on this occasion; patrio-
tism was less obviously at stake.[73] However, the use made of the
adjoining (New) Artillery Ground by the Company of that name
supplies that deficiency. The residents of Bunhill Row, who did not
yet include Milton, drew up a list of complaints when the Company
were granted this lease in 1641, specifying a number of evils which
would be attendant on the exercises of 'the military gentlemen of
London'.[74] However, the more prim inhabitants of Cripplegate seem
to have been markedly unsuccessful in keeping their parish free from
these indignities. Whatever the grounds of their objection, the playhouse or hospital or artillery ground duly appeared in the ward;
probably because the City authorities wanted such things kept well
away from the historic capital.

Some of the other uses to which Moorfields was put are thus
described by Denton:

> A more motley assemblage . . . than that which thronged Moorfields
> can hardly be imagined. The small penthouse shops which soon after
> 1600 began to spring up on the outskirts of the Moor, were tenanted by
> botchers . . . jobbing tailors, and renovators of old clothes, always
> ready to leave their shop boards and to join in the scuffles which went
> on before their doors. Under trees planted across the lower [southern]
> part of the Moor were stalls of second-hand booksellers, where anti-
> quaries rummaged for black-letter tracts . . . On lines stretched from
> tree to tree, slips of ballads fluttered in the breeze . . . In one corner

of the ground or another, wrestling matches gathered crowds of spectators for three or four centuries, and boxing and cudgel playing went on continually for the amusement of loiterers, and the advantage of the thieves who frequented these fields. Here, too, the place where the thief plied his vocation witnessed his punishment; for . . . Moorfields was chosen as the proper spot for publicly whipping the thief. A lock-up house for rioters, felons and other offenders . . . stood in these fields . . . Punch with his unfailing attractions, jugglers with their tricks of dexterity, and merry-andrews with their ready gibes, collect little crowds of idlers. Here, again, were ballad singers, sturdy beggars, and cripples, and at night . . . the prowling footpad and the burglar. . . .[75]

It is apparent that Pope knew what he was doing when he transferred the nerve-centre of the Dull from Rag Fair to a spot near Bedlam. The overtones are the same; a place of vagrancy, dissolute behaviour and crude physical action. Moreover, it is a simple metaphoric process to convert these ecological features into a critique of low professional scribbling. Writers (like the cheapjacks) deal in the second-hand; they are thieves; they are literary contortionists. At Moorfields (and, as we shall see, along the railings of Bedlam itself) lines of mean poetasters' wares were hung up like washing. The means of distribution – the 'point of sale' methods in use – reinforced Pope's point. Cheap literature was a commodity which had to be flaunted before the buyer's eyes like so much greengrocery. Its primary existence was one of visible, external substance;[76] as opposed to the inner life of true literature. The physicalities and literary fisticuffs of Pope's satire (e.g. in his prose pamphlets against Curll) are an image of Moorfields tumult, built into the artistic mode.

It is not hard to provide documentation of all the activities mentioned in Denton's account. The cheap stalls of Moorfields were mentioned by Garth; cheap meals were spoken of in 1755 as 'Farthing fries at Moorfields'.[77] (The Farthing Pye House, on the northern extremities of the region, will reappear presently.) Pepys describes the wrestling in 1661.[78] The cudgel players are mentioned by Shadwell. Throwing at cocks was another popular pastime, which thieves seem to have taken to around the turn of the century. Thirty years later we hear of strange wagers which were laid here.[79] As for the sturdy beggars to whom Denton refers, *A Trip through London*

(1728) has a phrase relating to 'the honest *Beggar* upon his *Truss of Straw* in *Moor-fields* . . .'[80] Again, the presence of low theatrical shows of one kind or another is attested by a number of sources. In 1739 the Grand Jury of Middlesex issued a presentment against the builders of booths erected in Moorfields, to which idle and disorderly people resorted to the disturbance of the peace. The constables of the Finsbury division were instructed to apprehend offenders. Similarly, in 1748 players were said to infest Moorfields daily.[81] The text of *The Dunciad* gives eloquent proof of what Pope thought about such Smithfield drolls (e.g. B.III.285ff.) Settle's prophecy envisages a day when

> . . . rais'd from booths, to Theatre, to Court,
> Her seat imperial Dulness shall transport. (B.III.299)

The movement of the poem, then, is from suburban fastnesses like Moorfields to the newly colonised areas of the West End.

The most direct link with literary topics, however, resides in the book trade. For example, the stalls which were cleared away from St Paul's Churchyard soon found a home elsewhere: 'by 1750 they seem to have congregated especially in Moorfields.'[82] About this time Gray wrote to Warton of the penny histories 'that hang upon the rails in Moorfields'. In Smyth's *Obituary*, an invaluable source for any student of Grub Street and its environs, we come on a bookseller at Bedlam who died in 1671; besides a variety of Moorfields residents in occupations ranging from hemp-beater to 'Ye City Painter'.[83] In *Trivia* the 'copious' stock market of Newgate is ranged with the fruit emporium of Covent Garden, whilst '*Moor-fields* [gives] old books; and *Monmouth-street* old suits.'

To these associations might be added such Moorfields specialities as itinerant preachers (Wesley and Whitefield used a shed in the old Canon Foundry on Windmill Hill, north of the fields towards the pest-house); brothels;[84] a dissenting academy which produced some of Samuel Johnson's early contacts in metaphoric Grub Street;[85] and the alehouses and singing-rooms which Pepys visited.[86] The stage of the Windmill tavern, opposite Bedlam, was used for strongman acts, whilst the Flying Horse in Little Moorfields was celebrated for music, merry andrews and cudgel play.[87] Finally there was a sad historical link with murder: in 1718 the public executioner, John Price, alias Jack Ketch, was hanged in Bunhill Fields for the brutal homicide of an old woman in Moorfields.[88]

This then was Moorfields in itself. That Dunces such as Ned Ward should have seen fit to set up their own taverns in the district was a further proof of that urban blight which Pope marked out as his special subject.[89] Again, it was more convenient than essential to the satirist's purposes that the disreputable Calves-Head Club, 'which caused scandal by celebrating the anniversary of Charles I's execution with ghoulish rites', should have been stated by a contemporary to have assembled 'in a blind alley about Moorfields'.[90] It all helped. But the major blot on this particular scutcheon was the existence of Bedlam.

Bethlehem Hospital had been founded in the thirteenth century, and stood originally near St Helen's, Bishopsgate. In 1675–6 a new building was erected by Robert Hooke, a short distance to the west. Stow refers to the narrow alleys surrounding the first hospital, 'of late time too much pesterd with people (a great cause of infection) up to the Bars'. Strype calls the original site an 'obscure and close Place, near unto many common Sewers'.[91] The new situation was generally considered to be better. James Ralph wrote in 1734, '*Bedlam* is very well situated in point of view and is laid out in a very elegant taste', although he deplored the 'near neighbourhood' of Moorgate as 'something of a blemish to this pile, because 'tis built in the same stile with it'.[92] The view from Bedlam was in essence the view from Grub Street. For completeness, it may be added that the hospital moved to St George's Fields, Southwark, in 1812–15, and occupied what is now the Imperial War Museum. The Bethlehem Hospital has since amalgamated with the Maudsley and has moved to Kent.

One striking visual aspect of Hooke's building was not precisely architectural at all; the two massive figures of Dementia and Mania (or 'Melancholy Madness' and 'Raving Madness') erected by Caius Gabriel Cibber, father of Colley Cibber, over the hospital gates. Pope, with his customary economy, utilised this feature of Bedlam in his revised *Dunciad*; whilst Hogarth is supposed to have parodied the figures in the background of his Bedlam scene in the *Rake's Progress*. This is a good clue to the importance of Bedlam in Augustan contexts. The significance it has in earlier literature has long been recognised; a monograph, indeed, called *Bedlam on the Jacobean Stage* contains useful information for our present purposes.[93] But there are several new components when we turn to Pope and Swift. Some of these relate to changing views of abnormal psychology, and to different provision for mentally sick persons. But other factors are connected with the new hospital itself, and its part in London life. There is a grim irony in the fact that a stately baroque mansion should have been dedicated to the task of housing the mad. According to Strype, 'Now those are judged the fittest Objects for this Hospital that are raving and furious, and are capable of cure . . . or if not, yet are likely to do mischief to themselves or others; and are Poor, and cannot be otherwise provided for.'[94] There was, as a matter of fact, a ward for incurables added, and this is shown in Hogarth's picture of Tom Rakewell. In general, however, Strype's account of the earlier dispensation fits the plan Pope had set out in his letter to Broome. He had stressed the age and penury of the 'tribe' of hack authors, and their claim to enjoy 'good looking after', Gildon and Dennis are to go out to stud, like Chelsea pensioners: their 'accommodation' is to be better than that experienced in Bedlam, by poets and others – but the implication is that the service will be of the same order.

In speaking of the treatment 'poets usually meet with in Moorfields', Pope undoubtedly had in mind the case of Nathaniel Lee,[95] who had been confined in the hospital from 1684 to 1688. This celebrated item of Grub Street mythology was of course as familiar to Pope as to anyone else. He seems, however, to have made only one explicit reference in an Horatian imitation (Sat.II.i):

> Whether the darkn'd Room to muse invite,
> Or whiten'd Wall provoke the Skew'r to write,
> In Durance, Exile, Bedlam, or the Mint,
> Like *Lee* or *Budgell*, I will Rhyme and Print.

The canard (retailed in the Twickenham edition, most recently) that Lee had written a twenty-five act drama in Bedlam serves to give

added point. Pope often links madness with poetry in his Horatian
essays, but nowhere else is certified lunacy tied so inextricably to
the production of mindless, unwanted verses. One more indirect
allusion comes in Ep.I.i, where Pope addresses Bolingbroke:

> You never change one muscle of your face,
> You think this Madness but a common case,
> Nor once to Chanc'ry, nor to Hales apply . . .[96]

Dr Hales is glossed simply as 'The Doctor of Bedlam' in Pope's note.

There had been one development, associated with the new
building, which had brought Bedlam and literary production further
together since the time of the Jacobean dramatists. This was the
practice of using the long railings fronting the hospital on the south
side as a publisher's billboard. Here books were advertised by the
simple expedient of displaying the title-page (a habit which Gay describes at the end of *Trivia*).[97] Unlike St Paul's Churchyard, Bedlam seems to have been a market chiefly for second-hand works.
Throughout the period from 1710 to 1786, books lined the perimeter
of the hospital. On the wooden palings outside, broadsheets were displayed, whilst next to the wall second-hand bookstalls were set up.
Pope himself alludes to this practice in the closing lines of his epistle
to Augustus:

> And when I flatter, let my dirty leaves
> (Like Journals, Odes, and such forgotten things,
> As Eusden, Philips, Settle, writ of Kings)
> Cloath spice, line trunks, or flutt'ring in a row,
> Befringe the rails of Bedlam and Sohoe.[98]

It was yet another way in which the Dunces' hide-out could be
associated with the shabby and the second-hand. In the first version
of Pope's poem, the cell of Dulness is situated near a well-known
mart for cast-off clothing. In the revised version, the Cave of Poverty
and Poetry is found near the bastions of Bedlam – indeed, the actual
walls (where the unwanted products of the duncely imagination
were on show) are mentioned at the outset:

> Close to those walls where Folly holds her throne . . .
> One Cell there is, conceal'd from vulgar eye . . .
>
> (B.I.29)

Characteristically, Pope has made dreary quotidinial reality foster the creative ends of satire. In the words of the poem he addressed to Fortescue, he has chosen to 'Publish the present Age'.[99] But ironically: the literal facts are drawn on, only in order to add weight to a grotesque fiction.

The singular preference Swift exhibits for the Bedlamite theme has not, I think, been sufficiently regarded. The biographic facts are plainly on record. We know that the Dean caused some consternation by his generous endowment of St Patrick's Hospital. It is also a matter of historical certainty that Swift (like his friend Atterbury) was appointed a governor of Bethlehem Hospital on 26 February 1714.[100] He is not recorded as having attended any meeting of the governors, which is accountable in view of his permanent departure for Ireland shortly afterwards. But again, in 1732, Swift received in a letter from Sir William Fownes detailed proposals for the establishment of a Bedlam Hospital in the city of Dublin, containing the interesting passage:

> I own to you I was for some time averse to our having a public Bedlam, apprehending we should be overloaded with numbers under the name of the mad. Nay I was apprehensive our Case would soon be like that in England.[101]

In other words, there can be no doubt that Swift was seriously interested in the problem of dealing with mentally sick patients.

But even without this documentation, there is plenty of literary evidence. In section IX–X of the *Tale*, Swift's obsession with this particular *topos* shines out very clearly. The '*Academy of Modern Bedlam*' is singled out in the Digression on Madness, and a description of an enquiry into the present state of Bedlam provided later. (In early editions this was garnished with a graphic illustration opposite the text.)[102] I shall return to this section subsequently (Ch.IV). More briefly, mention may be made here of the running conceit in the poem on 'The Legion Club', which identifies the Irish parliament with a madhouse, and the reference at the end of the 'Verses on the Death of Dr. Swift':

> He gave the little Wealth he had,
> To build a House for Fools and Mad . . .[103]

It is a familiar piece of social history that eighteenth-century men and women went along to Bedlam as to any other cheap pantomimic entertainment. Ned Ward described the scene in Part III of his *London Spy* (1698-9). As J. H. Plumb has written:

> Such strong passions could only flourish amidst a callous people, and it is not surprising that the popular sights of London were the lunatics in Bedlam, the whipping of half-naked women at Bridewell, the stoning to death of pilloried men and women, or the hangings at Tyburn, where a girl and a boy might be seen dangling between a highwayman and a murderer.[104]

Some of these occurrences were rare, as a matter of fact, but the show at Bedlam virtually never closed. It is also to the point that in one way or another the Dunces were connected with all four activities named. Bedlam it was, however, which was most conspicuously linked with literary folly. That was already true in 1742. The splendid imaginative stroke by which Pope made this connection actual in his *Dunciad in Four Books* has not had the critical recognition it deserves. To make Bedlam operative on the fringes of the actual plot was delicately arranged: for Grub Street, as the poem tells us, was itself flanked by that hospital.

Epic of Grub Street

One of the major changes in the revised *Dunciad*, as we have seen, is the shift of the centre of duncely operations from a spot near Rag Fair to one near Bedlam. I do not believe that the meaning of this alteration has been properly understood. Pope does not make such radical transformations idly. It is my view that the aim of this procedure is nothing less than the localisation of folly in Grub Street itself. What had been in the first version mere innuendo becomes finite, stated, *placed*.

The critical passage must be quoted in full if we are to understand the nature of this change:

> Close to those walls where Folly holds her throne,
> And laughs to think Monroe would take her down,

Where o'er the gates, by his fam'd father father's hand
Great Cibber's brazen, brainless brothers stand;
One Cell there is, conceal'd from vulgar eye,
The Cave of Poverty and Poetry.
Keen, hollow winds howl thro' the bleak recess,
Emblem of Music caus'd by Emptiness.
Hence Bards, like Proteus long in vain ty'd down,
Escape in Monsters, and amaze the town.
Hence Miscellanies spring, the weekly boast
Of Curl's chaste press, and Lintot's rubric post:
Hence hymning Tyburn's elegiac lines,
Hence Journals, Medleys, Merc'ries, Magazines:
Sepulcral Lyes, our holy walls to grace,
And New-year Odes, and all the Grub-street race. (B.I.29)

There are several important differences from the earlier version (quoted above, p. 39), apart from the shift of location. Pope has moved to a later position the reference to 'the imperial seat of Fools'; his note had suggested a parallel with the *Aeneid*, I.15–18. Literally this would have equated the cave of Dulness with Carthage, a somewhat distracting association as the poem develops. Secondly, the poet introduces mention of 'Bards' at the outset; this is to form an important part of his presentation of Duncehood. Thirdly, Pope has dropped the reference to the Quidnuncs, to the Guildhall and to Saint Cecilia's Day odes. (The first two are found at B.I.270.) He has substituted increased emphasis on the productions of folly ('Journals, Medleys . . .').

On the line 'One Cell there is . . .', the Twickenham edition has the following note, quoting at the start Warburton's gloss:

The cell of poor Poetry is here very properly represented as a little *unendowed Hall* in the neighbourhood of the Magnific *College* of *Bedlam*; and as the surest Seminary to supply those learned walls with Professors. For there cannot be a plainer indication of madness than in men's persisting to starve themselves and offend the public by scribling,

Escape in Monsters and amaze the town.

when they might have benefited themselves and others in profitable and honest employments. The *Qualities* and *Productions* of the students of this private Academy are afterwards described in this first book; as are also their *Actions* throughout the second; by which it appears, how near allied Dulness is to Madness. This naturally prepares us for the subject of the third book, where we find them in union, and acting in conjunction to produce the Catastrophe of the fourth; a mad poetical Sybil leading our Hero through the Regions of Vision, to animate him in the present undertaking, by a view of the past triumphs of Barbarism over Science. W[arburton]. [The Cell of Poverty and Poetry, situated in *Dunciad A* in the neighbourhood of Rag Fair, was shifted in *1743a* to the neighbourhood of Bedlam. Warburton's reference to 'a little unendowed Hall' is obscure; but, in view of the mention of 'Professors' immediately afterwards, the Hall may perhaps be identified with Sion College, close to Bedlam. Dr. Joseph Trapp, Professor of Poetry at Oxford from 1708–18, was, at the time Warburton's note was written, President of Sion College; and on April 26, 1743 he had published a *Concio ad Clerum Londinensem.* . . . He was a frequent subject of ridicule by the wits.][105]

I find this identification quite implausible. A much more obvious explanation of Warburton's 'obscure' allusion would be to take Grub Street as the seminary in question. Since it may appear highhanded to assume airily that all previous commentators have missed such an important point, I shall set out my reasons as fully and scrupulously as possible.

(1) Negatively. Trapp is an unlikely candidate for such a key role. Only once in all his work did Pope mention him: in the 1728 version of *The Dunciad*, at A.II.381, his identity was cloaked by the word '*T——*'. But this we learn from a manuscript source, since when the names were spelt out in full a year later, he had already been removed from the text. The only reference in Pope's correspondence dates back to 1710. Henry Cromwell had praised poems by Trapp included in Tonson's *Miscellany*: Pope replies less warmly, but adds that he does not have 'any sort of prejudice to him [Trapp] as a priest'.[106] Moreover, Trapp was an ardent Tory, and the butt chiefly of *Whiggish* wits – of Dunces such as Oldmixon, indeed. Swift may not have liked him very much, but Trapp certainly took the same side as he in various pamphleteering battles, notably in 1710–11.[107] It is hard to believe that so random and unformed a relationship should have been used to underpin the central attack on Dulness, when so many active enmities were available. Moreover Trapp was President only from 1742 to 1743, which would date the reference quickly.[108]

(2) Another negative point. The case is much the same with Sion College. This *was* near Bedlam, indeed Grub Street and Sion were almost equidistant from the hospital. On the other hand there are several arguments working against this identification. The College was not 'unendowed'. On the contrary, since its foundation in 1630, it had amassed amongst other things a notable library.[109] More important, it would be a most inappropriate setting for the 'scribbling' activities singled out by Warburton. Trapp was only one president amongst many, and neither starvation nor 'Journals, Medleys, Merc'ries . . .' were associated with this foundation. Sion could not properly be regarded as the 'home' of Cibber [B.I.266]; its potential resonance through the poem would be negligible, and it is certainly not mentioned by name anywhere – in text, notes, preliminaries or appendices. It never figures in the poems or correspondence of Pope, and to the best of my knowledge is not used with satiric intent by any major Augustan writer. Of course, the fact that it is not so used elsewhere does not prove that Pope could not have chosen to do so in this instance. But that, I think, is to multiply hypotheses beyond need – a fact that becomes apparent when we contrast the situation as it applies to Grub Street.

(3) As already shown, Grub Street was not merely near Moorfields and Bedlam; it was often so described. (As against Sion College 'lost' inside the City within the walls.) Grub Street might with perfect propriety be described as 'unendowed'; it was a poor region, and Pope never lets us forget that. The objection might be made that a street is not a hall. But Grub Street was constantly referred to by the satirists in such terms. Throughout his *Tale*, Swift speaks of the 'Society' of Grub Street, the 'Academy of Wits' located there, the 'College' of modern Aeolists, the 'Corporation of [hack] Authors', the 'Corporation of Poets', the 'Walks' of Wit, the 'spacious Commonwealth of Writers', 'Seminaries' planted by 'the *Grub-street* Brotherhood', and so on. As for professors, there is the familiar allusion to the '*Grubaean* Sages', with their 'Precepts and their Arts'. Again, in a work which has generally been taken as Swift's, the *Letter to a Young Poet*, the writer deplores the absence in Dublin of a Grub Street. He desiderates this institution by pointing to the existence of

parallel foundations ('a Court, a College, a Playhouse . . .'), and outlines a plan by which 'our poetical Vapours . . . might fall into one Quarter of the Town', instead of being scattered through 'every Street' at large. He proposes that 'some private Street, or blind Alley of this Town' should be set up as an 'apartment for the Muses'. This comes very close to Pope's idea of 'a bleak recess', 'conceal'd from vulgar eye'. In the case of the *Letter*, the application to Grub Street is made quite explicit. (See Ch.IV.)[110]

An even more striking piece of evidence can be found in the work of another Scriblerian: the preface to *John Bull* (1712), by Dr John Arbuthnot. I have used part of the passage as an epigraph to this chapter, but certain phrases may be singled out here: 'The whole University of *Grub-street*', 'the Matriculates of that famous University', 'O *Grubstreet*! thou fruitful Nursery of tow'ring Genius's!' Arbuthnot's narrator boasts of having received his education amongst 'the Learned of that Society', and laments the 'approaching Barbarity that is likely to overspread all its Regions' (cf. Warburton's note). He uses, too, the notion of the 'Brethren' of Grub Street, common to all such passages of satire, in which the street is institutionalised.[111] It is found, for example, in the preliminary material for Fielding's *Grub Street Opera* (1731), where the introduction is written by 'Scriblerus Secundus', a pseudonym indicating the extent of Fielding's debt to Pope and his friends.[112] (See p. 328 below.) Once again we see how the iconography of Grub Street, as it was customarily described, is matched by the details of the cave of Poverty and Poetry. The two localities can surely be merged into one.

(4) Grub Street was traditionally the 'home' of Dunces. The 'sacred Dome' of Dulness is specifically stated by Pope to be coterminous with the cave: and Cibber 'no sooner enters, but he Reconnoitres the place of his original'.[113] Grub Street was known for poverty, scribbling, calumny, 'Scribling' was its special occupation. It can be seen, then, that both the text and Warburton's note fit Grub Street snugly: neither suits Sion College, except by an effort of wrenching. Cibber had obvious links with Grub Street, none that is recorded with the College. Grub Street was a familiar recourse in contemporary satiric economy; its identity could be spotted by an

alert reader, whereas a joke resting on an allusion to Sion would be hard to penetrate, and not very pointed when grasped.

(5) The overriding reason stems from these facts. At the cave, the goddess shows her chosen king 'all her works' (B.I.273). These are without exception literary productions. Like the 'Journals, Medleys' and the rest, the list which Pope provides would suit an enclave of bad writers: scarcely, a theological backwater. Moreover, *The Dunciad* is stuffed throughout with references to 'bards' (at least six times), poets, authors, stationers, swans, muses, wits, critics, songsters, riddlers and the like. Their productions are named as images, similes, metaphors, tragedy, comedy, farce, epic, figures, odes, plays, lays, folio commonplace books, quartos and octavos, a birthday ode, long and painful pages, points, antitheses, puns, bawdry, Billingsgate, prologues, prefaces, notes, prose, verse, sermons, characters, essays, songs, sonnets, epigrams, and so on. The journey to the shades in Book III is led by what the argument calls 'a mad Poetical Sybil',[114] described in the text as one

> In lofty madness meditating song;
> Her tresses staring from poetic dreams . . . (B.III.16)

Similarly, the central vision of this book is that of Settle: a former City poet, not a superannuated select preacher. In other words, most of this material aligns very well with Grub Street; only contingently and fortuitously with Sion College.

Most recent critics, I think, have tended to play down excessively the direct *literary* satire of the poem. There is a metaphysical aspect to Dulness: but her principal avatars are always the writing profession. Warburton explains quite adequately, in my view, the trajectory of the poem; and if this is the case, then no other symbol could have been devised which would tie together the various layers of the poem than the home of bad poetry. Since 'the Restoration of the Empire of Dulness in Britain' is the theme (note to B.I.1), it is peculiarly just that this *coup d'état* should be organised from 'The College of the Goddess in the City, with her private Academy for Poets in particular'.[115] Only one place could reasonably be thought of as the habitat of the 'hacknied Town scribler' (note to B.I.37), and this of course was Grub Street.

(6) One item of external evidence may be mentioned. Not long after the first version of *The Dunciad* appeared, that strongly pro-Pope organ the *Grub-street Journal* began its career (cf.Ch.VI). In the issue for 20 August 1730, no. 33, an article was printed in the *Journal* entitled 'Proposals for erecting a College for the habitation of Grub-street Authors, by Giles Blunderbuss, Esq; Historiographer to the Grubean Society.' This mock proposal connects with Swift's many variants on the notion of a Grub Street academy. Here it is enough to note that 'Blunderbuss' suggests a removal from Grub Street itself to more spacious quarters nearby. These are to be near Fore Street, and Moorfields is fixed on as the ideal spot. Blunderbuss notes as a recommendation the proximity of the Artillery Ground ('that great famous seat of war') and, also anonymously, 'the vicinity of that college, which already occupies the south-side of those fields'. Among other details supplied in connection with the new Grub Street there is a reference to the walls as a 'station for booksellers after the old manner'. The article as a whole provides a series of parallels with the satiric practice of *The Dunciad*; here I wish merely to bring out its relevance to the topic we have been considering. Pope, I would contend, took the hint, but not quite *au pied de la lettre*. He moves the dome of the Dunces to new quarters in his revision, to be sure, and these are located within earshot of Bedlam. But they stand not in a new Grub Street, constructed on the great fen of Moorfields. If we are as readers alive to all the hints which the poem provides, the cave can be placed at no other point than the road which entered Fore Street a matter of two hundred yards westward: the 'old' Grub Street, of course.

Turning from the object of attack to the method, we ought to note the emphasis on 'the wond'rous pow'r of Noise' (B.II.222). Literary incompetence is imaged by cacophony; the two are actually forced together syntactically in phrases like 'Noise and Norton . . . Dennis and Dissonance' (B.II.238). It is therefore of special interest to find mention of Dulness summoning 'her own Grubstreet choir' (B.II. 123). Throughout the poem we have the swelling 'Chapel-royal throat' (B.I.319); the 'warble round' of the sirens (B.IV.541); and 'singing peers' (B.IV.49). There is the French horn (B.IV.278), trills and notes (B.IV.57), fiddling kings (B.IV.598), and 'loud Bow's stupendous bells resound' (B.III.278). Increasingly, these aural effects take on a sinister and less musical cast: 'warb'ling Polypheme' is taught to roar (B.III.305); screams issue forth (B.III.160, 306); 'chromatic tortures' threaten, as hums and snores break out (B.IV.55). Overtones of war are again present: the young rake, given a duncely education, 'stunn'd with his giddy Larum half the town' (B.IV.292). The Angel of Dulness, an *alter ego* of Cibber, 'wings the red lightning, and the thunder rolls' (B.III.256). If Handel is allowed his freedom to compose as he wishes, 'Jove's own Thunders follows Mars's Drums.' (B.IV.68). To counteract this threat, a last trump is blown, and all the retinue of Dulness assembled. Elsewhere, in an audacious pun, we hear 'the heavy Canon [of Christ Church] roll' (B.IV.247). The words *loud/loudly* are reiterated; terms like 'echo, hum, bray, bellow, strain, sound, bawl, peal' abound.

This richness of aural content serves two main functions. It fixes the Dunces as gibbering fools whose 'Music' never 'meanly borrows aid from Sense' (B.IV.64). The climatic moment occurs in Book II, with the shouting match and its accompaniment of grating catcalls. 'Tis yours to shake the soul' the Goddess tells her devotees:

> With Thunder rumbling from the mustard bowl,
> With horns and trumpets now to madness swell,
> Now sink in sorrows with a tolling bell;
> Such happy arts attention can command,
> When fancy flags, and sense is at a stand.
> Improve we these. Three Cat-calls be the bribe
> Of him, whose chatt'ring shames the Monkey tribe:
> And this his Drum, whose hoarse heroic base
> Drowns the loud clarion of the braying Ass. (B.II.226)

At that, a thousand tongues are heard 'in one loud din', and the famous passage of 'discordant' braying begins, with an unusual profusion for Pope of simple onomatopoeia (*chatt'ring, jabb'ring*). In the contest itself, Blackmore proves himself king brayer. Amidst all the 'moans' rending the welkin, and the 'harmonic twang' of the asses, the 'sonerous' poet carries away the prize, just as his voice carries to distant Tothill Fields, Hungerford and Westminster. The passage

reminds us that a Dunce is never more at home than when acting like
the donkey he is. Moore-Smythe has already been characterised
(B.II.45) by reference to 'empty words . . . and sounding strain'.
This is again a specifically literary emblem, though noisy inanity
might possibly have been applied to men and women in any walk of
life. Significantly, Bedlam was a byword for clamour: a contemporary
spoke of members of Parliament making 'a hideous noise like so many
Bedlamites'.[116]

Secondly, sound effects are used to drive home another prominent
motif, the idea of the factious, brawling crowd:

> Dire is the conflict, dismal is the din,
> Here shouts all Drury, there all Lincoln's-inn;
> Contending Theatres our empire raise . . . (B.III.269)

It is noteworthy that Drury Lane and Lincoln's Inn Fields had a
characteristic in common apart from housing a theatre. Each was
frequently the scene of affrays at this time. The 'din' thus becomes
representative of discord at large, as well as the quarrels between the
theatres. And 'discord', in this context, means not only the cosmic
breakdown, which recent critics have dwelt on so much – it points
once again to the noisy street battles of eighteenth-century London.
At best 'the noise of the streets was indeed deafening', what with the
clatter of the carriages and the cries of vendors. Sanity, in Pope's
poem, is forced to cover its ears against the hubbub, like Hogarth's
Enraged Musician.

There is a subsidiary point here. *The Dunciad* is to a remarkable
degree an *open-air* poem. A sense of expansiveness is apparent at all
times; something the constant iteration of place-names, spread across
the City, does much to promote. The text is littered with allusions to
St James's, the Fleet Prison, Hockley Hole (twice), Chancery Lane,
Guildhall, Ludgate, and so on. Sometimes the place is used with
little more than figurative intent (Billingsgate; Drury Lane, at
B.I.322). More often, however, the effect is to enhance the reader's
sense of an *alfresco* scene, where turbulence is the norm. It has been
wittily said, 'One of the few activities in which the upper and lower
classes could find a common, happy meeting ground [in the eighteenth

century] was street fighting.'[117] Here again the poem reflects the actuality of the age. A higher proportion of conspicuous life was led in the streets; historical events of consequence much more frequently took place out of doors. Public occasions, of ceremony or of function, went on in the streets. We need consider only the cases of Defoe, whose experience might be said to attain its most significant moments in the market place. His *Shortest Way* was burnt outsideWestminster Hall; he stood in the pillory in Cornhill, Cheapside and the Strand; he marched with a deputation into the Houses of Parliament. A few lines after mentioning the sight of Defoe in the pillory, indeed, Pope writes in the person of Curll:

> And oh! (he cry'd) what street, what lane but knows,
> Our purgings, pumpings, blankettings and blows? (B.II.153)

It is a rhetorical question. The cudgelling of publishers, the tossing of Curll himself in a blanket, were indeed quasi-public 'happenings', arranged for their display value. Yet they were also part of diurnal reality for the Londoner of 1740. Violence was a commonplace; perhaps Grub Street and its denizens were a little more at risk than the average.

Pope mentioned Grub Street by name only five times in the revised text. One additional reference (A.I.184) was dropped. In every case, the literal sense is present or available. (This is in contrast to his use of the term elsewhere, for example in the *Epistle to Arbuthnot*, where the figurative meaning is dominant).[118] Of these, the most valuable usage occurs in the third book, where Settle in his rapture compares Queen Dulness with Berecynthia:

> Not with less glory mighty Dulness crown'd,
> Shall take thro' Grub-street her triumphant round;
> And her Parnassus glancing o'er at once,
> Behold an hundred sons, and each a Dunce. (B.III.135)

Just as the bad poets aspiring to the art of sinking are allotted the 'Lowlands of Parnassus' as their quarters, so Dulness is assigned the lease of an actual plot of ground.[119] (Our key phrase never appears in *Peri Bathous*, though the topics and the individuals taken up are often identical. This suggests that it was the special needs of the plot, and the specially chosen setting, which dictate Pope's employment of the term in *The Dunciad*.) The simple truth is that Dulness *does* take 'her triumphant round' through Grub Street; the gallery of characters which follows (Ward, Jacob, Welsted, Dennis, Gildon, etc.) makes up a selection of first-choice Dunces. Ward is actually confronted with an ale-house (B.III.147), just like the one he had kept in Moorfields – another piece of live social history, to set against the stews, coalyards, and roundhouses mentioned elsewhere. Real poets went to Bedlam; real rioters practised cudgel-play or wrestling at Hockley Hole; real trainbands carried out their exercises on Moorfields (Cibber is ironically commended by Aristarchus for his knowledge of '*Old Battle-array*').[120] Real Dunces, like Defoe and Gildon, lived in the vicinity of Grub Street. The poem makes them re-enact these experiences at the removed (but no less painful) level of fiction. For all Pope's comic invention, the joke would have been much less good if there had been no reality on to which to base the grotesque transformation acts of his poem – no Bedlam, no city riots, no Grub Street.

*   *   *

As everyone knows, Dryden's *Mac Flecknoe* (1682) was the most important single model for the mock-heroic of *The Dunciad*. Apart from anything else, the earlier poem 'gave Pope the idea of a succession to the throne of Dulness'.[121] However, some of the implications of this carry-over have been missed, because one significant point of comparison has escaped detection. The throne of Thomas Shadwell is set up in the very same quarter of the town as the 'gorgeous seat' of Cibber (B.II.1). Cripplegate is the home of Dulness in both cases. It is no accident that Pope specifically recalls Dryden's poem at this moment: the seat 'far outshone/Henley's gilt tub, or Fleckno's Irish throne.'

At the outset there is a direct verbal recollection, not indicated in the Twickenham edition. When Pope describes the Dunces' cell, removed in the second version to the vicinity of Bedlam, he begins:

Close to those walls where Folly holds her throne . . . (B.I.29).

Compare the setting provided for Shadwell's imperial residence:

Close to the Walls which fair *Augusta* bind,
(The fair *Augusta* much to fears inclin'd)
An ancient fabrick, rais'd t' inform the sight,
There stood of yore, and *Barbican* it hight:
A watch Tower once; but now, so Fate ordains,
Of all the Pile an empty name remains.[122]

Dryden's archaising vein mirrors the dilapidated state of the place;
Dunces, like rats, infest decaying mansions. The passage continues:

From its old Ruins Brothel-houses rise,
Scenes of lewd loves, and of polluted joys.
Where their vast Courts the Mother-Strumpets keep,
And, undisturbed by Watch, in silence sleep.

In the light of Aubrey Williams's research, it is hardly necessary to
stress that Queen Dulness in Pope's poem functions as Magna Mater,
i.e., in one signification, mother-strumpet or madam. As with the
original site of the Dunces' cave, Rag Fair, a halo of brothels extends
around the sanctum of folly. That the watch turned a blind eye to
certain notorious areas of the town is well attested; some years later
party no. 7 of the Bow Street force was deputed to patrol this area,
but in 1740 the policing function was slackly performed – not to
speak of 1680.[123]

Dryden moves on to a splendid setpiece concerning the nursery
theatre briefly in occupation here during the Restoration. In this
house 'Queen's are form'd, and future Hero's bred'. Unfledged actors
are taught to rant and posture. Fletcher and Ben Jonson are banished
in favour of fairground drolleries:

. . . gentle *Simkin* just reception finds
Amid this Monument of vanisht minds:
Pure Clinches, the suburbian Muse affords;
And *Panton* waging harmless War with words.

Punning, we recall from Book IV, is a major acquirement of the
Dunces. And the 'suburbian Muse' is another word for the Smithfield Muses, the deities who preside over harlequinades, puppet-
shows or any other duncely spectacle.[124] In another sense, too, Pope
equally places his throne-room in a 'monument of vanisht minds' –
Bedlam.

On this spot, then, 'as a Place to Fame well known', Fleckno decides to set down Shadwell in readiness for his coronation. There is a hint that the dramatist Dekker has prophesied that 'in this Pile should Reign a mighty Prince', but as far as I can discover this is a facetious rather than a literal reference, corresponding to the vision of Settle in *The Dunciad*, Book III. At all events, the coronation is duly publicised throughout the town, and we are given one of those brief itineraries which are so characteristic of Augustan satire:

> Rows'd by report of Fame, the Nations meet,
> From near *Bun-Hill*, and distant *Watling-street*.

The City proper (Watling Street) is 'distant'; close at hand is the unmistakably suburban Bunhill Fields, where Cripplegate was in 1680 almost on the point of straggling into semi-rural scrubland. Bunhill Row had recent associations with John Milton; but equally to the purpose its southern end lay a bare hundred yards from the northern tip of Grub Street. And through that street the 'Nations' of bad authors would assuredly troop on their way to the coronation ceremony.

The remainder of *Mac Flecknoe* is familiar enough and need not concern us. The point is that Shadwell's far from peaceful province in 'Acrostick Land' turns out to lie within the limits of Cripplegate. Earlier commentators assumed that the theatre near the Barbican must have been the old Fortune playhouse, which had been situated north of the Barbican off Golden Lane. But some acute detective work by Leslie Hotson has shown that the Restoration nursery was situated elsewhere.[125] There was first of all a booth or playhouse built in Finsbury Fields, 'commonly called Bun hill', in 1671. For nine weeks that summer the nursery occupied that site until some of the young actors defected. But in October of the same year Lady Davenant's proposal to erect a playhouse in the Barbican was opposed by parishioners of St Giles'. They alleged that the foundation of the theatre would 'tend to the great evill and inconveniency' of the inhabitants, arguing that a playhouse should not be permitted 'so neere the Bowells of the City'. Nevertheless, the theatre was built and it is doubtless to this which Dryden alludes. Hotson argues with some cogency that the nursery stood south of the Barbican, in a court later named Playhouse Yard, and that the building was taken over by the Anabaptist meeting house which Rocque indicates on this site. This identification has the incidental merit of bringing the nursery closer to the city walls, and that is of some relevance in considering the thematic significance of the passage.

This section of *Mac Flecknoe* does indeed rehearse much of the satiric 'happening' which constitutes Book I of *The Dunciad*. The nursery was opposed by residents of Cripplegate on the grounds that it would lead to disorders. The theatre is itself an epitome of Dunce-hood in action; it rejects the honoured traditions of drama in favour of low pantomimic entertainments. Readers of Sybil Rosenfeld's enjoyable study of *The Theatre of the London Fairs in the Eighteenth Century* will know what that portends: for Dryden as for Pope, drolls were to legitimate drama as birthday odes were to Homer.

Secondly, the fact that the playhouse lay just outside the City walls is given deliberate emphasis. 'Augusta' had been 'much to fears inclin'd' around the time of the Exclusion Crisis and the Popish Plot. Yet the phrasing suggests a permanence in the situation – the absence of an auxiliary verb removes the notion as well as the gram-matical fact of tense. We are led to suppose that the city is in a con-stant state of siege and disquiet. The agencies of this unrest are concentrated *outside* the walls of the ancient Augusta – the use of the Roman term implies the integrity of the Roman settlement, rather than the modern city whose liberties extend further out. The nursery, unlike Bunhill Fields and the northern part of Grub Street, lay just inside the liberty of the city. But the 'suburban Muse' flourished in districts like Smithfield and Farringdon Without, which strictly came under the jurisdiction of the City – as well as places like Southwark which had their own ancient municipal life, yet remained wards of London without the walls. Suburban status, as today, was not a matter of administrative history, but of social and geographical reali-ties.[126] The growing suburbs had long been felt to constitute an obscure threat. Dryden and Pope may not have sided with the City Corporation on many political issues, but imaginatively they were at one with the ancient community here. The place of maximum squalor and lewdness, where policing is most inadequate, naturally lies away from the compact centre of organic 'London'. The same idea might be put in a slightly different way. Paradoxically the taint of urbanism, as Pope for one discerned it, lay most heavily on the fringes of the town, where haphazard development had proceeded, not unchecked but under too little restraint. The point of maximum danger, correspondingly, is the edge of the town, where callow urbanism is in process of destroying the age-old countryside. Not for nothing do Juvenal's Umbricius and Johnson's Thales deliver their philippics against the city from just outside its bounds – 'Indignant THALES eyes the *neighb'ring* town' (My italics).

The suburban muse, then, with all its baneful cultural implications, was properly set down in Cripplegate. Dryden used as its symbol a theatre in Paul's Alley. To find a more potent and expressive vehicle, Pope had only to shift the seat of Dulness two or three hundreds yard eastwards. Grub Street was half within the liberty of the city, half without: as literal a state of suburbia as one could ever imagine.

Men and Places

For the Dunces, the point of no return is the church of St Mary le Strand. Queen Dulness sets up her throne there (A.II.23):

> Amid that Area wide she took her stand,
> Where the tall May-pole once o'erlook'd the Strand;
> But now, so ANNE and Piety ordain,
> A Church collects the saints of Drury Lane.

According to Aubrey Williams, this siting of the action, just beyond the boundary of the City and Temple Bar, is 'highly significant, for at the Strand began the jurisdiction of Westminster'. He continues:

Then, where Drury Lane enters the Strand, the dunces enact their ludicrous parody of the epic games. The exact geography of the games seems partly determined by the fact that the Strand and Drury Lane were the actual sites of many printing-houses and theatres, and so could mark the encroachment of literary dulness on Westminster.[127]

All this, so far as it goes, is excellently said. But if we are to chart 'the exact geography' of the games, then there is much more to be said. On the negative side, it is not wholly true that many printing houses were located in the Strand. Booksellers' shops were numerous in Fleet Street particularly, and such famous members of the trade as the firm of Tonson were actually in business a few yards from St Mary's, 'over against Catherine Street', as many an imprint records. The printing trade as a whole was centred much farther east.[128] But there are more positive additions to be made. Firstly, the maypole (removed as lately as 1718) carries obvious associations of bawdy fun and pagan ritual. The Dunces act with the unthinking atavism of a Hocktide reveller. They do not know what their own jollities portend, but they indulge with religious fervour. More important is the range of ideas evoked by the mention of Drury Lane. As the mention of 'saints' (prostitutes) makes plain, the district north-westwards from the games' venue had an unsalubrious reputation. In particular, it was down in this direction that the Great Plague had spread. Drury Lane connoted only secondarily theatreland. Nor was the concentration of coffee-houses, which modern descriptions of the area tend to single out, its most marked feature for men and women of the time. Sociologically this district was rather heterogeneous; it had a genuine bohemian flavour, which the other haunts of Dulness lacked. Wits and aristocrats *would* have visited this part of town, whereas they would never willingly have strayed into Moorfields or Rag Fair. Despite that, it cannot be denied that for the most part Drury Lane was linked in the contemporary mind with organised vice. An early letter from Pope to Henry Cromwell makes the point. The issue is raised in prose: 'If I may be allow'd to object against any thing you write . . . it shou'd be that Passage in yours, where you are pleas'd to call the Whores of *Drury-Lane*, the Nymphs of *Drury* . . .' And then, amusingly, in verse:

> If Wit or Critick blame the tender Swain,
> Who stil'd the gentle Damsels in his Strain
> The Nymphs of *Drury*, not of Drury-Lane;
> Be this his Answer, and most just Excuse—
> 'Far be it, Sirs, from my more civill Muse,

Those Loving Ladies rudely to traduce.
Alleys and Lanes are Terms to vile and base,
And give Idea's of a narrow Pass;
But the well-worn Paths of the Nymphs of Drury
Are large & wide; *Tydcomb* and I assure ye.'[129]

The obscene touch here is only what contemporary readers would have expected every time the name 'Drury Lane' came up. Its squad of 'Loving Ladies' were for a long time the chief resident personnel. The topographic aspect is explicitly stressed on many occasions, so that we find references to 'a woman of great note in the hundreds of Drury' in the *Grub-street Journal*.[130]

For the severe moralist, the existence of the theatre did not improve matters, especially in the region about Russell Street. In 1730 the shopkeepers and traders appealed to the Westminster Sessions, in whose jurisdiction of course they lay:

> Several people of the most notorious characters and infamously wicked lives and conversation have of late . . . years taken up their abode in the parish. . . . There are several streets and courts such as Russell Street, Drury Lane, Crown Court and King's Court and divers places within the said parish and more particularly in the neighbourhood of Drury Lane infested with these vile people. . . . There are frequent outcries in the night, fighting, robberies and all sorts of debaucheries committed by them all night long to the great inquietude of his majesty's subjects.[131]

(Note, in passing, the word 'infested'.) Certainly this was no district in which to cultivate Thorowgood's bourgeois habits or to put the Protestant ethic into practice. Narcissus Luttrell describes a violent Jacobite riot which took place in Drury Lane itself in 1695,[132] and there were others later. Naturally the night-cellars and gaming establishments which had sprung up promoted crime, and it is interesting to note that Jack Sheppard began life as a carpenter's apprentice in Wych Street, off Drury Lane. He never moved his centre of operations very far away.[133] There was a cockpit in the street, too.[134] Whether Pope would align these features of the landscape with the theatre may be doubted. But he certainly knew the byways of the region. As we shall see, he gives as the address of one of Curll's authors Vinegar Yard, a mean court right up against the playhouse.

The whole district around Covent Garden and St Giles' requires a book to itself. Gay speaks of '*Drury's* mazy courts' and Garth of 'fam'd St *Giles*'s Pound'.[135] It was an area linked with rookeries and thieves' dens, around the crowded labyrinth of Seven Dials. Hogarth had set the first stage of cruelty in this vicinity, and the harsh image clung on. In fact St Giles' figures in the background of 'Noon', and one part of the parish forms the basis for Gin Lane.[136] The lodging-houses and gin-shops of this area were infamous even in a London less nice than our own; after the plague had gone, we find typhus setting in with peculiar virulence. Most of the houses were not especially old; it was a seventeenth-century development. But it was the worst part of the city as far as insanitary boarding went. Un-skilled Irish labourers, lascars, negroes flooded into the district. Coloured beggars even became known as 'St Giles' blackbirds'. As with the 'hundreds of Drury', adjoining the parish to the south-east, 'St Giles' in eighteenth-century art – literary or graphic – means trouble.[137] Dunces and highwaymen mingled there. The parish of St Paul's, Covent Garden, harboured at one time both the most infamous of bawds, Mother Douglas, and the most notorious of booksellers, Edmund Curll.[138] The sociological accident coincides with the literary assertion: to publish is to act as a pimp on behalf of artistic prostitution.

These associations can be traced in the work of many of Pope's contemporaries. But, to limit ourselves to his own circle of friends, Garth and John Gay had given recent expression to this view of Covent Garden and its environs. The former writes in *The Dispensary*:

> Long has this darling Quarter of the Town,
> For Lewdness, Wit, and Gallantry been known.

Whilst *Trivia* shows us a rowdy game of football, juxtaposed ironic-ally with Inigo Jones's 'famous temple'.[139] This blend of spacious amenity, as regards the actual buildings, with tumultuous and anti-social conduct furnishes just the kind of human oxymoron which the Scriblerians delighted to observe.

The St Giles' – Drury Lane – Covent Garden area, then, can be seen to contain the usual ingredients of a home of the Dull. It embraced a greater range of poverty and affluence than most districts of this kind. But the other characteristics appear as usual: connections with crime, plague black spots, organised vice, the visible squalor of Gin Lane, a high concentration of immigrant labourers, crowded housing, an abundance of night-cellars and garrets, labyrinths of impenetrable courts and alleys. The residence of particular minor writers whose genuine existence is attested seems almost an accidental addition.

Earlier we found similar circumstances in the case of other regions – Grub Street, West Smithfield and Rosemary Lane. I shall consider in Ch. II the extensive belt of poverty-line London which bordered on that notorious sink, the Fleet Ditch. Overall, we can distinguish four main centres of this kind. These regions adjoin one another and, in the case of Smithfield, they actually merge. However, they may be roughly divided as follows:

(1) ROSEMARY LANE. The parts just outside the City at the south-eastern corner, near the Tower. Mainly located in the parish of St Botolph without Aldgate, and Portsoken Ward. This district includes Rag Fair itself, the headquarters of the Dunces in the first version of the poem. It also embraces Goodman's Fields, the Minories, Nightingale Lane.

(2) ST GILES' CRIPPLEGATE. More or less coterminous with both the parochial and the municipal limits designated by that name. Contains Grub Street itself, and in addition Red Cross Street, Jewin Street, Old Street – as well as Moorfields and Bedlam. Joined with area (1) by Houndsditch and Petticoat Lane.

(3) FLEET *and* FARRINGDON. This is the largest area, covering most of Farringdon Ward Without, and also certain adjacent regions, notably the parish of St Andrew, Holborn. Skirts the western edge of the old City wall, and includes Bridewell, Fleet Street, Shoe Lane, the environs of Newgate, the Fleet Prison and the lower reaches of the Fleet River. Linked with area (2) by the notorious Smithfield slum, reaching as far as the southern tip of Clerkenwell, but all draining into the Ditch.

(4) ST GILES' *and* COVENT GARDEN. Includes Drury Lane and that part of the Strand immediately contiguous. Adjoins area (3) to the east.

It would be possible to devise other zones of this kind, most obviously in the Borough of Southwark – where the Mint served as an epicentre of the disease which was Dulness, not to mention other human disabilities. But these are the sectors of London most directly relevant to the imaginative working of *The Dunciad*.

It will be immediately apparent from the map that these four areas ring the ancient walled City. The point to be made is that they do not actually *invade* the limits so defined. This is not to say that they do not fall within the jurisdiction of the municipality. Actually, a high proportion of the first three areas lies within the 'liberties' of the City, i.e. parts within the 'rules' of the Corporation and its courts, but outside the walls. This is a significant fact. In the early eighteenth century, the heart of the City itself was not subjected to special strain. The population of the City within the Walls declined steadily over the course of the century. The City without the Walls, after growing in the Restoration era, remained fairly static. It was the outlying parishes which grew most quickly. Some of these in effect were surburban, and largely escaped the problems of poverty and sanitation associated with rapid growth. It was the zone surrounding the ancient City, the inner ring of parishes in such vicinities as Holborn, Stepney and Clerkenwell which felt these problems most acutely.[140]

It was in those secondary regions, surrounding the City Walls, where the Dunces were most highly concentrated. This point has been obscured by Aubrey Williams's reading of Pope, which – acute and valuable as it is – fosters one central misconception. Williams sees the gallery of Dunces as a literary embodiment for a process visible in the world at large – 'the extension of City standards into the court'.[141] He charts with some care 'the path pursued by the dunces in their riotous peregrinations about London' and implies that we can see this itinerary as an emblem for the passage of Troy-novant from the City to Westminster.[142] However this is to reckon only with a selection of the facts. It is important to recognise that the Dunces, for the most part, did not live in the City, narrowly defined. They cannot be simply equated with the brokers and stockjobbers, the merchants and importers, the shopkeepers and moneylenders: for the good reason that they themselves had no real stake in the life of the City. It is not just that they had no seat on the aldermanic bench of the Corporation. Many of them lived in Westminster (i.e. area (4)); many others resided in, and frequented, parts of the town nearer Whitehall than the new Guildhall which went up in the 1730's. The truth is that when the Dunces reached St Mary le Strand, and set up their maypole at that spot, they had returned to their own background. When they made their next halt, at Bridewell Bridge, they were virtually home. The journey from Mansion House to Fleet Ditch was not for them (as it *was* for the Lord Mayor and his party) a voyage out. It was not even an aimless peregrination. It was a homecoming.

Just how familiar Pope was with the haunts of his victims, and how carefully he plotted their movements, we can gauge from one striking piece of his evidence. This is to be found in his 'Further Account of the Condition of Edmund Curll' (1716). My analysis of the text is based partly on comments by Elwin and Courthope, and by Ralph Straus; but substantially the passage remains unexplicated. This is a great pity, for without assistance we can hardly make anything of Pope's satire. His interest in his literary opponents, *prior to* their transmutation into literary vehicles of his own manufacture, entails several obligations on us as readers. Unique amongst satirists, the Scriblerian group kept a detailed file on their victims over a period of many years. Their final satiric references are chosen with pointed accuracy. Indeed, there is a malicious brand of specificity which marks out all Pope's practice. It follows that we have to be alive to what may look at first to be the stray particulars, if we want to grasp the general implications of his attack.

The passage is occasioned by a determination of Curll (as Pope has it in his narrative) to summon his various authors for a kind of sickbed salon. The bookseller, in 'a lucid Interval' amid the fits of madness occasioned by the poison Pope had administered, sends out a messenger to call in his flock. There follow 'Instructions to a Porter how to find Mr. *Curll*'s Authors'. Delightfully circumstantial, these instructions provide us with Pope's first, and fullest, reference guide to his map of Dulness. In succession we are given the description of each needy hack and his likely whereabouts. Pope skips briskly from one address to the next; I shall follow at a more leisurely pace, proceeding not *seriatim* but taking the authors one by one. (Here we shall not be primarily concerned with the identity of these men and women, a question to be studied elsewhere.)[143]

The porter is to search first for the house historian, 'at a Tallowchandlers half way under the blind Arch'. This possibly refers to Petty France, Westminster, in view of the facts, first, that the parts of Westminster adjoining Tothill Fields were made up of mean streets at that time; and second, that Aaron Hill came to live in Petty France some years later.[144] (He had also written a history of the Ottoman Empire in 1709.) More probably, the location in mind is another Petty France, shortly to disappear, which at that time lay in Bishopsgate Ward Without, near modern Broad Street, and became 'New Broad Street'. The burial ground of St Botolph's lay here. The original Bethlehem Hospital had been sited here, though Bedlam now stood a few yards west. This is, in short, an archetypal duncely address, within easy reach of Grub Street, conveniently situated for access to Bedlam, and placed squarely within the liberties.

It is a short step to the second point of call, 'At the Bedsted and Bolster, a Musick-house in *Moorfields*, two Translators in a Bed together'. The two unfortunate hacks cannot be positively named, and I have not managed to locate the precise site of the music house. Ned Ward seems to have been connected with one such establishment.[145] Whether he can really be regarded as a translator (despite his version of *Don Quixote* 'Merrily translated into Hudibrastic Verse') is an open question. But there can be no two opinions about the character or social concomitants of the address supplied. Moorfields, as we have already seen, had a reputation for clandestine sexual assignations, orthodox or unorthodox. Again its proximity to Bedlam and to Grub Street was such that Pope and Swift appear to use the name as a mode of alternative description. Certainly a Dunce

domiciled in Moorfields had done nothing, by his choice of a residence, to infringe his status.

Thirdly, the porter is sent to 'the *Hercules* and *Still* in *Vinegar-
yard*', in search of 'a School-master with Carbuncles on his Nose'.
Who the latter was, I am not sure. Vinegar Yard is easier to identify;
this was an alley off Drury Lane, the very next along from Playhouse
Yard. In 1720 Strype described the alley as 'indifferent broad, but
ordinarily built and inhabited'.146 The topographer is careful in
choosing his words, and generally errs on the side of charity – somewhat by contrast with his predecessor, Stow. We may safely conclude
that Vinegar Yard was a narrow court, tainted by the local associations, likely to contain a 'bagnio' (or bordello) and inferior lodging-
houses. The tavern was doubtless as mixed in character and clientele
as was its very title. From its convenience for the theatre, it looks as
though the schoolmaster perhaps served on the dramatic side of
Curll's staff. But that is mere speculation. A more confident judgement would be that such denizens of the reigon contributed to the
tide of disease, immorality and dirt flowing down Drury Lane to the
Dunces' rendezvous at St Mary le Strand, a matter of two to three
hundred yards away.

The next two stopping-off points call for less comment. The first
is 'a Blacksmith's Shop in the *Fryars*', where a pindaric writer in red
stockings, almost certainly Ambrose Philips, may be found. The
district of Whitefriars, or 'Alsatia', long a refuge for every kind of
fugitive, is described in the next chapter. Pope suggests that the
writer of Pindarics is not merely in straightened circumstances, but
that he is fleeing from poetic justice: he is a fugitive from the civilised
standards and propriety of art, a debtor of the literary world. Following this, the porter is enjoined to visit 'the Calendar-mill-Room at
Exeter-change' in quest of a 'Composer of Meditations'. This again
places the action in the same quarter of London. The Exeter Exchange, not to be confused with the 'New' Exchange, down towards
Charing Cross, was likewise in the Strand. Until its demolition in
the early nineteenth century, it stood in the vicinity of the present-
day Exeter Street, the other side of Bow Street from Catherine
Street and Drury Lane – but again no more than three hundred

yards from St Mary's church. There is no doubt that many of Curll's authors survived, literally or imaginatively, to earn an entry for themselves in *The Dunciad*; in fact every writer unambiguously named in the 'Further Account' turns up in the later poem – Gildon, Oldmixon, Mrs Centlivre, Blackmore. With this in mind, it can fairly be said that several of the participants in the shouting-match outside St Mary's had indeed retired to their own parlour door.

The next reference is more puzzling. Curll is made to send his porter in search of his 'best Writer against *Reveal'd Religion*'. The address given is 'the three *Tobacco-pipes* in *Dog* and *Bitch* yard'. Despite extensive enquiries, I have not been able to locate this spot with any accuracy. There was an inn called the Three Tobacco Pipes, in a squalid district near Charing Cross which included part of what is now Trafalgar Square, as well as lower St Martin's Lane (where there was one of the ubiquitous, but none the less significant, streets by the name of 'Dirty Lane'.)[147] But I suspect, without having mustered clinching evidence, that Dog and Bitch Yard is more likely to have been situated in St Giles'. This is owing to a connection with Lewkners Lane, the next address to which I shall turn.

Here we have, indeed, the most interesting of all the localities, with the richest store of legendary association. It is worth quoting the entire paragraph: 'At Mr. *Summers* a Thief-catchers, in *Lewkners* Lane, the man that wrote against the impiety of Mr. *Rowe*'s Plays'. The individual concerned was almost certainly Charles Gildon, a Dunce of Dunces. More to the present purpose is the street itself. Lewkners Lane, sometimes spelt Lutenors, Leuknors, and similar variants, subsequently became known as Newtonhouse Lane and Charles Street. Ultimately, around 1878, it took its present name, Macklin Street. It was built on what had been the grounds of Sir Lewis Lewknor, who lived in Drury Lane about 1620.[148] Early in its existence the street acquired a bad reputation, which it was unable to slough off for the better part of two centuries. Even at this date, it is easy to find ample justification for this ill name, whether we consider literary or historical evidence.

Dryden was perhaps the first to use the street as a byword for loose living. In his early comedy, *The Wild Gallant*, the bawd Lady du Lake reluctantly admits, to the embarrassment of Loveby (the gallant of the title), that her lodgings are 'in St *Luknors* Lane at the Cat and Fiddle'. Two whores employed by this same procuress live respectively in Dog and Bitch Yard and in 'Sodom'. Loveby, shamed by this public avowal, exclaims 'I am ruined! . . . plague had you no other places in the Town to name but *Sodom*, and *Luknors-Lane* for Lodgings?' 'Sodom' is hard to fix exactly on the map – naturally it does not appear under that name! However, there are abundant indications that it was in the St Giles/Long Acre district: possibly eastwards towards Holborn. The latter was a centre of homosexual prostitution, and Jonathan Wild was to write of 'a noted house in Holborn' frequented by transvestites and known as 'the Sodomitish Academy'. I believe that the context suggests that Dog and Bitch Yard could also be found close at hand, and would be inclined to place it tentatively round about St Giles'. A few years after Dryden, Samuel Butler referred to Lewkners Lane in terms which leave no doubt as to its local character:

> The nymphs of chaste Diana's train,
> The same with those of Lewkner's lane.

An early commentator, cited by Zachary Grey, supplies an almost redundant gloss: 'Some years ago swarmed with notoriously lasciv-ious and profligate strumpets.' It was certainly not an address one would be proud to blazon as a letterhead.[149]

Roger L'Estrange said much the same thing: he called Lewkners Lane 'a rendezvous and nursery for lewd women, first resorted to by the Roundheads', a political slur Pope is not likely to have taken very seriously.[150] The point is made, but more subtly, in *The Beggar's Opera*. In direct imitation of the 'summons' technique employed by Pope, Gay has Macheath send a porter for the 'Ladies' he wishes to entertain. The assembled company, when the girls arrive, is made up entirely of the likes of Suky Tawdry and Jenny Diver. Apologising for a slight delay, the drawer at the inn tells Macheath, 'You know, Sir, you sent him as far as *Hockley in the Hole*, for three of the ladies, for one in *Vinegar Yard*, and for the rest of them somewhere about *Lewkner's Lane*.'[151] Literary men, it is plain, live in identical quarters with women of the streets – in some cases, one assumes, not just under the same roof. It is a simple but effective ploy. Yet again the Dunces are pressed into the army of poverty and vice.

If that had been all, however, they would have escaped more lightly than is the case. Lewkner's Lane was a haunt of tarts, certainly, and had its share of gin shops, night-cellars and similar establishments. Its real degeneration, and its real usefulness from the point of view of Pope, began about 1713. It was then that Jonathan Wild, shaking free of the Wood Street compter, and quitting his temporary abode in Cripplegate, came to live in Lewkner's Lane with his moll, whose favourite name seems to have been Mary Milliner. This formidable couple, lacking that collective unity of purpose which distinguishes Bonnie and Clyde, split up before very long. Within a year or two Wild had left his brandy shop in St Giles', and moved to a tavern in Little Old Bailey. However, it was in Cock Alley, a stone's throw from Grub Street itself, and Lewkner's Lane that he first made headway in his dubious business. And even in 1718, according to Charles Hitchen, Wild's brother Andrew kept a 'case' (brothel) in Newtenhouse Lane. Jonathan had left the street when Pope's 'Further Account' appeared. But there is no doubt who was the most celebrated thieftaker to have resided there in recent times: his name was not Summers. As we might expect, Jack Sheppard was just as closely connected with Lewkner's Lane. On one occasion, Defoe (?) tells us, he managed to dispose of stolen property at an ale-house in the Lane, 'a rendezvous of robbers and ruffians'. Sheppard is also said to have frequented a victualling house in this street, and to have met Edgeworth Bess there. Later the couple kept a small brandy shop there. Not surprisingly, the writer of Sheppard's dying confession makes him specify 'Lewknor's Lane' as one of 'the chief scenes of [his] rambles and pleasures.'[152] What company for the unhappy dramatic critic!

It will be possible to cover the remaining localities more briefly. The next relates to '*Tooting*' (presumably Tothill) Fields, in Westminster. However, the exact location is 'the Farthing Pye House', and that stood in the Tenter Fields, past Upper Moorfields at the edge of Cripplegate parish. Following that, in a garret 'up three pair of stair' at the laundresses 'at the Hole in the Wall in *Cursitors Alley*', the porter will find two more hacks employed by Curll, sleeping in one bed. (The volley of prepositions conveys just how remote and inaccessible the garret is: the syntax amounts to a flurry of gesticu-lated directions.) Cursitors Alley ran eastwards off Chancery Lane, through Castle Court, and turned north towards Holborn. It occupied the site of the Cursitor's Office, mentioned by Stow. Modern Cursi-tor Street corresponds broadly with the first section of the Alley. It is noteworthy perhaps that another fully paid-up Dunce, John Oldmixon, later lived in Southampton Buildings, a few yards further up Chancery Lane: he may possibly qualify for the role of 'Index-maker', named at this point.[153] Overall, this was perhaps not quite such an unsalubrious region as some of the others. But it did border on the heavily contaminated district surrounding the Fleet, i.e. area (3), and the narrow courts hereabouts must have been a suitable habitat for the hack author.

The remaining addresses are widely spread. First, the porter is to call on Mrs Centlivre in Buckingham Court, Charing Cross; her husband was a servant of the royal household at St James's. Next, he should visit Budge Row 'for the Gentleman you used to go to in the *Cockloft*. I have taken away the *Ladder*,' says Curll, 'but his Landlady has it in keeping.' Budge Row was situated just south of Poultry, running south-east towards Cannon Street out of Watling Street. Finally, a double item which is probably the best known of these directions: 'I don't much care if you ask at the *Mint* for the old beetle-brow'd Critick, and the purblind Poet at the alley over against St *Andrews Holborn*. But this as you have time.' Candidates offered here include John Dennis, Gildon again and Oldmixon. The Mint was, of course, a refuge for debtors in Southwark. A recent habitué had been Nahum Tate, Poet Laureate moreover, who had actually died there. Defoe had possibly spent at least one period in hiding there;[154] and there were doubtless others among contemporary men of letters who were acquainted with the Mint. As for the other ad-dress, it lies squarely within the confines of area (3), not far from Holborn Bridge, where the various confluent streams rolled into the Fleet – a moral, as much as a natural, phenomenon for Swift and Gay.

The complete list furnishes us with what is practically a working gazetteer of the subculture formed by professional writers at this time. It will be noted that the addresses are distributed all over the inner suburbs, except that the easternmost region (that of Rosemary Lane) is not represented. Otherwise, the locations are dotted about the infected areas which have already been described. It is apparent, too, that only one of the addresses falls inside the City walls, and yet that few of them lie very far from the boundary – several coming within the liberties of the City. Whether Pope invented these abodes with scrupulous care, or whether he simply used real addresses of real individuals, the effect is the same. His fastidiously precise directions further indicate the part played in the moral and imaginative life of his satiric drama by London topography. The distribution of Dunces is a clue to the marriage of character and setting. This chapter has, I hope, supplied evidence to support that contention. In the following chapters, I shall draw out more general implications from this state of affairs: implications bearing mainly on the way in which we should read Pope's verse.

Epigraphs (*i*) Taken from Stow, p. 122. The 'Birds' described are actually usurers; but since the location is Portsoken Ward, where the cave of Dulness was originally placed, I have ventured to apply the description to the Dunces. It was noteworthy that the needy hack, 'Omicron', who probably formed the basis of Hogarth's definitive portrait of 'The Distressed Poet', lived in Hounsditch. For Pope, such men undoubtedly constituted 'the black discredit of the Age'.

(*ii*) Arbuthnot, p. 194.

1. Bronson, 'When was Neo-classicism?' in *Studies in Criticism and Aesthetics 1660–1800*, ed. H. Anderson, J. Shea (Minneapolis, 1967), pp. 13–35 [quoted from p. 34].

2. Geoffrey Holmes, *British Politics in the Age of Anne* (London, 1967), p. 30; G. S. Holmes, W. A. Speck, *The Divided Society: Parties and Politics in England 1694–1716* (London, 1967), p. 66.

3. Ian Watt, 'Publishers and Sinners: The Augustan View', *Studies in Bibliography*, XII (1959), 17.

4. A. S. Turberville, *English Men and Manners in the Eighteenth Century* (New York, 1964), pp. 337–55. The quotations are from pp. 337 and 341; James Boswell, *The Life of Samuel Johnson* (London, 1963), II, 446.

5. Watt, p. 185.

6. R. Paulson, *Theme and Structure in Swift's Tale of a Tub* (Princeton, 1960), p. 170n.

7. E. A. Bloom, *Samuel Johnson in Grub Street* (Providence, 1957), e.g. p. 6: 'Despite the poverty which kept him [Johnson] in Grub Street, he was not a Grubean . . .'

8. See Nigel Barton, *The Lost Rivers of London* (London, 1962), p. 28; Stow, p. 475; S. E. Rasmussen, *London : The Unique City* (Harmondsworth, 1961), p. 76ff. Spate speaks of 'a mass of slums near the stagnant ditch of Moorfields' in O. H. K. Spate, 'The Growth of London, AD. 1660–1800', *A Historical Geography of England*, ed. H. C. Darby (Cambridge, 1963), p. 530.

9. Most of the facts mentioned in this paragraph are taken from Baddeley, pp. 4–5, 18–20, 203. See especially 'The Poor of the Parish', pp. 203–14.

10. T. C. Dale, *The Inhabitants of London in 1638* (London, 1931), I, 236–9, reprinting material from the Lambeth Palace Library. Grub Street itself contained only two houses of substance (one occupied by the celebrated recluse 'Mr. Welby') but even these were not exactly mansions. In Fore Street, the most considerable property, the Greyhound Tavern, was assessed equally with Welby's house, the most highly rated in Grub Street. Forty-six dwellings, of what description one can only guess, standing in Bullens Rents, off Grub Street, attained a grand total of £50 in the assessment. Very few properties in the immediate vicinity were worth a rental of £10. For the position in Pope's lifetime, see Appendix A.

11. William Kent (ed.), *An Encyclopaedia of London* (London, 1937), p. 158; Harben, p. 416. Eilert Ekwall, *Street Names of the City of London* (Oxford, 1954), pp. 85–6, deduces from a thirteenth-century source that the 'grub' = larva may be the origin of the name.

12. See Baddeley, op. cit., p. 2.

13. Quoted by George Poulson, *Beverlac : or, the Antiquities and History of the Town of Beverley* (London, 1829), II, 775n.

14. Stow, p. 122.

15. [Edward Hatton], *A New View of London* (London, 1708), p. 257. An earlier estimate is 6445 for the London portion in 1631 (quoted by Denton, p. 142). Denton provides figures to illustrate the decline in population during the nineteenth century (p. 143).

16. See George, pp. 410–11.

17. *New Remarks*, pp. 169–70.

18. Misprinted in George, p. 407, as 'Geo. III'. George quotes an estimate of 1710–11 (42000 for the joint parishes), which is 'clearly exaggerated' (pp. 408, 412).

19. John Timbs, *Curiosities of London* (London, 1855), pp. 335–7.

20. Denton, passim. Almost all the information in the following section derives from this source: separate references are not normally supplied.

21. The indented paragraph is from Denton, p. 16. Cf. Valerie Pearl, *London at the Outbreak of the Puritan Revolution* (Oxford, 1961), p. 13, on St Bride's, St Sepulchre, St Andrew's Holborn, and St Giles' Cripplegate 'already scarred with pestilential slum dwellings' before the Grand Rebellion. The following paragraphs are based on Denton. For a later theatre, see A. E. Wilson, 'Misfortunes in Grub Street', *East End Entertainment* (London, 1954), pp. 93–102. Actors had long been associated with Cripplegate (Denton, p. 157) and they were commonly regarded as mere vagabonds. Cibber, of course, was an actor.

22. Defoe, *A Journal of the Plague Year* (Harmondsworth, 1966), p. 57.

23. Baddeley, p. 192.

24. Baddeley, p. 196; Moore, *Citizen*, p. 340. Defoe tells the story (quoted by Moore, p. 315) of a sexton of Cripplegate who wanted the plague to continue, on account of the high burial fees he was receiving. In 1729 Bunhill Fields was the largest cemetery in London; Row's burial ground and Moorfields were also substantial; see Maitland, II, 741.

25. Baddeley, pp. 37, 208; Bayne-Powell, p. 241; Dale, pp. 238–9. There was a 'cage' for vagrants at Grub Street end mentioned in 1586 – Charles Pendrill, *Old Parish Life in London* (London, 1937), p. 203.

26. Oldmixon, p. 743.

27. Baddeley mentions 'a crack-brained enthusiast' who died in the parish and was buried in [Old] Bethlehem burial ground (p. 17). Cripplegate was notorious for such fanatics, and not merely for harmless eccentrics as Henry Welby. See also Baddeley, pp. 24, 36, 154–6, 157; George, pp. 331, 100–1, 125. Typhus was particularly virulent around 1800 in Old Street and Golden Lane (George, p. 94). By order of the Lord Mayor, houses in Cripplegate were pulled down in 1666 as part of an attempt to prevent the spread of the fire: Gomme, I, 158.

28. There is some discrepancy among the authorities, but this can be explained by changes as time elapsed. Malcolm, *London Redivivum*, (London, 1805), III, 280, gives these figures for 1710: three presbyterian meeting houses, three anabaptists, three independent. *New Remarks*, p. 167: five dissenting houses, plus a tabernacle where Anglican rites are performed. Maitland, II, 1189. See also Denton, p. 74.

   Other evidence of the dissenting influence resides in Dr Williams' Library, set up in Red Cross Street in 1729 (Presbyterian); and a school in Ropemakers Alley (Denton, p. 151).

29. See *Gentleman's Magazine*, LX (1790), 293.

30. The neighbouring properties included several breweries, notably Samuel Whitbread's on the north-west corner of the street (its site still, though the Barbican project has overwhelmed Grub Street). The best account is that

of Peter Mathias, *The Brewing Industry in England 1700–1830* (Cambridge, 1959), pp. 11, 262, etc.

31. Stow, p. 317. This corner of the City within the walls was associated with the first Earl of Shaftesbury (whose house had lain just off Aldersgate), and during the time of the Popish Plot had been regarded as a hub of protestant activity.

32. E. B. Chancellor, *The Literary Ghosts of London* (London, 1933), p. 57. For other literary connections, see Appendix B.

33. For Defoe see Ch. V: for Mandeville, Baddeley, p. 136. For Milton's residence in Jewen Street and Bunhill Row see *The Life Records of John Milton* (New Brunswick, 1958), IV, 377, V, passim.

34. *DNB*, s.v. Wild; F. J. Lyons, *Jonathan Wild Prince of Robbers* (London, 1936), p. 258 and passim.

35. Hatton is less informative, whilst Maitland derives largely from Strype. It should be noted that Strype's map of Cripplegate labels 'Moore Street' the stretch westwards from 'the Postern' to St Giles' church. This is normally referred to (as in Strype's text) by the name of Fore Street.

36. Strype, III, 93.

37. Strype, III, 93; IV, 60; Stow, p. 476.

38. Maitland, II, 906–7.

39. Stow, p. 318; Bayne-Powell, p. 167.

40. E. B. Chancellor, *The Pleasure Haunts of London* (London, 1925), p. 152.

41. Maitland, II, 908.

42. Baddeley, p. 7.

43. G. H. Cunningham, *London* (London, 1927), p. 368; *HMC* (Bath MSS) 58 (London, 1908), III, 506–7; Maitland, II, 908; William M. Sale, *Samuel Richardson Master Printer* (Ithaca, 1950), pp. 8–14. For other connections with the printing and book-selling trade, see H. R. Plomer, *A Dictionary of Printers and Booksellers 1668–1725* (Oxford, 1922), p. 150; and Henry L. Snyder, 'New Bibliographical Data for the Reign of Queen Anne', *The Library*, XXII (1967), 336–7, 345. Malcolm, *London Redivivum*, III, 306, records some improvements in and around Jewen Street on the site of formerly 'very wretched' houses. Oldmixon, p. 623, mentions the arrest of a Jacobite in his 'dirty lodging' in Jewen Street.

44. Henry Campkin, *Grub Street (Now Milton Street) London* (London, priv. prin. 1868), p. 6. A playhouse called 'the City Theatre' briefly stood in Milton Street in the 1830's (Chancellor, *Pleasure Haunts*, p. 133): a fact (had it existed earlier) which would have given an added touch to Pope's satire and would have locked the symbolism of his poem even more tightly together.

45. But see H. Bolitho, D. Peel, *Without the City Wall* (London, 1952), p. 18:

and p. 76 of an interleaved copy of G. B. Rawlings, *The Streets of London* (London, n.d.) held in Cambridge Public Library.

46. See Bryan Anstey, 'A Study of certain Changes in Land Values in the London Area in the Period 1950–64', *Land Values*, ed. Peter Hall (London, 1965), pp. 241–3, esp. map on p. 25.

47. Williams, pp. 14–15, 90ff.

48. Barton, pp. 28, 106; George, p. 91ff.

49. TE, V, 59, 267.

50. TE, V, 63–5.

51. Millicent Rose, *The East End of London* (London, 1951), p. 59. William Addison (*English Fairs and Markets*, [London, 1953], p. 75), implies that the fair is still held: but this appears to be a mistake. It should also be noted that fever was regularly transmitted through the poorer quarters via the old clothes in cast-off rags shops. See George, pp. 64–5.

52. Harben, pp. 514–5.

53. Strype, II, 13, 26–8.

54. Hawkins speaks, too, of a 'halo of bagnios' surrounding the theatre. *The Life of Samuel Johnson, Ll.D.*, ed. B. H. Davis (London, 1962), pp. 41–2.

55. See George, pp. 93, 95, 101, 345: for the low quality housing in the parish of St Botolph, Aldgate, see p. 100. On the 'rickety and verminous wooden houses' in St Katherine's by the Tower, see George passim and Rose, pp. 60, 200–1. On the dangers to be encountered round Nightingale Lane, which adjoined Rosemary Lane, cf. Chancellor, *Pleasure Haunts*, p. 176.

56. Irving, p. 260. See also Durfey, as quoted by Chancellor, p. 176.

57. George, pp. 100–1. See also p. 229.

58. *Colonel Jack*, ed. S. H. Monk (London, 1965), pp. 4, 8–9, 15. Monk is, however, wrong in suggesting that Defoe 'himself' had grown up 'in and about Stepney' (p. 312). There is no evidence to this effect.

59. *Romances and Narratives*, XVI, 182, 191, 192, 218.

60. *London*, ed. P. Cunningham (London, 1927), p. 572; W. C. Sydney, *England and the English in the Eighteenth Century* (London, 1891), II, 215; A. P. Herbert, *Mr. Gay's London* (London, 1948), p. 69; Radzinowicz, II, 175; Chancellor, *Pleasure Haunts*, p. 176; Defoe, *Tour*, I, 330; Marshall, p. 34; Straus, pp. 149–50; *New Remarks*, p. 398. For the bawdy houses around Goodman's Fields, see Marshall, p. 235. The *Observator* early in the century remarked the fact that the theatre in Goodman's Fields lay in the precincts of Rosemary Lane, which was a great convenience to the 'Ladies of Rag Fair' – see Malcolm, II, 124. Riots were frequent in the vicinity partly because of the existence of that perpetual target for destructive energies, the dissenting meeting-house. See Malcolm, II, 29, and Marshall, p. 34.

George Rudé describes the attacks on Irish alehouses in the district during the 'Mother Gin' riots of 1736, instancing the damage done to the

Bull and Butcher Tavern in Rag Fair. Curiously, he identifies Rag Fair not with Rosemary Lane but with Goodman's Fields. See *Paris and London in the Eighteenth Century* (London, 1970), pp. 201–21, esp. 208–11.

61. *Miscellanies. The Third Volume. By Dr. Arbuthnot, Mr. Pope*, and *Mr. Gay* (London, 1742), p. 62. Quoted by Johnson in the entry for Grub Street in his dictionary.

62. Boswell, II, 459.

63. Although a good deal of building was going on, as evidenced by Defoe, *Tour*, I, 375 ('A new street or range of houses taken out of the south side of the Artillery Ground near Moorfields, also an enlargement of the new burying ground, as it was formerly called, on the north side of the same ground'). See also R. J. Mitchell, M. D. R. Leys, *A History of London Life* (Harmondsworth, 1964), p. 179.

64. Pope, *Correspondence*, II, 3.

65. *Tale*, p. 181; *The Poems of Henry Carey*, ed. F. T. Wood (London, 1931), p. 151.

66. Rasmussen, pp. 76–81; Stow, pp. 301–2, 475. On the site of Moorfields proper were built Finsbury Square, Finsbury Circus and Lackington Street – the last commemorating a subsequent 'Temple of the Muses', the book-selling establishment of James Lackington which went by that name.

67. Quoted by Lyons, pp. 262–3.

68. See Patrick Pringle, *Stand and Deliver* (London, 1951), pp. 168–70; Mitchell, Leys, p. 179; Gomme, I, 161.

69. Sutherland, p. 4.

70. Defoe, *Colonel Jack*, pp. 43, 56.

71. Denton, pp. 103–4; Christopher Hibbert, *The Road to Tyburn* (London, 1957), p. 48; Jack Lindsay, *1764* (London, 1959), p. 259.

72. Denton, pp. 104, 114 (misnumbered 119). See also Max Beloff, *Public Order and Popular Disturbances 1660–1714* (Oxford, 1938), p. 82.

73. J. L. Hammond and Barbara Hammond, *The Skilled Craftsman 1760–1832* (London, 1927), pp. 206, 209.

74. Denton, p. 115.

75. Denton, pp. 104–6. A heap of charnel had been dumped on Moorfields in 1548 – perhaps as many as four or five hundred corpses. The mound lay just behind what was to become Whitefield's rostrum – Pendrill, pp. 141–2.

76. Cf. the comments of Emrys Jones on 'the gross materiality' of Grub Street poems, quoted on p. 309 below.

77. Thornbury, II, 197; Sydney, I, 65.

78. *The Diary of Samuel Pepys*, ed. H. B. Wheatley, (London, ed. 1952), I, 174, 250. (28 June 1661: 26 May 1662). Wrestling matches traditionally took place in Moorfields on the first three days of Bartholomew Fair – a further link with the Smithfield Muse. See Denton, p. 94.

79. Thornbury, II, 196; Malcolm, I, 91, 287.

80. *A Trip through London* (1728), pp. 52–3.

81. Sybil Rosenfeld, *The Theatre of the London Fairs in the Eighteenth Century* (Cambridge, 1960), p. 133.

82. Marjorie Plant, *The English Book Trade* (London, ed. 1965), p. 254; Plomer, p. 150. See also F. B. Tolles, *Meeting House and Counting House* (New York, 1963), p. 157.

83. *The Obituary of Richard Smyth*, ed. H. Ellis ([London], 1849), passim.

84. Denton, p. 115; Thornbury, II, 198. For Moorfields brothels, see Ned Ward's *Step to the Bath* quoted by Philip Pinkus, *Grub Street Laid Bare* (London, 1968), p. 203.

85. Sir John Hawkins, *The Life of Samuel Johnson, Ll.D.* (London, 2nd ed. 1787), p. 49.

86. Pepys, I, 214 (26 December 1661). For alehouses round Moorfields, see Besant, p. 640; and for music, Gomme, II, 137–8 and George, p. 306.

87. Denton, pp. 107–8. See also *Tricks of the Town: Eighteenth Century Diversions*, ed. R. Straus (London, 1927), pp. 74, 75. Tom Brown (quoted by Pinkus, pp. 162, 174) refers to 'Moorfields sharpers'.

88. Radzinowicz, I, 188; *Calendar*, I, 37–9; Horace Bleakley, *The Hangmen of England* (London, 1929), pp. 12–19. The execution followed a procession past the Artillery Ground. Radzinowicz also tells (I, 196) of a bookseller who had committed murder and then suicide in prison (1755). He was buried at a crossway in Moorfields with a stake through his heart. For the Artillery Company's annual march through London from Moorfields, see Read's *Weekly Journal*, 24 May 1718.

89. See H. W. Troyer, *Ned Ward of Grub Street* (Cambridge, Mass., 1946), p. 159.

90. See Holmes, Speck, p. 41; *Catalogue of Prints and Drawings in the British Museum* (London, 1873), II, 303.

91. Stow, p. 175; cf. p. 172, on Petty France; Strype, I, 192.

92. Ralph, *A Critical Review of the Publick Buildings . . . in . . . London and Westminster* (London, 1734), pp. 7–8. Defoe admired Moorgate, once it had been rebuilt and enlarged 'to give room for the city Train'd Bands to go through to the Artillery Ground, where they muster, and that they might march with their Pikes advanc'd . . .' (*Tour*, I, 354). This confessed aim allows Pope to drive a satiric coach and horses through the gateway to Bedlam.

93. By R. R. Reed (Cambridge, Mass., 1952); see esp. Ch. I, pp. 1–39.

94. Strype, I, 195.

95. See *DNB*, s.v. Lee.

96. Butt, pp. 616, 630.

97. Faber, p. 87. See also *Tatler* no. 174, and E. G. O'Donoghue, *The Story of*

Bethlehem Hospital (London, 1914), p. 252. O'Donoghue (pp. 240–2) comments on the literary associations of Bedlam, notably those with Ned Ward and Tom Brown. *Journal* (probably in the person of Defoe) satirised a Curll author who was to be given 'a safe conduct to the structure in Moorfields' :– Lee, II, 48, quoting *Journal* of 28 June 1718.

98. Butt, p. 649.

99. Butt, p. 615.

100. O'Donoghue, pp. 249–51; *Journal*, I, 122n.

101. Swift, *Correspondence*, IV, 65–70.

102. *Tale*, pp. 175–6.

103. Swift, *Poems*, p. 512.

104. Plumb, *The First Four Georges* (London, 1967), p. 16. For Johnson's visit to Bedlam in May 1775, see Boswell, I, 565. Curiously Boswell does not mention this visit in his journal, as published from the Boswell papers at Yale.

105. TE, V, 271–2n.

106. TE, V, 147n, 457; Pope, *Correspondence*, I, 106.

107. See for example Oldmixon's *Critical History of England* (1724–26), I, 270; II, 270; *History* (1735), p. [633]: and *Essay on Criticism* (1728), pp. 49, 56, among many similar references.

108. E. H. Pearce, *Sion College and Library* (Cambridge, 1913), pp. 347–8, lists the names of the Presidents at this period.

109. Stow specifically observes, 'To this Library there have been already [1633] divers bountifull and well disposed benefactors, who have given large sums of money towards the furnishing it with books . . . [seven named] besides divers others; whose names, legacies, gifts, and bookes bought therewith: are (by way of a gratefull memoriall) registred in a fair Booke kept in the Library' (pp. 304–5).

110. See Swift, *Prose Works*, I, 341–2.

111. *Miscellanies*, pp. iv–vi.

112. Fielding, IX, 209–10.

113. Note at B.I. 265. The 'fogs' of Dulness (B.I. 262) would be appropriate to the traditionally marshy area of Grub Street. Incidentally, the original word for the fen ('More') happens to be the name Pope gives to the first individualised Dunce (other than Cibber) whose actions are described – James Moore Smythe (B.II. 35). The first 'Poet's form' set before us is his – 'A Wit it was, and called the phantom More.' (B.II. 50). Again bad poetry is identified with the bogs of Moorfields, the most un-bracing and soporific climate in all London.

114. TE, V, 319.

115. 'Argument to Book the First', TE, V, 266.

116. Holmes, p. 304.

117. L. C. Jones, *The Clubs of the Georgian Rakes* (New York, 1942), p. 27. On the noise of the streets, see M. Dorothy George, 'London and the Life of the Towns', in Turberville, II, 171–2.

118. Butt, pp. 601, 610.

119. Steeves, p. 5ff.

120. TE, V, 263.

121. TE, V, xxxviii–xxxix. Cf. Ian Jack, *Augustan Satire* (Oxford, 1952), pp. 116–18.

122. *The Poems of John Dryden*, ed. J. Kinsley (Oxford, 1958), IV, 1917.

123. Radzinowicz, II, 257.

124. For Simkin and Panton, cf. *Poems*, ed. Kinsley, IV, 1918 and *English Satiric Poetry*, ed. J. Kinsley, J. T. Boulton (London, 1966), 27.

125. See Leslie Hotson, *The Commonwealth and Restoration Stage* (Cambridge, Mass., 1928), pp. 176–94. This treatment supplants that of W. J. Lawrence, *The Elizabethan Playhouse and other Studies/Second Series* (Stratford, 1915) – see pp. 237–9 for an account of the Fortune theatre – and 'A Forgotten Restoration Playhouse', *Englische Studien*, XXXV (1904).

126. It is arguable for instance that present-day Watford is at least as much a suburb of London (demographically or economically considered) as is Feltham. Yet the latter lies within the GLC administrative area, the former some way outside. For the general character of the suburbs and parishes in Stuart London, and a discussion of their particular social problems, see Valerie Pearl, pp. 23–37.

127. Williams, p. 36.

128. Macky's *Journey through England* (1714–22) tells us that the main centre of the book trade had shifted from Little Britain to Paternoster Row. Certain sections of the trade were conducted chiefly in the vicinity of Temple Bar. See F. A. Mumby, *Publishing and Bookselling* (London, 1949), p. 141. However, a quick census of the printers listed by Plomer and by William Sale suggests that the actual printing shops were chiefly located nearer the heart of the City.

129. Letter of 25 April 1708: Pope, *Correspondence*, I, 47.

130. Quoted by Paulson, I, 147, from the issue of the *Journal* for 24 September 1730.

131. Quoted in George, pp. 92–3.

132. Entry in Luttrell's *Relation* for 11 June 1695, quoted by Holmes, Speck, pp. 78–9.

133. *Romances and Narratives*, XVI, 173, 214.

134. Bayne-Powell, p. 169.

135. Faber, p. 84, and see the reference to 'the rounds of *Drury-lane*' in the following section on 'how to know a Whore'; *The Dispensary* (8th edn., 1718), p. 29.

136. See Paulson, I, 168, 210–1; Wheatley, pp. 138, 155. The badges which the charity boys wear in Hogarth's prints, as in the case of Tom Nero, mark them as educated in the rough school of life, after the manner of St Giles in the Fields.

137. For other information see Paulson, I, 179; Wheatley, pp. 132–7, 285; E. B. Chancellor, *The Eighteenth Century in London* (London, n.d.), p. 134.

138. Chancellor, *The Annals of Covent Garden* (London, n.d.), pp. 61–2, 106, 198, 240–1. It is fair to record that there was at least one association of a happier kind: Robert Harley, later first Earl of Oxford, was born in Bow Street. Some other indications: a pillory was set up at the heart of St Giles', that is Seven Dials, in 1733. It was an unfortunate place for any man who happened to have incurred unpopularity, rather than glamour, by his crimes. Wild would not have survived long there. John Thrift, a mid-century hang-man, was accused of murdering a Jacobite in Short's Gardens, Drury Lane, in 1750; not surprisingly, he got off when the affair reached the Old Bailey. Two years later, Thrift died at his home in Coal Yard, also off Drury Lane. The parishioners of St Paul's, Covent Garden, were strongly opposed to his burial in their consecrated ground; hangmen, like Dunces, were rudely bundled from one parish to the next. See Bleakley, pp. 62, 85–9. For other crimes and disorders of St Giles', extracted from the proceedings of the Commissions of the Peace, and Oyer and Terminer for the City of London and County of Middlesex, see Herbert, pp. 14, 31, 100, etc. For references to the whores of the 'hundreds of Old Drury', see the *Weekly Journal* for 28 May 1721; cf. Virginia Cowles, *The Great Swindle* (London, 1960), pp. 120, 174. According to Miss Cowles (p. 147), after the South Sea Bubble crash there were rich liveries on sale in the old clothes markets of Long Lane, Monmouth Street and 'Regent Fair'. The last seems to be an error for Rag Fair.

139. Garth, *The Dispensary*, p. 40; Faber, p. 73. It should be noted that the one place Gay hits on, to localise prostitution in a city teeming with prostitution, was the *exact* site of the Dunces' games – 'Where *Katherine-street* descends into the *Strand*' (Faber, p. 84).

140. George, p. 17. The same writer states (p. 78): 'The poorest parts of eighteenth-century London – the dilapidated courts and alleys, the crumbling tenements and the dangerous districts – were chiefly in the belt which had grown up round the City between the reign of Elizabeth and the end of the seventeenth century.'

141. Williams, p. 38.

142. Williams, p. 30ff. The author asserts that 'in Book II . . . contemporary London topography is an essential, meaningful part of the poem.' It is my view that this significance prevails from the very first line of *The Dunciad*, from the moment Smithfields, Rag Fair, Bedlam, and so on, are introduced.

143. Pope, *Prose Works*, I, 278–9. I am preparing a separate account of the passage, with a view to identifying the various writers.

144. Cf. Pope, *Correspondence*, III, 371.

145. H. W. Troyer, *Ned Ward of Grub Street* (Cambridge, Mass., 1946), p. 159.

146. Strype, VI, 75.

147. LCC *Survey*, XVIII (London, 1937), p. 129.

148. LCC *Survey*, V: ii, p. 30; Cunningham, p. 433.

149. *The Works of John Dryden*, ed. J. H. Smith, D. MacMillan (Berkeley/Los Angeles, 1962), VIII, 59–60; Lyons, pp. 279–81; *Hudibras*, ed. Z. Grey (London, 1799), II, 176 [Part III, Canto I, 11.865–6]).

150. Quoted by Chancellor, *Pleasure Haunts*, p. 175.

151. Faber, p. 504. Similarly Macaulay speaks of 'painted women, the refuse of Lewknor Lane and Whetstone Park': *History of England* (London, 1906), I, 286.

152. Lyons, pp. 70, 244; *DNB*. s.v. Wild; *Romances and Narratives*, XVI, 180, 194, 198, 230. There *was* a real 'Somers a Thief-taker in Newtner's Lane', mentioned in Applebee's *Weekly Journal*, 8 September 1716 – Wild figures in the same story. But Wild was already the bigger fish.

153. See *Weekly Miscellany*, 20 June 1733, quoted in *Gentleman's Magazine* (July 1733), III, 336.

154. Sutherland, p. 43.

II

The Plagues of Dulness

All, that they boast of Styx, of Acheron,
Cocytus, Phlegeton, our have prov'd in one;
The filth, stench, noyse: save only what was there
Subtley distinguish'd, was confused here.

Ben Jonson, 'On the famous Voyage'

Besides those overt-acts of treason now recounted, the most of all of which the insurgents were guilty of, they were guilty of several acts of felony, such as burning private property, and demolishing private houses, and committing several acts of robbery and open violence. . . . The crime, as applied to the fact, is palpable and direct; pulling down all inclosures, demolishing all brothels or bawdy-houses, or chapels, making insurrections, in order to redress grievances, real or pretended, is levying war within the realm, and against the King, though they have no design against his person. . . . The rabble had augmented their numbers by setting the felons at liberty. If the military had not been called in, none of your lordships can hesitate to agree with me, that within a very few hours the capital would have been in flames, and shortly reduced to an heap of rubbish.

Lord Mansfield, speech in the House of Lords, 1780

The birth of the eighteenth century was attended with four searing memories, which can fairly be called traumatic. Within the lifetime of men and women who were still active, four great events had impinged deeply on the national consciousness. I mean the Civil War, the Great Plague, the Fire of London and the Glorious Revolution. These happenings had personal and imaginative repercussions which were to last for generations; and not even the Restoration or the Dutch wars, the Popish plot or the Monmouth rebellion, made quite the same durable impact. The importance of the constitutional upheavals from the point of view of literature has often been emphasised. I do not think, however, that the impress on writers of the other two events has ever been satisfactorily described. My aim here is to sketch out some of the ways in which these occurrences prolonged their resonance within a single major form, satire, with special reference to Pope, Swift and Gay. This is a study (in A. C. Charity's expressive phrase) of events and their afterlife.

The Plague and the Fire had several conspicuous features in common.[1] Apart from their propinquity in time – they were separated by a bare twelve months, if we regard the epicentre of the plague as the end of August 1665 – they both came to be regarded as a divine visitation. Each was interpreted as a prophecy, as a warning, as a blight ordained by the Almighty; each was surrounded by numerological speculation and gnostic prediction. Equally, the spread of both events was seen as an act of sabotage by Papists, Dissenters, freethinkers, the French, the Italians and whomever one chanced to dislike. Both brought sudden destruction to the capital in the autumn of the year. Both involved evacuation on a massive scale. Both centred closely on the City of London and its immediate environs. Both spread at an accelerating tempo and smouldered for some time before gradually dying out.

The two main verbs in that last sentence are worth picking up, although I did not choose them with any extraordinary care. They lead towards a less literal-minded basis of comparison, which is itself the guiding idea of this chapter. Both plague and fire, then, are phenomena which can be described in terms of raging, consuming, seething, blazing, inflaming, and so on. Both can be called virulent or, by extension, voracious. Amongst their shared connotations, three ideas seem to be overlaid. The first is that of spreading; the second is that of destruction; and the third is that of corrosion or some form of impairment by heat. Semantically, words associated with disease have, for obvious historical reasons, come to overlap with those suggesting burning. This is an ineluctable fact of language. Its convenience for the Augustan satirists, as regards their wider rhetorical ends, will be illustrated shortly. For the moment, I want to insist on the historical and literal applicability of such notions at the end of

95

the seventeenth century. Images of disease and of fire required only a very short fuse to activate them into poetic life. They carried with them a potent imaginative charge, derived from the recent memory of the twin cataclysms of 1665–6. If, as I shall contend, these images became the climactic symbols of Augustan satire, then they would gain additional force from their links with two climactic events of the age immediately preceding.

It is now widely agreed that Augustan rhetoric employs a defensive idiom. Jeffrey Hart, for example, has pointed out in an illuminating essay that whereas Donne, Marvell and Milton seek to create coherence through their imagery, their successors attempt rather to assert and defend an existing order. The pattern is already established, the harmony is already a going concern. Dryden's characteristic operation, says Hart, is 'to exclude, rather than to assimilate, whatever would disturb the balance of mind or state . . .' In a similar way, tone in Augustan poetry 'hold[s] in balance those disparities in experience which the metaphysical conceit would have attempted to depict as analogical identities.'[2] In other words (to extrapolate from what Hart says), Augustan idiom does not fuse but holds in equilibrium; does not create new identities but safeguards old identities. The integrity to be preserved is the one that was already observable and observed before the artistic construct was fashioned, or indeed contemplated.

Seen in this light, it is easy to deduce how the phraseology of satire in this period should revert so often to terms implying contagion, destruction, morbidity, virus and the like. Relatively little comment appears to have been made on this obsession with disease, apart from the hostile remarks of those deploring Swift's coprophilia and Pope's nastiness. The defence of these writers has, in recent years, been mainly conducted on other grounds. Yet if one wanted a quick run-down of the governing metaphors to be found in their work, one could scarcely do better than turn to Roget's *Thesaurus*, and consider the entry for 'Disease'; I append a selection from this sub-heading.

Disease; illness, sickness . . . morbidity; infirmity, ailment . . . disorder, malady; distemper. Visitation, attack, seizure, stroke, fit, epilepsy, apoplexy . . . atrophy; indigestion . . . decay . . . decline, consumption . . . paralysis . . . taint, pollution, infection, contagion . . . epi-, endemic; murrain, plague, pestilence, virus, pox. Sore, ulcer, abcess, fester, boil . . . imposthume, issue; rot, canker, cancer, carcinoma, caries, mortification, corruption, gangrene, leprosy, eruption, rash, breaking out, venereal disease. Fever, calenture; inflammation . . . galloping consumption, churchyard cough . . . neurasthenia; idiocy, insanity . . . cripple, invalid, sickroom, hospital.[3]

The relevance of these words (and others I have omitted) to such works as *The Dunciad, A Tale of a Tub* and many more, is surely very obvious. Here I wish to draw attention chiefly to the term 'calenture', as holding within itself the basic coupling of heat and pestilence. Other items such as 'morbidity', 'epilepsy', 'taint', are equally significant. Pope and Swift, as we know, tended to image religious fanaticism as a febrile kind of disorder, rising and subsiding spasmodically with the lunes. It is interesting to note, therefore, that Wyld's *Universal English Dictionary* glosses 'contagions' with a secondary, figurative meaning, 'catching, liable to spread from one person to another', and gives as instances 'enthusiasm, laughter, gloom, mirth, religious fervour &c.' Either the modern or the ancient sense of 'enthusiasm' will do. The point is that moral and social decay was, for the Scriblerian group, *catching*; and the enthusiast was only a particularly striking case of the way in which folly was transmitted by contact with the foolish. His fits might be especially noteworthy for their epidemic character – but then all Dulness was epidemic, because all Dulness was pestilential. The metaphor of plague explains the phenomenon; at the same time, it acts as an icon for the condition. I do not go so far as to say that Pope and Swift chose the image because of the dominance of the Great Plague, and its forerunners, in the national imagination; and that their idiom therefore predetermined their human outlook at large. That is the *reductio ad absurdum* of rhetorical criticism. Professor Wimsatt once referred scathingly to 'the confident school of ritual origins (where the myth of American Independence might be derived from firecrackers on the Fourth of July) . . .'[4] And there is, quite seriously, some danger that our present approach to satire, with all its virtues, may produce a situation where attitudes to folly in the post-Renaissance phase of humanism are seen to derive from the availability of the *Encomium Moriae* framework. But, having said this, I do believe that the eighteenth-century satirists were, at some level, impelled to dramatise their moral dialectic along the lines they did because of the potency of certain images at that precise moment in history. An obvious example is the pox. Swift's ready recourse to this idea, culminating in his mock-panegyric, 'Pethox the Great', can easily be misinterpreted if we forget the virulence of the disease at this time – the facility with which it could be picked up, the difficulty with which it could be cured, the frequency of hereditary conditions, the savage side-effects it carried with it, and so on.

I am arguing three things. Firstly, that the recollection of the disasters of a generation before still operated powerfully in people's minds at the opening of the eighteenth century. Secondly, that the characteristic idiom of Augustan satire (whether the actual vocabulary, at a local level, or the wider rhetorical and fictional resources used) makes use of this residual memory, though often at a subliminal level. And thirdly, that the images centrally derived from the historical events (plague/epidemic/burning etc.) were peculiarly suited to the things these satirists actually wanted to say – peculiarly effective weapons for exposing the kind of danger they saw in the contemporary world.

But it is possible to go farther than this. I want now to suggest that the conditions of life in London at this period were such as to reinforce this choice of idiom. I wish to propound, by means of concrete illustrations studied in some detail, the view that the Scriblerian party – though they may have borrowed their controlling metaphors from the events of Restoration London – developed their central dialectic with close reference to the London of fifty years later. Of course, one specialised instance is provided by Grub Street, a district with its own peculiar human ecology and satiric economy.

The great satirists were born in the century of revolution. Within their lifetime they experienced every kind of disturbance which a nation can undergo. There was international conflict, with the struggles between states exemplified by the War of Spanish Succession and that of Jenkins' Ear. Far from achieving peace in their time (the plan for perpetual peace which the Abbé de Saint-Pierre drew up in 1715 was a symptom of the general bellicosity of the age), men saw Europe constantly riven by turmoil. Swift was conceived whilst the Dutch wars smouldered: he lived on to see the relatively marginal Jenkins' Ear affair escalate into the War of Austrian Succession.[5] But it was internal dissent which most characterised the period. Pope was born in London almost with the Revolution. As a man of twenty-seven he was an interested bystander as the first considerable Jacobite rebellion was put down.[6] He died at fifty-six, a single year too early to witness the second. These rebellions were not, to contemporaries, the pitiful sallies of a hopelessly lost cause which they have become in modern eyes. Both the Fifteen and the Forty-five were less romantic, less operatic, less chivalric than legend instructs us. For the men and women of Pope's generation they represented a genuine threat to the stability of the Hanoverian regime.[7]

But it is not only the major flashpoints which make an age or a society insecure. As well as the big constitutional upheavals, there was a steady undertow of popular disturbance. Seditious movements ranged from the alleged plots to assassinate William III in the 1690's to a series of minor affrays set off, for instance, by the Gin Act (1736). I shall argue that *The Dunciad* offers us, on one level, an imaginative reconstruction of an eighteenth century riot. In the following sections I shall develop this point with reference to two particular outbursts of violence, which illustrate the passion and enthusiasm with which people took sides in a century once regarded as the epitome of torpor. First the premonition, then the enactment.

The Crowd in Action

I have borrowed this heading from George Rudé's suggestive book, *The Crowd in History*.[8] Its appropriateness stems from the fact that *The Dunciad* is, apart from anything else, a poem about civil commotion. Not only the riotous gathering in the streets which occupies much of Books I and II, but also the later parade of 'Farces, Operas, and Shows', and the complex action of Book IV, are relevant to this theme. There can be few poems which are richer in crowd scenes. A number of scattered instances may be named at random:

> And now had Fame's posterior Trumpet blown,
> And all Nations summon'd to the Throne.
> The young, the old, who feel her [Dulness's] inward sway,
> One instinct seizes, and transports away.
> None need a guide, by sure Attraction led,
> And strong impulsive gravity of Head:
> None want a place, for all their Centre found,
> Hung to the Goddess, and coher'd around.
> Not closer, orb in orb, are seen
> The buzzing Bees about their dusky Queen.
>   The gath'ring number, as it moves along,
> Involves a vast involuntary throng,
> Who gently drawn, and struggling less and less,
> Roll in her Vortex, and her pow'r confess. (B.IV.71)

> Dire is the conflict, dismal is the din,
> Here shouts all Drury, there all Lincoln's-inn;
> Contending Theatres our empire raise,
> Alike their labours, and alike their praise. (B.III.269)

> Thro' Lud's fam'd gates, along the well-known Fleet
> Rolls the black troop, and overshades the street,
> 'Till show'rs of Sermons, Characters, Essays,
> In circling fleeces whiten all the ways:
> So clouds replenish'd from some bog below,
> Mount in dark volumes, and descend in snow. (B.II.359)

> And thou! his Aid de camp, lead on my sons,
> Light-arm'd with Points, Antitheses, and Puns.
> Let Bawdry, Billingsgate, my daughters dear,
> Support his front, and Oaths bring up the rear:
> And under his, and under Archer's wing,
> Gaming and Grub-street skulk behind the King. (B.I.305)

The work is filled with references to the 'crowd', or similar terms. Confining ourselves to the revised version of the poem, we find mention of 'the vulgar herd' (B.IV.535); the 'sable shoal' and 'black blockade' formed by 'a hundred head of Aristotle's friends' (B.IV. 190), described by Aristarchus as 'that rabble' (B.IV.209); the 'hundred sons' of Dulness, mentioned with careful emphasis twice in five lines (B.III.134); the 'sea of heads' belonging to the sleeping Dunces (B.II.410); the 'black troop' with their 'show'rs' of sermons and essays (B.II.360); the 'desp'rate pack' of mud-divers (B.II.305); the 'guild' awoken by the shouting-match (B.II.250); the 'industrious Tribe' of authors (B.II.33); the 'mass of Nonsense' (B.I.241); the 'progeny' of the Dunce, Cibber (B.I.228); the 'Mob of Metaphors' (B.I.67); whilst the word 'crowd' actually occurs seven times. Every manifestation of Dulness indeed – whether pedantry or venal bookselling or the promotion of opera – is characterised by a tropism towards such aggregative units. Dunces find safety in numbers.

Nor are these collectivities either neutral or inert. Their 'union' is illusory: it promotes anarchic disorder. To quote the 'harlot form' of opera:

> O *Cara! Cara!* silence all that train:
> Joy to great Chaos! let Division reign . . . (B.IV.53)

There is something oppressive about all these assemblies ('Now crowds on crowds around the Goddess press . . . Dunce scorning Dunce beholds the next advance . . .') (B.IV.135). They are not merely 'clam'rous' (B.II.385); they are bent on displacing others:

> In flow'd at once a gay embroider'd race,
> And titt'ring push'd the Pedants off the place . . . (B.IV.275)

At times the imagery takes on even more sinister overtones:

> Then thick as Locusts black'ning all the ground,
> A tribe, with weeds and shells fantastic crown'd . . . (B.IV.397)

The bellicose nature of the Dunces is suggested by Pope's phrasing:

> Around him wide a sable Army stand,
> A low-born, cell-bred, selfish, servile band,
> Prompt or to guard or stab, to saint or damn,
> Heav'n's Swiss, who fight for any God, or Man. (B.II.355)

Elsewhere the language resounds with contempt:

> Millions and millions on these banks he views,
> Thick as the stars of night, or morning dews,

As thick as bees o'er vernal blossoms fly,
As thick as eggs at Ward in Pillory. (B.III.31)

Once again the last line brings back the poetic context from apparently free-ranging metaphor to closely specified contemporary actuality: the actuality of crime and punishment which lies so close to the duncely milieu. Finally, the fullest description of the crowd's composition, which comes after Queen Dulness has proclaimed her games:

They summon all her Race: An endless band
Pours forth, and leaves unpeopled half the land.
A motley mixture! in long wigs, in bags,
In silks, in crapes, in Garters, and in rags.
From drawing rooms, from colleges, from garrets,
On horse, on foot, in hacks, and gilded chariots:
All who true Dunces in her cause appear'd,
And all who knew those Dunces to reward. (B.II.19)

One could scarcely have a more explicit statement in poetic terms of the sociology of Duncehood.

It is interesting to compare the picture thus built up with Rudé's analysis of the pre-industrial crowd. He begins, it is true, by excluding from consideration

crowds that are casually drawn together like sight-seers; crowds assembled on purely ceremonial occasions or crowds taking part in religious or academic processions; or 'audience' crowds . . . who gather in theatres or lecture halls, at baseball matches or bullfights, or who used to witness hangings at Tyburn Fair . . . Equally, we should generally exclude those more active, or 'expressive' crowds that come together for Mardi Gras, participate in dancing orgies or student 'rags', or attend revivalist meetings to hear Billy Graham or Father Divine, as they listened two hundred years ago to George Whitefield and the Wesleys.

Now all of these (except perhaps the first) are categories into which one *could* fit the crowd movements of *The Dunciad*. There is a strong processional flavour to the Dunces' own itinerary, as was appropriate to a parodic Lord Mayor's Show; and in so far as Dulness partakes of both academic and religious vices, Rudé's phrasing meets the case. Again, the crowd in the poem does spend a good deal of its time listening to their Queen or to other spellbinders. The element of a sporting contest is unmistakable; and the road to Tyburn is a very short one indeed. Orgiastic symptoms are just as unmistakable, and not only in the second book. Lastly, what Rudé says about revivalist meetings comes especially close because such events did indeed take place in the neighbourhood of Moorfields. In the British Museum Print Room there is an engraving of 1739 called, appositely enough, 'Enthusiasm Displayed: or the Moorfields Congregation'. This is an attack on Whitefield. But in another sense the scribblers of Grub Street formed a standing Moorfields congregation.

Despite these considerations, I think it is plain that the goings-on in *The Dunciad* fall into the residual categories, as well, found in Rudé's analysis. The historian states that 'main attention will be given to political demonstrations and to what sociologists have termed the "aggressive mob" or the "hostile outburst" – to such activities as strikes, riots, rebellions, insurrections, and revolutions'.[9] The activities Pope recounts are not in any obvious sense political. That they are often aggressive or hostile has already been indicated. That they have the character of an outburst, a riot or an insurrection may be less easily granted. Again, a somewhat exhaustive tabulation of particular references is the best way of carrying forward the argument.

Apart from the allusion to the 'sable Army', we find many other points at which Pope emphasises the quasi-military aspect of the events. Thus the contentiousness which is endemic to folly is satirised by means of the ancient disputes concerning the date of Easter:

> . . . Happy! had she seen
> No fiercer sons, had Easter never been.
> In peace, great Goddess, ever be ador'd;
> How keen the war, if Dulness draw the sword!
> Thus visit not thy own! on this blest age
> Oh spread thy Influence, but restrain thy Rage. (B.III.117)

Pope's note runs, 'Wars in *England* anciently, about the right time of celebrating *Easter*'. War and ceremonial are thus connected; the plea made by Settle's ghost in this passage is to be in vain, for Dulness has already drawn her sword in effect. Her final triumph, moreover, is one based on superior numbers, like any ordinary military success.

Later on in the same book, Settle refers to the aldermen of the City in significant terms, speaking of

> Their full-fed Heroes, their pacific May'rs,
> Their annual trophies, and their monthly wars . . . (B.III.281)

'Peaceful' is little more than a sneer, harking back to the 'bloodless swords and maces' of B.I.87. 'Monthly wars', as Pope's note tells us, refers to the periodic exercises of the City trainband 'in the *Artillery Ground*'. This was located – where else but in Moorfields? The cockpit of civic fribbles is near the arena of literary foolery: appropriately, since the 'monthly wars' could just as well mean the periodical infights of Grub Street, too.

Settle constantly recurs to the theme of dissension among the retinue of Dulness. On the surface he deplores it: but that is only Pope's way of making him testify to its existence:

> Ah Dennis! Gildon ah! what ill-starr'd rage
> Divides a friendship long confirm'd by age?
> Blockheads with reason wicked wits abhor,
> But fool with fool is barb'rous civil war.
> Embrace, embrace my sons! be free no more!
> Nor glad vile Poets with true Critic's gore. (B.III.173)

As a matter of fact the only embracing going on (as the next line reveals) is a homosexual coupling. But Dunces are inalienably at war: if not amongst themselves, with 'wicked wits', that is genuine literary talent or true social propriety. The atavistic return of 'barb'rous civil war' in the mentality of these satirists is something I shall turn to presently. Likewise the dominating imaginative role played by the notion of consumption by fire:

> All sudden, Gorgons hiss, and Dragons glare,
> And ten-horn'd fiends and Giants rush to war.
> Hell rises, Heav'n descends, and dance on Earth:
> Gods, imps, and monsters, music, rage, and mirth,
> A fire, a jigg, a battle, and a ball,
> 'Till one wide conflagration swallows all. (B.III.235)

No giants, outside Settle's crazed prophecy, but only pigmy batallions of Dunces 'rush to war' in the event. At the end the fires are all dimmed. '*Art* after *Art* goes out' (B.IV.640), the precise result of war, according to many versions of cultural history available to Pope. Similarly we find Settle speaking of the lawless insurgence of the bad poets, 'Each Songster, Riddler':

> Some free from rhyme or reason, rule or check,
> Break Priscian's head, and Pegasus's neck;
> Down, down they larum, with impetuous whirl,
> The Pinders, and the Miltons of a Curl. (B.III.161)

If that is not a riot, it is uncomfortably like one. Not even the eighteenth century accepted headbreaking in the streets as a part of ordinary civilised behaviour, lax as they were in these matters. One is less sure in the case of the fierce logicians (that epithet occurs frequently) who 'Came whip and spur, and dash'd thro' thin and thick' (B.IV.197), something the young blood might have attempted without the militia's being called out.[10]

Pope puts into a more express form his sense of the Dunces as taking part in a revolution against good sense. The main evidence comes in Book IV. Here we have a portrait of the crowd in action which approaches the analysis of Gustave Le Bon. As Rudé puts it, not unfairly, Le Bon

> was inclined to treat the crowd . . . as irrational, fickle, and destructive; as intellectually inferior to its components; as primitive or tending to revert to an animal condition. His prejudices led him to equate the 'mob' with the lower classes in society; and . . . [he] claimed [the French revolutionary crowd] tended to be composed of criminal elements, degenerates, and persons with destructive instincts, who blindly respond to the siren voices of 'leaders' or 'demagogues'.[11]

So, long before Taine or Le Bon, contemporaries saw it, much as it depresses the modern liberal historian. Large sections of *The Dunciad* are applicable, as I read the poem: the destructive element is most apparent at the end of the poem, the irrationality perhaps most in Book III. But to see how Pope shows us a crowd 'intellectually inferior to its components', easily hoodwinked by a leader, and bent obscurely on rebellion against it knows not what, we must look at one particular episode in the last book. There is indeed so much evidence that my quotation must be highly selective:

> The young, the old, who feel her inward sway,
> One instinct seizes, and transports away.
> None need a guide, by sure Attraction led,
> And strong impulsive gravity of Head:
> None want a place, for all their Centre found,
> Hung to the Goddess, and coher'd around.
> Not closer, orb in orb, conglob'd are seen
> The buzzing Bees about their dusky Queen.
>   The gath'ring number, as it moves along,
> Involves a vast involuntary throng,
> Who gently drawn, and struggling less and less,
> Roll in her Vortex, and her pow'r confess.
> Not those alone who passive own her laws,
> But who, weak revels, more advance her cause.
> Whate'er of dunce in College or in Town
> Sneers at another, in toupee or gown;
> Whate'er of mungril no one class admits,
> A wit with dunces, and a dunce with wits.
>   Nor absent they, no members of her state,
> Who pay her homage in her sons, the Great;
> Who false to Phoebus, bow the knee to Baal;
> Or impious, preach his Word without a call . . .
> . . . There march'd the bard and blockhead, side by side,
> Who rhym'd for hire, and patroniz'd for pride . . .
> . . . When Dulness, smiling – 'Thus revive the Wits!
> But murder first, and mince them all to bits . . .
> Let standard-Authors, thus, like trophies born,
> Appear more glorious as more hack'd and torn . . .
>   Leave not a foot or verse, a foot of stone,
> A Page, a Grave, that they can call their own . . .
> And while on Fame's triumphal Car they ride,
> Some Slave of mine be pinion'd to their side.' (B.IV.73–134)

With proleptic accuracy, this horrifying picture serves as a kind of warning against the Gordon riots.[12] The sluggish but unstoppable impetus of the crowd;[13] their social heterogeneity; their complement of 'mongrel' outcasts; their delight in rapine and destruction; their pathetic search for trophies and effigies; their careful choice of victim and rancorous envy – all this and more corresponds with what we know of the eighteenth-century city riot. When there is added the sustaining parallel between Cibber and the arch-rebel Satan (so brilliantly elucidated by Aubrey Williams), the importance of the 'riot' theme begins to show up.[14] Palpably, the civil broil has become an image of the breakdown in intellectual order which the poem takes as its subject.

There are further similarities. The Dunces obscurely imagine themselves to be oppressed (by merit), which Rudé – following Lord Granville in 1737 – sees as a characteristic of the rebellious crowd. Again, Rudé writes that the people may rise, amongst other reasons, 'because it has some deep social grievance, because it seeks an immediate reform or the millenium, or because it wants to destroy an enemy or acclaim a "hero"; but it is seldom for any single one of these reasons alone.' The social grievance of the Dunces is the strong antipathy of bad for good. The milleniary and destructive ambitions of the crowd, and their desire to do honour to their leader, are apparent on the most cursory reading of the last two books. The chiliastic fervour of Cibber is matched by the hero-worshipping zeal of the mass of Dunces:

> . . . All eyes direct their rays
> On him, and crowds turn Coxcombs as they gaze.
> His Peers shine round him with reflected grace,
> New edge their dulness, and new bronze their face. (B.II.7)

Again, the charismatic presence of Dulness herself is everywhere apparent. She glories in the absolute tyranny of King Mob:

> For sure, if Dulness sees a grateful Day,
> 'Tis in the shade of Arbitrary Sway.
> O! if my sons may learn one earthly thing . . .
> 'The RIGHT DIVINE of Kings to govern wrong.' (B.IV.181)

There is a parallel, too, with a series of riots led by 'Rebecca' and her daughters in the next century. Here we have a (spuriously) female leader, whose name has biblical overtones: a Magna Mater claiming allegiance from her 'children'. The religious connection is interesting, in view of the sacerdotal implications which have been discovered in *The Dunciad* by Williams and others. According to Rudé, the French

Revolution 'saw a remarkable upsurge of new religious cults; and solemn ceremonies, accompanied by all the *mystique* of the old religious practices, were dedicated to new local "saints".' In *The Dunciad*, as Williams puts it, Pope 'constructs a negative image of Christian theology, fashioning an inverse paradigm of creation with a deity in it who parodies antithetically the Christian deity.' Doubtless it was a byproduct of Pope's main imaginative purposes – a sort of artistic parergon – by which the ceremony and practices connected with the cult of Dulness came to link the central business of the poem even more firmly with the revolutionary crowd. But so it was.[15]

Other specialised points of comparison may be isolated. For example, Rudé mentions that the Common Council of the City 'most often gave the lead' in London riots. 'The City, which prided itself on its political independence, opposed the policies of Westminster and St James's almost continuously throughout the century, and more particularly between 1730 and 1780; and . . . it became the real political educator of London's "lower orders".' In this light it takes on a special interest that bards and aldermen should be so intimately connected in the passage of Book IV from which I took the last extensive quotation. As pointed out elsewhere, the Dunces did not actually inhabit the City within the walls, and their literal association with the Corporation was slight. But they could be seen as 'pupils' of the pseudo-educators, the embattled guildsmen bent on opposing St James's and Westminster, and such tutelage would bear fruit chiefly in the context of a riot. Secondly, Rudé refers to an 'elementary form of social protest' found in the 'gay abandon' of the Wilkite demonstrators. The Dunces are perhaps more abandoned than gay, but broadly it fits. Thirdly, the location of riots and the provenance of those taking part deserve a word. In his chapter on 'The City Riot of the Eighteenth Century', Rudé names Rosemary Lane (Rag Fair) as a major centre of activity of the anti-Irish riots in 1736, just halfway between the two principal versions of *The Dunciad* (1729–43). There were a great many Irish in Cripplegate and one might have expected some trouble there: the only evidence of this kind I have found during the period concerns the demolition of an Irish alehouse in Golden Lane. Rudé also singles out the silk-weavers of Moorfields as especially persistent and violent protesters on labour matters. Equally to point, he notes the 'surprising fact that the most riotous parts of London . . . were not the crowded quarters of St Giles-in-the-Fields or the shadier alleys of Holborn but the more solid and respectable popular districts of the City, the Strand, Southwark, Shoreditch, and Spitalfields.' The Dunces often lived in St Giles' or Holborn, but their riots take place in the City and around the Strand.[16]

Three final points. As to the composition of the crowd, Rudé sets out to refute the assumption of historians such as Dorothy George and Dorothy Marshall that the mob 'was in large measure composed of social dregs, pimps, prostitutes, thieves, and receivers.' Throughout this book I have attempted to show that Pope does indeed seek to associate his Dunces with such people, mainly by use of the actual physical environment. But, as the quotations must have made clear, he is far from asserting that all Dunces were 'social dregs' by origin. Secondly, it is notable how many eighteenth-century London riots were anti-Catholic in inspiration. The best-known instances postdate *The Dunciad*, but not by any means all. This was a fact of which Pope, even though he left Lombard Street in infancy, cannot have failed to be aware. Thirdly, it is fascinating to observe how closely 'the common pattern of the eighteenth-century city riot', as Rudé describes it, conforms to that of the poem. In the cases Rudé studied, the rioters 'operated in itinerant bands, marching (or running) through Shoreditch, the City of London, Westminster or Southwark, gathering fresh forces on the way.' So do the Dunces 'march' (B.II.423; IV.101) through the City to the boundary of Westminster, as a 'gath'ring number' (B.IV.81). The running seems to be confined to the foot races of Book II.[17]

I do not claim, of course, that Pope was so prescient that he foresaw all the historical parallels which can now, with hindsight, be drawn. I do believe that he instinctively turned to a conspicuous breach of public order when he wished to project imaginatively his sense of a breakdown in social values. As I shall argue presently, rebellion meant to the Augustans something more than the cultural lesion which it connotes for writers of this century (and indeed, to some extent for Arnold too, protected from the more violent continental *coups* of the nineteenth century). In 1740 rebellion still sparked off in men's minds the idea of desperate constitutional collision – a fissure, not in social consensus but in the rule of law itself: brother killing brother. If this is so, then it is fair to see in *The Dunciad* the image of a febrile state, on the verge of a reign of terror:

> Beneath her foot-stool, *Science* groans in Chains,
> And *Wit* dreads Exile, Penalties and Pains.
> There foam'd rebellious *Logic*, gagged and bound,
> There, stript, fair *Rhet'ric* languish'd on the ground. (B.IV.21)

Dulness, the great insurrectionist, is also the great tyrant, commissar of the secret police. So it will always be, Pope implies. This is not by way of literal prediction, of course. The poetry is simply that much more effective because of the immediacy with which civil war then seemed to threaten, and because of the way contemporaries thought about such turmoil.

There is a danger that we shall exaggerate the importance of this element in the total workings of the poem, once we have discovered it: as with the topographic background. This is a risk which attends most attempts to explicate poetry written in such different conditions from our own. By isolating the submerged religious allusions in Pope, we are liable to falsify his intent: not because they are not there, but just because they *are*, so self-evidently to a reader of Pope's day. As soon as we pick out a strand in his thought or imagery, which has passed from automatic reception to recondite 'demonstration', we tend to give that strand more significance than it should really possess. But this is one of the penalties of exposition.

Nor do I wish to suggest that the reading of the poem I have offered, with its emphasis on the seething crowd, furnishes what critics of the age called 'a complete key' to *The Dunciad*. The view of Pope's work which is made possible by reference to documentation and analysis of the eighteenth-century urban riot is only a partial vision. But I would contend that it does harmonise with the insights we already bring to that work, based on more familiar responses and bodies of information.

The events of *The Dunciad* call to mind another form of urban protest or demonstration. As well as the riot, they suggest the political procession or symbolic carnival which was the Augustan equivalent of a modern sit-in. The processional element in the poem has not been very fully explored; it can, I think, be illuminated by considering two external factors.

The first concerns a reference in a letter by Alderman John Barber. Surprisingly, this immensely helpful clue seems to have been disregarded by all previous commentators, yet it has been in print more than a century and a half. Neither the Twickenham editor nor Aubrey Williams mention this letter, even though it would strengthen much of what they say. Barber was printer of the *London Gazette*, a leading figure in the Stationers' Company, and Lord Mayor of London in 1732–3. Writing to Swift on 24 August 1732, he alludes to the coming Lord Mayor's Day (30 October) and continues:

> It would add very much to my felicity, if your health would permit you to come over in the spring, and see a pageant of your own making. Had you been here now, I am persuaded you would have put me to an additional expense, by having a raree-show (or pageant) as of old, on the lord mayor's day. Mr. Pope and I were thinking of having a large machine carried through the city, with a printing-press, author, publishers, hawkers, devils, etc., and a satirical poem printed and thrown from the press to the mob, in public view, but not to give offence; but your absence spoils that design.[18]

Or did it? These words were written five years after Pope had been in the throes of composition; but its suggestion of medieval guilds, Terrae Filius and public display may well have been in Pope's mind much earlier. The difference was that in 1732 there was a Lord Mayor, who was a Tory and a friend of the Scriblerians. Barber was a friend of Swift of very long standing – he had suffered for his part in putting out *The Public Spirit of the Whigs* in 1714 – and he was no bumbling alderman to be taken in by a passing joke. The poem to be thrown to the mob may not have been *The Dunciad* – something more within the compass of a broadside sheet would be required – but it would be a work of the same order. In the event, Pope's satirical offering to the mob, guying the literary profession in a 'public' mode, was circulated in a more conventional fashion. The procession of hawkers was simply built into the internal structure of the poem (A.II.13ff.).

Second, there is the annual procession to commemorate the Popish Plot. This was instituted in 1679, possibly with the knowledge of Shaftesbury, and every November right into Hanoverian times it was re-enacted to the accompaniment of bonfires, huzzas and side-skirmishes. The torchlit caravan began, appropriately, at Moorfields, and moved via Bishopsgate, Hounsditch, Aldgate, Leadenhall Street and Cornhill through Cheapside down to Temple Bar. There the waxwork figure of the Pope which had been carried along would be burnt, his richly dressed body having been lifted down from its chariot. On the bar itself, as reconstructed by Wren, one of the embossed figures was that of Queen Elizabeth; and on to this statue a shield would be placed, bearing the legend 'The Protestant Religion, Magna Charta.'[19] No one born a Londoner, least of all a Papist, could fail to be aware of this yearly ritual.[20] I do not suggest that Pope was necessarily conscious of the custom when he devised his supreme poetic fiction; though there is nothing in psychological or aesthetic theory which would rule that out. It does seem possible, to put it no higher, that subconsciously he had the memory of this gruesome procession activating his imagination when he sent his own troop of Dunces marching through the City. Two mental tricks, by no means uncommon, could have aided this process. To start with, it would not be fanciful to suppose that Pope at some level may have identified his own persecuted church with his own name (his opponents could never resist such an easy pun). An army of zealots bearing a stuffed Pope to ceremonial carnage at Temple Bar would therefore easily serve as a surrogate for an army of Dunces bent on the ritual destruction of Alexander Pope. Secondly, we might recall a familiar fact which has been given prominence by recent experiments. This is the tendency of the mind, when abstracted by sleep or some other preoccupation, to confuse words which sound nearly alike. Thus the subjects of psychological research have been found to dream of door-keys when the name 'Torquay' is repeated quietly to them as they sleep. Could it be that the vowel-quantities in another pair of words were close enough for Pope to make an imaginative transference – Magna Charta: Magna Mater? The shibboleth of the anti-Papists, and the talisman of the anti-Popists, mentioned in the very first line of the revised poem. It is a remote possibility, but instructive to contemplate.

To see this potential symbolism realised in literature, we have only to turn to the *Tatler*. A fairly early number by Steele is No. 41, which appeared on 14 July 1709.[21] The paper describes an exercise of arms by the Artillery Company a fortnight previously. Steele recounts the march of a body down Moorgate from the Artillery Ground, through the City, and then their return via Aldersgate Street, the Barbican and Red Cross Street. Here the force drew up, and subsequently moved up Beech Lane (then a twisting alley, later improved as Beech Street) before taking up position in White Cross Street. Here a sort of tactical exercise was conducted, with the Lieutenant-General's contingent retreating into Chiswell Street. The action of this curious wide-game was concentrated in a zone centring on Grub Street, the radius being about two hundred yards. Forays are made through Red Lion Court, over by the Artillery Ground itself; ambushes are laid in Black Raven Court, off Golden Lane; Bunhill Row is fiercely contested. Two divisions are deployed in Grub Street, and the entire affair takes place within shouting range of that unruly citadel. Steele ends with the level-toned irony he commanded so well: 'Happy was it, that the greatest part of the achievements of this day was to be performed near Grub Street, that there might not be wanting a sufficient number of faithful historians.'

Here was one lead for Pope: it was a paper he almost certainly read. The divisions of Grub Street are the forbears of the war-like Dunces, parading through London. The conducted tour of Cripplegate is, at the close, related directly to the other forms of aggressive life which flourished in the parish. In other words, Steele emphasises the happy accident by which military pageantry and pompous trainband zeal had its expression in the Quartier Scriblerian, where instant history was made by the hack chroniclers. It is a key instance of a literary joke which depends on (and is accompanied by) a close itinerary of this single, unsubstitutable area. From the start, Grub Street was a better joke because its geographical setting was so familiar, so available and so endlessly appropriate. Pope, of course, improves on the joke; but he does so by developing, not muting, its existing implications.

The Rage and the Rabble

The vocabulary of Augustan satire, then, carries within itself a buried layer of allusion to civil unrest. The 'premonition' is imagistic and rhetorical, rather than literal; but it is still true that this body of writing prefigures an important development in populist activity, indeed in social history at large. The Scriblerian lexicon anticipated events.

The clue to this state of affairs is to be found in the terror and revulsion with which Pope and Swift looked on faction. This is now a grey little word with little power to alarm us. But at a historical moment when schism appeared the great threat to progress in political, economic and cultural life, the term had a sharper ring. Not for nothing does Ricardus Aristarchus, in introducing the later *Dunciad*, refer to 'the party of Dulness'.[22] The poem itself incorporates a visionary account of a malicious faction destroying itself, and others, in pursuit of private goals. The chiliastic fervour of the Dunces leads them to parrot mindless slogans; their fierce conviction induces them to swamp London with their noxious and debilitating exhalations. They are a party.

The phrase 'cultural life' was perhaps ill-considered. It is doubtful whether the eighteenth-century mind truly recognised such a category at large. And assuredly the thinkers of the age did not regard crime or public affray as social lesions, as many people would today. They had not read their Matthew Arnold, and for them a riot in Hyde Park was only secondarily – if at all – to be deplored because it showed a lack of personal cultivation on the rioters' part. It was to be reviled as threatening an actual breakdown in the rule of law. The Augustans, we should recall, read Cicero not merely as a graceful moralist; they still combed his works for lessons in political prudence.

The tendency to read *The Dunciad* as an exploration of a gap in 'communication' betrays a similar distortion of the period. The first thing to say about the eighteenth-century notion of communication is that, broadly speaking, no such theory existed. By importing our modern categories, we give a spurious lucidity to some aspects of the age. But we blur its outlines, too, and soften its asperities. On the whole the Augustan mind was not well attuned to 'cultural' considerations. Both Pope and Swift, I believe, harboured deeper fears than the mere loss of cultivation in personal living. It is a pardonable exaggeration to say that their literary forebodings project a state of affairs almost exactly equivalent with that of the actual French Revolution, as it impressed itself on the mind of their successor Burke. They feared the storming of the English Bastille.

More significant, then, than any 'cultural' development is the growing importance of the popular affray as a *political* instrument in the eighteenth century. Historians disagree as to the precise nature of this change, and it would be rash to place too much weight on the 'partisan' basis of riots at large. But in using the term I do not mean that all disturbances were motivated by a straight Whig/Tory clash, though some were: the Mug-House riot of 1716 would seem to be one. Nor do I postulate any definite ideological alignment in such persistent troublemakers as the Spitalfields weavers. The point is not that these varied groups all had a common 'radical' banner – clearly they did not. But behind the different religious, economic, racial or social issues which stimulated disorder, there is one shared characteristic. All the rioters believe that by carrying out a public demonstration, as a group, they will be able to further their ends. Almost invariably, their demonstration ran into pillage, arson or both. Pope implies that the Dunces are experts in '*Battle-array*', like their leader, Cibber (who actually 'met the *Revolution* at Nottingham face to face', as Pope jibingly puts it).[23] The phrase is hardly metaphoric at all; and as usual the biographic hint is to the purpose. Dunces are heirs of the armies of the seventeenth century, which had laid waste so much of the country. They are destroyers by profession.

Symptomatically, the age which was so fertile in riots gave us the Riot Act. This was indeed among the very first measures of the first

Hanoverian king. It is 1 George I, stat. 2, c. 5 (1714), and survived in England and Wales right up to the Criminal Law Act of 1967. Eighteenth-century jurists were much concerned to provide a workable definition of the various modes of unlawful assembly. A rout, for instance, has been held to mean an affray caused by an assembly on the move – like, let us say, the Gordon rioters or the Dunces. Riot itself has been interpreted to refer to a 'tumultuous disturbance of the peace by three or more with an intent mutually to assist one another against any who oppose them, in the execution of some enterprise of a private nature.' (The last phrase is designed to exclude the notion of insurrection, where some public cause is at issue.) But all modes of affray must be shown to induce 'the terror and affright of the people' for a prosecution to lie.[24] It is hardly necessary to remind ourselves of the nature of the duncely 'enterprise', or the horrific quality of the 'dread Empire' of Chaos (B.IV.653) with its promise of unending night.

Among popular disturbances of the age, two are of special interest. Both link Grub Street even more firmly with tumult. The Wilkite affrays of 1768, which have been so thoroughly explored by George Rudé, confirm Pope's imaginative thesis in a variety of ways. We find Wilkes greeted by huzzas at the junction of Chancery Lane and the Strand; by St Clement's church, his supporters actually went so far as to take over as carriage-horses in their delight. The resemblance to the cries of 'God save King Cibber!' (B.I.320), or the brays which roll down Chancery Lane (B.II.263) are too obvious to need emphasis. The hacks' quarter of St Giles' and Drury Lane was, inevitably, convulsed during the riots. St Bride's, in the vicinity of the Fleet Ditch, was a parish which resounded again and again to the cry of 'Wilkes and Liberty'. Wilkes indeed was elected as alderman for the ward of Farringdon Without (the corresponding civic division) in January 1769. It is interesting to note that the popular hero had been born in St John's Square, Clerkenwell, in 1725: little more than a decade later, Samuel Johnson was to be in occupation of the nearby St John's Gate – profession, hack writer. It is not a very long step to Grub Street proper: a bare quarter of a mile from Wilkes's birthplace to the parish of Cripplegate.[25]

No less interesting, though more indirect, are two other features of Professor Rudé's research. He quotes Alexander Wedderburn, writing to George Grenville on 3 April 1768:

> [the south of England has become] a great Bedlam under the dominion of a beggarly, idle and intoxicated mob without keepers, actuated solely by the word *Wilkes*, which they use as better savages do a walrus to incite them in their attempts to insult Government and trample upon law.

The phraseology here is a standing testimony to the imaginative accuracy of the poem Pope had written over a quarter of a century earlier. The noisy and inebriated Wilkites mouthing their shibboleths are at one with the devotees of Colley Cibber. Secondly, it is intriguing to note that many of the citizens arrested in 1768 for riotous assembly, or similar offences, prove to have been parishioners of St Giles', Cripplegate or St Luke's, Old Street. Perhaps they did not have so far to march as others – but that in itself made the inner suburbs a home of the riotous. Among those listed by Rudé, we find a lighterman of Old Street, convicted of breaking windows at the Mansion House riots, and given one of the stiffest sentences. Another given to protest by defenestration was a watch-finisher of Jewin Street. A weaver of Golden Lane is also named. Moving slightly further afield, we encounter a porter of John Street, Clerkenwell, and the wife of a clothes-dealer in Nightingale Lane – a street abutting on Rosemary Lane, where old clothes and Dulness alike proliferated.[26] It would appear that whenever serious disturbance broke out in London, Cripplegate could be relied on to supply its quota of hooligans and hoodlums.

It is the Gordon Riots, however, twelve years later, which supply the most striking authentication of Pope's charge. In a number of ways the events of June 1780 sum up the history of popular insurrection in the eighteenth century. It cannot fail to impress us, then, that they prove equally to enact many of the implied predictions of *The Dunciad*. Of course, I do not mean that Pope literally divined the shape of things to come, as Burke perhaps did in the case of French history. I am suggesting rather that the poet's creative mind shaped events along lines that were, so to speak, already immanent in history. His poem acts out fictively a myth of social disorder, which the anti-popery riots chance to follow with curious mimicry. But this is a contingent fact: *The Dunciad* would still be an impressive vision of the anarchic city even if the Protestant Association had never existed. We are being neither perverse nor anachronistic, then, if we congratulate Pope on writing better than he knew. Events come to his support so often because he went so often (and at such an early imaginative stage) *to* events in the devising of his myth.

A single piece of evidence gives eloquent proof of the relevance of the happenings of 1780. It was only at this juncture that Samuel Johnson for the very first time planned to visit Grub Street. He was over seventy years old; he had been living in London continuously for more than half that span; and he was in no doubt that he ought to have paid his respects before this time. Fanny Burney tells the story to Mrs Thrale:

> Since that time, I have had the pleasure to meet him [Johnson] again at Mrs. Reynolds's, when he offered to take me with him to Grub Street, to see the ruins of the house demolished there in the late riots, by a mob that, as he observed, could be no friend to the Muses! He inquired if I had ever yet visited Grub Street? but was obliged to restrain his anger when I answered 'No', because he acknowledged that he had never paid his respects to it himself. 'However,' says he, 'you and I, Burney will go together; we have a very good right to go, so we'll visit the mansions of our progenitors, and take up our own freedom together.'[27]

Typically, the comic byplay illustrates a larger truth. The septuagenarian writer, once a hack domiciled over the way from Cripplegate, invites the young author of *Evelina* to inspect 'the mansions of [their] progenitors' – the only bit of London literary men could call their own. And when, we may ask, does he feel impelled to do so? Why, when the street is recovering from the after-effects of a riot. Grub Street was in a proper state to receive its own at such a moment: conflict and destruction were its lifeblood.

Johnson had taken a close interest in the progress of the riots. He noted in a letter to Mrs Thrale on 9 June 1780 that a masshouse in

Moorfields had been burnt down (conceivably the same 'house' he was to visit with Fanny Burney). Three days later he inquired with an air of some desperation, 'Who can guess the caprice of the rabble?'[28] It is a refrain taken up by others. Horace Walpole, an equally interested spectator, had been using similar phrasing for some time. During the Wilkite troubles, he had written to Mann, 'Since our riots and tumults, I conclude you are glad when you do *not* hear from me; it is a symptom that we are tolerably quiet; for you can have no fear of me, who live out of the storm. It is true, our mobs are subsided . . .'[29] The word 'mob' is ubiquitous. A concordance of Walpole's work – which would be a most valuable operation if enough computer-programmers could be recruited at Yale – would show how often he falls back on the word around this period. Johnson did not live 'out of the storm', and his fears were almost as marked. Even men of great physical courage found themselves beset by apprehension. For a time it must have seemed as if the empire of Chaos had indeed come: the destruction of Lord Mansfield's famous library must have appeared as a ghastly fulfilment of Settle's demented prophecy:

> Heav'ns! what a pile! whole ages perish there,
> And one bright blaze turns Learning into air. (B.III.77)

By one of those strange connections which begin to look less and less like pure coincidence, William Cowper chose to single out Pope and Swift amongst the many valuable books destroyed. His poem was enclosed in a letter dated 22 June 1780:

On the Burning of Lord Mansfield's Library : Together with his MSS. By the Mob, in the Month of June 1780.

> So then – the Vandals of our isle,
>   Sworn foes to sense and law,
> Have burnt to dust a nobler pile
>   Than ever Roman saw!
>
> And MURRAY sighs o'er Pope and Swift,
>   And many a treasure more,
> The well-judged purchase and the gift
>   That grac'd his letter'd store.

Their pages mangled, burnt, and torn,
    The loss was *his alone ;*
But ages yet to come shall mourn
    The burning of *his own.*[30]

Cowper here associates vandalism, burning, mangling, as common foes of the tradition represented by Swift, Pope and Mansfield himself. The 'mob' are by implication *un*lettered, incapable of the 'storing' function which humanist lore revered (as with Swift's bee). The Gordon riots, in other words, operated as an agency of Dulness. The populace, volatile and doomed to the temporary, takes its revenge on the stable and the permanent. It has but one weapon: indiscriminate carnage. That a mob bent on throwing Pope, along with other Catholics, to the flames should concentrate many of its activities in Cripplegate is almost too apt to be credible.

A lively, though not meticulously accurate, account of the disturbances has been given by Christopher Hibbert in *King Mob.* To set his narrative alongside *The Dunciad* is to become aware of an uncanny prescience on the part of Pope. The most striking way of making the point, indeed, will be simply to juxtapose quotations, with brief reference to other surveys of the riot.

The trouble first reached serious proportions on Friday, 2 June, with the meeting at St George's Fields. This was a large open space in Southwark, and as Hibbert says,

> By night it was a dangerous place and only the most foolhardy citizens took a short cut across it unarmed. In daylight gangs of streetboys chased each other around the wooden shacks of beggars and the bushes near stagnant ponds, while apprentices from the workshops at Newington Butts and from the maze of streets between Bandly Leg Walk and Angel Street ['angel' doubtless connoting prostitutes], came out to play football or to make love in the long grass. For many years it had been a favourite place for open air meetings, demonstrations and religious meetings . . .

It was, in other words, exactly like Moorfields on the other side of the river. The riots started in a natural habitat of Dulness. Similarly the gangs of Dunces chase one another round London, after emerging from their shacks in the 'maze of streets' in St Giles', and recreate themselves with boisterous athletics round the stagnant pool that was the Fleet Ditch. They demonstrate with religious fervour and quasi-erotic immodesty. After this assembly, the rioters marched (as do the Dunces) to the West End. They moved down Fleet Street to the Strand, towards Charing Cross. Whenever they passed a church they would give three cheers (exactly so, the acclamations and bawlings of Pope's poem take place outside St Mary le Strand). The rioters progressed a little farther, since Westminster was their destination; the Dunces are content to petition Parliament with noise:

> Thames wafts it thence to Rufus' roaring hall,
> And Hungerford re-echoes bawl for bawl. (B.II.265)

Whilst the rioters were hanging about outside the House of Lords, awaiting news of how their petition had been received, they began to 'jeer or laugh' at the Foot Guards, who retorted with a somewhat impotent charge.

> This treatment [writes Hibbert] while enraging many of the demonstrators made others laugh so much that they could not get up from the ground, where they rolling about in paroxysms of infectious laughter.

It seems hardly necessary to remind ourselves that an identical blend of rage, laughter, reeling and paralysis runs through *The Dunciad*:

> Heav'n rings with laughter: Of the laughter vain,
> Dulness, good Queen, repeats the jest again. (B.II.121)

Many of the rioters were drunk, of course. Many lay down at Westminster, as do the drugged circle of Dunces at the end of their games. Samuel Romilly, on his way to listen to the debate in the Lords, encountered a group of people

> assembled round a female preacher who by her gestures and actions seemed to be well persuaded, or desirous of persuading others that she was animated by some supernatural spirit.

At one point Dulness does actually change from a false deity into a priestess:

> The Goddess then, o'er his anointed head,
> With mystic words, the sacred Opium shed. (B. I.287)

Like all proselytisers, Dulness has her 'Chosen' (B.I.273); she pours her 'Spirit' over the land (B.I.8).

Again, the link with Bedlam is explicit. Horace Walpole had written of Lord George Gordon as the 'lunatic apostle', and added:

> It is to be hoped this man is so mad that it will soon come to perfection unless my plan is adopted of shutting up in Bedlam the few persons in this country that remain in their senses. It would be easier and much cheaper to confine all the delirious.

When the Protestant Petition was presented at the House of Commons, a certain Colonel Holroyd told Gordon that initially he had regarded the leader of the rioters as mad 'and was going to move that you might be sent to Bedlam'. But now, he went on, he saw that there was method as well as madness, and if Gordon went once more to the mob, he would move that the Tower, instead, should receive him. If Gordon was not completely dissociated at this stage (Dickens perhaps exaggerates the wildness of his fanaticism), he was certainly a man of marked neurotic tendency; in later years he was simply mad. But this is not all. During the riots themselves, there had at first been a plan to release the lunatics along with the convicts. This was abandoned; but witnesses testify to the reactions of the inmates of the hospital. The Bedlamites, excited by the glare and the noise, shrieked deliriously; many danced with glee. There is a deep poetic accuracy in Dickens' choice of a hero for *Barnaby Rudge*.[31]

It was on the following day – Saturday, 3 June – that Grub Street itself became involved. About nine o'clock in the evening violence flared up near Finsbury Yard, in Moorfields. Hibbert comments:

> Moorfields was one of the poorest districts, just to the east ['some way to the north-east'?] of the ragged tumbling slum quarter of St Giles', portrayed in Hogarth's 'Gin Lane', and north of Bedlam. It was a part of London where many Irish labourers had lodgings and where the doss-houses were frequently full of Irish vagrants who paid a penny a night to sleep on the lousy, rat-ridden straw.

A merchant 'of Irish extraction' called Malo was the target for the mob. He seems to have been singled out not principally because he was a Catholic (some of the victims of the depredations were in fact themselves of the Protestant faith), but because he was believed to favour the employment of Catholics, generally Irishmen. The rioters, not altogether without justification, saw this as a threat to their own livelihood. As we saw earlier, there had always been a high proportion of unskilled Irish labourers in Cripplegate Ward. In 1740 this had been one more way in which the rich connotations of the opprobious term 'Grub Street' could be filled out. In 1780 the circumstances came home to roost: the first serious damage done by the Gordon rioters was that wreaked on Grub Street and its immediate environs.

Thanks more to the irresolution of the crowd than to any preventive measures (though seventy-three militia-men were belatedly called in from the Tower), comparatively little physical harm was done on the first night. But on the Sunday, things changed – as Hibbert explains.

It was a hot dry day with not a breath of wind in the air, and the people seemed content to sit idly around on doorsteps and in the streets and to lie on the hot dry ground in Middle Moor Fields and the Tenter Grounds. They seemed unwilling, a Guards Officer noted, to wander far away from the district and the Artillery Ground usually crowded on a Sunday afternoon was strangely quiet.

As the evening cooled the excitement mounted. At about eight o'clock the crowds converged, as if instructed during the day to do so, on a Catholic chapel in Ropemakers Alley. Some women who lived next door to the chapel leaned out of a first floor window and begged the people below to be careful. Their entreaties were greeted with a hail of stones and brickbats, which had been collected to smash the windows of the chapel, and the women hastily withdrew and fled in terror from the back door of their house.

The intoxicating sound of smashing glass was the awaited signal. Hundreds of street-boys and girl prostitutes ran excitedly up and down Ropemakers Alley and the courts adjoining, shouting that the fun had started.

It continued unabated in Moorfields for two horrifying and long-remembered days and nights. Every Catholic chapel in the district was burned to the ground; Irishmen were attacked with sticks and knives whenever they were recognised; quiet and inoffensive Catholics were insulted, spat upon and their clothes torn off their backs; their houses were broken open and their furniture and books and pictures and carpets were tossed on to raging bonfires in the middle of the streets.

Cellars were invaded and food and wine were brought up to be consumed in Bacchanalian parties around the fires; while the Pope and St Patrick were burned in effigy on the sites of burned-out chapels and Irish taverns.

This was indeed the party of Dulness let loose. A riot of destruction and gluttony, sustained by perverted religious principles.

How keen the war, if Dulness draw the sword! (B.III.120)

It was this scene, in and around Grub Street, which suggested to Dr Johnson that he might go and acknowledge his descent from the hacks of yesteryear. It was this scene, too, which Dickens described in a paragraph of impassioned energy in *Barnaby Rudge* (Ch. III), and which Hablot K. Browne illustrated with a kind of maniacal comedy. This is the hellish city of the eighteenth century satirists come to life.

According to J. P. de Castro, a Catholic pawnbroker in Golden Lane was amongst the worst sufferers. His house was pulled down and, not content with that, the mob burnt all his goods in their store at Old Street. Catholic property in Bunhill Fields was also gutted. Thus two streets associated with the most resolute Protestants among major English authors, Milton and Defoe, were ravaged in the cause of anti-popery. It is a matter for gratitude that Bunyan's grave in Tindall's burial ground, just next to Bunhill, was not desecrated by some meandering rioter. The Catholic chapel seems to have been situated in White Street, off Little Moorfields, parallel with Ropemakers Alley. It was in this street, curiously, that the leader of the Cato Street conspirators was found and arrested in 1820. Forty years earlier a bonfire was set up in White Street. In Moorfields itself four young men were strung up after conviction for taking part in the riots. Grub Street continued its unhappy alliance with jailbirds, rakehells and small-time anarchists. The prophecy uttered by Settle in which Dulness is apotheosised contains only the prediction that Rome will be brought low; the rioters attempted to bring down her church too. The minister of the Catholic church died two months later; his death, the *Annual Register* thought, had been hastened by the events in June. He had begun his career as minister when the chapel stood in Butler's Alley, directly off Grub Street itself. When Pope wrote his poem, that is, the main target of the rioters would have lain in the very precincts of Grub Street. Their centre of operations was deflected a couple of hundred yards when the chapel moved, possibly to the site of the former Anabaptist conventicle in White Street, at some date subsequent to 1765.[32]

The bonfires in Moorfields having lit the way, the riot now spread to other parts of the City. For the remainder of that ugly week, we hear little of the region. On the Wednesday night we catch a glimpse of Gordon himself 'haranguing the multitude' there, in a vain attempt to stem the tide and to get them to disperse. On the same evening, according to one story, the party who assailed the Bank dragged off one man to Moorfields in order to ensure his secrecy on an embarrassing discovery he had made. But there is little firm evidence.

However, this is not all that can be said on the subject of the Gordon riots. Again and again in descriptions of the events we come on phrases which instantly call up the world of *The Dunciad*. To take a few examples more or less at random – there is the poet Crabbe observing of the rioters, 'They boldly paraded the streets with colours and music.' Compare the triumphal progress of Cibber to St James's:

> Lift up your gates, ye Princes, see him come!
> Sound, sound ye Viols, be the Cat-call dumb!
> Bring, bring the madding Bay, the drunken Vine . . . (B.I.301)

Cibber's minions 'shine' with reflected grace and bronzed face (B.II.9); their 'motley' troop pours forth in garish abundance, with 'silks, crapes, Garters' as well as rags (B.II.21). Crabbe saw the parade on the morning of Tuesday, 6 June; later that day the rioters carried off Lord Gordon in his chariot (the Dunces had their quota of those: B.II.24). The route taken was up Whitehall, along the Strand and Fleet Street, down Cheapside and Poultry to Mansion House. Not even Pope, with his inventive mock-heroic mind, dreamt up so total an invasion of the Lord Mayor's procession. Here fact does more than underline Pope's joke: it gives it another, uncovenanted, level of meaning.

We may pass over such obvious items of information as the fact that prostitutes were amongst the earliest recruits to the army of destruction. Or that the prisons, bordering the Fleet for the most part, were the major focus of attention for much of the time. Or that the garrets of Smithfield were searched, not for hacks (who could certainly have been found there on occasion) but for fugitives. Or that one of the largest vigilante corps, said to be two thousand strong, had to be set up in Cripplegate. Or that dead bodies were dumped into that universal receptacle, the Fleet Ditch. It is more interesting to note, first that the riots were said to provoke the 'largest exodus since the plague', and second that the riots, like the Fire, were initially blamed on foreign *provocateurs*. Historical evidence is only documenting a connection which poetic imagery had long before asserted.[33]

Fire and Fever

Bonfires raged through the Gordon riots – and other eighteenth-century insurrections – as they blaze through Augustan literature. Combustion was at once the symbol and the agency of anti-popery. The zeal of the anti-Pope faction, that is the Dunces, was likewise attended with conflagration. That crowds and fires went together had been noted by Samuel Johnson as early as 1738: at a time when Grub Street was in a sense his spiritual home, five years before the revised *Dunciad* appeared. His Juvenalian picture of the capital, *London*, contains the thought:

> Here malice, rapine, accident, conspire,
> And now a rabble rages, now a fire . . .[34]

The very grammar links *rabble* with *fire*, whether or not the second is actually caused by the first. As a student of Jacobean city comedy has written, London backgrounds reflect 'the intricacies and unpredictable though constant hazards of the city, which is at once familiar yet hostile and impersonal.'[35] A major hazard of the time was the loss of property by fire, either by accident or malicious arson. Physical fire protection was only just growing up, and insurance was still in its infancy. The mob accordingly had a strong weapon in their hands when they resorted to fire-raising, as the Sacheverell riots in 1710 conspicuously illustrated. A natural visitation could also become a convenient means of offence for the disaffected. An act of God might be taken over to further the actions of the godless.

Naturally a good deal of contemporary concern with the matter can be traced back to the Great Fire. The fear of a recurrence of that disaster shaped the attitude of all Londoners. So we find reprints of a book like *An Account of the burning of the city of London, as it was published in . . . 1666*, which was issued in its third edition (1721) with the 'opinion of Dr. [White] Kennet . . . and Dr [Laurence] Eachard', expert witnesses in theological rather than pyrotechnical matters. Defoe characteristically has a good deal to say on the matter. One of the most obvious examples occurs in his section on the city of London in his *Tour*. He devotes a number of paragraphs specific-ally to the new buildings erected after the Fire, and discusses the changes in the urban landscape which have resulted. Then, a few pages later, he reverts to the theme:

> And as I am speaking of Fire and burning of Houses, it cannot be omitted, That no where in the World is so good Care taken to quench Fires as in *London*; I will not say the like Care is taken to prevent them; for I must say, That I think the Servants, nay, and Masters too in *London*, are the most careless People in the World about Fire, and this, no doubt, is the Reason why there are frequently more Fires in *London* and in the Out-parts, than there are in all the Cities of *Europe* put them together; nor are they the more careful, as I can learn, either from observation or report, I say, they are not made more cautious by the inumerable fires which continually happen among them.

Defoe goes on to list the factors which make London particularly 'well furnished for the extinguishing fires when they happen.' These include the number of water-courses and piped water supplies; the great number of 'admirable engines' owned by the parishes; and the care of well-equipped fire insurance offices. Defoe had earlier listed the four principal societies, and estimated that more than seventy thousand separate properties in the metropolis were now covered against fire risk.[36]

I have not been able to ascertain whether Defoe's claim regarding the high rate of fire-damage, relative to other European cities, is as much of an exaggeration as it looks. Early actuarial figures are not complete enough to make such comparisons reliable. But it does appear that, on a subjective plane, the inhabitants of London *thought* they were uniquely exposed to loss and danger from this source – an understandable legacy in their minds from the calamity of 1666.

Pope was never one to waste such a psychological circumstance. His poem reverberates with the words *fire*, *flames*, *flamy*, *burns*, *smokes*, *blaze conflagration* and so on. One trivial instance will exemplify the way in which he utilised topical facts to his own artistic purposes. I quote from the earlier version, although both text and note survive intact in 1743.

> Grubstreet! thy fall should men and Gods conspire,
> Thy stage shall stand, ensure it but from Fire. (A.III.309)

Pope's note at this point may be supplemented by the Twickenham editor's helpful gloss:

> In *Tibbald's* Farce of *Proserpine* a Corn-field was set on fire; whereupon the other Playhouse had a Barn burnt down for the recreation of the spectators. They also rival'd each other in showing the Burnings of Hell-fire, in Dr. *Faustus*. [Twick.ed: On Oct. 26, 1727 – just about the time that these words were written – a riot occurred at the opening performance of Cibber's *Henry VIII* at Drury Lane, owing to a cry of 'Fire!' raised among the audience. Several people were injured, and one woman crushed to death . . . Pope may have had the circumstance in mind.]

It is worth stressing that the two playwrights involved here, Theobald and Cibber, were the two successive King Dunces. Pope's point is clear. Grub Street in its theatrical aspect – Drury Lane, say – deals in the perishable, like its literary organ; even though here there are no physical copies, but merely plays, to undergo the process of destruction. As everyone knows, eighteenth-century theatres were notoriously likely to go up in flames. Pope therefore gets further satiric purchase by associating theatres and fire. It is a reminder that the actual buildings in which the harlequinade and operas of the Dull were performed were as short-lived as their repertoire. Slightly earlier, in 1721, there had been fears that Drury Lane was in danger of falling down; whilst in 1722 one of the common playhouse 'riots' (the normal word used) erupted against Cibber himself.[37]

Much the same innuendo is found in Book I. There, the chosen bard (let us take Cibber) retires to his library and runs his eyes over his unique collection of trash and showily-bound lightweight authors. To this 'Gothic Library' his fellow-hacks are admitted:

> Here all his suff'ring brotherhood retire,
> And 'scape the martyrdom of jakes and fire. (B.I.143)

Their wretched productions, if not granted the sanctity of their King's library (there is possibly a joke on Bentley here, who had come to prominence while keeper of the royal collection), will suffer one of two fates. Either they will be reduced to the arse-wiping function or else they will be used to light fires. I do not think there is any strong sense here that the books will burn on account of heretical content, i.e. will be placed on the index.

It is this very same library, of course, which provides the kindling for the great ritual bonfire in this book. The pyre is carefully built up, in a manner the Smithfield Muses who are invoked at the start might well approve; for was not Smithfield the place above all in England to carry out a ritual cremation?

> Of these twelve volumes, twelve of amplest size,
> Redeem'd from tapers and defrauded pies,
> Inspir'd he seizes: These an altar raise:
> An hecatomb of pure, unsully'd lays
> That altar crowns: A folio Common-place
> Founds the whole pile, of all his works the base:
> Quartos, octavos, shape the less'ning pyre;
> A twisted Birth-day Ode completes the spire. (B.I.155)

Cibber goes on to address these volumes:

> 'O born in sin, and fourth in folly brought!
> Works damn'd, or to be damn'd (your father's fault)
> Go, purify'd by flames ascend the sky,
> My better and more christian progeny!
> Unstain'd, untouch'd, and yet in maiden sheets;
> While all your smutty sisters walk the streets.' (B.I.225)

As often, there are important biographic allusions here, which have been well explained by the Twickenham editor.[38] But the wider effect of this 'tender and passionate Apostrophe', as Pope calls it, is to link Dulness even more closely with the life of the streets. At the moment in which purification should be taking place, by ceremonial sacrifice, we are forcibly reminded of the filth that surrounds folly. Fire and dirt go together, as they are generally made to do.

Shortly afterwards, the ceremony proper:

> And thrice he lifted high the Birth-day brand,
> And thrice he dropt it from his quiv'ring hand;
> Then lights the structure, with averted eyes:
> The rowling smokes involve the sacrifice.
> The op'ning clouds disclose each work by turns,
> Now flames the Cid, and now Perolla burns;
> Great Caesar roars, and hisses in the fires;
> King John in silence modestly expires;
> No merit now the dear Nonjuror claims,
> Moliere's old stubble in a moment flames.
> Tears gush'd again, as from pale Priam's eyes
> When the last blaze sent Ilion to the skies. (B.I.245)

Ironically only Dulness herself can douse the flames. It would take a whole campaign of extended forays in practical criticism to tease out all the meanings here, quite apart from the Ovidian and Virgilian recollections. Pope himself supplies further jokes in his annotation, bringing in asbestos amongst other things. It is enough, perhaps, to mention the brilliant metaphysical wit enshrined in the phrase, 'Moliere's old stubble' to which the note adds, 'A Comedy thrashed out of Moliere's Tartuffe.' Pope's imagination dances from one variety of fire to the next: at one moment we have a smouldering cornfield after the harvest, at another a Guy Fawkes celebration, at another possibly a royal fireworks display ('the Birthday brand') – or might this indeed suggest a child lighting candles on a cake?[39]

By this means the poet has linked the Dunces with a rather grisly rite. But he has also shown us their works as ripe for incineration; and he has prepared us for the rumbustious crowd scenes of the following book. Cibber's face, at the start of Book II, is itself a sort of burning-glass; and throughout the section we are given constant reminders of this trope. Of Curll's urine, for example, we are told,

> His rapid waters in their passage burn. (B.II.184).

It is Settle's prophecy in Book III, however, which takes up the notion most centrally. The apotheosis of Dulness involves an extension of territorial rights, to regions

> Where spices smoak beneath the burning Line (B.III.70)

and reaches even Tartary:

> Heav'ns! what a pile! whole ages perish there,
> And one bright blaze turns Learning into air. (B.III.77)

There is a paradox here. Queen Dulness, herself, a heavy cloud-compelling monarch, tedious and cold, can yet 'burn' up learning and civility, as a very cold object burns by the transference of heat.

At the climax of Settle's vision, we see the progress of barbarism as Gothic ignorance settles over Rome and even the Popes themselves become instruments of destroying ancient civilisation.

> Padua, with sighs, beholds her Livy burn,
> And ev'n th' Antipodes Vigilius mourn.
> See, the Cirque falls, th' unpillar'd Temple nods,
> Streets pav'd with Heroes, Tyber choak'd with Gods:
> 'Till Peter's keys some christ'ned Jove adorn,
> And Pan to Moses lends his pagan horn;
> See graceless Venus to a Virgin turn'd,
> Or Phidias broken, and Apelles burn'd. (B.III.105)

It is unlike Pope, who has justifiably been termed the most consistently varied of our poets, to repeat a key rhyme-word at so close an interval. Here the idea of 'burning' seems to have taken so compulsive a hold on his imagination that no alteration, no elegant variation, no more or less accurate synonym would do. The simple monosyllabic word comes back with heavy insistence to clinch this horrific description of the self-induced ruins of Rome.[40]

At the very end of the poem, with the triumph of Dulness, eternal night comes to quench the fires of learning with its own black combustion. To a Hanoverian, this must have suggested the trampling down of civic and political morality by the jobbing administration (as Pope thought of it) of Robert Walpole, and later Henry Pelham. The passage is so well known that selective quotation should be enough:

> Before her, *Fancy*'s gilded clouds decay,
> And all its varying Rain-bows die away.
> *Wit* shoots in vain its momentary fires,
> The meteor drops, and in a flash expires.
> As one by one, at dread Medea's strain,
> The sick'ning stars fade off th'ethereal plain . . .
> Thus at her felt approach, and secret might,
> *Art* after *Art* goes out, and all is Night . . .
> *Religion* blushing veils her sacred fires,
> And unawares *Morality* expires.
> Nor *public* Flame, nor *private*, dares to shine;
> Nor *human* Spark is left, nor Glimpse *divine*! (B.IV.631–52)

Wit has become a frenzied, irregular kind of flame; its luminosity is no longer steady or controlled. The Queen of Ignorance has assumed absolute power, and with that London becomes a city very like Hell – a point that emerges most plainly from Aubrey Williams's reading. The city of endless night is, in fact, dark as Milton's Hades is dark: the flames are sensible ('felt') but not visible.

This emphasis on the destructive power of fire could be further explored along two different lines, one broadly 'rhetorical' in character, the other historical or documentary. Under the first aspect, we might recall the statement by Jeffrey Hart which I quoted earlier (p. 96). Fire is a powerful emblem of a process which serves to 'disturb the balance of mind or state' (thus one speaks of a rebellion breaking out, catching alight, spreading like wildfire, razing institutions to the ground, and so on). More specifically, fire came to be associated with religious zeal, that is enthusiasm. And possibly because of the Gunpowder Plot, the notion seems often to have been associated in the seventeenth and eighteenth centuries with constitutional upheaval:

> True Zeal is an *Ignis lambens*, a soft and gentle Flame, that will not Scorch one's hand; it is no predatory or voracious thing: but *Carnall and fleshly Zeal*, is like the Spirit of Gunpowder set on fire, that tears and blows up all that stands before us.[41]

This is Ralph Cudworth, preaching to the House of Commons as early as 1647. But eighty years later, it is still apt to think of the zeal of the Dunces as being 'like the Spirit of Gunpowder set on fire'. The 'bright blaze' which destroyed Rome, which 'turns Learning into air' (B.III.78) and which reduced Lord Mansfield's library to ashes are one and the same. All can be seen as ceremonial fireworks lit as part of the triumph of Dulness.

This leads us to the historical aspect. The only preservative against Popery which the Gordon rioters could think of was to demolish Catholic churches. Equally, in 1710, the pro-Sacheverell mob had gutted meeting-houses and conventicles to proclaim its horror of dissent. Even the Spitalfields weavers, those ubiquitous protesters (often, significantly enough, choosing Moorfields as their venue),[42] engaged in fire-raising. Their normal method of destroying Irish properties, for instance in the riots of 1736, was to break down the house with crowbars and other non-inflammatory tools. But they did burn an effigy of an unpopular master on other occasions;[43] and if the damage was less, the symbolism is hardly impaired. That the demolition of chapels was an invariable accompaniment of any sizeable riot in the eighteenth century is illustrated by the very terms of the Riot Act itself. Section IV proclaims:

> And be it further enacted by the authority aforesaid, That if any persons unlawfully, riotously, tumultuously assembled together, to the disturbance of the publick peace, shall unlawfully, and with force demolish or pull down any church or chapel, or any building for religious worship certified or registred according to the (Toleration Act) . . . or any dwelling-house, barn, stable or other out-house, that then such demolishing, or pulling down, or beginning to demolish, or pull down, shall be judged felony without benefit of clergy, and the offenders therein shall be judged felons, and shall suffer death as in the case of felony, without benefit of clergy.[44]

This was the act which was read (or more strictly its critical passage read) before the Spitalfields rioters in 1736,[45] and on subsequent occasions through the century. Looting, as with the Dunces, was secondary. The rioter engaged in destruction principally with regard to public or official residences (as with that of the Lord Chief Justice in 1780), and this indicates that he was dealing out a symbolic blow rather than seeking personal gain. Very rarely did the mob attack a bank, possibly because this institution had not yet become in the mind of the underprivileged an agency of repression. Religious buildings were the most regular target, and it is in connection with religion that Pope mentions duncely conflagrations (not without a private joke). Settle is made to boast:

> '. . . long my Party built on me their hopes,
> For writing pamphlets, and for burning Popes . . .'
> (A.III.282)

The note explains this juxtaposition of hack literature and ritual cremation:

> He (Settle) had managed the Ceremony of a famous Pope-burning on *Nov.* 17, 1680 . . .

This whole note, retained in the later version of the poem, is worthy of attention. Its astonishingly minute information should flatten at one blow the view that knowledge of the life-histories of the Dunces is extraneous to any literary assessment of the work.

Two final points may be mentioned. First, it is interesting that the fire insurance companies, so highly extolled by Defoe, were concerned over the prevalence of arson at this period. In 1716, for instance, two offices jointly announced a reward for information leading to the discovery of certain active fire-raisers.[46] This makes it all the more suitable that the King Dunce should be presented as a pyromaniac by inclination as much as by profession. Second, fire had long been linked imaginatively with portents and monstrous prodigies – as in, say, *Julius Caesar*. It is Settle, once more, who makes clear that the literary or theatrical aberrations of Grub Street are infractions of the natural order: breaches of cosmic order heralded by roaring flames, as breaches of civil order were announced by bonfires in the streets.

> Another Aeschylus appears! prepare
> For new abortions, all ye pregnant fair!
> In flames, like Semele's, be brought to bed,
> While op'ning Hell spouts wild-fire at your head. (B.III.313)

At the very jaws of the underworld, Dulness like a savage dances round the flames she has conjured up.

The threat of fire was insistent, and the memory of the events of 1666 recent enough to cut deeply into men's minds. But on the whole it was a threat either to property or to the peace;[47] law-abiding people could generally think that it wouldn't happen to them, and except in a very extreme case, such as the Gordon riots, the person of a private individual was unlikely to be in jeopardy. But not so with the other great nightmare – the plague. This could strike at anyone, however he or she might attempt to stay out of trouble. Appropriately, the Great Fire had stopped short at the very edge of Grub Street: Cripplegate church had had its windows scorched, but the structure had stood.[48] On the other hand, the Great Plague had raged through the parish for weeks on end.[49] As we have seen, disease had always been hard to combat in the fenny ground by Moorfields. If a writer wished (as many did) to present London as a breeding-ground for pestilence of every kind, Fleet Ditch was his most obvious symbolic recourse. But as far as actual mortality figures go, Cripplegate was as bad as Farringdon Ward Without.[50]

In 1728 there appeared under the imprint of James Roberts – sometime associate of Curll, publisher of Dunces but also of their chief enemies – a pamphlet called *A Trip through London*. This is an orthodox exercise in a genre owing something to the Roman satirists, something to Ned Ward and something to serious topography. Its opening words are representative:

> *London*, like the Ocean, that receives the muddy and dirty Brooks, as well as the clear and rapid Rivers, swallows up all the Scum and Filth, not only of our own, but of other Countries . . . continually emptying and discharging themselves into this grand Reservoir, or common Sewer of the World.

The writer's progress takes him from near Charing Cross, where a shower typically takes place, down the Strand and Fleet Street, through Little Britain into Cripplegate. Now we begin to realise the nature of the 'Scum and Filth' on the surface of London society. '*Hackney-Coachmen*, *Porters*, and all sorts of *Handicrafts* abound in *Cripplegate* Parish.' We are told that 'Mechanicks of both Sexes' are rife in its population. Its low literary productions are mentioned and its resident collection of quacks and frauds too. A whole paragraph is devoted to 'the Beggars of this Parish'. All round we are left in no doubt as to the social character of the region.[51]

This emphasis on low surroundings is important. It was a commonplace of the literary imagination. Writers constantly saw disease as coming to silent life in unobserved crannies, the hidden ulcers of the city. The trope could be applied to the spread of both the Plague and the Fire. For the latter, we need only recall Dryden's *Annus Mirabilis*:

> Such was the Rise of this prodigious fire,
> Which in mean Buildings first obscurely bred,
> From thence did soon to open Streets aspire
> And straight to Palaces and Temples spread.[52]

The bacillus of Dulness, 'bred' in the nooks and alleys of Cripplegate, 'conceal'd from vulgar eye' (B.I.33), aspires to the open street – the broad Strand for instance – and finally reaches St. James's, the Chapel Royal, seething Westminster. The 'reservoir' of filth is likewise described as a receptacle for thieves and prostitutes. A City Marshal who certainly knew the underworld well was Charles Hitchen, the homosexual and corrupt officer familiar to students of the career of Jonathan Wild. In his attack on Wild, *The Regulator* (1718), Hitchen apostrophises the city whose good order he was supposed to maintain:

> *O London! London!* so much fam'd for thy good Order, by what Means is it now come to pass, that thou art become a Receptacle for a Den of Thieves and Robber, and all sorts of villainous Persons and Practices.[53]

Admittedly, this is hollow rhetoric, cheap and insincere into the bargain. But it shows precisely exactly the kind of moral topos available to Pope when *The Dunciad* was taking shape; and it is this which lies behind the calculated obscenities of the poem, as of those of *Peri Bathous*.

A more substantial debt is to a work once greatly admired – perhaps excessively so – and now, as is the way, unduly deprecated. Samuel Garth's *Dispensary* deserves more than its routine textbook mention, if only because its satiric plant was so valuable when Pope retooled, as it were, for *The Dunciad*. Well, no: not only because of that, for it is a spirited and well sustained piece of mock-heroic poetry in its own right. But it *is* a fact that Pope continued to respect Garth long after the first burst of esteem for *The Dispensary* had been forgotten. Not the least pertinent factor here, I would suggest, is the manner in which Garth invokes Disease, 'most propitious Pow'r', and relates this to the social geography of London. He writes of the bills of mortality for St Giles' parish, the 'dreadful Shambles' round about the Fleet Ditch, and the 'Lewdness' of Covent Garden. In other words, he showed how health as a moral concept might be shadowed forth through the facts of what would later have been called public health. Thus to relate ethics and ecology is the special achievement of *The Dunciad* – but Garth had given the clue. Sometimes the allusiveness comes close to Pope's own, though the cadence is still that of Dryden:

> So thus at *Bothos*, when the *Gyants* strove
> T'invade the Skies, and wage a War with *Jove*;
> Soon as the *Ass* of old *Silenus* bray'd,
> The trembling Rebels in confusion fled.

But it is above all for his evocation of 'that devouring Harpy call'd *Disease*' that Garth was useful to the later poet.[54]

It would be possible to go through many minor productions of the Augustan era with the aim of illustrating the tenacity of the 'disease' image. But such tabulation is of limited utility, unless we can show that currency implies imaginative charge, as well as mere voltage in the circuit waiting to be switched on. One or two striking examples should suffice. There is, for example, a glaring fact on which I have never seen a comment. The historic Jonathan Wild was born in Wolverhampton about April 1683. This fact was well enough known to contemporaries: Defoe (if it is he who wrote the life mentioned earlier) gets the place and year both right. Captain Alexander Smith, who it is pretty safe to say was not Defoe (though one can never be sure) says 1684. Occasionally 1682 is found. Fielding, however, in his very free biography, substitutes a more evocative date:

To omit other stories, some of which may be perhaps the growth of superstition, we proceed to the birth of our hero, who made his first appearance on this great theatre the very day when the plague first broke out in 1665. Some say his mother was delivered of him in an house of an orbicular or round form in Covent Garden, but of this we are not certain. He was some years afterwards baptized by the famous Mr. Titus Oates.[55]

Now it is conceivable that the text signifies 'on the anniversary of the outbreak of the plague'. But note first, that Fielding explicitly removes his account from the realms of legend (he means to be believed, he implies): second, that a fictitious London address is given for the accouchement, which any reader of the Defoe life – or its numerous rivals – would *know* to be fictitious. The joke about the roundhouse, or parish gaol, suggests that truth is being handled with some discretion. And then it would be unlike such a careful ironist as Fielding to leave an ambiguity like this if he didn't want it there. We are surely justified in concluding that this is one of the signs of a notable birth, to which Fielding has just been alluding, and that he intends the sentence to convey the meaning 'in the year 1665, around the end of April' (when the Plague did set in with increased virulence). If that is so, then the further deductions need little comment. Fielding is associating the reign of the Great (Bad) Man, the arch-criminal, the commandant of the underworld, with the phenomenon of bubonic plague. Wild hits London in its seamiest quarters, just as the plague did: both began on the same day.

Jonathan Wild came out, in the *Miscellanies*, too late to be useful to Pope. Its hero had been named once or twice by Pope, in the conventional equation with Walpole:

> Down, down, proud Satire! tho' a Realm be spoil'd,
> Arraign no mightier Thief than wretched *Wild*,
> Or if a Court or Country's made a Job,
> Go drench a Pick-pocket, and join the Mob.[56]

Other references to disease in the writer's works are comparatively muted. 'Plague' and 'sore' are used in close proximity to 'Fool' in the fourth satire of Donne imitated: more neutrally, in the same poem, we have 'The whole Artill'ry of the Terms of War,/And (all those Plagues in one) the bawling Bar . . .' In the second Donne satire, poetry is said to be 'Catch'd like the plague, or love, the Lord knows how . . .', where the subliminal notion is that of venereal disease. Similarly in the *Epistle to Arbuthnot*, the 'Plague' is that incident to poets, i.e. the constant desire of his inferior brethren to badger him with their own lines. In the *Epistle to Bathurst* there is a bare reference to 'Some War, some Plague, or Famine they foresee.' Fever and pox appear together in the imitation of Swift.[57] But over all it is an unimpressive list, nothing beside Swift's catalogue of physical ailments and debilities. The truth is that Pope evolved a more indirect way of dealing with the 'unhealthy' implications of Dulness.

The language of *The Dunciad* is deeply infested: there are poetic 'Maggots', crawling about the crannies of the Cave, along with 'spawn' waiting to be hatched by 'a warm Third day'. There are showers of sermons, replenished like clouds 'from some bog below' (B.II.363). There is mention of ordure, evil vapours, a strange mutant 'vast egg': it is like a biological catastrophe brought about by the on-set of Dulness. One has the sense as one reads of observing weird medical research through a microscope:

> None want a place, for all their Centre found,
> Hung to the Goddess, and coher'd around.
> Not closer, orb in orb, conglob'd are seen
> The buzzing Bees about their dusky Queen. (B.IV.77)

This buglike quality of the Dunces is dramatically effective for more than one reason; but I draw attention to it here as it contributes to the disease motif – the festering, germ-ridden insect-world of the scribblers.

But the main hint was given by Gay, with the episode of Cloacina in *Trivia*. There is a particular link here, with the localisation of the episode in the vicinity of the Fleet Ditch (see the next section); but the device of projecting squalid, anarchically sexual, morbid Dulness through a mud-besmirched underworld landscape is of general interest. The joke exploits a psychological, if not then a verbal pun. At that date the predominant meaning of 'underworld' was the nether regions, Hades. An older usage, that of the lower world, i.e. this earth, survived as late as Rowe. But primarily the term connoted hell. Only

in the nineteenth century did the modern sense of 'the lowest stratum
of society' develop, according to *OED*. Nevertheless, it is not too
hazardous to suggest that the 'nether world' of Hades and the nether
world of criminal society had some imaginative fusion in Pope's
mind. In *The Rape of the Lock*, canto IV, the 'dusky' spright Umbriel
visits his home in the infernal regions, and

> Down to the Central Earth, his proper Scene,
> Repair'd to search the gloomy Cave of Spleen.
>   Swift on his sooty Pinions flits the *Gnome*,
> And in a Vapour reach'd the dismal Dome.
> No cheerful Breeze this sullen Region knows,
> The dreaded *East* is all the wind that blows.
> Here, in a Grotto, sheltred close from Air,
> And screen'd in Shades from Day's detested Glare,
> She sighs forever on her pensive Bed,
> *Pain* at her Side, and *Megrim* at her Head.
>   Two Handmaids wait the Throne: Alike in Place,
> But diff'ring far in Figure and in Face.[58]

The resemblance of this passage to the description of the cave of
Dulness (that is, I have argued, Grub Street) is very marked. That
description has already been quoted (p. 57), and here I shall merely
pick out a few of the more striking parallels. The home of Dulness,
like that of Spleen, is called a 'Dome' (B.I.265). Both cells are 'conceal'd from vulgar eye' (B.I.33), or screened from the light. Each
is racked by 'keen, hollow winds' (B.I.35); one is a 'sullen Region',
the other a 'bleak recess'. One is termed a 'Grotto', the other – with
little more than elegant variation – as 'Cave' (B.I.34). Queen Dulness is attended by four guardian virtues; her rival Spleen has two
handmaidens. In the earlier poem one of the attendants, Ill-nature,
has her bosom filled with lampoons: in the later, there are allusions
to Curll's chaste press, 'sepulchral Lyes' and 'all the Grub-street
race'. With the Cave of Spleen 'A constant Vapour o'er the Palace
flies'; with the Cave of Poverty, we are told, 'In clouded Majesty
here Dulness shone'. Spleen changes bodies 'to various Forms', and

> Strange Phantoms rising as the Mists arise;
> Dreadful, as Hermit's Dreams in haunted Shades,
> Or bright as Visions of expiring Maids.[59]

'Fiends' and 'Spectres' throng the cave. Compare *The Dunciad*:

> All these, and more, the cloud-compelling Queen,
> Beholds thro' fogs that magnify the scene.
> She, tinsel'd o'er in robes of varying hues,
> With self-applause her wild creation views;
> Sees momentary monsters rise and fall,
> And with her own fools-colours gilds them all. (B.I.79)

With the exception of a few details of special significance (the 'momentary' monsters of Grub Street, say), these descriptions are interchangeable. That could be put another way: Pope bridges the gap between the eighteenth century and the modern senses of the word 'underworld'. He asserts, poetically, that the Hades of his time is the squalid 'Chaos dark and deep' infected by rogues, vagabonds, pimps, prostitutes – and hack writers. Hell, indeed, has its urban ghetto very much like Grub Street. The voyage from this world to the next in *The Dunciad*, significantly, takes the form of a descent into the filthy depths of the Fleet Ditch; the voyager is Jonathan Smedley. I shall return to this passage in the next section. At this point I stress only the explicit way in which the inferno is identified with the dirt of contemporary London. Pope's season in hell is spent on the shores of the Thames, shared by 'all from Paul's to Aldgate' (B.II.346).

It is tempting to recross some familiar ground, and illustrate the appositeness of the satire from eighteenth-century conditions. But this would be otiose. *The Dunciad* is not a report of the sanitary commissioners, and a detailed account of London squalor would not add very much to our appreciation of the poem. It is enough to accept the broad outline, as many authorities have handed it down to us. The streets were noisome in every respect; stench, ordure, germs, decomposing bodies of animals, malarial pests, slime and vomit – with such candidates as these, it is impossible to draw up an order of offensive magnitude. If things were bad in the daytime, they were worse at night. It did not need the Scourers or the Mohocks to make going abroad a perilsome affair. There were virtually no street lights; an attempt had been made to provide these in 1684 but 'the experiment was not a success . . . the fat used was derived from animals' intestines.' In 1734 a new scheme was introduced which 'dispelled some of the nocturnal gloom.' But in general London streets in Pope's day were dark as well as 'squalid and pestiferous'.[60]

Some parts of this general picture are relevant to the theme of this chapter, and these may be examined a little more closely. For example there is the condemnation which had been issued in 1636 by the College of Physicians (an institution bordering almost on the Fleet Ditch), regarding the spread of the plague by 'the neglect in cleansing sewers and town ditches, the presence of standing pools of foetid water, uncleanliness of the streets, the toleration of laystalls so near the living quarters, especially on the City's northern side . . .'[61] As we have seen (pp. 46–7 above), Moorfields was especially noted for this latter inconvenience. It is well known that foul ditches and sewers did much to encourage the plague in Shakespeare's London, but it may be forgotten that the notorious outbreaks of the infection in Jacobean and then in Restoration London were only the most serious among many. Somewhere on the continent, the plague was always raging fiercely; and epidemics, major or minor, persisted in England throughout the seventeenth century. In 1720 the plague flared up in the South of France. A national hubbub ensued, with a hotly contested Quarantine Bill and a series of warnings from Defoe among the consequences. Pope's great friend, Dr Arbuthnot, was called in by the Government to give advice. Later typhus, or 'gaol fever' as it was popularly named, became a greater scourge. This was a libel, inasmuch as the prisons were not the only insalubrious parts of the city. Contagious disease might just as aptly have been called 'suburban fever'. It was the malarial marshes on the outskirts of the ancient settlement – the ring of liberties between the walled city and the outparishes – which recorded the heaviest casualty figures every time the plague struck. And it struck often. Smallpox, too, had a high incidence rate in these districts. Several times I have referred to drains and ditches. The 'kennel' down the middle of the street was the most obvious form these took; but there were other conduits of one kind or another, filled with stagnant water and disagreeable jetsam. They ranged from the mighty Fleet Ditch, the great sink of London, to small culverts winding through the backways of the poorer districts. Many were, of course, literally sewers: all fulfilled this function to some degree. Two important riders follow from the point of view of the satirist. Firstly, there was a built-in joke in the name 'Grub Street', whether the writers knew it or not. The place incorporated in its very title (grub=ditch) an allusion to the major single blot on the London landscape, and one of the main agencies of disease.[62] Secondly, the presence of so many drains supplied the basis for a striking satiric *motif* – the cloacal trope so widely encountered in Augustan contexts.

Ian Watt has written that 'the whole subject of the cloacal image in Augustan polemic cries out for the attention of some curious and intrepid scholar.'[63] This is not the place for a full enquiry into the subject, even supposing my qualifications matched, as they do not, Watt's desiderata. Nonetheless, it is possible to suggest lines for research, and to list in a tentative way some of the rhetorical needs which the figure met, in its graceless but effective fashion. Consider this brief outline:

(1) The image served once again to link moral 'health' and sanitary welfare. It utilised the readily available facts of contemporary existence, known to all readers, in order to enforce a wider social, ethical or artistic judgement. A sewer, to put it crudely, would be a much less potent image today because we rarely if ever see such a thing; it has become another mode of the 'underworld', as distant from most people's experience as Styx or as hell. (2) There was a long tradition of idiomatic usage. The Cloaca Maxima had been as notorious in its way as the Fleet Ditch, and Roman authors had developed its figurative applications – thus Plautus uses 'cloaca' of the stomach of a drunken woman. (But the serious anatomical sense appears to have grown up only in English.) Moreover, there was at least one famous aphorism – 'A woman is a temple built on a sewer' – which carried the right overtones of slightly comic disgust. Swift, as we shall see, was to develop this idea with telling particularity. The basis for the notion is very obvious: the orifice which both receives one kind of effluvium and disgorges its own. The drain collected its filth 'down below', as, according to this view, the female pudenda did. A ditch could run beneath imposing buildings, as a

fair countenance concealed the nastiness below. (3) A sewer was a kind of public receptacle, into which any man could drop his own personal excretions; it was known to spread illness; if often flooded right over, and forced a channel into previously pure streams; and it was a tunnel between the upper and the lower world, between the city and the great river. Open sewers indeed were among the few direct communicating links from one part of London to another, in some areas of the town where the streets were little better than a maze. For all these reasons the 'cloaca' could easily be used to symbolise the way of life of the dregs of society, either morally or sociologically. In particular, it connoted, almost without the author's consciously desiring it, a measure of *sexual* corruption.

It was the Fleet Ditch above all which contained in itself these various implications. Or, to put the matter another way, it was the Ditch that dramatised in real life the imagistic possibilities of the term. On a third level, the mythological aspect was represented by the tutelary goddess of all sewers, Cloacina. John Gay had annotated *Trivia* thus: 'Cloacina was a Goddess whose image Tatius (a King of the Sabines) found in the common-shore, and not knowing what Goddess it was, he called it Cloacina from the place in which it was found, and paid it divine honours.'[64] Pope writes more curtly, 'The *Roman* Goddess of the Common-shores'.[65] Initially, however, she had been Cluaca Venus, the purifier. The satirists treat her as a kind of befouled Venus; the writers who are her devotees (living, as it were, on the edge of her mansion) likewise besmirch a noble name – that of literature.

In the ditches of London we find the Dunces plunging and wallowing and floundering. Like the strange water-beasts of *Peri Bathous*, they pride themselves on their capacity to sink ever more deeply into the mire. There are, to be sure, moral implications here – to dive headfirst, with one's backside uppermost, was to assume the very posture of folly – but mainly the value of this picture is a *comic* one. The Dunces are forced to suffer the indignities meted out by farce in every age. Instead of custard-pies in the face, Curll receives 'brown dishonours', having just slipped on a pool of urine made by his mistress. With such a passage, though it would technically be possible to relate the phraseology to the commonplaces of Augustan thought, it seems more tactful simply to leave unqualified the sheer bawdy exuberance:

> A place there is, betwixt earth, air, and seas,
> Where, from Ambrosia, Jove retires for ease.
> There in his seat two spacious vents appear,
> On this he sits, to that he leans his ear,
> And hears the various vows of fond mankind . . .
>   In office here fair Cloacina stands,
> And ministers to Jove with purest hands.
> Forth from the heap she pick'd her Vot'ry's pray'r,
> And plac'd it next him, a distinction rare!
> Oft had the Goddess heard her servant's call,
> From her black grottos near the Temple-wall,
> List'ning delighted to the jest unclean
> Of link-boys vile, and watermen obscene;
> Where as he fish'd her nether realms for Wit,
> She oft had favour'd him, and favours yet.
> Renew'd by ordure's sympathetic force,
> As oil'd with magic juices for the course,
> Vig'rous he rises; from the effluvia strong
> Imbibes new life, and scours and stinks along;
> Re-passes Lintot, vindicates the race,
> Nor heeds the brown dishonours of his face. (B.II.83–108)

Here Pope makes an equivalence between Curll's fishing the 'nether realms' of Whitefriars for wit and sexual intercourse with Cloacina; such congress drugs him for the race ahead, as with a Tour de France cyclist. Characteristically Pope introduced into the later version the allusion to the 'Temple-wall'. This localises the event in the vicinity of Fleet Street, an area to which we can now turn more directly.

Artery of Dulness

If there had been no Fleet Ditch, the satirists would have had to invent one. The existence of such a notorious sore on the surface of London life proved to be an immense, though uncovenanted, gain to the Scriblerian party. The Ditch served their rhetorical needs perfectly. It symbolised, with an extraordinary fineness of imaginative 'tolerance', the squalid nature of Dulness. There are two main reasons for this special aptness.

(A) In the first place, the Ditch simply *was* all the things which Pope wishes to imply the home of the Dull should be. It was the literal embodiment of a cloacal metaphor. It did run beneath the street in places and so did constitute a link with the 'underworld'. It was a carrier of disease, smelly, unsightly, opaque with dirt, infested not only with bacteria but with hogs and human carcasses. The great Lord Clarendon seems to have been among the first writers (in that *History* which Tories of Pope's generation so venerated) to spell out the associations of the City of London into a moral formula: 'The Sink of the ill-humour of this Kingdom'.[66] A succession of later authors developed this hint with special reference to the Ditch until its name became a synonym for social, as well as physical, malady. Pope, Swift and Gay are notable for the literary effectiveness of their use of the idea, and not because they devised it.

It is important to remember just what purposes a ditch, any ditch, then served. The 'grubbe' of Grub Street would be first of all a water supply, for all its impurity. But in addition it might be used for a variety of functions, ranging from the burial of suicides to the demarcation of parish boundaries.[67] The Fleet itself was commandeered for every undignified need urban man can mentally compass. It was a latrine, a pigsty (or residential trough, one might say), a criminal escape-route, a primitive fire-precaution, and several other things as well. Of the portion of the ditch which ran through the Smithfield region, Mrs George observes:

> The Field Lane district was intersected by the filthy channel of the Fleet ditch (called in 1722 'a nauceious and abominable sink of nastiness'), into which the tripe dressers, sausage makers and catgut spinners, who shared the Lane with professional thieves, flung their offal.[68]

For centuries rubbish had been thrown into the Ditch, an existing right which men and women of the eighteenth century jealously preserved. It is natural that the Plague was particularly destructive along this appalling watercourse.[69]

For generations, there had been a vague resolve to do something about it. Stow records an effort to cleanse the 'dike' in 1502 and 1589, and efforts to remove the mills which had operated along the upper stretches, contributing further to the contamination of the stream.[70] The later developments have been summarised by T. F. Reddaway, and his account may be given verbatim:

In former times the Fleet river had been navigable up to Holborn Bridge, but as the years passed it had gradually deteriorated into a shallow and evil-smelling sewer. Navigation had ceased and, in the middle of the seventeenth century, a not overparticular age, its condition had been described as 'very stinking and noisome'. Silt from the upper reaches, and mud and refuse from the growing streets in its valley had gradually choked it, with the result that, despite occasional cleansings, its condition more or less regularly troubled the minds of those in authority. During the reign of James I various projects had been put forward for clearing out accumulations down to the true floor of the channel, embanking its sides with brick, stone or timber, and then flushing it out at intervals from a reservoir constructed above Clerkenwell. The most detailed had envisaged grates on the upper waters to intercept debris and silt, a warden to remove carrion and bulky matter when the tide was out, and a vast grate at Bridewell to stop the Thames bringing up filth on the rising tide. Little seems to have come of them, and as the years passed an expanding population had added to the difficulties. The Commissioners of Sewers (in 1653) . . . clearly set out the evils which had arisen from this last cause. The river, they declared, from Hockley in the Hole to the Thames, was 'by many encroachments thereupon made by keeping of Hogs and Swine therein and elsewhere neer to it, the throwing in of Offals and Garbage . . . and by reason of many houses of office erected built and standing upon and over [it] and otherwise not only stopped . . . and become unpassable with boats . . . but also become [a] very . . . great prejudice . . . not only to the neighbourhood . . . but to the City of *London* and County of Middlesex.'[71]

Pope, we may interpose, did not invent the link between excretion and the Ditch which his poem joyfully celebrates.

As Reddaway continues, this valley 'where the crowded poor bred plagues, and divided authority clogged the wheels of reform, was something that the planners of 1666 could not possibly overlook.' Accordingly they drew up plans in due course for a canalised river, forty feet wide, navigable up to Holborn Bridge. There would be wharves on each bank and severe building restrictions in the environs. Compensation for lands adjoining the Fleet which had, in effect, to be compulsorily purchased caused some difficulty and delay; but ultimately work was started on the new scheme with plans drawn up by Robert Hooke, under the oversight of Wren. Even now there were a number of practical problems which impeded the project. This was despite the unusual lack of corruption displayed by the main contractor, Thomas Fitch. As Reddaway observes,

> throughout [the contract] he was hampered by the mud and refuse coming down from Turnmill Brook [that is, precisely the outflow from Smithfield which Swift describes in his 'City Shower'] and the streets round the channel. Piles of rubbish, wood and building materials, illicitly left on the wharves he was levelling were almost as great a hindrance . . . Warfare and weather both affected progress. Heavy storm caused floods in Turnmill Brook, and war with the Dutch brought the ravages of press-gangs.[72]

Thus once again we find the connection between the seamier parts of London with the depredations of war, coupled here with a reference to the city shower which Swift was to convert into a Virgilian image of Grub Street.

Nevertheless, Fitch went about his duties in a conscientious way, and by 1674 the work was completed. Unfortunately, the costly and imaginative enterprise of building the canal was not a success. The district soon reverted to its character; in Reddaway's words,

> In an area with all too few open spaces the broad stretch on each side of the channel was a temptation too great to be resisted. They were used as standing-grounds for carts, as storage places for timber, and as dumps for rubbish . . . Carts and coaches alike passed so often . . . that the pavements were broken and the roofing of the vaults threatened.

There were many critics of the scheme, Ned Ward among them, who gave as his view the statement that the cellar warehouses were so damp as to be useless 'except to Frogs, toads, and other vermin.' Thus did a duncely haunt revert to type, with an ecological shift not unlike the 'entropy' which Edwards sees as the process of Dulness in its metaphysical aspect. It quickly emerged that there was much more need for a north-west thoroughfare at this point than for a canal, which benefited only a limited number of coal merchants. Shoe Lane, of which more presently, was the main road then in existence, and it was not much of a street. Ultimately the authorities bowed to the inevitable, and just after the first version of *The Dunciad*, in 1733, the canal was arched over from Holborn Bridge down to Fleet Bridge. The central strip became a covered market. Then in 1766 the remainder of the canal, down to the Thames, was covered in, shortly before that hotly debated architectural feature, Blackfriars Bridge, went up. The Fleet Market survived till 1829 (the year before Grub Street, as such, disappeared), when Farringdon Street was built. The Canal, then, must be accounted a failure. Reddaway believes that 'an evil slum had been made attractive', and that the balance is in favour of the scheme.[73] But there is plenty of contemporary evidence that the region of the Fleet Ditch was still regarded as a fetid, rank and disagreeable place after the construction of the Canal. Certainly Pope and his friends found it no less available for their satiric purposes.

(B) This circumstance can only be understood in the context of another factor which gave the Ditch its peculiar applicability. The fortunes of the Fleet River have been encapsulated in a neat formula, that is decline from a river to a brook, from a brook to a ditch, and from a ditch to a drain. But this drop in the world was not entirely a function of what went on in, or on, the channel itself. A good deal of the disrepute into which it sank can only be explained by reference to the places it ran through or near or alongside. The Fleet, in a word, was a conduit which linked virtually all the most wretched corners of the city.

A few examples should suffice. The Ditch did not actually drain Grub Street, since it was the Walbrook which arose in the Moorfield swamp and flowed sluggishly down to the Thames near London Bridge, some half a mile to the east of the Fleet's own 'estuary'. But there was scarcely any other haunt of the Dunces which was not transversed by the Fleet or its tributary streams, as it meandered down from Hampstead through King's Cross, Clerkenwell, Holborn and Blackfriars. For example:

(a) Prisons. A representative list is Defoe's survey of 'Public Gaols' in his *Tour*. Four important prisons named in the first six – Newgate, Ludgate, the Fleet, and Bridewell – were all immediately contiguous to the Ditch. The 'New-Prison' and 'New-Bridewell' were both in Clerkenwell, near to the stinking middle stretches of the Fleet. There were roundhouses in Farringdon Ward Without.[74]

(b) Smithfield, with all its unpleasant associations (see pp. 37–38) was drained by Turnmill Brook, which fed the Ditch. Because of the lie of the land, a great deal of refuse was shipped out of this region (notably the offal of slaughter-houses) along the same undesirable waterway.[75]

(c) To the north lay Clerkenwell, with an almost equally repugnant set of associations, ranging from bear-baiting and cudgel-play to organised crime. Here too many writers found their home (see below pp. 159–60).[76]

(d) The whole of the ward of Farringdon Without was an epitome of the worst sides of eighteenth-century London life. Holborn with its notoriety for sexual irregularities of every kind; the area round Lincoln's Inn Fields, where riot and violence were daily phenomena; and the region round Fleet Street itself, where the less reputable side of the publishing trade was established and every kind of crime flourished: these and districts like them made up the ward.[77]

There were other, special, reasons for the bad character of the region. Whitefriars, for instance, had for centuries been a licensed refuge of the dissolute. There was Bridewell, too, which as a house of correction combined some of the sadder features of Bedlam with those of the ordinary gaol. In short, had the Ditch been as limpid and sparkling as Helicon, it would have had a bad name. The guilt it bore by association was that attaching to places such as Newgate, Saffron Hill, Smithfield, Whitefriars and Holborn. The Newgate Calendar recorded the daily experience of men and women who lived by the Fleet. In turn, the humours of the Fleet cling round many a Newgate pastoral, for it was across the Ditch that the road to Tyburn ran; just as these same humours eddy thickly round the Goddess Dulness herself. Rising fogs prevail in every quarter which the Fleet reached; its moist influence, 'cloud-compelling' like that of the Queen, 'spawns' pests and 'maggots' such as nonsense took to itself. To beat the bounds of the parish of St Bride's or St Dunstan's,[78] to make a perambulation of the Fleet Rules, was to take a walk on the wild side. We need look in detail at only a limited number of the named localities to see the distressing reality which lay behind the vibrant metaphor Pope made out of the Ditch.

If we begin at the mouth of the Fleet river, near to the point where the Dunces gathered for their games, there was on the right (western) bank the precinct of Whitefriars.[79] On this region Macaulay has written a superb passage, blending as usual massive and calculated overstatement with delicate precision of detail:

> We may easily imagine what, in such times, must have been the state of the quarters of London which were peopled by the outcasts of society. Among those quarters one had attained a scandalous preeminence. On the confines of the City and the Temple had been founded, in the thirteenth century, a House of Carmelite Friars, distinguished by their white hoods. The precinct of this house had, before the Reformation, been a sanctuary for criminals, and still retained the privilege of protecting debtors from arrest. Insolvents consequently were to be found in every dwelling, from cellar to garret. Of these a large proportion were knaves and libertines, and were followed to their asylum by women more abandoned than themselves. The civil power was unable to keep order in a district swarming with such inhabitants; and thus Whitefriars became the favourite resort of all who wished to become emancipated from the restraints of the law. Though the immunities legally belonging to the place extended only to cases of debt, cheats, false witnesses, forgers, and highwaymen found refuge there. For amidst a rabble so desperate no peace officer's life was in safety. At the cry of 'Rescue' bullies with swords and cudgels, and termagant hags with swords and broomsticks, poured forth by hundreds; and the intruder was fortunate if he escaped back into Fleet Street, hustled, stripped and pumped upon.[80]

In placing the pindaric writer (Ambrose Philips) at an unseemly address in Whitefriars (see p. 78), Pope was suggesting that the hack writer wished 'to become emancipated from the restraints' of poetic law. It is notable that Cripplegate was likewise renowned for its population of forgers and highwaymen. 'Alsatia', as the district was also known, was long celebrated for street brawls; Shadwell's fine comedy *The Squire of Alsatia* (1688) fills out some of these associations. In Hogarth's *Industry and Idleness*, Plate 9, Tom Idle is shown betrayed by a prostitute in an infamous house of Blood Bowl Alley (later Hanging Sword Alley), in the heart of Alsatia.[81]

More directly relevant are the literary associations. In earlier years a good deal of the book trade had been centred in Whitefriars, and it is still common to find printers settled in this area at the time of *The Dunciad*. Stanley Morison records several cases where the imprint of a newspaper indicates Whitefriars as its provenance. John Ogilby was in business here; John Purser, another printer of the period, had establishments successively in Shoe Lane, just across Fleet Street, and in Salisbury Court. From 1724 onwards this latter square had a more distinguished member of the trade as an occupant, namely Samuel Richardson. At first the famous printer-novelist took a house 'in the centre' of the Court; but by 1755 this structure was unsafe, at any rate for the purpose of carrying on the printing trade, and Richardson did not renew the lease. Instead he built a new printing plant, with an adjoining residence, on the north of Salisbury Court, reached from Fleet Street via Whitefriars Street. Among writers, both Shadwell and Dryden lived in this district; whilst there is a persistent, if unconfirmed, story that Defoe fled to the sanctuary of Alsatia to escape his creditors. Amongst Pope's acquaintances the printer William Bowyer, jr., was living in Whitefriars around 1740, as an extant letter from the poet makes clear.[82]

Here we have the classic set of duncely circumstances – crime, debtors, prostitutes, street-affrays, the book trade, minor authors and the rest. It is almost as if the baneful influence of the Fleet had predetermined the character of the region. Much the same applies to Bridewell. The infamous House of Correction is mainly of interest with regard to Swift. But it figures too in Defoe, in Hogarth's *Harlot's Progress*, in Ned Ward's *London Spy* and elsewhere. It was closely associated with Bedlam on the one hand and with the other gaols of the Fleet on the other: indeed, as the Webbs showed many years ago, the distinction between the prison proper, intended for the reception of felons, and the house of correction, intended for vagabonds and the incorrigibly idle, gradually vanished over this period.[83] The hospital was largely destroyed in the Great Fire, but was speedily rebuilt. Among the new developments was a new stone bridge, erected to replace the former wooden Bridewell Bridge. This was apparently designed by Wren himself, possibly on the model of the Rialto at Venice. It was this graceful footbridge which can be seen in Hayman's illustration of the mud-diving episode of *The Dunciad*; the artist has even perched the Goddess herself on the parapet of the bridge.[84] It is a succint comment on the connotations of Bridewell. Pope selected the venue with several obvious considerations in mind. There was the 'flagellation' of naked men and women (mentioned at B.II.270); the links with the Fire, with Bedlam, with vagrancy and idleness (Pope and Swift are generally ironical when they imply that they wish to find a good 'hospital' where superannuated Dunces may rest their bones); and above all the proximity of the Ditch (Stow in fact calls it Bridewell Ditch). A sizeable portion of the land belonging to Bridewell had to be taken to enlarge the quay when the Fleet Canal improvements were under way. This cannot have improved the vicinity to any marked degree: Bridewell Lane was generally clogged with debris and rubbish. Finally, had Pope known about it, he would undoubtedly have found applicable the events of 1780, when the Gordon rioters opened up Bridewell and the militia were forced to maintain a presence there for some two months. There were many felons active in this district during the riot, possibly because it was the custom to dispatch transported convicts from Blackfriars Stairs. With his customary propriety Pope has his Dunces gather at a place of assignation otherwise reserved for jailbirds.[85]

Moving up the Fleet we encounter a succession of such milieux. Fleet Street itself carried over many of the darker doings of Whitefriars. Beggars or vagrants were strongly in evidence, streetfights were commonplace, printers and journalists were already concentrated here. Curll had several places of business in and around the street; Lintot, Gilliver, and Jacob Robinson all set up shop there; Pope, indeed, used Robinson's shop as a sort of poste-restante for Warburton's correspondence in 1740.[86] At least one celebrated woman criminal, Sarah Malcolm, familiar through Hogarth's graphic study, was executed in Fleet Street;[87] a few years before Moll Frith had operated her thief-taking business from the same address.[88] The district from Temple Bar to the Ditch was notorious for alehouses and brandy shops, as Jonathan Wild's reply to Hitchen indicates;[89] drunks regularly fell right into the Ditch, and came up probably little less besmeared than Pope's divers. In 1756 it was stated that 'the most flagitious of the poor' lived in this locality.[90] Inevitably, the Plague was especially virulent 'in dirty alleys and festering courts about the Fleet River and the debtors' prison, horrible for their mixed poverty and dissoluteness'.[91] The prison itself stood a little way off, to the north-east of the modern Ludgate Circus. It was destroyed in the Fire, and again during the Gordon Riots. Supplies for the Prison were brought up the Ditch,[92] and the stench of the place must have penetrated into the heart of the gaol.

The Fleet was, of course, the debtor's prison first and foremost. The common side was especially notorious on account of the wretched conditions in which its inhabitants lived. It was here that Pickwick found Alfred Jingle, reduced to a shadow of his previous plausible substance. The existence of great cruelties in the fearsome dungeons of the Fleet was brought to light just as *The Dunciad* came to birth. A commission of enquiry headed by the philanthropist Oglethorpe was appointed in 1727, and in due course they produced a horrifying indictment of the way in which debtors' prisons – notably the Fleet – were managed. Much of the blame fell on the Warden of the Prison, Bambridge, whose name has gone down to history with no happy associations thanks to Hogarth's painting which depicts Bambridge's appearance before the Committee in 1729.[93] However, the severities of the gaol were by no means confined to the extortions of a single warden of sadistic character. Within a few years, well before the appearance of the revised *Dunciad*, Hogarth had added further dimensions to the iconography of the Prison. Tom Rakewell is seen in Plate VII of the *Rake's Progress* confined to a stone cell and attended by three gruesome personages.[94] His debts had been contracted in another duncely environment, St Giles': his only remaining port of call was to be Bedlam. The Fleet was the road to Bedlam, as it was to every place of ultimate humiliation in eighteenth-century London. In Defoe's *Complete English Tradesman* (1725), we are told of the wit turned tradesman whose saga ends in bankruptcy, with 'the Epilogue in the *Fleet Prison* or the *Mint*'.[95] The social prejudices of Defoe and of Pope were not, of course, identical. None the less this decline in fortune resembles that suffered by many a Dunce; as we have seen, hack writers did find themselves in the debtors' sanctuary at the Mint, and several, including Defoe, Settle and Theophilus Cibber, underwent confinement in the Fleet Prison.

Other gaols within close proximity of the Ditch were Ludgate, Newgate (where Tom Idle lay in fiction, Jack Sheppard in reality, and Defoe found himself on two occasions at least),[96] the House of Correction in Cold Bath Fields, west of the Ditch, and the two Clerkenwell prisons. There was, too, the Old Bailey, which owned a variety of associations with the most desperate malefactors of the age. Modern Fleet Lane, in the shadow of Holborn Viaduct station, lies at the very centre of this region.[97]

No contemporary could fail to be aware of the pageantry of Newgate. The 'Memoirs of Malefactors', published by successive Ordinaries of Newgate Prison (among whom was Thomas Purney, listed by Pope as one of Curll's authors), constituted one branch of literary Dulness in action. We recall, too, the dying confessions of men like Sheppard and Wild which are numbered amongst Defoe's contributions to the literature of roguery. Pope specifically mentions this practice in a note to the 'Epilogue to the Satires', Dialogue II:

> *Fr.* Yet none but you by Name the Guilty lash;
> Ev'n *Guthry* saves half *Newgate* by a Dash.
> Spare then the Person, and expose the Vice.[98]

'Lash' is a graphically appropriate verb, since it calls up so many of the brutal connotations of the gaol. It is striking that Pope adumbrates such a topic – central to any assessment of the artistic ends of *The Dunciad* – with reference to the habits of the underworld, social and literary. The fact is that Pope regularly frames a response to his

155

most basic dilemmas as an author in terms of concrete allusion to the actuality of his times. We recall, too, that Newgate was the place of confinement for the most desperate and dangerous criminals; and that gaol fever raged there on many occasions.[99]

One custom overshadowed all others, as regards the criminal ecology of this part of London. This was the almost royal progress of a condemned criminal from the prison to the scaffold at Tyburn. The ostensible business was simply to convey the convict from Newgate gatehouse, at the edge of the ancient city, to the junction of Tyburn Lane and the Oxford road – that is to say, to present-day Marble Arch. In reality the procession was ritualised into a kind of black mass version of the journey to Calvary.[100] The extent of the parody may be gauged from the fact that, amongst the stations of this particular journey, there was a halt at the Bowl on the corner of St Giles' High Street and Hog Lane. Here the convicted man would be offered a drink, almost as Christ was given wine mixed with gall prior to His crucifixion. (A popular highwayman could also count on a following of 'a great multitude of people, and of women who bewailed and lamented him,' as St Luke has it.) The other circumstances of this journey will be taken up in relation to Swift's 'City Shower'. Here it is sufficient to remark that the major ceremonial acts were performed around Holborn Bridge, on Snow Hill or outside St Sepulchre's church. Old Bailey, where Jonathan Wild set up his thieftaking business, ran south from this point, parallel to the Ditch on the other side of the Fleet Prison. From 1752 the body of the criminal was brought back for dissection to Surgeon's Hall in Old Bailey. Prior to that, as in the case of Tom Nero, the anatomy was conducted in Monkwell Street, over towards Cripplegate.[101]

There were plenty of other reasons why a well-bred young person would not have been conducted to this district. The reputation it bore is well caught in a passing remark by Boswell when he first came up to the capital: 'I then thought of having obscure lodgings, and actually looked up and down the bottom of Holborn and towards Fleet Ditch for an out-of-the-way place. How very absurd are such conceits! . . . When a man is out of humour, he thinks he will vex the world by keeping away from it . . .'[102] Of course, many Dunces likewise looked up and down the Ditch for a lodging; the difference was that they were seeking not isolation from their 'world' – duncely society flourished in this very quarter – but a cheap place to rest their head. As we have seen, one of Curll's authors, very likely John Old-mixon, is located by Pope 'at the alley over against St *Andrews Holborn*'. Professional writers slightly higher in the social scale, such as John Hughes, might take up residence in the better addresses over Holborn, in this case Red Lion Street.[103] Most inhabitants of Far-ringdon Ward Without, nevertheless, occupied less auspicious quar-ters. Hogarth places his second stage of cruelty outside Thavies Inn; whilst the area round about Lincoln's Inn was infamous for many generations as a scene of riot, dissolute behaviour and rob-bery.[104] As to Holborn itself, it had acquired a special name for the practice of unnatural vice. When Thomas Amory, in *John Buncle*, said of Curll that his translators 'lay three in a bed at the Pewter Platter Inn in Holborn', one suspects that there may be more behind the joke than innocent rumour.[105] Curiously enough, one writer I have definitely located as a native of Farringdon Ward was the ally of Pope, and principal informant on the doings of the hacks; namely Richard Savage, who was born in Fox Court, Holborn, and baptised at St Andrew's.[106] His birth, however, was somewhat exceptional in its circumstances. Certainly it was a common exercise for respectable people to find the quickest way out of Farringdon. Miss Sterling, in *The Clandestine Marriage*, would list it among the dull districts she wanted to quit for the dear regions of Grosvenor Square; whilst the author of *A Trip through London* (1728) makes his representative *parvenu* a citizen of the ward. Since it also included such black-spots as Shoe Lane, with its sponging-houses, its cockpit, its prosti-tutes and its nooks and alleys; as well as Stonecutter Street, where dark deeds were accepted as part of life – in this light, it is obvious why the effective parish of the Fleet was shunned by the better classes.[107] To do them justice, the Dunces would possibly have shunned it too, if they could have afforded to.

To the north of the ward lay Smithfield. The numerous unhappy associations of this district have been noted. The name had indeed become a sort of semantic coral reef, in which there were encrusted myriads of fossilised allusions, practically all of them pejorative in character. When Pope used this proper noun in the first couplet of his great poem, he was gaining the effect otherwise attainable only by a string of opprobious epithets. It is true that these submerged meanings were quite outside the control of the satirist to make or unmake. The point is that he did nothing to neutralise them or to silence them. Primarily we are to think of the low farces of Bartholomew Fair, to which Pope directs our attention in his note. At the same time, the attentive reader is perfectly free to summon in his mind any number of notions connected with Smithfield – the thieves' kitchen, the legacy of Jonathan Wild, the crowd of aliens among the inhabitants, the filth and garbage of the market, the wretched living conditions. It should not occasion surprise by now that after the Gordon riots the officers charged to seek out the main culprits reported back dolefully from Smithfield: Chick Lane and its environs made up 'almost a town in itself' where a republic of thieves lived securely isolated.[108] Pope, of course, rams home the message. He remarks in a note (A.III.281) that Elkanah Settle 'kept a Booth at *Bartlemew-fair* . . .', and at length was charitably received into the nearby Charterhouse. When we add that Turnmill Lane became known as 'Sodom', the picture is nearly complete.[109] It seems almost inevitable that a writer of the time (actually in the *British Journal* of 24 April 1728) should compare 'the Droves that are carried to Tyburn with those sent to Smithfield for the same purpose.'[110] The Fleet Ditch bore along with its sluggish flow a perpetual slaughter-house, both animal and human.

Such then was the ward of Farringdon Without. Its main constituent parishes all had the Ditch as an eastern boundary at some point although St Bride's straddled the Fleet. St Dunstan's ran as far west as Temple Bar, which might indifferently be caparisoned with the head of a highwayman or a Jacobite.[111] St Andrew's, Holborn, stretched from Holborn Bridge to Chancery Lane; it included part of Smithfield, as did St Sepulchre's. By a species of urban blight, familiar to modern sociologists, the baneful influence of the Ditch seeped damply over the most remote parts of each parish.[112] It could be felt almost as far as it could be smelt.

Technically, the Fleet Rules stretched rather less than a mile,[113] though it is doubtful whether unfrocked clergymen performing unlicensed marriages in the Prison worried about the matter. As a result, the upper reaches of the River, above Holborn Bridge, were less immediately thought of in connection with the squalor that the name portended. All the same, Clerkenwell was traversed by the same fearful sewer as Blackfriars and Holborn. In some ways, this part of London serves as a link between the Fleet and Cripplegate. Its overall character was perhaps a little less unsavoury than that of its southern neighbourhood. But it was nothing to boast of; and a minor writer like Henry Carey who came to settle there,[114] or a hack like John Duick who eked out a precarious livelihood in the district, would be unlikely to advertise the fact.[115] The most celebrated literary connection of Clerkenwell was St John's Gate, the home of the *Gentleman's Magazine* from 1731. Here Johnson worked for some time; in nearby St John's Street Dr Thomas Birch kept his no doubt disorderly household. Charles Ackers, a printer of more than one duncely production, operated from St John's Close.[116] The man whom Johnson has immortalised, out of the Dunces' rank where he perhaps belongs, Richard Savage, frequented the Cross Keys Inn opposite St John's Gate.[117] James Bailey, a leading member of the Stationers' Company, lived in St John's Square.[118] To shift personalities a little, it is intriguing to recall that Moll Flanders, on the run from a husband for once, took lodgings in St John's Street, or 'as it is vulgarly called, St Jones', The two prisons of this quarter also figure in Defoe's narrative of Jack Sheppard, who made his escape from the New Prison via the yard of the adjacent Bridewell.[119]

Above all, there was Edward Cave, who set up the *Gentleman's Magazine* from the old gatehouse of the Knights of St John of Jerusalem. In this incongruous setting Samuel Johnson, as his best modern biographer has it, 'found out what it was like to be a hack writer'. Such an initiation naturally took place a matter of yards from the Ditch. Cave's connection with that ever-present symbol is even more direct, however. In 1740 he dammed up a part of the Fleet near his establishment, on the northern edge of Smithfield, and built a mill to drive a newfangled spinning machine. Many people including at least one Dunce (James Ralph) thought it would have been a good thing if the whole Ditch were filled in for good. But that event had to wait till 1766; a blessing for the satirists, if for nobody else.[120]

The first writer of distinction to accept the gift offered up by the local *cloaca maxima* was Ben Jonson. His poem, 'On the famous Voyage', appeared in his *Epigrammes* of 1616. Not exactly satiric, this is rather a species of whimsical mock-heroic: daringly contrived, but not altogether successful. Two revellers, having dined well in the City, 'propos'd to goe to Hol'borne in a wherry' from Blackfriars, or more strictly from a 'Docke'

> . . . that called is Avernus,
> Of some Bride-well . . .

This is the precise site of the goings-on in *The Dunciad*; and Pope, too, could have spoken of 'The many perills of this Port'. The intrepid voyagers encounter stench, mud, oozing gases. Jonson's description isolates many of the features which the Augustan authors were to attribute to every Grubean environment:

> . . . an ayre, as hot, as at a muster
> Of all your night-tubs, when the carts doe cluster,
> Who shall discharge first his merd-urinous load:
> Through her wombe they make their famous road,
> Between two walls; where, on one side, to sacramen,
> Were seene your ugly Centaures, yee call Car-men,
> Gorgonian scolds, and Harpyes: on the other
> Hung stench, diseases, and old filth, their mother,
> With famine, wants, and sorrows many a dosen.
> The least of which was to the plague a cosen.

Though the poetic manner is consciously archaic, the range of implications achieved by Jonson points forward and not back. This is a journey from this world to the next, a visit to the shades; but it is at the same time a conducted tour of the parishes round the Fleet. There is a Virgilian downpour, whereby the travellers are 'shitten'; as with Swift's *Tale*, the great natural phenomena are reduced to a fart. Besides the open coprophilia, there are several hints of a sexual meaning; indeed, it is a cause for wonder that the Freudians have never got to work on this poem. Throughout, classical mythology is used to underpin the fiction; inevitably, the gods are a little soiled in the process, but such deflation does not seem to be Jonson's main purpose.

At length the voyagers reach 'the Stygian poole', where 'thicke frequente mists' such as envelop Dulness prevail. They pass on from Styx to Acheron, 'the ever-boyling floud'. Here 'your Fleet-lane Furies' dwell; the image changes from that of a sewer to that of a kitchen, where offal is put into a 'pastie' and the scalding steams 'make the place hell'. This is a region where (remembering that latrines were generally built over a watercourse)

> . . . each privies seate,
> Is fill'd with buttock [.] And the walls doe sweate
> Urine and plaisters [.] when the noise doth beate
> Upon your eares, of discords so un-sweet?
> And out-cryes of the damned in the Fleet?
> Cannot the Plague-bill keepe you backe? nor bells
> Of loud Sepulchres with their hourely knells,
> But you will visit grisly Pluto's hall?
> Behold where Cerberus, rear'd on the wall
> Of Hol'borne (three sergeants heads) lookes ore,
> And stayes but till you come unto the dore!

Privies, discord, noise, the Fleet Prison, plague, the bells of Old Bailey tolling for the condemned man – it is more or less an induction to Popian comedy. In the last few lines of his poem Jonson introduces an ale-house keeper, a role fit for Dunces such as Ned Ward. The very last line ends with the crude dismissive pun, '[the Muse] that sung A-JAX.' It is not the *Iliad* but a later heroic poem which Jonson brings to our mind in the event.[121]

The leap forward to Pope's lifetime involves no great feat of imaginative yoking. At the turn of the seventeenth century, Samuel Garth was to write in *The Dispensary* of 'those dreadful Shambles' round about the Ditch. Apothecaries' Hall he locates in the familiar mythological terms:

> Nigh where *Fleet Ditch* descends in Sable Streams
> To wash his Sooty *Naiads* in the *Thames*;
> There stands a Structure on a Rising Hill,
> Where *Tyro*'s take their Freedom out to Kill.

The Hall stood in Water Lane, Blackfriars. After this a whole series of poems were devoted to the humours of the Fleet. As W. G. Bell has said, 'A collection of Fleet Ditch odes would not be edifying.'[122] Even after the first portion of the Ditch had been filled in, we find references to 'that drain'd barren Sluice'.[123] The best of these poems is perhaps Arthur Murphy's 'Ode to the Naiads of the Fleet Ditch' (1761), a reply to Churchill: but this does little more than fill out Garth's conceit.

In fact Pope had only one important source among contemporaries; and that was his friend Gay. In 1720 Gay added to the second book of *Trivia* an episode of some one hundred and twenty lines concerning the goddess Cloacina. In fact, he devised a fable which serves to distance the narrative and to put the poem into a timeless continuum. Both the tone and content of *Trivia* have misled readers into imagining that its leading strategies are journalistic. Yet, as perceptive critics have recently drawn to our attention, it is a complex feat of rhetorical engineering. In one way the poem plays the usual mock-heroic game according to the standard rules (that is, a squalid and debased present is belittled by implied comparison with an heroic past). But *Trivia* is no more a straightforward mock-heroic than it is straight reportage. As with Pope, Gay takes the actual and topical as a limiting case: the poetry employs social observation to make permanent moral comment; it employs moral emblems, such as the Fleet, to state a sociological truth. In variety of resource and panache of detail, *Trivia* is great poetry; and it is time we acknowledged it as such.

Gay starts with a misleadingly conventional bit of mythologising. Just as Jove had been wont to range 'this nether world' (i.e. the earth, but a possible ambiguity is already created), so the fashion spread to 'vulgar Deitys'. Amongst them, Cloacina '(Goddess of the tide/Whose sable streams beneath the city glide)'. She falls in love with a 'mortal scavenger'. On hearing his 'cart' she approaches him, adopting the airs of a 'night-wandring harlot' and the disguise of 'the black form of a cinder-wench'. The assignation is conducted in a dark alley. Its predictable outcome, after nine months have elapsed, is the birth of a boy, 'dropt' beneath a bulk. Bulks figure largely in the legend of Grub Street, since many hacks, from Savage on, were alleged to spend their nights sleeping on them. At all events, the 'beggar's brat' thus sired grows up in the streets of London. He becomes a shoe-shine boy in a stall in the vicinity of the Fleet. Idle through lack of business, standing above 'the black canal of mud,/ Where common-shores a lulling murmur keep,/Whose torrents rush from Holborn's fatal steep,' he bemoans his sad condition. This is extremely dense poetry. The first joke, of course, is to refer to the stagnant Ditch in terms appropriate to a clear mountain stream in Arcady; 'fatal' because of the link with the procession to Tyburn. The common-shores are initially 'the land on both sides of the Fleet-ditch, where refuse gathered or was dumped until the tide came up and washed it away.' But by this time the moral overtones of the phrase were strongly evident. The open channels of refuse became a shorthand term for filth of every kind, as in Air XXI, 'Oh Mr. Constable', of Fielding's *Author's Farce* (1730).

Cloacina feels pity for her deserted child, and obtains help from the other deities in preparing a new japanning oil which will easily bring a fine polish to the most heavily besmeared shoes. She descends to the earth, and 'shoots beneath the tides' of the Ditch to await the morning, when she can make her epiphonal entrance.

> The Goddess rose amid the inmost round,
> With wither'd turnip tops her temple crown'd;
> Low reach'd her dripping tresses, lank, and black
> As the smooth jet, or glossy raven's back;
> Around her waste a circling eel was twin'd,
> Which bound her robe that hung in rags behind . . .
> The Goddess plunges swift beneath the flood,
> And dashes all around her show'rs of mud:
> The youth strait chose his post; the labour play'd
> Where branching streets from Charing-cross divide;
> His treble voice resounds along the *Meuse*,
> And White-hall echoes—*Clean your Honour's shoes.*

Thus the orphan achieves independence. It is impossible to believe that Pope did not have this passage in mind when he came to write his description of the Goddess Dulness, her robes and her rags; or the bawling contest, where Westminster and Hungerford 're-echo' (A.II.254) – Hungerford market stood almost exactly where the boy took his station – or the account of the Dunces who themselves 'plunge beneath the flood'. Gay's anecdote can be read as a charming fancy, along the lines of Thomas Parnell's treatment of the Pandora's box theme in 'Hesiod'. But there is more to it than that. The myth of Cloacina articulates a strand of thought otherwise present in the poem only inchoately. The episode, in brief, suggests that there is something energetic and life-giving about the currents of filth that course beneath the streets of London (or beside them). Gay makes something almost pretty out of the showers of mud that bespatter citizens; the dirt can perhaps be identified with the lower segments of society – it has certainly become part of the moving stream of the city, a kind of urban hormone which sets the activity of the whole town in motion.[124]

Pope approaches similar ideas in a very different way. Nevertheless there are enough points of connection to make the transition a fairly easy one. The events of *The Dunciad* are even more accurately placed than those of *Trivia*:

> This labour past, by Bridewell all descend,
> (As morning pray'r, and flagellation end)
> To where Fleet-ditch with disemboguing streams
> Rolls the large tribute of dead dogs to Thames,
> The King of dykes! than whom no sluice of mud
> With deeper sable blots the silver flood. (B.II.269)

The Fleet is king of dykes in the sense that Cibber is king of poets. Behind the last line we can discern a host of earlier lines, celebrating such tributaries of the Thames as 'The blue, transparent Vandalis'.[125] It is in this carefully defined location that the venal bookmakers compete to discover 'him who dives the best'. There is a culminating example here of Pope's ability to make the facts of geography body forth a degrading critique of the ways of the Dunces. To take the first to hand, there is (in the second version) the miscellaneous compiler Oldmixon, who would turn his hand to scandalous memoirs, secret history, court tales or whatever the booksellers would buy:

He said, and clim'd a stranded lighter's height,
Shot to the black abyss, and plung'd down-right.
The Senior's judgement all the crowd admire,
Who but to sink the deeper, rose the higher. (B.II.287)

I hope it is not too pedantic to add that a number of coal-barges
actually *were* stranded periodically in the canal.

The next diver is Smedley, round whom 'the quaking mud' closes.
He is given up for lost, but significantly the contest goes on – hacks
are always dispensable. However, the disreputable clergyman re-
appears after a succession of plunging prelates and precipitately dull
scribblers have made their attempt. Smedley relates 'the wonders of
the deep' in a parody of a time-honoured literary device, the vision
of the underworld:[126]

First he relates, how sinking to the chin,
Smit with his mien, the Mud-nymphs suck'd him in:
How young Lutetia, softer than the down,
Nigrina black, and Merdamante brown,
Vy'd for his love in jetty bow'rs below,
As Hylas fair was ravish'd long ago.
Then sung, how shown him by the Nut-brown maids
A branch of Styx here rises from the Shades,
That tinctur'd as it runs with Lethe's streams,
And wafting Vapours from the Land of dreams,
(As under seas Alphaus' secret sluice
Bears Pisa's off'rings to his Arethuse)
Pours into Thames: and hence the mingled wave
Intoxicates the pert, and lulls the grave:
Here brisker vapours o'er the Temple creep,
There, all from Paul's to Aldgate drink and sleep. (B.II.331)

This is the authentic Popian effect. A brutal and jolting contrast is
set up between the pleasant endowments of myth (including even
the mellifluous proper names) and the jagged asperities of London
reality, summed up in the glottal Saxon sounds of 'Aldgate'. Eternal
sleep is the ultimate condition of Dulness, its Nirvana and its
ideology. Shortly the entire gathering of Dunces will be reduced to a
drugged trance by the tedium of the final contest – appropriately held
between academics, that new breed of non-literary literary men

whom Pope so presciently feared. With deft economy, the poet has related this circumstance to the fetid air around Blackfriars. The 'pert' will not survive for long; it is the irremediably Dull who will feel the breath from Lethe and spread their influence over London and then the whole nation. That is what Settle prophesies in the next book; that is what happens in the final book. The Fleet Ditch, agency of disease, harbinger of poverty, home of both crime and punishment – this is, too, the great artery of Dulness through London and the first place to give itself up to that everlasting sleep which the Dunces so earnestly crave.

This unfortunate quarter witnessed, then, every plague that beset men and women of the time, both literal and metaphorical. As such, it was fit domicile for the forces of Dulness: for that condition is but a literary rephrasing of the experience of a London slum-dweller in the eighteenth century. Pope's myth of social disorder consigns his victims to a world of darkness, poverty, squalor, idleness, vice and ignorance. The rise of a scribbling gentry, indigenous to garrets such as the ramshackle lath-and-plaster tenements of Grub Street afforded, was a circumstance Pope knew well how to utilise. He collaborates imaginatively with history. And for this purpose, it was ideally suitable that his controlling metaphor should remain – as it was before the poem was ever conceived – a real part of real London. Not Aeneas, but Rome, is the final, unstated subject of *The Aeneid*; and it is not Queen Dulness, but her Grub Street realm, whose epic destiny Pope recounts to us.

Epigraphs (*i*) 'They' refers to the ancients, 'our' to modern worthies. Phlegeton, or Phlegethon, was of course a river of liquid fire in Hades. Quoted from *Poems of Ben Jonson*, ed. G. B. Johnston (London, 1954), p. 69.

    (*ii*) See note 44 below.

  1. I have used for general reference three serviceable books by W. G. Bell: *The Great Plague of London in 1665* (London, ed. 1924); *The Great Fire of London in 1666* (London, ed. 1923); and *Fleet Street in Seven Centuries* (London, 1912). Other specialised sources are referred to in the notes below.

2. Hart, 'Some Reflections on Johnson as Hero', *Johnsonian Studies*, ed. M. Wahba (Cairo, 1962), pp. 28–9.

3. Quoted from the Penguin edition of *Roget's Thesaurus* (Harmondsworth, 1953), pp. 221–2.

4. W. K. Wimsatt, jr., *The Verbal Icon* (New York, 1958), p. 124.

5. Penfield Roberts called his study of the diplomatic events in Europe *The Quest for Security 1715–1740* (New York, 1963). This phrase could be transferred from the sphere of foreign policy and international alignments to that of personal psychology.

6. Pope's concern is evidenced by his own letters during 1715 (e.g. that to the retired diplomat Trumbull, on 16 December – 'Fire and sword, and fire and faggot, are equally my aversion . . .'), and also by those addressed to the poet by his closest friends (notably that of Blount on 11 November). See Pope, *Correspondence*, I, 307–24 especially. Among the better known Dunces, Defoe and Cibber were active followers of William III on his arrival; Oldmixon witnessed the events at Sedgmoor.

7. This aspect of the Jacobite risings has been stressed by several modern historians. See for example C. B. Realey, *The Early Opposition to Sir Robert Walpole 1720–1727* (Lawrence, Kansas, 1931), p. 53.

8. *The Crowd in History* (New York, 1964), pp. 47–65. In eighteenth-century usage, 'crowd' meant a bustling, pressing concourse – one could say 'there were many people present but no crowd' (=crowding). See Susie I. Tucker, *Protean Shape* (London, 1967), p. 160.

9. Rudé, p. 4; British Museum, *Catalogue of Prints and Drawings*, III, 302.

10. On the difficulties of maintaining the peace in the eighteenth century, see Radzinowicz, IV, 105–57 ('The Control of Crowds').

11. Rudé, p. 9.

12. During the Gordon riots there were rumours that lions had been let loose from the Tower and that lunatics were to be released from Bedlam. This is analogous to the fictional riot of *The Dunciad*, where (in the first version) the menagerie of Dunces are set free from their 'cell' near the Tower; and where (in the second version) the lunatic corps engulf the city from their 'cell' near Bedlam.

13. Dulness 'includes . . . Labour, Industry, and some degree of Activity and Boldness: a ruling principle not inert, but turning topsy-turvy the Understanding, and inducing an Anarchy or confused State of Mind' (note to B.I.15). The turbulent, anarchic forces of Dulness seek to overturn the due order of things, much as a mob of levellers would subvert the rule of law. Yet, for all their momentum and massiness, there is a sort of drugged or stupefied quality in the band of Dunces, such as crowd psychologists have detected.

14. Williams, pp. 131–58.
15. Rudé, pp. 7n. 217, 233; Williams, p. 143.
16. Rudé, pp. 51, 225, 54, 72, 61, and cf. p. 204; George, p. 125.
17. Rudé, pp. 198, 62, 59. The same writer observes (pp. 59–60) that the riot- ing bands (a noun Pope uses of his Dunces) 'were frequently "captained" by men enjoying temporary authority.' Now in one sense Cibber's eleva- tion is permanent; but in another, his authority derives from the Settle succession, i.e. the City Poet whose term of office is confined to the single occasion of the Lord Mayor's Show. (Though a re-election could be made each year in practice.) More generally, Pope contrives, by linking Cibber's apotheosis to the specific post of laureate which he had obtained, to suggest that his kingship had as short a term as his own poetic works.
18. Swift, *Correspondence*, IV, 62: cf. II, 12n, 15n. Pope had dealings with Barber at least as early as 1714: Pope, *Correspondence*, I, 444.
19. On the procession see for example Malcolm, II, 15–18; Thornbury, I, 26–7. Both accounts probably incorporate fable as well as fact. See also the poem to Francis Child, in the *Grub-street Journal*, reproduced as Appendix C. Swift refers to the procession in his *Journal* on 17 November 1711.
20. For an account of the procession in 1679, attended by an alleged 200,000 persons, and of the activities of the mob, see David Ogg, *England in the Reign of Charles II* (Oxford, 1963), II, 595–6.
21. *The Tatler*, ed. G. A. Aitken (London 1898–9), I, 333–5. It may be perti- nent to add that the Artillery Ground was the venue for another stirring contest at arms in the year of Pope's death, just after the revised *Dunciad* made its appearance. This was the celebrated match between Kent and All England, on 18 June 1744: the first representative game of cricket, and the first for which detailed scores were preserved. It even stimulated a mock- heroic poem by James Love. See H. S. Altham, E. W. Swanton, *A History of Cricket* (London, 1947), pp. 34–6. For Pope's reference to the ground, see above, p. 104. Jokes at the expense of the 'Cripplegate Grenadiers' were common: e.g. Read's *Weekly Journal*, 16 January 1720.
22. TE, V, 260.
23. TE, V, 263.
24. Cf. Ian Brownlie, *The Law Relating to Public Order* (London, 1968), pp. 201, 37–59; Radzinowicz, II, 164; Holdsworth, X, 705–6.
25. Rudé, *Wilkes and Liberty* (Oxford, ed. 1965), esp. pp. 17, 58–73, 153.
26. Rudé, *Wilkes*, pp. 76, 173, 220–1.
27. *Diary and Letters of Madame D'Arblay*, ed. A. Dobson (London, 1904), I, 438. According to Austin Dobson, Johnson never did *afterwards* visit Grub Street. The letter is dated about 15 July 1780; cf. *Dr. Johnson and Mrs. Thrale*, ed. C. B. Tinker (London, 1912), pp. 118–19. It might perhaps be a day or two earlier.

28. *The Letters of Samuel Johnson*, ed. R. W. Chapman (Oxford, 1952), II, 368–71.

29. *The Yale Edition of Horace Walpole's Correspondence*, ed. W. S. Lewis et al. (London, 1967), XXIII, 39: cf. p. 221. Similarly the Duchess of Devonshire speaks of 'a violent mob in Moorfields' at the start of the Gordon riot: Iris Leveson Gower, *The Face Without a Frown* (London, 1944), p. 55. Gibbon writes of the mob in a letter of 6 June 1780, the 'tumult' caused by the 'scum' on the surface of 'this huge Cauldron (London) . . . every Gentleman . . . must extinguish the flame . . . Col. H. was all last night in Holborn, among the flares . . .' *The Letters of Edward Gibbon*, ed. E. J. Norton (London, 1956), II, 243–4.

30. *The Complete Poetical Works of William Cowper*, ed. H. Hilford (London, 1907), p. 306.

31. Hibbert, *King Mob* (London, 1958), esp. pp. 27, 32, 34, 39, 44, 45, 48; see also J. P. de Castro, *The Gordon Riots* (London, 1926), p. 140.

32. Hibbert, pp. 56ff: de Castro, p. 105: Denton, pp. 176–8.

33. Hibbert, pp. 98, 102–3, 109, 117, 122, 125.

34. *The Works of Samuel Johnson, Ll.D.*, ed. A. Murphy (London, 1824), I, ii, 4.

35. Brian Gibbons, *Jacobean City Comedy* (London, 1968), p. 155. According to Gibbons, the London setting in one representative play 'is accurately achieved with many placing references to streets and district names, to attract local interest' (p. 23). Again, he contends that '. . . the detailed setting of Cony-Catching episodes in specific parts of London was similarly intended to give sensational interest to otherwise very commonplace material' (p. 140). As is, I hope, apparent from the text, I believe that the topographic basis of Augustan satire is far from being confined to questions of mere 'local colour': it is a device for moral insight and revelation.

36. Defoe, *Tour*, I, 351; cf. pp. 326–7, 341.

37. See R. H. Barker, *Mr. Cibber of Drury Lane* (New York, 1939), pp. 127–8, 140. Riots at Drury Lane were common throughout the century; there was a bad outbreak in 1744, and a curious step was then taken. 'In order that grievances might have expression and that excesses might be avoided, a spokesman for the public was appointed in or about 1744, and regularly attended the pit on all important occasions.': W. J. Lawrence, 'The Theatre', in Turberville, II, 178. There could scarcely be a clearer demonstration of the tumultuous and divisive nature of eighteenth-century society than the recurrent party squabbles in places of entertainment, or than the need to appoint a kind of industrial conciliation officer in the theatre. Spikes even had to be placed across the proscenium arch, leaving the theatre almost in the condition of a South American football ground. See Marshall, p. 183, where details of a riot at Drury Lane in 1737 are supplied.

38. TE, V, 287.

39. Sutherland's note (TE, V, 288–9) is particularly helpful at this point.

40. See also B.III. 253 ff, and B.III.315–6. The evocation of 'one wide conflagration' occurs at B.III.240.

41. Cudworth, *A Sermon preached before the Honourable the House of Commons* . . . (Cambridge, 1647), pp. 63–4. To cite a modern instance, Dorothy Marshall (pp. 236–7) speaks repeatedly of 'the spark that lit the flame', 'inflamatory pamphlets', a populace 'inflamed' by 'fiery' gin.

42. J. L. and Barbara Hammond, *The Skilled Labourer 1760–1832* (London, 1927), pp. 206, 209.

43. Hammond, p. 205, where the writers also record the fact that the weavers donned masks and other disguises prior to wreaking violence.

44. *The Eighteenth-Century Constitution 1688–1715*, ed. E. N. Williams (Cambridge, 1965), pp. 414–7. For Mansfield's speech in the Lords on the application of the Act during the Gordon riots, see pp. 417–20. See also *English Historical Documents 1714–1783*, ed. D. B. Horn, M. Ransome (London, 1957), pp. 271–9.

45. Rudé, *The Crowd in History*, p. 54.

46. Cf. Radzinowicz, I, 8–9: 'Few other offences induce the same degree of public alarm' as arson. See also the quotation from Pollock and Maitland, p. 8.

47. On the predominance of property considerations, cf. the quotation from Basil Williams in Radzinowicz, I, 34.

48. J. J. Baddeley, *An Account of the Church and Parish of St Giles, without Cripplegate* (London, 1888), p. 24.

49. See Denton, pp. 122–34.

50. Defoe's *Journal* mentions the heavy inflictions of the plague on the parish of St Giles' Cripplegate: e.g. (Harmondsworth, 1966), p. 36. See also his 'Due Preparations for the Plague', in *Romances and Narratives*, XV, 59ff.

51. *A Trip through London* (8th ed., 1728), pp. 1, 52–3.

52. *The Poems of John Dryden* (London, 1910), p. 39.

53. Hitchen, *A True Discovery* (1718), p. 7, quoted by Radzinowicz, II, 1; cf. F. J. Lyons, *Jonathan Wild, Prince of Robbers* (London, 1936), p. 225.

54. *The Dispensary* (ed. 1718), pp. 28–9, 36.

55. *Jonathan Wild* (New York, 1962), p. 28: cf. *Romances and Narratives*, XVI, 241–2.

56. Butt, p. 696 ('Epilogue to the Satires', II, 38).

57. Butt, pp. 577, 598, 676, 681–2.

58. Butt, pp. 232–3.

59. Butt, p. 233.

60. J. H. Plumb, *England in the Eighteenth Century* (Harmondsworth, 1950), p. 13.

61. Bell, *Plague*, pp. 275-6. Another report by the Commissioners, in 1653, alluded to the practice of keeping swine in the Fleet River: T. F. Reddaway, *The Rebuilding of London after the Great Fire* (London, 1940,) p. 202.

62. "Is there not as much skill in making Dikes, as in raising Mounts?", asks Martinus Scriblerus in Ch. IV of *Peri Bathous* (Steeves, p. 15). For Swift's use of the motif of ditches, see Ch. IV below.

63. Watt, 'Publishers and Sinners: The Augustan View', *Studies in Bibliography*, XII (1959), 14.

64. Faber, p. 68.

65. TE, V, 108.

66. *The History of the Rebellion* (Oxford, 1702), I, 158. Cf. Valerie Pearl, *London at the Outbreak of the Puritan Revolution* (Oxford, 1961), p. 1, and Marshall, p. 11.

67. Nigel Barton, *The Lost Rivers of London* (London, 1962), Ch. IX ('The Uses of the Lost Rivers'), pp. 65-100, is of help here. See also Ch. X ('Disasters, Diseases and Drains'), pp. 101-126. Not surprisingly the Fleet figures prominently in this latter.

68. George, p. 94.

69. Bell, *Plague*, p. 276.

70. Stow, pp. 9-10: Reddaway, p. 201, says 1502 and 1606.

71. Reddaway, pp. 201-2.

72. Reddaway, pp. 202-15.

73. Reddaway, pp. 220-1; Barton, p. 77.

74. Defoe, *Tour*, I, 355-6.

75. The notorious Saffron Hill district, infamous into the time of Dickens, adjoined Smithfield proper. The liberty lay in the parish of St Andrew's Holborn. It was associated with prostitutes, with poor Irish immigrants, with disease (e.g. typhus) and with crime: see George, pp. 91, 92, 121, 130, 351; E. B. Chancellor, *The Pleasure Haunts of London* (London, 1925), p. 176.

76. Further north still the Ditch ran near Hockley in the Hole, famous for boistrous sport, and mentioned in *Trivia* as well as in the *Dunciad* (B.I. 222, 326). Clerkenwell sprawled on the slopes of the Fleet Valley, 'a district of innumerable twisting lanes and alleys': O. H. K. Spate, 'The Growth of London A.D. 1660-1800', *A Historical Geography of England*, ed. H. C. Darby (Cambridge, 1963), p. 534.

77. On Lincoln's Inn Fields, see George, pp. 106-7, 342 (a particularly telling instance), 350. Just by the Fields lay Whetstone Park, a leading feature of London night-life for those who were not particular with whom they slept. Prior writes of 'that hallow'd Ground/Of *Temple-Walks*, or Whetstone's Park' as haunts of the prostitute: 'The Antiquated Coquet', in his *Poems on Several Occasions* (London, '5th' ed., 1767), II, 332.

78. A convenient guide is *New Remarks of London . . . Collected by the Company of Parish Clerks* (1732), which sets out the streets and alleys in each parish. It is to be feared that the parish of St Dunstan's was not always very scrupulously managed; at least, the scandal of holding an expensive feast when the officers met to settle the poor book suggests as much: see Dorothy Marshall, *The English Poor in the Eighteenth Century* (London, 1926), p. 64. A century before St Bride's had already been 'scarred with pestilential slum dwellings' which the Fire, unfortunately, could not reach: Pearl, p. 13.

79. Opposite lay Blackfriars, a scarcely more salubrious district. It was described in 1756 as filled with 'laystalls and bawdy houses, obscure pawnbrokers, gin-shops and ale-houses; the haunts of strolling prostitutes, thieves and beggars . . .' (George, p. 339).

80. T. B. Macaulay, *The History of England* (London, 1906), I, 290–1.

81. Cf. Wheatley, p. 398.

82. Stanley Morison, *The English Newspaper* (Cambridge, 1932), p. 93n; W. M. Sale, *Samuel Richardson Master Printer* (Ithaca, 1950), esp. pp. 10, 61; Chancellor, *Pleasure Haunts*, pp. 64, 76ff; Dobson, *Samuel Richardson* (London, 1902), pp. 174–6; Pope, *Correspondence*, IV, 338; see also R. J. Blackham, *The Story of the Temple Gray's and Lincoln's Inn* (London, n.d.), pp. 54–9.

83. Webb, VI, 12ff. In a characteristic 'Preface' to this work, Bernard Shaw wrote, 'If the prison does not underbid the slum in human misery, the slum will empty and the prison will fill' (p. xi). This is a particularly suggestive statement with regard to the Fleet (debtors') Prison and its environs.

84. Reproduced by Barton, opp. p. 80. Perhaps this shows some authorial backing for this location, though Aubrey Williams (pp. 38–9) seems to be following the text when he places the games at the very outlet of the Fleet into the Thames.

85. De Castro, p. 268: E. G. O'Donoghue, *Bridewell Hospital* (London, 1929), passim.

86. Pope, *Correspondence*, IV, 233–4. It was said that one in six of those who passed Temple Bar was a writer by profession: Thornbury, I, 45ff. But it cannot have been true.

87. Radzinowicz, I, 300; Wheatley, p. 395, places this execution of 1733 at the Fetter Lane end of the street, opposite Mitre Court.

88. Christopher Hibbert, *The Roots of Evil*, (London, 1963), p. 48.

89. See Lyons, pp. 270, 273, etc. For Shenstone's comments to Richard Jago on the prevalence of armed footpads in the region of Fleet Street around 1744, see Hibbert, *Roots*, p. 50.

90. O'Donoghue, II, 188.

91. Bell, *Plague*, p. 276.

92. Barton, p. 75.

93. Wheatley, pp. 388–92; Webb, VI, 8, 26.
94. Wheatley, pp. 392–3.
95. J. T. Boulton (ed.), *Daniel Defoe* (London, 1965), p. 237.
96. Moore, *Citizen*, p. 47.
97. For a gruesome story set in a garret in Stonecutter Street, see Bayne-Powell, p. 81.
98. Butt, p. 695.
99. Webb, VI, 30–1, mention the famous occasion in 1750 when judges, aldermen and counsel perished along with prisoners from the disease. For Boswell's visit to Newgate's 'dark mansions' and dismal cells in 1763, see his *London Journal*, ed. F. A. Pottle (London, 1950), pp. 251–2. Savage and Wycherley were confined there.
100. Radzinowicz, I, 168ff, gives a great deal of interesting evidence on the subject; see also Dorothy George, in Turberville, I, 175. The biblical parallel is my own.
101. Wheatley, pp. 402–3.
102. Boswell, *Journal*, p. 214.
103. Pope, *Correspondence*, II, 29, 34, is the authority.
104. Cf. George, pp. 106–7, 342–3, 350; as well as Macaulay, *History*, I, 277, for a description of Lincoln's Inn Fields, with its rubbish, its beggars and its rough sports.
105. Cf. Lyons, p. 279; F. A. Mumby, *Publishing and Bookselling* (London, 1949), p. 154ff.
106. *DNB*, s.v. Savage.
107. On Shoe Lane, see Irving, pp. 139, 259; George, p. 93. For the large number of alehouses in Holborn, see Radzinowicz, I, 400; for rioting there, see Dorothy George in Turberville, I, 193. It should be recalled that Dr. Johnson, in his young and far from affluent days, lived twice in Holborn as well as in Fetter Lane, Bow Street and other streets in the vicinity long before he came to relative comfort in Gough Square.
108. Radzinowicz, II, 310.
109. Irving, p. 260.
110. Quoted by Radzinowicz, II, 23. Some time earlier (see p. 255) John Oldham had linked Tyburn with Grub Street; one could almost set the imaginative connection out in the form of a syllogism or proportion sum:

Smithfield: Tyburn
Grub Street: Tyburn
thus Smithfield: Grub Street.

111. Defoe stood in the pillory for the third and last time by Temple Bar. For the extent of the parish of St Dunstan's (which contained Whitefriars as an 'extraparochial' district), see *New Remarks*, pp. 159–62.

112. Other unfortunate connections, of a more or less serious kind, were a wax-work show near St Dunstan's Church, for which see A. J. Sambrook (ed.), *The Scribleriad* (Los Angeles, 1967), p. ix; the legacy of the theatre which had stood in Dorset Gardens in Restoration times (theatres nearly always sent down the tone of a neighbourhood, for reasons that are only partly intelligible today); and the noxious Bugg Alley, alias Harp Alley.

113. M. D. George, *Hogarth to Cruickshank* (London, 1967), pp. 33-4.

114. Carey was buried in St James' church in 1743: *The Poems of Henry Carey*, ed. F. T. Wood (London, n.d. (? 1930)), p. 12.

115. Clifford, p. 180.

116. Morison, p. 324.

117. E. B. Chancellor, *The Literary Ghosts of London* (London, 1933), p. 171.

118. Sale, p. 26.

119. Defoe, *Romances and Narratives*, XVI, 179. The House of Correction was in Clerkenwell Close, next to the New Prison in Clerkenwell Green (*New Remarks*, p. 215).

120. Clifford, p. 180; Barton, p. 88; *DNB*, s.v. Cave; Ralph, *A Critical Review* (1734), p. 23.

121. *Poems of Ben Jonson*, pp. 69-75.

122. *The Dispensary* (ed. 1718), p. 29; Bell, *Fleet Street*, p. 417.

123. James Miller, 'Art of Life' (1739), quoted by Irving, p. 86.

124. Faber, pp. 69-70.

125. Butt, p. 207. The poem is 'Windsor Forest'.

126. Among other connotations of 'hell' at this period, it may be worth mentioning, were gambling dens (regularly so described: see for instance the Newgate *Calendar*, III, 179ff) and, in legend if not in reality, the underground lairs of such disreputable groups as the Medmenham 'monks'. It is not necessary to give credence to stories such as the one that there was at Medmenham 'a marble outhouse, beautifully designed, called "The Temple of Cloacina" . . .' – thus retailed by Daniel P. Mannix, *The Hell-Fire Club* (London, 1961), p. 24. It remains a clear fact that people of the time *did* refer in a shocked sort of way to various 'Hell-Fire Clubs', real or imaginary, whether those putatively established by Dashwood, by Philip Wharton or by others. Black magic rites and illicit sexual dealings were frequently located on the linguistic map in close proximity to Hades. However apocryphal the tales, it can hardly be gainsaid that satanic cults were identified in the popular imagination with subterranean caves which, more often than not, were described as 'hells'. In addition, 'Hell' seems to have been used in prostitutes' argot for the female pudenda – another useful connotation as far as the iconography of the Fleet was concerned. See Tom Brown, quoted by Pinkus, p. 45.

III

The Criteria of Duncehood

But then it is not every Knave, nor (let me add) every Fool, that is a fit
subject for a Dunciad.

Ricardus Aristarchus, 'Of the Hero of the Poem',
The Dunciad in Four Books

Nature, said William Godwin, never made a dunce.[1] Whatever the
truth of this proposition at large, it is broadly accurate as regards
that species of Dunce whom Pope and the other Scriblerians recognised. They took their Dunces where they found them; and generally Nature had little to do with the matter. A few Dunces were
born. Most, however, were made: they earned their title by a series
of identifiable choices and actions. Some, such as James Ralph,[2]
had their Duncehood thrust suddenly upon them. But even this
latter class did not find themselves pressed into the retinue of Queen
Dulness without some contributory negligence on their part. There
was, in fact, no single way of winning admission. You could not
guarantee inclusion in *The Dunciad* even by attacking Pope or his
friends. John Hughes wrote a satiric piece, 'Advice to Mr Pope, on
his intended Translation of Homer', in 1714:[3] a fact of which Pope
probably was aware by 1735. He never incorporated Hughes into his
gallery of literary rogues (as he could easily have done). Either this
was out of respect for Hughes' memory – the other had died in 1720
– or else some private, 'irrelevant' factor allowed Hughes to scape
whipping. At the same time you could not buy immunity by desist-
ing from attack. It can none the less be shown that there was a broad
pattern of criminality which made your chances of subsequent conviction a good deal higher. It is my aim here to sketch in the main
lines of this 'pattern of criminality'.

Strangely, the only recipe for Duncehood available is that of Pope and Swift themselves.[4] The statements of the Scriblerian party have ordinarily been taken as sufficient accounts of the matter. Yet it is evidently possible to apply other tests. In recent years many outstanding passages of criticism have been written on *The Dunciad*. Without exception, these analyses accept as given Pope's stated criteria of Duncehood; and they then go on (profitably and properly) to consider the action of the poem itself. George Sherburn has illuminated what might be called the *mise-en-scène* of *The Dunciad*; Aubrey Williams, Thomas Edwards and others have described the principles of Popian production; Alvin Kernan, Hugo Reichard and others have assessed the choreography of this duncely drama.[5] In short, the staging and production are now very fully understood. But all this assumes that the casting has already been carried out. Whereas the truth is (as the older critics, whatever their lapses into *parti pris*, did sense) that the choice of Dunces was one of the major creative tasks facing Pope. To revert to the earlier metaphor, the success of the performance depends not only on the antics which the characters are called upon to perform in the course of the poem. It depends also on the fitness of the actors for their role; on the variety and interest of those making up the *dramatis personae*; and on the tractability of the cast, individually and collectively, to Pope: Pope who, Orson Welles-like, functions as producer, director, scriptwriter (the Dunces get few of the best lines), stage-manager, lighting engineer and master of ceremonies.[6]

Portraits in Dulness

It is, of course, important to realise that Pope transmutes his victims into fictional constructs. Modern critics such as Aubrey Williams have expressed the matter well: 'Very few of the dunces were as interesting in real life as they are after Pope has retouched and given a lustre to their dulness.' Professor Williams speaks of the 'realm of half-truth' assigned to the brood, and this we can accept. It is, however, another thing to assert a 'serious impairment of the victim's historical status'.[7] Only the most blinkered concentration on the text as a self-contained monad will obscure the plain truth that Dunce hood was a recognised historical phenomenon. It would have survived, in a less remarkable form to be sure, if Pope had never written a word of his projected 'Dulness'. Like Swift, Pope inherited certain models when he came to anatomise literary folly. He took over ready-made a number of unmissable targets such as Shadwell, Blackmore, Settle and Flecknoe.[8] His chief benefactors here were Marvell, Dryden and Swift; but there were many others, *including some actual Dunces* who had unwittingly prepared the ground for him.[9] When Professor Sutherland remarks, 'Such a comic butt as Tom Durfey is introduced, not because Pope felt spiteful towards him, but because almost every one was prepared to treat Durfey as a joke,' I believe the admission is more significant than he realises. The point is a double-edged one: it is made to indicate that Pope's victims are often 'mythical' rather than individual. But equally the firm historical reality of Tom Durfey, playwright and songwriter, stands out (it is enshrined, by the way, as near at hand as the 'Biographical Appendix' to Professor Sutherland's edition).[10] Durfey was not merely a well known writer. He was a well known Dunce. Just as the contemporary 'celebrity' is well known for being well known, so the Dunce was celebrated on account of his Duncehood. It was a fact about him which coloured and pre-empted any other judgment; literary, social or whatever. Consequently, Pope's decision to use notorious figures of this kind among his cast serves to *fix* the developing narrative within a historical context, rather than to liberate it from such a context.

His resolute determination to name names has a similar effect. It is worth recalling that when *The New Dunciad* appeared, contemporary readers found considerable difficulty with the new method of employing a sobriquet, such as 'Mummius', instead of a real name:

The Censure [the critics of the town] pass is, That the *Satire* is too *allegorical*, and the *Characters* he has drawn are too *conceal'd*: That *real Names* should have been inserted instead of *fictitious* ones.[11]

I shall not dispute the justice or injustice of this criticism. It is enough that here we have clear factual evidence that a radical change in reading habits was called for. The first three books, for good or ill, employed many actors type-cast for their role. These were old favourites of the audience, to be greeted with a comforting sense of familiarity as they made their appearance. It is no good pretending that there is no difference, *under this precise aspect*, between Timon, Atossa and Sir Balaam on the one hand, and on the other

> Norton, from Daniel and Ostroea sprung,
> Blest with his father's front, and mother's tongue . . .
> (A.II.383)

Timon may be legion: anybody or nobody. Norton has got to be Benjamin Norton Defoe, first and foremost.[12] Otherwise all satiric thrust is dissipated; and any symbolic existence we like to annex to his character is stifled at birth. More than that, the moral character-istics stressed in Timon or Atossa are linked only contingently with their role in life. Timon might be a profligate landowner whether or not he were a peer, a grasping ex-Paymaster or a pretender to taste in music and the arts. But it is of the essence of Norton that he should be a starveling writer, in or out of the precise poetic context. His whole title to inclusion in *The Dunciad* rests on that fact. One of the main functions of the notes by Martin Scriblerus is to assert a *dramatic* propriety by insisting on the real-life career of the victim – the real Duncehood, we might say without begging any question.

In this connection it is worth recalling Thomas Edwards' point, to the effect that the Dunces 'take on a disturbing dignity from being a part of a long historical sequence' of bad writers[13] and, it might be added, *recognised* bad writers. So they do. Pope, needless to say, turns this ineluctable condition to his own advantage. It is surely impossi-ble to argue, however, that such a dignity, quasi-mythical as it is, would survive intact the discovery, shall we say, that Elkanah Settle never lived. Swift once managed to convince the world, by the brilli-ant operation of his satiric wit, that John Partridge had departed this life. Not even a Scriblerian, however, could deny the historical exis-tence of a Dunce by the mere *ipse dixit* of a mock-heroic. Heidegger becomes a sort of mythical beast, but he still lives, and still lives as a Dunce. There are limits to the alchemy of satire.

I have implied that recent critics have not troubled themselves with the truth or otherwise of Pope's portraits. And it is the case that they are not usually concerned, even within the imaginative fidelity of a particular dramatisation, with the duncely career which lies behind it. On occasion, nevertheless, they are betrayed into hasty acceptance of Pope's word. Hugo M. Reichard, for example, has written sensitively of 'Pope's Social Satire', focussing with especial clarity on the treatment of poverty in *The Dunciad*. I shall return to this discussion later. At the moment I wish to indicate a separate fact. Reichard writes at one juncture, 'If one may take as a criterion Johnson's longer and graver account of Savage's tribulations . . . Pope's descriptions of literary temperance and prudence must be pronounced accurate.'[14] Well, of course, one can't take Johnson as gospel on this question: his own purposes were to some degree polemical. Beyond that, it is noteworthy that Reichard has suddenly switched to a totally fresh test of 'accuracy'. It is open to the critic to assert that he will have no truck with concepts of historical truth or falsity. In consistency, he cannot suddenly raise the issue when he thinks he has a way of 'establishing' the accuracy of Pope's presentation, as soon as such fidelity strikes him as a merit. Elsewhere Reichard shows no interest in tracking down whatever evidence may be available concerning the social ecology of Grub Street. As this book should indicate, there is a lot of evidence: far more, at all events, than is usually brought to bear on the study of *The Dunciad*.

In fact the proposition that 'the Poem was not made for these Authors, but these Authors for the Poem' is double-edged.[15] One implication might be that the Dunces were mere instrumentalities, unidentified lackeys of a higher poetic cause. On the other hand, the phrase could be construed to work the other way – to confer a new importance and a new individuality on these special, custom-designed antitypes. Quite apart from their historical lineage, the Dunces took on significance by the very fact that they were named. According to Gilbert Highet, Pope 'felt the paradox implicit in his work and the work of many satirists, that he was expanding his genius on giving a kind of immortality to the unimportant and the ephemeral.'[16] Swift, of course, had insisted on the need to spell out 'the names of those scriblers printed indexically', and had written, 'Again, I insist, you must have your Asterisks fill'd up with some real names of real Dunces.' But in an even more famous passage he warned Pope against the operations of Highet's 'paradox';

> Take care the bad poets do not outwit you, as they have served the good ones in every Age, whom they have provoked to transmit their Names to posterity Maevius is as well known as Virgil, and Gildon will be as well known as you if his name gets into your Verses; and as to the difference between good and bad Fame is a perfect Trifle . . .[17]

The rhetorical dilemma facing Pope was this. He had to make his Dunces emblematic of a real threat and a real active power; they had to be recognisable and menacing in their capacity as destructive, anti-literary forces. Yet obviously he did not want them to become too approachable to the reader. His problem was to give them a bad eminence without imparting the idea that they might claim (actually or potentially) an eminence independent of this badness.

The dilemma had come up in a slightly different form some years earlier. In 1716 Swift replied to a letter of Pope's, lamenting the many sufferings he (Pope) endured 'as an Author militant'. Swift retorts:

> And who are all these enemies you hint at? I can only think of Curl, Gildon, Squire Burnet, Blackmore, and a few others whose fame I have forgot: Tools in my opinion as necessary for a good writer, as pen, ink and paper.
> [Elwin reads 'Fools . . . are as necessary . . .'][18]

Both men agreed on the necessity for having enemies, and keeping one's enmities in good repair. The practical utility of this is indicated by Pope's remarks concerning Ambrose Philips, which reveal a manifest desire that history shall follow the course satire had decreed ('if they don't promote him they'l spoil a very good conclusion of one of my Satyrs . . .')[19] We are back to the position sketched in just now. Pope wished to allow his Dunces the anonymity of myth;

but he also wished to utilise their acknowledged *historical* vulnerability. Philips became more available as a Dunce to the extent that he entered the public domain of notoriety. The better recognised his face became, the more suitable a model he was for the impersonal grimace of Duncehood.

It has been very widely agreed in recent years that Pope and Swift were sincere in claiming that literary disrespect came before personal dislike, and that the two modes of criticism need not always go together. 'My name', wrote Pope, 'is as bad a one as yours, and hated by all bad Poets from Hopkins and Sternhold to Gildon and Cibber.'[20] Once again he has recourse to well sanctioned rosters of literary iniquity. It is on the basis of these remarks that critics such as Geoffrey Tillotson have concluded, 'In Pope's eye a man, otherwise inoffensive, might offend through his badness as a writer. For Pope, a bad author was to literature what a fool or a knave was to life. *The Dunciad* attacks the denizens of Grub Street not as men first of all but as authors.' Similarly W. L. Macdonald has written, 'It can be said with some reservations that Pope satirised contemporary writers because he thought their work insipid or plain bad, and not because he detested them personally.'[21] Granted: but the relation between literary incompetence and personal insufficiency is one of the identifications which *The Dunciad* strives, through its own rhetorical energy, to assert. It is necessary to look into this point more fully before we concur, too readily, in the words Pope gave to William Cleland: 'On his principle of attacking few but who had slander'd him, he could not have done it at all had he been confin'd from censuring obscure and worthless persons, for scarce any other were his enemies.'[22]

Firstly, it is observable that Pope wished to make this equivalence in every context. The letter to Swift in which he announces the change of title, from *Dulness* to *Dunciad*, is a case in point:

> As the obtaining the love of valuable men is the happiest end I know of this life, so the next felicity is to get rid of fools and scoundrels; which I can't but own to you was one part of my design in falling upon these Authors, whose incapacity is not greater than their insincerity, and of whom I have always found (if I may quote myself)

That each bad Author is as bad a Friend.
This Poem will rid me of those insects . . .[23]

The poem, on this showing, is to be a literary machine for pest-destruction. And the manner of destruction is to be an equation of 'fools and scoundrels'. The work will hint incapacity by asserting insincerity, and vice versa. That is, known personal defects will be exploited in the poem to heighten the specifically literary misdemeanours of the authors and booksellers presented. Other failings, diagnosed under the cultural aspect, will be dramatised to reinforce the personal innuendo against a particular figure. This seems to me to relate more directly to the actual workings of the poem than the pious sentiment certain recent commentators attribute to Pope. The truth is, that if he had taken as little care as they suggest he did in *choosing* his Dunces, his 'invention' would have been that much impaired. Equally, if we as readers concern ourselves as little with the sample of Duncehood offered us, in the way these critics recommend, we limit our response to the moral and human perspectives which *The Dunciad* opens up. Pope was no doubt serious when he wrote to Judith Cowper, in a non-polemical context.

> Not that I woud place all my Pretensions upon That Poetical foot, much less confine 'em to it; I am far more desirous to be admitted as yours on the more meritorious title of Friendship. I have ever believd this as a sacred maxime, that the most Ingenious Natures were the most sincere, & the most Knowing & Sensible Minds made the best Friends. Of all those that I have thought it the felicity of my life to know, I have ever found the most distinguished in Capacity, the most distinguished in Morality: and those the most to be depended on, whom one esteemd so much as to desire they shoud be so.[24]

Nevertheless, it was an obvious satiric convenience that Mrs Haywood's private life should be as suspect as her scandalous books; that Budgell should have compounded his Buttonian literary position by leading a life of irresponsibility and muddle; that Oldmixon's books should have been as virulent as his private affairs were debased.

Secondly, it is apparent that Pope uses irrelevant factors, strictly defined, in building up his portraits in Duncehood. This point seems to me evaded by this piece of advice from R. K. Root:[25]

> Most readers of today will best appreciate the Dunciad by keeping its general significance in mind, and regarding the individual Dunces as types rather than individuals. They may even amuse themselves by substituting for these forgotten persons of long ago their own pet aversions in the literary world of the present [1929].

There are, it seems to me, several difficulties here. In the first place, however much we bend them Mrs Pix and Roome and Charles Johnson will not squeeze into a recognisable likeness of Mencken or James Hadley Chase or Elinor Wylie. Too much had changed between these two ages for such simple swaps to be possible. In the second place, it seems odd to recommend distractions on the side to a reader of *The Dunciad*: few poems require more concentrated attention, few provide more opportunities for integral, one might say *structural*, amusement. Amusement is, indeed, part of the experiential phenomenon which constitutes a reading of *The Dunciad*. Lastly, the argument thus far should have indicated that the Dunces are indeed types; but types whose clarity of presentation and immediacy of character derive from a real individuality, amounting at times to idiosyncracy. The fact that critics debate the propriety of Cibber's substitution for Theobald represents a tacit admission that questions of dramatic suitability are not out of court. Actually, many of the commentators who are most insistent that we should take a cavalier attitude towards the identity of specific Dunces are amongst those to make the loudest shout concerning Cibber's unfitness for the role of the new King Dunce. Many individual thrusts in the poem reflect particular characteristics (Heidegger's uncouth appearance; Curll's 'size' – stature literally, though there is obviously an innuendo concerning his genitals; the 'plunging Prelate' Sherlock; and many more.)[26] Clearly these graphic touches add to the dramatic impact of the poem. But equally they take away some typical significance. It is open to a critic to say that this is a pity, that this fact limits the appeal of *The Dunciad*, or indeed that it converts the work into a different kind of poem. What he cannot do is simply to ignore the presence of such individualised vignettes within the organisation.

Pope wrote a poem about corrupt, mischievous and stupid people involved in, or hanging on to, the world of letters. His fictional constructs derive part of their title from a most undivine succession, the hereditary right of Dulness. They draw some of their obscene and farcical squalor from the actual goings on within the poem. But – the fact remains – they take much of their colouring from their real-life counterparts. Curll in the poem, as Williams suggests, is more than Curll in actuality. But it would be a pretty arbitrary and pointless joke, barely satiric in any sense, if there were no Curll in real life at all. The energy comes from the transmutation: not the bare presentation of a bookseller of the age.

Professor Tillotson wrote in a later book: '[Pope's] presence is as strongly felt in many of his poem's as a jailer's in a jail: a strong reason why he is never absent from his *Dunciad* is because it is he who has put in all the other writers.'[27] This is so; and it might be recalled that prisoners receive not only the general issue of uniform (which marks them off as convicts) but serial numbers (which serves to identify one from another). If, then, it may be provisionally granted that Pope did incarcerate his victims for particular reasons, and not merely out of some atavistic hatred for any bad writer, we may enquire what exactly the grounds of conviction tended to be. Inevitably we shall find that there were several indictable offences, ranging over many parts of the literary life. At the most extreme level, you could find yourself committed into custody partly because your name itself was right. If your career was broadly suitable, you might earn a mention whenever the demands of the rhyme, of alliteration, or a sort of ironic euphony required your presence:

> And Noise and Norton, Brangling and Breval,
> Dennis and Dissonance, and captious Art,
> And Snip-snap short, and Interruption smart . . .

Here the cadence is such that one reads 'Snip-snap' exactly as though he were a minor poet.

> A Gothic Library! of Greece and Rome
> Well purg'd, and worthy Settle, Banks, and Broome.

The jarring half-rhyme (though it may have been nearer perfection in Pope's day) symbolises well enough the descent implied in the couplet, the failure of the moderns to live up to their high pretensions and lofty models.

> A past, vamp'd, future, old, reviv'd, new piece,
> 'Twixt Plautus, Fletcher, Shakespear, and Corneille,
> Can make a Cibber, Theobald, or Ozell.

Again, in the passage beginning 'Three wicked imps, of her own Grubstreet choir', the major writers retain the solidity of repute (Congreve, Addison, Prior, Gay). The hacks (Mears, Warner, Wilkins; Breval, Bond, Besaleel; an empty Joseph) take on the role of mere items in a sound progression: participants in a phonetic dance, they cavort in grotesque helplessness.[28]

The Dunce in Action

But generally the grounds of admission were more serious. In order to bring out some of the major duncely characteristics, it may be worth prefacing any full-scale review with a more limited enquiry. I shall take as a concrete instance of the Dunce in action the case of John Oldmixon. He is a worthy representative of the breed on several counts. His writing career was exceptionally protracted; his *oeuvre* astonishingly miscellaneous even for an age so little given to specialisation. His dealings with Pope, though extensive, were reasonably tidy and distinct, in terms both of time and causation. There was never a standing Pope-Oldmixon 'situation', such as long prevailed between Pope and Dennis.[29] Finally, it is possible to be a good deal more specific with regard to Oldmixon's claims to Duncehood than is the case elsewhere. He was a brave and imprudent man, not addicted to trimming his sails. No sign that he had incurred the disapproval of the cultural or political establishment; no indication that Pope or Swift had taken umbrage: no advance warning of his satiric liabilities – nothing could deter him. Doggedly he went on his way. Long before the first version of *The Dunciad* he had given abundant hostages to fortune. After his inclusion in *Peri Bathous* he showed no inclination to play for safety. Nor was he one of those deliberately to apply for admission to the Dunces' gallery. Unlike James Ralph, a fellow client of George Dodington, and one who afterwards was to comment on the hardship of Oldmixon's lot[30] – unlike Ralph, he gave Pope no deliberate provocation. He simply went ahead, abusing, sneering, expostulating, whining, wheezing. If a literary form were anathema to the Scriblerian group, he was sure to practise it. Did a peer excite Pope's scorn, he was sure to have composed eulogistic addresses to that peer. If an unknown writer called out Pope's admiration, he was sure to have singled out the obscure author for comment of special savagery. He was, in fact, the living embodiment of the Dunce. Not merely because he clashed personally with Pope: though he did. Not merely because he took the opposite side on political and historical issues: though he did. Not merely because the tone and content of all his writings were at odds with all Pope's standards: though they were. Not merely because he lived in social regions alien to Pope and made his living in a manner despised by Pope: though these things were so. Not merely because he was a professional Grub Street hack, even. His suitability for the role allotted to him in *The Dunciad* includes, and transcends, all these factors.

A few commentators have paused to reflect on the rightness of Pope's decision to put him in the poem. The first was probably William Ayre, who may or may not be Edmund Curll. '*Oldmixon* comes in most naturally' to the revised *Dunciad* (i.e. from 1735 onwards). According to Ayre, Mr Pope, 'being willing to take a little of the Load off poor old *Dennis*, claps it on the shoulder of *Oldmixon*, who, next to Mr *Dennis*, was the most ancient Critick of our Nation then living.' Here dramatic propriety does relate to observed historical fact; for Oldmixon, earlier known for a variety of achievements, became much better known as a critic in the period immediately subsequent to the first edition of *The Dunciad* (where he figures as 'Oldmixon the Poet', patron-hunter). Ayre bases his attack mainly on the notes to the Variorum *Dunciad*. He adds one or two barbed comments of his own: 'This Mr *Oldmixon* pretended to be a Writer of Secret History; but as his History (if such a Lump of Lies deserves that Name) has been hiss'd out of the World . . .' Again: 'Author of what he calls *A critical History of England*, and others call a heap of Scandal and Lies . . .' Two years later, incidentally, Warburton, the prime influence on this attitude to the Dunces, was himself responsible for a sneering allusion to Oldmixon.[31]

In the nineteenth century Leslie Stephen instanced Oldmixon, 'a hack writer employed in compilations', as a natural object of Pope's attack. For Stephen, the Dunces in Book II of the poem 'were all hateful, partly because they were on the side of Walpole, and there-fore, by Pope's logic, unprincipled hirelings, and more, because in that cause, as others, they had assaulted Pope and his friend.' It is scarcely necessary to add that this is to simplify matters.[32] A few years later T. R. Lounsbury briefly referred to Oldmixon's share in the poem, and used his name, misleadingly, to support the conten-tion that the Dunces managed to prosper in later years despite the notoriety Pope had bestowed on them.[33] Professor Sutherland has produced evidence to the contrary; and certainly Oldmixon's case is less useful to Lounsbury's argument than he seems to have thought.[34] In the 1730's Oldmixon found considerable difficulty in finding a bookseller to float his massive histories. He complained that this was because a malicious rumour had been spread abroad that he was a 'court writer' – a hack directly subsidised by Walpole, like Arnall. There was probably something in this complaint.[35] At the same time, it seems likely that the trade shied away from Oldmixon for a quite different reason. His massive histories must have been hard to shift, even on a subscription basis. This contrasts with the situation in 1724, when the *Critical History*, Volume I, enjoyed a ready sale. It is easy to imagine a cause for this change: the disrepute Oldmixon had incurred in the dispute over Clarendon's history; and (linked to that) the public degradation he had suffered in *The Dunciad*, especially the Variorum edition with its damaging notes.

One of the few recent critics to take up the issue of Oldmixon's place in the poem is Austin Warren.[36] He sees Oldmixon, 'one of these unfortunates who figured in the *Dunciad*', as a sort of outsider. On this reading, Oldmixon, excluded from 'the charmed circle', resented the cosy bonhomie of the in-group – Pope, Swift, Gay,

Addison – writers of classic status, who were also personally familiar to one another. 'Every classical age has had its similar "circle" of the eminent; and no doubt in every age there have been Oldmixons to suspect their eminence.' I do not find this entirely convincing. Quite apart from the fact that Addison was scarcely a close literary ally of the other men after about 1713 (Oldmixon, on the other hand, knew him quite well and solicited his aid as late as 1717),[37] I feel that the account distorts Oldmixon's motivation in attacking the coterie. His basic psychological configuration was made up of envy, bitterness, pride, pugnacity and simple good sense. In his *Memoirs of Somers* (1716), he sneers at the polite writer in his brocade gown, lolling in a chariot, and contrasts this pose to that of the working professional, clad in calico. This particular piece of rhetoric was directed against Addison, who had written disparagingly of Grub Street biographers in the *Freeholder*.[38] There is, however, no real evidence that Oldmixon wished to join the charmed circle of leisure. He wanted, principally, better financial rewards; secondarily, at best, greater social respect. In addition he may have hoped for a modicum of political influence. It is going beyond the facts to assert that he resented the coterie as such. If the coterie were made up of the right people (the Junto Lords: Garth, Maynwaring, etc.), he was ready enough to accept its cultural and social hegemony.

Actually, the forces of social exclusion operating on Oldmixon were rather more subtle, rather less personal. The point has been suggested in an outstanding essay by Ian Watt. 'The social historian', Mr Watt writes, 'may see the legend of Grub-Street primarily as an early and revealingly hostile social definition of a new professional class.' Further, he describes Theobald and Cibber as both 'unauthorized professional intruders into the republic of letters': Theobald was an attorney, a trained pedant, whilst Cibber was a vagabond player turned theatrical manager turned autobiographer.[39] This is not far from what James Sutherland has written:

> . . . Pope, no doubt because he lived at the beginning of a new era of popular publishing and weekly journalism, took a firm stand against the upstarts whom he saw invading the enclosed territory of literature. In the *Dunciad* of 1729 it is partly the *type* that he is attacking: the

pedantic scholar like Hearne or Theobald; the weekly journalist like Roome and Concanen; the party hack like Oldmixon; the popular writer like Mrs Centlivre, Mrs Haywood, Ned Ward, or the author of *Robinson Crusoe*; the shameless publisher like Edmund Curll.[40]

There are two overlaid senses of 'professional' here. In the first place, we have the regular, paid hack who depends wholly on fugitive writing for his livelihood. Pope scorns such a man because his stake in literature is inalienably commercial. If the hack does not deliver the goods, he will not eat; consequently, he is bound to accept any commission, however unworthy, and cannot conduct that free-ranging search of topics, themes and styles which Renaissance theory demanded as a prelude to worthwhile imaginative writing. His subject-matter and his manner of treatment are generally preordained. Secondly, there is the other kind of professional. The category described by Watt includes a number of persons with vested interests in the escalation of vapid bookmaking. The standard example of this type today would surely be the academic. In Pope's time, as Watt indicates, the world of literature was threatened by a new breed of non-literary literary men. Pope had himself remarked on the willingness of commentators on Homer to discuss anything rather than the poetry as such. In men such as Bentley or Dr Freind, he saw a similar commitment to the world of letters without any vital engagement in the human and moral qualities which books existed to proclaim. The new 'professionals', second sense, are therefore men with a positive vocation – unlike the opportunistic hack. On the other hand, their cultural interests are as it were contingent. They do not necessarily possess, and Pope contends they generally *will* not possess, the deep personal attachment to good writing which the true poet or true critic must nurture. They will respect neither the mystery of the craft nor the spiritual value of the art. Seen in this light, Pope's attitude is very far from the mere 'amateur' snobbery which Austin Warren's comments might suggest. His exclusiveness is dictated not by the new social structure as such, but by the cultural process of which a powerful secular middle class is but a symptom.

Oldmixon is the first kind of professional, hardly the second. His pretensions as a historian and as a full-dress critic, for example, do not quite constitute the unsubstantiated claim for literary status which I have been describing. The case is clearer, perhaps, with Cibber. The latter's birthday odes are venial, comparatively: hack-like effusions proper to that removed *banlieu* of Grub Street assigned by royal will to the laureate. Against this, his pronouncements as a man of the theatre, or his solemn autobiographical meanderings, stand out as just targets of satire. Pope dislikes something we have long taken for granted: the fact that books are attended to less for intrinsic merit than for the cultural stance of the author, his role in the social system which encloses the world of letters.

That Pope despised Oldmixon as a party hack, according to Sutherland's formulation, is true enough. Again, however, the issue is larger than the simple recognition that Oldmixon accepted the programme of a given political group and set out to defame its opponents. Nor is the economic factor strongly present here – it is doubtful if Oldmixon got much reward for the majority of his Whiggish polemics. To an extent Pope scorns the mercenary, *ipso facto*, and sees the 'professional' (first sense) party writer as corrupted by financial necessity.[41] More significantly, he recognises a form which of its nature makes for infractions of literary decorum. The virulence of Oldmixon's writing is an emblem of his commitment, one might say his avocation, against art. That he should (as Pope believed) have put his pen out to hire was a further symptom of his corruption, and not its efficient cause.

What then, concretely, did Oldmixon do to earn Pope's opposition? The factors may be roughly divided into two categories, biographic and literary. Under the first head, a number of items spring readily to mind. Oldmixon had never been to a university – it was a frequent jibe by controversialists ranged against him – and had expressed a good deal of contempt for such institutions. Pope, much as he execrated pedantry, the learned lumber of those who stayed too long, had the uncritical respect for conventional education which only someone deprived of its benefits could maintain. Oldmixon was a provincial by background, but he soon became associated with the world of London garrets and commercial life.[42] Even when he left London again in middle life, he did so not for the sake of rural retirement but as a minor government functionary in a distant, rather unlovely country town. Again, he had been brought up in the household of a dissenting merchant. Pope's feelings towards trade were ambiguous rather than hostile; but his own rather similar background (in one way) made him less worshipful of self-made magnates of the City. In addition to holding an unimposing post in government service, Oldmixon acted as an informer for the ministry with respect to alleged Jacobite plots. If Pope by any chance came to know of this, his dislike for Oldmixon would have grown. There is little doubt that he shared Swift's prejudice against this activity, manifested both in *Gulliver's Travels* and in the celebrated published letter to Pope (10 January 1721), where there is reference to 'the whole Tribe of Informers, the most accursed, and prostitute, and abandoned race, that God ever permitted to plague mankind.'[43] Oldmixon committed other misdemeanours. It is doubtful whether his sturdy loyalty to men like Maynwaring meant much to Pope, and his temporary allegiance to the Duke of Chandos was in too menial a capacity to infect him with Timon's vices. On the other hand his indiscriminate support for all varieties of Whig must have struck Pope as eccentric as well as misguided. In the first few years of George I's reign, for example, Oldmixon dedicated with equal fluency to Sunderland, Cadogan and other Marlbrugians on the one hand, and Walpole, Argyll and the Prince of Wales on the other.[44] If it was a way of hedging his bets, it proved conspicuously unsuccessful. Later on, Oldmixon did obtain a small favour from Walpole, through the intercession of Queen Caroline and James Johnston (cordially disliked by his Twickenham neighbour). Pope may have believed that Oldmixon was one of Walpole's band of hired writers, but almost certainly this was not so. Throughout his life Oldmixon found his patrons in men who had incurred Pope's satire at one time or another – George Duckett [?], George Dodington, William Benson, Walpole and others.[45] It is true that he also addressed work to Cobham, recipient of a more distinguished epistle from Pope's hand; and to the Duchess of Marlborough, with whom Pope was on good terms towards the end of his life. It remains the case that the lifelong exercise in patron-hunting which Oldmixon's circumstances demanded gave Pope an excellent opportunity to get him into *The Dunciad* – if excuse were needed.

On the literary side, two main classes of misdemeanour may be distinguished. Firstly there are direct personal affronts to Pope and his circle of friends. These include the publication of Pope's tavern piece in Oldmixon's miscellany of 1714; the unauthorised issue of *Court Poems*; the ballad, *The Catholick Poet*;[46] the assault on Pope in *The Arts of Logick and Rhetorick*; the riposte to *Peri Bathous* printed in the *Flying Post*; and a number of incidental references. In addition, Oldmixon kept up a running attack on Swift in the period when Pope first made the latter's acquaintance – beginning with the *Medley*, and moving on to such pamphlets as *Reflections on Dr Swift's Letter*, *Remarks upon Remarks*, and so on. Bolingbroke invariably comes in for savage treatment at the hands of Oldmixon. Gay, Prior, Atterbury and several members of the Harley family suffered equally from Oldmixon's shrill invective. Pope would doubtless consider Oldmixon to have been guilty of an especially vile and unmanly slander in his accusations against the aged and exiled Bishop of Rochester. Oldmixon brushed more lightly with Lord Lansdowne, 'Granville the Polite'. It must be confessed that so pugnacious a man as Oldmixon was bound to clash with many whom Pope respected, at one period or another in his long career; as a matter of fact, he also fell foul of several individuals whom Pope reviled with equal warmth. Despite that, we may justifiably conclude that the balance of 'personal' controversy totted up to a heavy adverse sum in Oldmixon's ledger. And Pope, like many book-keepers, was better at remembering the identity of debtors than those of creditors.

Secondly, there are the more general offences. Oldmixon attempted a number of high literary forms, such as pastoral, without the equipment for such exacting creative undertakings. He chanced to embark on a number of enterprises Pope was later to make central to his own achievement. Worse, he participated in a collective version of Ovid in which Pope had a share. Oldmixon sought the dignity of prestigious literary company without the proper credentials: he not only sought Jacob Tonson's aid in his bid to become Poet Laureate (which Pope must have found a good joke) but actually wanted

Tonson to bring out a volume of his own miscellaneous work – for all the world, as if he had been Matthew Prior![47] On the other hand, he debased the weighty historiographic kind by his violent and partisan volumes. These histories were also very bulky folios, which Pope would have seen as a triumph of pedantic Dulness in itself.[48]

However, Oldmixon committed at one and the same time errors of a directly opposite sort. He practised low and venal modes of authorial enterprise. Oldmixon was not merely the 'hypercritical Historian' introduced in the 'Testimonies of Authors', prefaced to *The Dunciad*. He was also a specialist in secret history, a form given some vague classical precedent by Procopius, but by this time hopelessly degraded in polite literary circles. (Swift alludes to the 'Roguery and Insolence' of those who practised the form.) In the first place, Swift and Gay were to satirise the notion of 'secrecy' as a political necessity, equating this quality with low cunning.[49] More particularly, secret history had come to mean scandalous accounts of private caballing, hole-and-corner intrigue, backstairs diplomacy. No one could deny that Oldmixon's pages contain a good deal of these things. When we recall Swift's contempt for 'arcana' of every sort, it is amusing to note Oldmixon's serious use of the word in the title of *Arcana Gallica* (1714). Two related genres were those of political allegory, exemplified by *The Court of Atalantis*, and of the instant biography. The view which the Scriblerians took of these 'new terrors of death' needs no rehearsal here. It might, however, be recalled that Cleland's 'Letter to the Publisher' contains this passage:

> Then I thought . . . that it was an act of justice to detect the Author's not only on this account [i.e. their having previously attacked Pope], but as many of them are the same . . . whose prostituted papers (for one or other Party, in the unhappy Divisions of their Country) have insulted the Fallen, the Friendless, the Exil'd, and the Dead.[50]

Oldmixon was ready enough to attack all these categories; he had recommended in *The False Steps of the Ministry* (1714) harsh reprisals against the fallen ministry, and warned against over-leniency. He had not minced words in describing the conduct of Bolingbroke and Atterbury. His insults to the dead were many; and they possibly included, for Pope, his 'memoirs' of leading figures in politics or literature who had gone to their grave. At this date we can identify only three such books with complete confidence: the lives of Maynwaring, Wharton and Somers. The fact that Pope held a poor opinion of the first, and doubtless shared Swift's views with regard to the second, would scarcely influence his attitude to the scurrility of the genre. In addition, the second Earl of Oxford thought Oldmixon had written a life of Halifax, and though this is uncertain Pope is likely to have accepted any such ascription by his friend. There are the memoirs of Congreve, often attributed to Oldmixon with some show of plausibility. And lastly there is the 'Conduct' of the Earl of Nottingham, which was suspended before publication and of which Pope somehow got wind.[51] The evidence makes it certain that the Scriblerian group would think of Oldmixon as a leading practitioner of that Curllian branch of literature they so heartily despised: partly because they feared at some future date to constitute themselves the occasion of such a work.

Other crimes of this sort can be detected. By 1728 Oldmixon was well known as a professional critic: hence his new role in the revised *Dunciad*. This was in any case a very dubious vocation. We can gauge from *A Tale of a Tub* and 'On Poetry: A Rapsody', what Swift thought of this parasitic activity.[52] Moreover Oldmixon had inevitably put himself in a succession of notorious Dulness. As far as Pope and other contemporaries were concerned, the 'critic' connoted less than Dryden than Rymer, Dennis, Gildon. The rhetorical needs of *The Dunciad* prompted the substitution of Oldmixon for Dennis in the revised text. But the dramatic *rightness* of this change partly issues from the fact that such a substitution had already, historically, occurred. Oldmixon *had* taken over from the departed Dennis as 'senior critic' of the nation. It was almost as if Cibber, to augment his earlier crimes, had actually produced an edition of Shakespeare, the better to fit Theobald's shoes. A Dunce might appeal against the findings of *The Dunciad*, in so far as they represented his capers in an unfriendly or misleading light. He might not appeal against historical fact. That was part of the strength of Pope's position. Hence the importance of his original 'casting' procedure.

Finally, it is worth noting that Oldmixon's ambitions had undergone a steady atrophy. He had begun as a lyric poet and dramatist composer of pastorals, Anacreontics, versions of Boileau, funeral idylls and the like. He had intervened in the Collier controversy on the side of the champions of polite letters, notably Congreve and Vanbrugh. By the 1720's his creative urge was all but spent. Now he was seen as a compiler, an historical drudge, an indexer (a sphere of his activity his opponents liked to stress), and a publisher of other men's works – openly, as with Maynwaring, or surreptitiously, as with *Court Poems*. Even a bad tragedian could claim a certain kind of status. Even a purveyor of that abhorred form, the opera, required a certain kind of 'original' gift. But the party hack, the journalist, the editor of literary miscellanies, the compiler of keys, the abridger of Daniel's chronicle: this was quite a different matter. The point is put, lightheartedly to be sure, in a letter from Pope to Caryll in 1722:

> I must again sincerely protest to you, that I have wholly given over scribbling, at least any thing of my own, but am become, by due gradation of dulness, from a poet a translator, and from a translator, a mere editor.[53]

The tone is amused and mock-regretful. But there is a serious element underlying it all: Pope's genuine sorrow, and guilt, on realising that the best years of his life have been given over to secondary pursuits, whether the version of Homer or the edition of Buckinghamshire. His real mission in life has not been accomplished; his highest literary appetencies have not been satisfied. Tomorrow he must go off and write Essays on Man. This serious application is focused in the phrase 'due gradations of dulness'. There *was* a duncely career, a typical life-cycle embracing high initial aspirations, gradual disenchantment, acquiesence first in the mediocre and then in the downright venal. Oldmixon embodies, in his own biography, the stages of such a descent into Dulness. His progressive tropism away from creative writing and towards compilation exemplifies the 'due gradations' which Pope observes.

Crime and Punishment

Clearly there were other factors, less narrowly personal. A Dunce was convicted partly on the evidence of guilt by association. It was accordingly very unlucky for Oldmixon that he was inextricably linked with the Grub Street milieu. Pope had done a good deal himself to see that this was so. In 1716 he had portrayed Oldmixon as one of the 'beggarly brood' of Curll's authors. Two effective pamphlets had juxtaposed Oldmixon's name with that of Gildon and Sewell.[54] Moreover, crushingly explicit directions had been given concerning the habitation of these writers, so that the reader was left in no doubt as to the disreputable locality or the seamy mode of life which went on there. Once again there was a kind of feedback effect. Oldmixon was presented as a needy hack, surrounded by dissolute and grovelling creatures who were terrorised by their master Curll. The picture took on life; and Oldmixon found his reputation lowered, not only with the reading public, but also among his potential employers, the bookselling trade. As we shall see in a moment, it was in any case a grievous blow to a writer to find himself publicly branded as a tool of such scurrilous publishers as Curll. The combined effect of this process was to *ensure* that Oldmixon should increasingly be limited in his literary opportunities. He was, so to speak, the victim of Pope's self-fullfilling prophecy.

To be forcibly enlisted into this 'Rabble Rout of Writers' (Ayre's phrase) carried with it various implications. Pope stressed the internecine battles of the Dunces: their irresistible urge to combat; the fact that they feed on personal abuse, and cannot live in any other element. According to George Sherburn, such men were libellers by avocation: invective was their automatic response in any situation:

When we get to Curll, Oldmixon, and possibly Gildon, we have reached the hireling class, who had no personal acquaintance with Pope and who wrote simply for their daily bread . . . Because of their lack of social position and their lack of much personal knowledge of Pope, their venal quills were recklessly abusive and untruthful.[55]

This perhaps overstates the case. Literally it cannot be shown that Pope was personally a stranger to Curll or Oldmixon. They had a good many acquaintances in common, and in the narrow world of literary London it is possible that Pope came into contact with both men several years before the episode of the emetic. It is also noteworthy that Pope somehow came to know of the suppressed 'Conduct' of Nottingham – an event so private that Pope's allusion has never been explained hitherto.[56] However, details aside, the analysis Sherburn provides is valuable in throwing light on Pope's *poetic* procedures. On the whole he liked to have the Dunces throw dirt at one another. He took advantage of their natural propensity to quarrel,[57] and dramatised this by the fictional device of the contests in Book II. This method suited his purposes, in that it appeared to leave his own hands clean. Part of Pope's design was to give the impression that he was simply *recording*, and not devising, the grotesque antics of Duncehood. He sought to distance himself from the proceedings, and ostentatiously proclaimed his own lack of first-hand acquaintance with the objects of his satire. Witness the 'Advertisement' to the poem:

> In some Articles, it was thought sufficient barely to transcribe from *Jacob*, *Curl*, and other writers of their own rank, who were much better acquainted with them than any of the Authors of this Comment [i.e. Commentary] can pretend to be. Most of them had drawn each other's Characters on certain occasions; but the few here inserted, are all that could be saved from the general destruction of such Works.[58]

Once again Pope contrives to suggest that the Dunces are constantly at loggerheads with one another. It becomes almost an act of kindness on his part to protract the fragile existence of their productions by quoting from them in his notes to the poem. Pope was uneasy at one time concerning the role allotted to Thomas Cooke, author of *The Battle of the Poets*. Cooke's letters of private apology brought no respite in the Variorum *Dunciad*; but they did occasion a statement of Pope's views in a letter to Samuel Wesley.[59] In general, however, he had little direct traffic with his Dunces (Savage probably gave him such firsthand information of Grub Street as he possessed).[60] Their backbiting pamphlets were merely *used* as evidence of their warlike disposition. With typical economy Pope forces the Dunce to convict himself out of his own mouth, whilst the author himself remains seemingly detached.

Along with belligerence went a taste for faction, something Swift emphasises in his *Tale*. Pride, obscurantism, apostasy, plagiarism, ignorance and scurrility are qualities which follow not far behind: all are anatomised in the *Tale*.[61] In addition, Dulness has the power of intensifying a defect. It magnifies a vice and brings latent faults into sudden combustible life, like a burning glass. Thus the *Essay on Criticism*:

> No Pardon vile *Obscenity* should find,
> Tho' *Wit* and *Art* conspire to move your Mind;
> But *Dulness* with *Obscenity* must prove
> As Shameful sure as *Impotence* in *Love*.[62]

(Pope typically makes his point about obscenity with a slightly risqué simile.) Most of these flaws are associated with the practice of criticism, as in *The Battle of the Books*: which made it surer than ever that Oldmixon had it coming. In its narrow literary aspect, as in the wider philosophic context of Book IV of *The Dunciad*, it is characteristic of Dulness to attempt sublimity and achieve bathos. The hack aspires above his proper level, in the very choice of form and in his putative models. Again Oldmixon was fair game. His elective affinities were to be with Bouhours, Addison, de Thou and Rapin. The effects he achieved, Pope indicates, were those of Gildon, Dennis and Welsted.

The recent flowering in our scholarly knowledge of *The Dunciad* – its background and its method – has meant that we have now before us a long list of duncely characteristics. Mostly these definitions concentrate on what might be termed the metaphysical aspects of Duncehood; they tend to draw their supporting evidence from the last book, and they accept Courthope's view that the term connotes 'every sort of rebellion against right reason and good taste'.[63] I need select only a brief sample of representative comments. Alvin Kernan emphasises the optimism of the creed: 'Marching under the banner of progress, dullness is always incurably optimistic about its ability to rework nature into a brave new world and to make itself over in the image of its own desire.' The same critic draws attention to what he calls the 'energy of dullness', and makes apposite reference to the note at line 15 of Book I (1743 ed.).[64] This is the fullest statement we have on the point, with any authorial sanction; surprisingly, comparatively little has been made of the passage:

> 15. *Laborious, heavy, busy, bold, &c.*] I wonder the learned Scriblerus has omitted to advertise the Reader, at the opening of this Poem, that Dulness here is not to be taken contractedly for mere Stupidity, but in the enlarged sense of the word, for all Slowness of Apprehension, Shortness of Sight, or imperfect Sense of things. It includes (as we see by the Poet's own words) Labour, Industry, and some degree of Activity and Boldness: a ruling principle not inert, but turning topsy-turvy the Understanding, and inducing an Anarchy or confused State of Mind. This remark ought to be carried along with the reader throughout the work; and without this caution he will be apt to mistake the Importance of many of the Characters, as well as of the Design of the Poet. Hence it is that some have complained he chuses too mean a subject, and imagined he employs himself, like Domitian, in killing flies; whereas those who have the true key will find he sports with nobler quarry, and embraces a larger compass; or (as one saith, on a like occasion)
>
> > Will see his Work, like Jacob's ladder, rise,
> > Its foot in dirt, its head amid the skies. BENTL.

As Martin Price observes, 'All this energy is perfectly consonant with a moral inertia.'[65] The activity of Duncehood is non-functional, purposeless, finally inhumane. Whilst a man is not on his oath in impersonating Bentley (and, for a moment, proleptically, Coleridge – 'a ruling principle not inert') we may fairly take this as Pope's own considered view.

Another influential reading has been that of Thomas Edwards. He isolates a similar phenomenon, which he calls the 'entropy' of Dulness. Its aim, he suggests, is 'sameness, the utter absence of differentiation that makes order possible.'[66] Austin Warren had earlier identified just this deadening, narcotic power of Dulness, when he said that the poem, 'a kind of anti-masque, is a series of ritual tableaux and pageants and processions, chiefly sluggish of movement and visually dusky.' For Edwards, Pope's work is marked by an 'increasing willingness to disturb the dramatic propriety of his poems.' If this means that the rhetorical purposes wrench the means from their easygoing placidity ('There comes a time when urbanity cannot deal with evil'), I agree. But if the implication is that the choreographed sequence, so well described by Warren, is acted out behind masks – that all Dunces are, in a word, faceless – then I believe the judgment will not stand unqualified. There is a pervasive ambiguity surrounding the poem: H. H. Erskine-Hill speaks of 'a double response' on Pope's part to the world he has created: 'A response which could at once deplore such a world, and yet endow it with surrealistic strangeness, grandeur or beauty.'[67] Yet in many ways no satiric target, or series of targets, could be more clearcut than the line of contortionists and clowns who parade before us. Part of the seductive appeal of Dulness lies in the fact that its avatars are so unselfconsciously, so solipsistically, so splendidly *themselves*. The Dunces, unlike poor aspiring humanity at large, can imagine no other existence – certainly no higher existence – than their own. Once more this rooted quality in Pope's victims can be related to their historical dimension. A Dunce is a Dunce, largely because he is a specified and identifiable figure in the first place.

I said just now that the representatives of Dulness were guilty of solipsism. This is an important consideration for both Pope and Swift. The last book of *The Dunciad* could be read as a conducted tour of the new literary world,[68] where communication has broken down and the 'uncreating Word' holds sway:

> 'Tis true, on Words is still our whole debate . . . (B.IV.219)

In the same way, the hack-narrator of *A Tale of a Tub* has lost touch with the social function of literature, treasured so jealously by the humanist tradition. Speech is speech *to* nobody; the hack doesn't require an audience at all. His vein is self-expression. Where Pope and Swift see the work of art as an object to be fashioned carefully to achieve a set rhetorical end, the new men of letters are interested only in giving rein to their own vapid sentiments. A Dunce embodies in his nature the fault of pride or self-sufficiency:

> Find, Virtue local, all Relation scorn,
> See all in *Self*, and but for self be born. (B.IV.479)

In just the same way, he embodies in his literary technique a dis-regard for the public duties of a writer. His compositions will be non-functional, private, self-enclosed.

Linguistic decay was another, more concrete ground for Pope's fears. Swift had deplored in many places 'the ignorance and caprice' which had permitted corruption of the language to set in. He was also to make Simon Wagstaff, in the introduction to *Polite Conversation*, commend 'those two illustrious Writers, Mr *Ozel*, and Captain *Stevens*':[69]

> These, and some others of distinguished Eminence, in whose Company I have passed so many agreeable Hours, as they have been the great Refiners of our Language, so it hath been my chief Ambition to imi-tate them. Let the *Popes*, the *Gays*, the *Arbuthnots*, the *Youngs*, and all the rest of that snarling Brood burst with Envy at the Praises we re-ceive from the Court and Kingdom.[70]

That there was a connection between ignorance, the invariable mark of the mercenary hack, and such linguistic decay. Swift had alleged as early as 1710, in his *Tatler* paper 'On Corruptions of Style': 'These Two Evils, Ignorance and Want of Taste, have produced a Third; I mean, the continual Corruption of our English tongue . . .'[71] Swift goes on to speak of 'false Refinements' now in vogue: the sort that Ozell or Stevens might perpetrate in the delusion that they were adding beauty to their style. Pope would have agreed. A Dunce is a man who cannot control or even understand the workings of language – the very medium he professes to employ. He is a servant of litera-ture whose practice threatens the very existence of literature: a user of English whose barbarian style heralds the demise of English as an instrument of thought.

This aspect of Dulness has taken us into less metaphysical regions, and it might be appropriate to consider some of the more down-to-earth associations the word has. Miriam Starkman, after noting the startling heterogeneity of Swift's victims in the *Tale* (Bentley and L'Estrange lying side by side), goes on to contend that 'as Swift uses the term Grub Street, it is pejorative rather than descriptive.'[72] I am not convinced this is wholly accurate with regard to Swift. Applied to Pope, it would certainly be no better than a half-truth. For Grub

Street does have a physical presence in his work. The entire *mise-en-scène* of *The Dunciad* is designed to bring before us the human geography of Dulness. Its fondness for malodorous, squalid surroundings; its connections with the City and mercantile affairs generally; its desperate ambitions to rise in the world, and to spread its infective presence into the West End; its dependence on one particular trade, the illiberal and ungentlemanly pursuit of bookselling; its delight in low-life jollity; its indecency – all these and many other facets are made plain. I should contend that the poem constitutes, amongst its many other artistic tasks, a sociological report on the conditions of Dulness; and, further, that this imaginative account draws a good deal of its vigour and immediacy from its basis in the social ecology of *real* men at this time. I do not assert, of course, that the day-to-day life of a professional writer exactly resembled the series of events enacted in the poem. For one thing, the duncely goings-on there are occasioned by the fact that it is a holiday, the Lord Mayor's Feast day to be precise. (How appropriate that the festival of Dunces should be the one kept by the trading community at large!) But I do believe that there is a broad imaginative link.

One of the features which has most bothered critics and readers of Pope has been the issue of poverty. As stated earlier, Hugo Reichard has written most illuminatingly on this issue.[73] But a few things more may be said. First of all, we should note Swift's considered statement at the start of *The Battle of the Books*:

> Whoever examines with due Circumspection into the *Annual Records of Time* will find it remarked, that *War is the Child* of *Pride*, and *Pride the Daughter of Riches*. The former of which Assertions may soon be granted, but one cannot so easily subscribe to the latter; the *Pride* is nearly related to Beggary and Want, either by Father or Mother, and sometimes by both; And, to speak naturally, it very seldom happens among men to fall out, when all have enough; Invasions usually travelling from *North* to *South*, that is to say from Poverty upon Plenty.[74]

The relevance of this for Swift's immediate tactical purposes is easy to see: the quarrelsome Moderns will pick a fight out of envy and intellectual penury. But the formula 'pride is nearly related to beggary and want' applies more generally. Looked at from the other end, it suggests 'Poverty leads to, entails even, pride.' I do not think, therefore, that we can wholly accept Aubrey Williams's view that poverty is often seen as a mitigating factor. Williams is thinking of such notes as that at A.II.270:

> Our indulgent Poet, whenever he has spoken of any dirty or low work, constantly puts us in mind of the Poverty of the offenders, as the only extenuation of such practices. Let any one but remark, when a Thief, a Pickpocket, a Highwayman or a Knight of the Post is spoken of, how much our hatred to those characters is lessen'd, if they add, a needy Thief, a *poor* pickpocket, a *hungry* Highwayman, a *starving* Knight of the Post, &c.

He comments that such a reference 'further embarrasses the position of the dunces, but it does so in terms which also extenuate their deeds.'[75] I am unable to see any lightening of the load at all here. Pope supplies the very obvious innuendo that he has himself been speaking of needy rogues, literary pickpockets and so on; and any apparent 'extenuation' is purely nominal. Pope's basic point seems to me, on the contrary, toughminded – almost brutally so. We often regard poverty as a mitigating factor, he says, but in fact it is one of the main symptoms of wrong-doing. It is in the nature of a thief to be needy; he cannot by definition make his living in any worthy manner. Similarly, poverty is the proper livery of Dulness, since Dulness is but literary vagabondage.

'If Poverty be a Title to Poetry,' says the Beggar in Gay's *Opera*, 'I am sure Nobody can dispute mine.' Pope accepts the implications of this proverbial saw. He sees a measure of indigence as the necessary, not merely the contingent, accompaniment of the life of a professional writer. According to Reichard, 'rags implicate morals more than caste' in *The Dunciad*.[76] The truth is perhaps that both are implicated (or indeed *implied*, if that is what Reichard means.) A starveling writer in the poem, to be sure, inhabits a morally questionable district. But he also inhabits a district which is socially and economically inferior, as the whole fiction serves to bring out. One of the key metaphors of the poem, round which both plot and idiom gravitate, is that of *infection*. The Fleet Ditch is an emblem of the contagious effect of Dulness:

> . . . To where Fleet-ditch with disemboguing streams
> Rolls the large tribute of dead dogs to Thames,
> The King of Dykes! than whom, no sluice of mud
> With deeper sable blots the silver flood. (A.II.259)

This corrupting power has its agents, who are the Dunces: and it is central to Pope's dialectic that they live sordid and ill-regulated lives. Their surroundings are insanitary; their habits are filthy; their privacy is minimal; their public behaviour is shamelessly obscene. All these are characteristic of the lowest social classes, the derelicts who inhabit our modern twilight areas as much as the pariahs who wander *The Dunciad*. Nor is evidence of this fact confined to the games in Book II, though the mud-diving and urinating contests obviously supply a good deal of it. To compete in order to find out 'who the most in love of dirt excel' is surely to indicate one's social caste, apart from anything else. But elsewhere in the poem we get plenty of hints as to the social condition of Dulness:

> Where wave the tatter'd ensigns of Rag-Fair,
> A yawning ruin hangs and nods in air;
> Keen, hollow winds howl thro' the bleak recess,
> Emblem of Music caus'd by Emptiness:
> Here in one bed two shiv'ring sisters lye,
> The Cave of Poverty and Poetry. (A.I.27)

'Music caus'd by Emptiness' – there is duncely utterance epitomised. The noise and clatter they all make, often stressed by Pope, proceed from their empty bellies. Poverty *is* a salient expression of Duncehood. Swift wrote to Pope when he had received *The Dunciad* that the Dublin edition in octavo had 'sold wonderfully, considering our poverty, and dulness, the consequence of it.'[77] Similarly, Savage (at this time among Pope's closer associates) wrote of John Dennis that he was:

> Secure in dulness, madness, want, and age.

If you were in want, then, your chances of recognition as a Dunce were perceptibly increased. Pope might wish you a dinner, and sit still (for a while). He might even, as a benevolent man, write a prologue for your benefit concert. But he would not impair his poetic integrity by striking your name off the role of Dunces. Dickens could afford to be kind to individuals when he had caused them pain by his fictional representations of their life. Pope dare not relent: individuals around him were the stuff of his art.

The position of the bookselling trade requires a few words to itself. Ian Watt has written so well on this topic that little beyond marginal gloss is required. He quotes a letter from George Cheyne to Samuel Richardson, alleging that 'all booksellers I fear are Curlls by profession.'[78] So it must have seemed to Pope and his circle. Gay wrote to him at the time of *The Dunciad*, 'All I could hear of you of late hath been by advertisements in the news-papers, by which one wou'd think the race of Curls was multiplied.'[79] For the Scriblerians, bookselling was of its nature a mechanical occupation. That a few individuals approaching gentlemanly respectability carried it on (such as Jacob Tonson sen.) was an accident. The typical product of the trade was, in Watt's description, the 'scandalous contemporary memoir, biography or secret history, especially that which took the form of the unauthorised publication of private letters'.[80] Now Oldmixon was a leading exponent of all three duncely genres set out here; and in addition he published a poem of Pope's without authority. But Oldmixon's sometime employer, Curll, was an even bigger threat. As Swift had written to Pope as far back as 1716:

> . . . However, I will grant, that one thorough book-selling Rogue is better qualified to vex an author, than all his cotemporary scriblers in Critick or Satire, not only by stolen Copies of what was incorrect or unfit for the publick, but by downright laying other mens dulness at your door. I had a long design upon the ears of that Curl, when I was in credit, but the rogue would never allow me a fair stroke at them, though my penknife was ready and sharp.[81]

'Downright laying other mens dulness at your door' – it is a significant phrase. A hack writer can spread abroad his pestilential influence in his books and pamphlets. But a bookseller is not only the author of Dulness in his own person, he can father the disease on to others. If, as I suggested, the image of contagious fever, *plague*, is central to *The Dunciad*, it is easily apparent how such a capacity would mark the bookseller out for special obloquy. In real life, as Professor Watt indicates, Pope devised strategems to circumvent this dependence on an illiberal profession he despised. In the fictive life of his poem, he devised rhetorical stratagems to ensure that not only Curll, but also 'Mears, Warner, Wilkins', Mist, Osborne, Dunton *et al.* stand at the centre of the picture. The nature of Curll's pre-eminence is left in no doubt: 'Still happy Impudence obtains the prize.' (A.II.178.) A bookseller, in short, was an *ex officio* Dunce.

Briefer mention may be made of certain characteristics found in the breed at large. The City connections of the Dunce shade into a Whiggish hue, often detected by the Tory satirists. When Bays, in the first book of the revised version, is debating whether to betake himself to the church, to gaming or to party-writing, he lets fall a revealing momentary idea:

Dulness! whose good old cause I yet defend . . . (B.I.165)

Now Pope does not explicitly say that Duncehood goes with Whiggery; but there is certainly a hint to that effect. The old enthusiastic breed of republicans, puritans, covenanters and other concealed enemies of the nation are indicated as the sort of men likely to be ensnared by Queen Dulness. Her votaries are the heirs of Achitophel; they are the dupes of Oliver Cromwell, who later whistled the foolish tune of 'Lilliburlero' at Thomas Wharton's bidding. Secondly, a Dunce is likely to be socially ambitious, at least in his own sphere. He will aspire to the Laureateship, an office for which (so Swift told Gay) the heroes of Pope's poem fell into contention, on Eusden's death in 1730.[82] Once again John Oldmixon had marked himself out as a suitable recipient of the accolade.[83] Lastly, the Dunce is likely to be a professional 'Answerer' of the kind marked out in *A Tale of a Tub*. He will, for instance, attempt to pay back Pope in his own coin, however unsuitable his qualifications. Like John Dennis, he will contend that Pope (not Theobald) should be 'advanced to the Throne [of Dulness] by Right Hereditary and Right of Merit'.[84] Like Charles Johnson, he will dispute Pope's claim to literary dictatorship.[85] Like John Oldmixon, he will occasion ridicule by attempting to rival Pope by an *Essay on Criticism* or a projected treatise 'On the Art of Sinking in Reputation'. The Dunce's readiness to do these things springs partly from his lifelong vocational commitment to the 'countercheck quarrelsome'.

Background and Biography

I have set out two main arguments. The first is that the identity of the specific authors pilloried in *The Dunciad* is of some importance. This fact colours the entire poem, and affects the artistic working at several points. Secondly, that the social ecology of Dulness is filled in with care and relish. Putting these two contentions together, it would be logical to expect that the actual life-histories of prominent Dunces would display many features in common with those just described. We should anticipate a characteristic duncely milieu, in real life as well as within the poem. We should look for a pattern of literary and personal experiences analogous with that I have just attributed to the Dunce. And we should be ready to find a criminal biography to match, in broad outline, the charge-sheet drawn up by Pope in *The Dunciad*.

In fact, I believe that these expectations can be fulfilled. Naturally, Pope heightens the iniquity of his chosen malefactors; he telescopes their careers and takes a long series of crimes into consideration at the same hearing. Nevertheless, a profile can be drawn with some accuracy; and the features fit those of known individuals with astonishing regularity. This has been obscured hitherto by the dearth of solid research on smaller figures in the Augustan literary landscape. However, scholarly biographies do exist in the case of Dunces like Susanna Centlivre, Leonard Welsted, John Dennis, Aaron Hill, Ned Ward, Lewis Theobald and Eliza Haywood. This compensates to some extent for the disappointing shortage of work on Gildon, Arnall, Ralph and others (although in some cases unpublished theses are available here). On the basis of such biographies, together with standard works of reference, I have assembled a number of observations on Duncehood in action.

The typical background for the hack is not, as might be expected, a deprived childhood. Some professional writers had known penury all their lives, but more came into the occupation as their social and financial circumstances *were declining*. Peter Motteux was a Huguenot refugee;[86] otherwise it is hard to think of a writer of his standing who did not enjoy a more fortunate boyhood than that of Matthew Prior. Few of the writers satirised in *The Dunciad* suffered from a home background as disturbed as Swift's, or as persecuted as Pope's. It is true, as we shall see, that in many cases the Dunce was born into a family already losing caste. All the same, not even the most liberal criminologist would be able to find much evidence to suggest that men setting out on a life of literary law-breaking (to adopt Pope's viewpoint) could urge a broken home as their excuse. The truth is that the hack embraced poetry as a means of disgrace. Grub Street was a haven of the damned, rather as Calais became for nineteenth-century reprobates.

A few examples should suffice. Leonard Welsted came of good family; his father was a highly respectable clergyman, who (like his son) received his education at Westminster School, a breeding ground for poets and politicians alike. Welsted, like so many of his school-fellows, was intended for Trinity College, Cambridge; but he seems not to have proceeded there, perhaps owing to an early and imprudent marriage. Incidentally, his godfather was Thomas Stavely, a lawyer and historian. It is a solid middle-class background in every respect.[87] Secondly, consider the case of Lewis Theobald. His father was an attorney. (The dominance of the law in these biographies is a matter for comment.) Bred for the same profession, Theobald was educated privately at Isleworth. He first entered the literary world as a translator for Lintot, and soon gravitated to weekly journalism and pantomimic entertainments, both very dubious territories in Pope's estimation.[88] Next, there is Aaron Hill. He, too, was the son of an attorney; apparently a man of some substance, with definite pretensions to gentility. Unfortunately the lawyer's affairs miscarried and he became embarrassed financially. Just the same, young Aaron went to Barnstaple School (where John Gay was a schoolmate), and proceeded to Westminster. He then went on a tour of Turkey, an adventurous course at this time for one so young, and became that stock eighteenth-century equivalent of the governess in Victorian times: a tutor to a nobleman on the Grand Tour. Hill had at least one influential kinsman, Lord Paget, whose favour he sought with great assiduity. Subsequently he became secretary to the Earl of Peterborough, a friend of Pope and Swift.[89] John Dennis was another to serve as a tutor, this time for Lord Seymour. The son of a soldier, he had been educated at Harrow Grammar School and Caius College.[90] Oxford was the Alma Mater of Duncehood at large, however (only Bentley stands out as a conspicuous exception). It is more than a pun, rather a genuine imaginative connection in Pope's mind, which links the Alma Mater and the Magna Mater named in the very first line of the poem. At all events, hack writers like Tom Brown could be found who had been at Christ Church, along with more distinguished followers of literature. Brown's father was possibly a farmer, possibly a tanner; at the least, good yeoman stock, and the likelihood is, something better than that.[91] Colley Cibber was of course the son of a celebrated sculptor. His father had started out as a cabinet-maker; but he had achieved some notice from wealthy patrons by the time of Colley's birth, which took place in the fashionable quarter of Southampton Street. After a period at the free school in Grantham, Colley Cibber stood for election to Westminster, but was rejected. He then joined the forces of the Prince of Orange, but saw no action, and entered the household service of a peer. It was at this point that he took himself off to the life of an actor.[92]

In the case of the women, a less secure background is observable. This is natural: the opportunities for a single woman to climb an authorised professional ladder, in almost any field, were non-existent. As a result, for a woman to become prominent at all (unless she had exceptional advantages of birth) implied unconventionality. Susanna Centlivre started with more disadvantages, apart from her sex, than any of the other writers who have been mentioned. Both her parents died while she was still young. She had little formal education and started out as a strolling actress. Nor did her marriage – the one hope of a major improvement in status, for most women – give Mrs Centlivre any real social standing. The case is different with Mrs Haywood. She appears to have enjoyed a better education than most girls were permitted. Married by the age of twenty to a clergyman, a life of dull and onerous respectability stretched before her. After ten years of such constraint, she eloped, something I cannot find it in myself to deplore very strongly. She too became an actress, and then embarked on her successful and prolific career as a novelist.[93]

To these instances, two more may be added. Charles Gildon came of a good Catholic family, but again one declining in the world. According to Curll, it was Gildon whom Pope meant when he wrote in 1709 of one 'who is every way a Scoundrell but that he has the luck to be born a Gentleman'.[94] Gildon was the son of a member of Lincoln's Inn, studied at Douai; and married at twenty-three, having already lost the money he inherited. He early branched into miscellaneous writing, editing, compiling, performing the various functions allotted to a hack. He ended his life blind, poverty-stricken and resentful. Much the same is true of John Oldmixon. Possessor of an ancient lineage, he was unfortunate in that his father, who died when he was six, suffered a good deal of money troubles and may indeed have gone bankrupt. He was sent to live with his uncle, the prominent City trader Sir John Bawden, Alderman and Dissenter. Both his mother and his uncle died before he was sixteen; and henceforward he was on his own. The currency difficulties in the 1690's complicated matters further, and by the time he was twenty-five Oldmixon had been forced to sell his patrimonial estate, bearing the family name, near Weston-super-Mare. He had already commenced as an author; and from now on this distant kinsman of the Earl of Wharton was committed to making his livelihood by this means. (Though he evidently dabbled in trade for some years.) At first he attempted the politer forms, as mentioned; but within a few years he found his pen given over to historical compilation, periodical journalism, translation, biography, in a word hack-writing. The 'due gradations of dulness' had succeeded one another with mechanical regularity.[95]

These case histories do, I think, add up to strong evidence that there was a common pattern for the fulltime professional writers who were to be christened Dunce in later life. (The women present a slightly different picture.) Their origins are not especially humble, as a rule. The most frequently encountered background is a good middle-class home, sometimes with more aspirations to gentility than current affluence. Education is usually orthodox and thorough, and rarely differs markedly from that received by the distinguished men admitted to Pope's friendship (most members of the Harley family, for example, went to Westminster School). In the same way, it is seldom that we find a Dunce whose formative years were burdened by religious persecution or political vendettas: unlike Pope's own. A premature marriage and financial loss often combine to make matters worse – as with Defoe. The truth is that a Dunce only becomes a social pariah as a result of his misadventures in the literary profession. Once he has embarked on his writing career, all his personal disasters, marital misfortunes and social gaffes become relevant considerations. He is now a member of an insecure profession, whose incidental escapades the satirist can properly record. Indeed, the poet can put these mishaps into his fiction, suitably garnished and transmuted. Osborne did indeed compete unsuccessfully with Curll in shameless obscenity, as *The Dunciad* makes him do again. Oldmixon did indeed pay assiduous court to well-known patrons, who bestowed their largesse instead on stripling writers 'unknown to Phoebus'. It was a fact that rankled with him, before ever it got into *The Dunciad*. Cibber was indeed advanced to an eminence few had anticipated for him; he was indeed given to public capers, to unconcealed plagiary, and to the direction of literary entertainments. Once again we see that the fictional lines of the poem have been in part laid down by the facts of real life: which is not, of course, to say that they are determined by *realistic* considerations. The poem dramatises the ludicrous mishaps attendant on the hack's way of life. For farce is, in the context of satire, the most damning form of criticism.

Very few attempts have been made to consider the standing of Pope's victims in detail, under any aspect. W. L. Macdonald did carry out a rough count of Pope's friends and enemies,[96] characterising them by party affiliation and by headings such as 'Writers', 'Unclassified', and so on. The methodology was, confessedly, unsophisticated; and the value of the results may be gauged by noting that Steele and the Duchess of Marlborough are omitted, whilst many interesting relationships (e.g. with Hugh Bethel) are tamely deposited in the 'unclassified' section. None the less, Macdonald's table does illustrate the fact that Pope's satiric animus was by no means casually *dispersed* over society as a whole, regardless of its original motivation.

There is one final way in which Dulness could be illuminated. This would be by considering later applications of the term, in the work of writers who saw themselves, more or less optimistically, as carrying on Pope's battle for him. I shall not explore this approach at length, but notice three instances. Pope's protégé, Walter Harte, wrote an *Essay on Satire* (1730), possibly touched up by the great man. This includes the lines, 'True Dulness nods, reclining and reposed . . . Sense, grace, nor harmony, ne'er enter there,/Nor human faith, nor piety sincere.' Harte emphasises the gracelessness of the Dunce; his 'artistic' productions and his life exhibit the same angular, unlovely, charmless quality. Secondly, a better poet, Paul Whitehead, produced his *State Dunces* in 1733. This is a more imaginative development. Here the Dunces have gravitated to court, senate and drawing-room; to bench, bar and church. As Whitehead describes 'The big, Rich, mighty, Dunces of the State,' the picture grows almost as horrific as Pope's original vision of eternal night.[97]

Lastly, a brief look at Christopher Smart's *Hilliad* (1753). From the preface to this vigorous lampoon on the quack John Hill comes the following:

> For a clear vein of thinking, easy natural expression, and an intelligible style, this pretender [Hill] has substituted brisk question and answer, pert, unmeaning periods, ungrammatical construction, unnatural metaphors, with a profusion of epithets, inconsistent for the most part with the real or figurative meanings of his words, and in short all the masculine beauties of style are likely to be banished from among us by the continuation of his papers for almost two years together.

Hill, we are made aware, possesses all the 'constituent qualities . . . of the lesser Epic Hero . . . Vanity, Impudence, and Debauchery', on which Ricardus Aristarchus had insisted. (Note once more the mingling of literary and personal qualities.) Hill is charged by Smart with immorality and malice, and finally the complete bill is brought in: 'Pertness, dullness, scandal and malice, &c. being the very constituents of an hero for the mock heroic . . .' Smart proceeds to invoke the precise metaphor I have isolated as vital to the workings of *The Dunciad*: 'the rising generation will be totally infected . . .' Here the rhetorical procedures of *The Dunciad* live on with its spirit. How suitable that the attack should be carefully based on the known facts regarding a living individual.[98]

Duncehood was an honour to be won by many different routes. Most of the qualifying offences, however, were the special liability of professional authors; partly because of their actual undertakings in the world of letters, partly because of the position in society which such a career marked out for them. Swift wrote in his 'Rapsody' of the ambition to 'purchase fame by writing ill'.[99] This was what the Dunce initially did. But there were all sorts of ways in which he could compound his felony; and the structure of Pope's poem was flexible enough to allow the fictional line to be bent to accommodate a particular figure. That is part of the irony. To achieve social status through literary merit was not easy: the Scriblerians were amongst the few to manage it. But Duncehood, through Pope's kind offices, was a *carrière ouverte aux talents*.[100]

1. Quoted by L. I. Bredvold, *The Brave New World of the Enlightenment* (Ann Arbor, 1961), p. 106.
2. On Ralph's bid (apparently deliberate) to incur a hostile reference by Pope, see TE, V, 452.
3. *Poems and Translations*, ed. J. Oldmixon, p. 245. The work appeared in Hughes' posthumous *Poems on Several Occasions* (1735), II, 90: an edition to which Pope and (unknowingly) Swift subscribed.
4. Or provided by others under the aegis of Pope: a case in point is Richard Savage's *Author to be Let* (1729).
5. Sherburn, 'The *Dunciad*, Book IV', *SE*, XXIV(1944), 174–8; Williams, pp. 87–103 and passim; Thomas R. Edwards, jr., *This Dark Estate* (Berkeley/Los Angeles, 1963); Alvin Kernan, *The Plot of Satire* (New Haven, 1965); Hugo M. Reichard, 'Pope's Social Satire', *PMLA*, LXVII (1952), 420–34. All these studies except Williams's, are represented, either in full or in extract, in Maynard Mack (ed.), *Essential Articles for the Study of Alexander Pope* (New York, 1965), henceforth cited as 'Mack'.
6. It is important, of course, that we are not trapped by the useful analogy

with the stage. *The Dunciad* is, literally, a poem; and however many comparisons we may trace with a theatrical production, however many dramatic ingredients we may find embedded in its narrative, this residual *nondramatic* fact remains. Nevertheless I believe that Sherburn's essay, in particular, supplies a most valuable mode of entry into the workings of *The Dunciad*, which it would be churlish to forego on pedantic grounds of literary taxonomy.

7. Williams, pp. 62–70.

8. TE, V, xiv.

9. Oldmixon, for instance, had bestowed unflattering comments on Blackmore, Settle, Gildon, Ward, Durfey and others. Few, indeed, were more insistent on the reality and pervasiveness of Duncehood than other Dunces, anxious to exempt themselves from the general condemnation.

10. TE, V, xlv, 439.

11. Quoted by Sutherland, TE, V, xxxi.

12. On Norton Defoe, see TE, V, 437.

13. Edwards, in Mack, p. 177. See also *Peri Bathous*: Steeves, p. 24ff.

14. Reichard, in Mack, p. 692.

15. Cf. TE, V, xliv.

16. Highet, *The Anatomy of Satire* (Princeton/London, 1962), p. 17. Highet remarks that men like Ralph, Morris and Welsted are today 'quite unknown' to us. Logically, the question remains open whether in such circumstances we are fully equipped to understand the poetic effects Pope has designed, in their richest implication at any rate.

17. See Pope, *Correspondence*, II, 343, 504. On another occasion Swift wrote to Gay (*Correspondence*, II, 475), 'Why does Mr Pope not publish his dullness, the rogues he mawls will dy of themselves in peace, and So will his friends, and So there will be neither punishment nor reward'. See also Swift's *Poems*, p. 36; *Prose Works*, V, 201.

18. Pope, *Correspondence*, I, 358–9.

19. Pope, *Correspondence*, II, 332.

20. Pope, *Correspondence*, II, 334.

21. Tillotson, *On the Poetry of Pope* (London, 2nd ed., 1962), p. 35: Macdonald, *Pope and his Critics* (London, 1951), p. 67.

22. TE, V, 18 ('A Letter to the Publisher').

23. Pope, *Correspondence*, II, 481. The quotation is from the *Essay on Criticism*, l. 519 (Butt, p. 160).

24. Pope, *Correspondence*, II, 138–9. For an excellent statement of Pope's equation of 'hacks, Hanoverians and Low Churchmen', see Thomas Maresca *Pope's Horatian Poems* (Ohio, 1966), pp. 46–7.

25. R. K. Root (ed.), *The Dunciad Variorum* (Princeton, 1929), p. 21. It was, of course, tactically convenient to Pope and his supporters to have opponents

branded as a rabble of anonymous nincompoops, whose individual identity was of no serious interest. See William Ayre, *Memoirs of the Life of Alexander Pope* (London, 1745), I, 91; and Owen Ruffhead, *The Life of Alexander Pope Esq.* (London, 1769), p. 351.

26. *Dunciad*, A.I.244, II.162, B.II.323.

27. Tillotson, *Pope and Human Nature* (Oxford, 1958), p. 146.

28. *Dunciad*, A.I.240, II.115ff, II.230, B.I.146.

29. The trouble perhaps began when Oldmixon was permitted to join Pope among the translators of Ovid's *Heroides*, in Tonson's edition of 1712 (*Ovid's Epistles*, pp. 172–81).

30. *The Case of Authors by Trade and Profession* (1758), pp. 3–4n.

31. Ayre, I, 320–1.

32. Stephen, *Pope* (London, ed. 1909), p. 122.

33. Lounsbury, *The Text of Shakespeare* (London, 1906), pp. 208, 274.

34. TE, V, xxiii, 452.

35. See Oldmixon, *Memoirs of the Press* (1742), pp. 5, 50–1, 59, and passim.

36. Warren, *Alexander Pope as Critic and Humanist* (Princeton, 1929), p. 258.

37. See a letter of 1 June 1717, PRO SP 79/8.

38. Oldmixon, *Memoirs of Somers*, p. 3.

39. Watt, 'Publishers and Sinners: The Augustan View', *PBSA*, XII (1959), 3–20.

40. TE, V, xlvi.

41. Cf. *Dunciad*, B.IV.502.

42. For Oldmixon's resentment towards those who thought that 'Trade and Letters, were incompatible,' see *The British Empire in America* (2nd ed., 1741), II, 53–4: Oldmixon was evidently engaged in the West Indies shipping trade. For the importance of the rural/urban issue in religious affairs, see R. N. Stromberg, *Religious Liberalism in Eighteenth-Century England* (Oxford, 1954), p. 26n; for its relevance to politics, see J. H. Plumb, *The Growth of Political Stability* (London, 1967), p. 8.

43. Pope, *Correspondence*, II, 71. For Oldmixon as an informer, see PRO SP 35/15/119, 129; SP 35/16/16; SP 35/27/23, 59.

44. On divisions at court among the Whigs at this period, see J. M. Beattie, *The English Court in the Reign of George I* (Cambridge, 1967), p. 224ff.

45. For an MS version of the *Epistle to Arbuthnot* linking Duckett's name with Oldmixon, see E/C, III, 261n.

46. Discussed in my article 'John Oldmixon's Attack on Pope', *Bodleian Library Record*, viii (1971), 277–84.

47. See letter of 29 October 1720, BM Add.MS 28275.

48. Cf. *Dunciad*, A.II.351.

49. Swift, *Prose Works*, xi, 184. Besides numerous examples in Swift, see Gay's

ironic treatise on the subject in a letter to Arbuthnot: *The Letters of John Gay*, ed. C. F. Burgess (Oxford, 1966), pp. 13–14.

50. TE, V, 13. For Fielding's satire on Oldmixon as a historian, see my art'cle in *PQ*, XLIX (1970), 262–6. See also *Society*, I, 246.

51. The facts referred to here are set out in my articles in *Notes & Queries*, n.s. XVII (1970), 293–300: *RES*, XXI (1970), 175–81; and *MLX*, XXXI (1970), 330–44.

52. The qualifications of a critic are set out by Martinus Scriblerus as 'smartness, quick censure, vivacity of remark, certainty of asseveration, . . . acerbity' – TE, V, 53.

53. Pope, *Correspondence*, II, 140. Cf. his remarks (I, 307) on his 'dwindling' from a poet into a news-writer.

54. See 'A Full and True Account' and 'A Farther Account' of the emetic episode, in Pope's *Prose Works*, I, 257–66, 273–85.

55. Ayre, I, 247. Sherburn, p. 184.

56. See my article in *RES* XIX (1970), 175–81, for an elucidation of these events.

57. This trait is also emphasised in Swift's 'On Poetry: A Rapsody'. See Swift, *Poems*, p. 578, and Ch.IV.

58. TE, V, 9.

59. See Pope, *Correspondence*, V, 7.

60. TE, V, xxv.

61. See Miriam Kosh Starkman, *Swift's Satire on Learning in A Tale of a Tub* (Princeton, 1950), p. 108. It should be recalled that in Fielding's *Pasquin* the 'society' of Grub Street plead to be allowed to unite with the court of Queen Ignorance: *Pasquin*, V, i, in Fielding, XI, 225.

62. Butt, p. 160.

63. E/C, IV, 28.

64. Kernan, pp. 37, 4.

65. Price, *To the Palace of Wisdom* (New York, ed. 1965), p. 225.

66. Edwards, p. 127ff.

67. Warren, in Mack, p. 94: Edwards, p. 99: Erskine-Hill, in Mack, p. 813.

68. Cf. Erskine-Hill, in Mack, pp. 809–10.

69. For Stevens, see Ch. V, below.

70. Swift, *Prose Works*, IV, 118. See also Ch. IV.

71. Swift, *Prose Works*, II, 174ff.

72. Starkman, p. 108.

73. Reichard, in Mack, pp. 689–98.

74. Swift, *Prose Works*, I, 141.

75. Williams, p. 80.

76. Reichard, in Mack, p. 691.

77. Pope, *Correspondence*, III, 64.

78. Quoted by Watt, p. 20.

79. Gay, *Letters*, p. 77.
80. Watt, p. 14.
81. Pope, *Correspondence*, I, 359. For Fielding's portrait of the domineering Bookweight, in *The Author's Farce*, II. iv, see Ch. V and Fielding, VIII, 218–23.
82. Pope, *Correspondence*, III, 151.
83. See his letter of 13 December 1718, BM Add.MS 28275.
84. Dennis, *Remarks upon several Passages in the Dunciad* (1729), pp. 1–2.
85. See Maurice M. Shudofsky, 'A Dunce objects to Pope's Dictatorship', *HLQ*, XIV (1950), 203–7.
86. See R. N. Cunningham, *Peter Anthony Motteux 1663–1715* (Oxford, 1933), pp. 1–8.
87. Daniel A. Fineman, *Leonard Welsted/Gentleman Poet of the Augustan Age* (Philadelphia, 1950), pp. 17–40.
88. Richard F. Jones, *Lewis Theobald* (New York, 1919), pp. 1–30. It is true that 'the attorney's was not an eminent calling in eighteenth century England'; but it became, for the most part, a respectable and secure profession. See B. H. Davis (ed.), *The Life of Samuel Johnson, Ll.D.*, by Sir John Hawkins (London, 1962), p. viii.
89. Dorothy Brewster, *Aaron Hill* (New York 1913), pp. 1–27.
90. H. G. Paul, *John Dennis: His Life and Criticism* (New York, 1911), pp. 1–6.
91. Benjamin Boyce, *Tom Brown of Facetious Memory* (Cambridge, Mass., 1939), pp. 1–18.
92. R. H. Barker, *Mr Cibber of Drury Lane* (New York, 1939), pp. 3–9.
93. J. W. Bowyer, *The Celebrated Mrs Centlivre* (Durham, N. C., 1952), pp. 3–14; G. F. Whicher, *The Life and Romances of Mrs Eliza Haywood* (New York, 1915), pp. 1–6.
94. Pope, *Correspondence*, I, 73.
95. See especially my article in *Notes and Queries*, n.s. XVII (1970), 293–300.
96. Macdonald, pp. 54–9.
97. Alexander Chalmers, *The Works of the English Poets* (London, 1910), XVI, 208, 351–2. According to Harte, 'Blundering is the essence of a dunce.'
98. Chalmers, XVI, 43–4.
99. Swift, *Poems*, p. 579.
100. Throughout I have capitalised the substantives 'Dunce, Dulness, Duncehood', etc., in order to mark off the special, quasi-technical sense of this term in literary usage. I do not imply by this device any prosopopoetic quality in the term.

IV

Swift and the Scribbler

A regiment is a corporation which consists of individuals detached
from Bridewell, the Queen's Bench, Fleet, Newgate and the Counters.
Ned Ward, Mars stripped of his Armour

———————◆◆◆◆———————

Writers at all times have been conscious of the Grub Street fraternity.
That is, major authors – satirists especially – have been aware of a
horde of disgruntled literary aspirants baying at their heels: men of
slender talent or none at all, racked by envy and embittered by failure. At certain periods this insistent murmur becomes louder, till it
almost drowns the voice of the major writer. The early eighteenth
century was one such period. We *need* to know something of the
lesser fry if we are to understand the procedures or appreciate the
rhetoric of the great Augustans. They were all taken up, at a deep
level, with the activities of their emulators and detractors. The
legend of Grub Street which they did so much to create testifies to
the importance that the scribblers had in their mind. Parody, paraphrase, burlesque, mock-encomia, tongue-in-cheek 'answers' – these
are the weapons of the Scriblerians. They might also be seen as a
kind of devious tribute to Grub Street.

So much is true in general outline; but Swift remains unique. No
other great writer, surely, can have made his name by producing a
deliberately bad book: a work whose content, structure and style
alike reproduced the worst features of contemporary Grub Street
writing. *A Tale of a Tub* is not, of course, a faithful transcript of
Grubean composition in every single detail. As with all effective
parody, the *Tale* distorts, heightens, extends, telescopes. Nevertheless, the book does, by its form and matter, provide us with a sharp
insight into the eighteenth-century hack: his motivation, his personal

and literary goals, his foibles and his pathos. It took a modern critic to designate the narrator of the *Tale*, with clipped finality, *the* Hack, as though there were no other. But Ronald Paulson was right, as the widespread currency of his term has shown; the Hack *is* an archetypal figure, Everyman under the Grub Street aspect.

Let us think for a moment what the term connotes. Johnson's *Dictionary* entry for 'hackney' moves from the sense of a hired horse (with an example from *Hudibras*) to that of a prostitute to 'any thing let out for hire' (both the latter illustrated from Pope) to 'much used or common'. 'To hack' is defined as 'to turn hackney or prostitute'. We notice at once the sexual innuendo in the word and its derivatives: something lost, I believe, to most present-day readers. To be a hack, then, was to traffic commercially in something fundamentally admirable, and thus to sully it. It was to do for literature what prostitution did for sex. Hence the great advantage to the satirist in being able to suggest that the scribbling profession lived cheek by jowl with the whores. Needless to say, whores abounded in eighteenth-century London; and they abound in Swift's work, too. The facts of the language were such that Swift could convincingly present Grub Street as a brothel; as Pope had done, with his secluded 'cave' presided over by that awesome madam, Dulness.

In certain respects Swift's response to the seething world of actuality was even more immediate than that of Pope; and his compulsion to manufacture fiction of power and sometimes beauty from this unlovely reality was quite as marked. To think of the Dean's entire corpus of writings is to call up pictures of sturdy beggars, of rainstorms in the City, of litter in the streets, of quacks at Bartholomew Fair and servants below stairs. And his climactic figure of folly, outside the pages of *Gulliver's Travels* at least, is a nakedly human personage. Pope embodies the ultimate stage of folly in a quasi-mythological symbol, Queen Dulness; even if he does provide her with a closely observed social milieu for her domain. But with Swift the casting is brutal and unavoidable. The great exemplar of literary iniquity is the hack in his garret; the setting is a London as real and unmistakable as if John Rocque had drawn a map for frontispiece to the *Tale*.[1]

Likewise, Swift's poetry is rich in allusions to Curll, Lintot, Temple Bar, Ludgate, Duck Lane, cellars and attics, sponging-houses and pastry-cooks, doggerel and the *Craftsman*. It is not, of course, mere reportage; its social brightness and topicality are not those of the gossip column, and its realism is not to be confused with straight naturalism. Despite that reservation, it would be fair to say that Swift makes more *poetic* capital out of the raw material offered him by real life than any other writer of his time. If we take 'real life' to mean, for the moment, the daily round of eighteenth-century urban dwellers, then Swift, far more than Prior or Gay, is the poet of real life. His poems reflect the same power of eager observation as his portrait of the Grub Street Hack; the same power to make of the temporary a solid vehicle for the permanent.

Grubean Spokesman

A Tale of a Tub is a revelation of the complex fate of Duncehood.[2] The modern scribbler is anatomised both through direct reference and through self-betrayal on the part of the putative author. Before we have left the very title-page, a strain of megalomania has appeared: a bibliographical formula conveys this literary vainglory nicely – / / / A / TALE / OF A / TUB. / Written for the Universal Im- / provement of Mankind. / / And so on. Opposite the title-page in early editions was found a list of 'Treatises wrote by the same Author, most of them mentioned in the following Discourses [oh dear, yes!]; which will be speedily published.' These classic works of the un-learned include 'A Character of the present set of *Wits* in this Island' along with (what is much the same thing) 'A Dissertation upon the principal Productions of *Grub-Street*.' Thus early is the haunt of folly identified. Later in the list occurs 'A Description of the Kingdom of *Absurdities*', and it is already plain that the capital of this realm of nonsense is to be London. A few years afterwards, a tract was to appear – possibly, as we shall see, by Swift; if not, certainly inspired by him – in which the absence of a Grub Street in Dublin was lamented. Only London was so privileged; and, to move from metaphor to history, it could be said that in 1700 only London had reached the condition of modern urbanism. The person of quality from '*Terra Australis incognita*' who is to make a voyage into England (another tome advertised in the list) will find in its capital city an unparalleled degree of crime, turbulence and overcrowding. He will also find Dulness in its finest expression.

The elaborate preliminaries to the *Tale* are led off by the author's 'Apology' from the fifth edition of 1710. There is, of course, plenty of disagreement as to the intent of this section. For the present I shall remark only that the literary meanings of the book are emphasised quite as sharply as the religious. The writer singles out 'those heavy, illiterate Scriblers, prostitute in their Reputations, vicious in their Lives, and ruin'd in their Fortunes, who to the shame of good Sense as well as Piety' write against religion and morality. The books of these men are condemned as exhibiting 'Errors, Ignorance, Dullness and Villany'. The first writers mentioned by name, who are inevitably connected by the reader with this general condemnation, turn out to be Dryden, and L'Estrange – 'who having spent their Lives in Faction, and Apostacies, and all manner of Vice, pretended to be Sufferers for Loyalty and Religion.' His style in the Introduction, he explains, parodies such writing.

Another form of parody appears in the dedication to Lord Somers. Unlike some satirists, Swift did not choose to supply a comic invocation to the man in the moon or some such figure of myth. He chooses to write in the person of the bookseller to the great patron and bibliophile Somers. And although the writer is presented as both foolish and ignorant, he is at least allowed to make this eminently sane decision to inscribe the book to Somers. Instead of the hack's own absurd Prince Posterity, the dedication is really to go to the worthiest recipient. That is the point of the joke. Despite the bookseller's fawning, his pathetic civic ambition 'to grow an Alderman' (the verb nicely suggesting a sort of unhaltable bourgeois progression, something fundamentally *unearned*), and despite his niggardly commercial caution, he has at least more sense than the allegedly 'professional' hack whose work he is vending. He knows who collects books and encourages literature. Swift's recourse to Somers, then, is no back-handed compliment: the parody of a very bad dedication to a very good patron is the most effective satire he could have devised.

The bookseller, like many writers of dedications in this age, remarks on the tired conventions of the genre – it *was* a minor literary genre of some interest: 'I should now, in right of a Dedicator, give your Lordship a List of your own Virtues, and at the same time, be very unwilling to offend your Modesty . . .' Most people mention such conventions in the course of explaining that they will avoid such falsities. The bookseller, however, proudly continues that he really was going to to 'peruse a hundred or two of Dedications, and transcribe an Abstract, to be applied to your Lordship . . .' He was sidetracked only by the mysterious words *'Detur dignissimo'*. None of his authors can, of course, understand the Latin phrase – although, as the bookseller ruefully observes, 'I have them often in pay, to translate out of that Language' – and he has to go to a curate. Having established the sense of the words, the bookseller calls at 'a Poet's Chamber (who works for my Shop) in an Alley hard by'. The poet names himself as the likeliest candidate, with Somers as second choice; and a similar result ensues after visits to other wits 'with no small Hazard and Weariness to my Person, from a prodigious Number of dark, winding Stairs'. 'Poor authors', runs a note in the 1720 edition, 'generally lodge in Garrets.' The bookseller concludes that Somers must be the intended dedicatee. But, 'being very unacquainted in the Style and Form of Dedications', he is forced to return to the scribblers for a panegyric on Somers. Predictably, the authors bring him a standard encomium, so blatantly plagiarised that even he can see it. 'So that I look upon my self, as fifty Shillings out of Pocket, to no manner of Purpose,' the bookseller adds with intended pathos. He despairs of changing the name and using the panegyric again on another occasion, since its terms fit only the matchless Somers. A genuinely delicate compliment is fashioned out of this graceless narrative. Moreover, the dedication shows us Swift aligning commercial motives with ignorance, impudence and fraud. The environment, needless to say, is that of the garret in the back-alley. We are in the purlieu of Grub Street, ecologically and morally.

In the absurd Epistle Dedicatory which follows, the first piece of the putative author's own handiwork, Swift introduces the central idea of his satire. The writer explains how Time has intervened to forestall any sight by Posterity (who is the recipient of the letter) of the numerous 'Studies' by contemporary hacks. Time, indeed, has insolently thinned the ranks of 'our vast flourishing Body' of authors, on account of 'a peculiar Malice' he bears against this class. In a splendidly funny passage, the hack-figure creates a vision of thousands of fugitive writings condemned to an early grave, stifled in their cradles or frightened into convulsions. Then he shifts to a more businesslike vein:

> But the Concern I have most at Heart, is for our Corporation of *Poets*, from whom I am preparing a Petition to *Your Highness*, to be subscribed with the Names of one hundred and thirty six of the first Rate, but whose immortal Productions are never likely to reach your Eyes, tho' each of them is now an humble and an earnest Appellant for the Laurel, and has large comely Volumes ready to shew a Support to his Pretensions. The *never-dying* Works of these illustrious Persons, Your *Governour* [Time], Sir, has devoted to unavoidable Death . . .

There is a pomposity here ('an humble and an earnest'), a quasi-legal air at times, an impression of not having quite learnt what some words mean ('devote'): it all suggests the trade unionist satirised by Peter Sellers. Nor is this inappropiate: since the poets are leagued together in a mutual-protection organisation. Like the Dunces, who coalesce in a seething mass of corrupt humanity (B.IV.77), the poets have incorporated themselves to disguise their individual frailty. They are, in the Webbs' sense, an association of producers:[3] another proof of the professionalisation of letters, that movement towards a scribbling bureaucracy which the Tory humanists so much feared. One element of the whole Grub Street fiction, indeed, is that poor writers are now banded together as an institutionalised estate of the realm; they operate in contemporary culture as a perversely anti-educative and anti-literary force. They resemble the least enlightened City companies; they form a *corporation*.

The dedicator goes on to speak of a list of (duncely) 'Titles' which were 'posted fresh upon all Gates and Corners of Streets.' In a few hours these were all torn down: all trace of the existence of these works had been lost. The question naturally arises, 'What is then become of those immense Bales of Paper, which must needs have been employ'd in such Numbers of Books? Can these also be wholly annihilate . . .?' The answer, though the writer professes some hesitation about revealing the details to so high a potentate as Posterity, is that the sheets have been allocated a use in a jakes, an oven, in 'the Windows of a *Bawdy-house*, or . . . a sordid *Lanthorn*. Books, like Men their Authors, have no more than one Way of coming into the World, but there are ten Thousand to go out of it, and return no more.' The quality of the wit here is distinctly seventeenth-century and metaphysical. The conceit, it need hardly be added, serves to ally literary production with the dark corners of life: scribblers are waste-makers above all.

The next passage incorporates a roll-call of the deserving moderns. They are, in order: Dryden; Nahum Tate; Tom Durfey; the critics Rymer and Dennis; 'a Person styl'd Dr *B*[en]*tl*[e]*y*'; and William Wotton, who played such a major part in the Ancient and Moderns controversy. All these writers have produced works which the world unaccountably disregards. To remedy this situation, the author plans to write 'a Character of the present Set of *Wits* in our Nation.' Meanwhile, he is content to put before Prince Posterity a 'faithful Abstract' of modern learning – the *Tale of a Tub* itself.

There follows yet another in the series of preliminary puffs. This one is called a preface, though it serves the same naïvely self-advertising function as the others. The 'Design . . . [of] the Treatise' is soon announced, in a passage central to the understanding of Tory satire in this era.

> It is intended that a large Academy be erected, capable of containing nine thousand seven hundred forty and three Persons; which by modest Computation is reckoned to be pretty near the current Number of *Wits* in this Island. These are to be disposed into the several Schools of this Academy, and there pursue those Studies to which their Genius most inclines them. The Undertaker himself will publish his Proposals with all convenient speed, to which I shall refer the curious Reader for a more particular Account, mentioning at present only a few of the

Principal Schools. . . . No Person to be admitted Member into any of these Schools, without an Attestation under two sufficient Persons Hands, certifying him to be a *Wit*.

Here is the germ of the Grand Academy of Lagado, of the intellectual enquiries of Martinus Scriblerus, of the 'regular Institutes' of the lowlands of Parnassus, set out in *Peri Bathous*. The idea of an academy is perhaps so dominant because of the impression made by the Royal Society on men's minds. But whatever the source of the concept, and however we try to locate these Scriblerian fancies in the tradition of learned wit, the fact remains it was a small group of writers – Swift, Arbuthnot, Pope – who saw the potential in this idea. The exact term used varies: college, seminary, lyceum, even hospital, are among the descriptions encountered. In each case, however, the sense is of folly institutionalised. Dulness, once a matter of individual quirks and personal inadequacies, has now organised itself into union militancy. Moreover, the aspirant writer is bred up by a distorted *alma mater*, supplying the place occupied in the Renaissance dream of learning by the university. The success of the Grubean academy is, amongst other things, an indictment of the ancient English universities, given over to pedantry, faction and soft living.

It might also be noted that the writer describes himself as an 'Undertaker', a word then carrying suggestions of graft – a City magnate such as Sir Henry Furnese, who amassed great wealth after engrossing the contracts for paying the army abroad during Marlborough's campaigns, would be a representative figure of this kind. And we know that Swift's circle had no high opinion of Furnese.[4] After this, the author utters his apothegmatic statement on the 'Walks and Purlieus' of wit, quoted as an epigraph to the Introduction. It is, of course, further proof of the connection between topographic and literary matters. Far from being a global village, London was then a kind of rustic metropolis: its cultural life curiously atomised by modern standards.

Finally, in this preface of garrulous non-progression, the author lets slip that 'the shrewdest Pieces of this Treatise, were conceived in Bed, in a Garret: At other times (for a Reason best known to my self) I thought fit to sharpen my Invention with Hunger; and in general, the whole Work was begun, continued, and ended, under a long Course of Physick, and a great want of Money.' This explicit admission that the *Tale* was composed in a garret under needy circumstances should not be overlooked. The book is a product of indigence, and that fact colours its entire artistic and moral identity. By the end of these introductory sections, then, we have already been alerted to the status of the author, and the nature of his 'undertaking'.

It is not possible, or necessary, to make a detailed survey of the *Tale* proper. Rather, we may isolate the themes already noticed as they make their reappearance. In the introductory chapter, the scribbler describes various kinds of oratorial machine, including the stage-itinerant. This last serves as 'the great seminary' for the pulpit and the execution-ladder: that is, 'the Mountebank's Stage, whose Orators the Author determines either to the Gallows or a Conventicle.' It can be shown that dissenting houses were concentrated most thickly in the haunts of Dulness; whilst dissenting academies thronged the Grub Street/Moorfields area. Swift goes on to explain the 'physico-logical' scheme of oratorical machines as conveying an analogy 'to the spacious Commonwealth of Writers, and to those Methods by which they must exalt themselves to a certain Eminency above the inferiour World.' The pseudo-mysticism of the hack author is thus converted to the ends of direct literary satire.

A paragraph or two later, the subject is revealed in a still more explicit manner:

> Under the *Stage-Itinerant* are couched those Productions designed for the Pleasure and Delight of Mortal Man; such as *Six-peny-worth of Wit*, Westminster *Drolleries*, *Delightful Tales*, *Compleat Jesters*, and the like; by which the Writers of and for *GRUB-STREET*, have in these latter Ages so nobly triumph'd over *Time*; have clipt his Wings, pared his Nails, filed his Teeth, turn'd back his Hour-Glass, blunted his Scythe, and drawn the Hob-Nails out of his Shoes. It is under this Classis, I have presumed to list my present Treatise, being just come from having the Honor conferred upon me, to be adopted a Member of that Illustrious Fraternity.

The writer has just been admitted to the fraternity of Grub Street, as one would be admitted to the freedom of the City. His treatise is a kind of commemorative offering: the gift one bestows in some pagan *rite de passage*. Yet his pride is mixed with a certain apprehension:

> Now, I am not unaware, how the Productions of the *Grub-street* Brotherhood, have of late Years fallen under many Prejudices, nor how it has been the perpetual Employment of two *Junior* start-up Societies, to ridicule them and their Authors, as unworthy their established Post in the Commonwelath of Wit and Learning.

(Note the epithet 'established'). These upstarts are the Royal Society and Will's coffee-house, the leading place of resort for literary and theatrical men at this time. The scribbler has more than one ground for resentment against these 'Societies', not least their manifest ingratitude:

> For, how can it be forgot by the World or themselves, (to say nothing of our own Records, which are full and clear in the Point) that they both are Seminaries, not only of our *Planting*, but our *Watering* too?

If the respective contributions of Grub Street and the new societies are compared, as to both weight and number of their books, Grub Street will easily carry the day – always provided that an impartial judge shall decide 'which Society each Book, Treatise or Pamphlet do most properly belong to . . . For, We are ready to produce a Catalogue of some Thousands, which in all common Justice ought to be entitled to our Fraternity, but by the revolted and new-fangled Writers, most perfidiously ascribe to the others.' Such has been the scale of the intrigue among the new academies that a huge defection has been induced from Grub Street to its rivals: 'the greatest part of our Society hath already deserted to them, and our nearest Friends begin to stand aloof, as if they were half-ashamed to own us.'

This section is usually read, and correctly, as a satire directed against Will's and the Royal Society. It is certain that these historical gatherings of intellectual London form the principal target at this point. But, semi-fictional as it may have been, Grub Street is more than simply the vehicle of a satiric metaphor. The insult to the Royal Society is as cutting as it is because Swift could rely on a ready assent to the identity of the Grub Street fraternity.

The word 'seminary' has occured two or three times. It may be recalled that in the *Memoirs of a Woman of Pleasure* Fanny Hill refers to the brothel in which she was lodged as an 'academy', with cognate usages such as 'professors of pleasure'. This mode of speech may have been connected with the mock-solemn rites of Medmenham and Crazy Castle. At all events, it is apparent that words to do with educational establishments could be applied, without much of a semantic leap, to places of immoral behaviour. 'Seminary' today has a rather neutral air to it. In the eighteenth century, it was poised ready to form combinations like 'seminary of vice'. When Arbuthnot, then, gave vent to his exclamation, '*O Grubstreet*! thou fruitful Nursery of tow'ring Genius's!' he, was taking advantage of an image already partly degraded. Others apart from the persona who masks Arbuthnot's identity in *John Bull* had the 'good Fortune to receive [their] Education there' – Grub Street was a sort of extension college.[5] It was all the better that many hacks turned out, in the 1720's and 1730's, to have attended John Eames's academy in Moorfields (Ch.I).

The narrative now moves to a celebrated passage in which the writer describes the indirect methods adopted by 'the *Grubean* Sages' (a Swiftian coinage) to convey their deep ideas. The scribbler puts foremost among the reasons for the bad press which 'the Writings of our Society have formerly received' the unwillingness of the reading public to delve into the hidden meaning of things. The only remedy for this lack of comprehension is 'a compleat and laborious Dissertation upon the Prime Productions of our Society, which besides their beautiful Externals for the Gratification of superficial Readers, have darkly and deeply couched under them, the most finished and refined Systems of all Sciences and Arts . . .' The language here is alive with innuendo and veiled malice. 'Beautiful externals' perhaps hits at the ugly chapbooks, wretchedly printed with crude woodcuts as illustration, which formed a considerable part of the Grub Street output. The word 'couched' manages to hint slily that the deep systems are after all *sleeping* in their subterranean hideout. The dissertation will of course be 'laborious' to read as well as to compile. And so on.

Not surprisingly the works of vast erudition to be studied in this critical survey prove to be on the level of *Reynard the Fox*, *Whitting-*

ton and his Cat and *Tom Thumb*. With an extra touch of scorn, Swift adds *The Hind and the Panther*, 'the Master-piece of a famous Writer now living, intended for a compleat Abstract of sixteen thousand Schoolmen from *Scotus* to *Bellarmin*.' Scotus, of course, was the primal Dunce. Additionally, William Wotton is indicated as a leading member of the scribbling fraternity. Otherwise the drift is general rather than particular. It is necessary, however, for the hack author himself to make clear his credentials for the job. He mentions his 'unfortunate Life', with 'a Quill worn to the Pith in the Service of the State', i.e. in controversial pamphlets on the Popish Plot and similar events. As a (would-be) climax, he launches into a self-pitying autobiography:

> From an Understanding and a Conscience, thread-bare and ragged with perpetual turning; From a Head broken in a hundred places, by the Malignants of the opposite Factions, and from a Body spent with Poxes ill cured, by trusting to Bawds and Surgeons, who (as it after-wards appeared) were profess'd Enemies to me and the Government, and revenged their Party's Quarrel upon my Nose and Shins . . . four-score and eleven Pamphlets have I written under three Reigns, and for the Service of six and thirty Factions.

There are elements of this account which fit Dryden, and something of his occasional self-justificatory vein. Yet the main satiric energy works in a different direction. This is Scriblerus Everyman, turn-coat, opportunist, loose liver, but always industrious. The task most suited to such a writer is the archetypal duncely endeavour of com-piling an abstract. Grub Street abstracts and dissects: hence its cousinhood to the anatomy hall at the College of Physicians.

This appears most clearly in the 'Digression in the Modern Kind', with the scheme to make a kind of balsam from the works of modern learning, which would then be inhaled every morning. As a result 'you immediately perceive in your Head an infinite Number of *Abstracts*, *Summaries*, *Compendiums*, *Extracts*, *Collections*, *Medulla's*, *Excerpta quaedam's*, *Florilegia's* and the like, all disposed into great Order, and reducible upon Paper.' You will be, in other words, qualified to take up residence in Grub Street.

To return to the society itself: at the opening of the Digression in Praise of Digressions, we hear of the 'Commonwealth of Learning' whose taste for literary medleys and '*Ollio's*' Grub Street, her seat of government, has done so much to promote. The 'Society of Writers' is mentioned shortly afterwards, and later on the 'Corporation of Authors' busy producing their collections and commentaries and lexicons. In this section, as well as in the Digression on Criticks, Swift takes no pain to conceal his scorn for the literary middle-men of his age. Humanist ideology revered the scholar when he was about his true business of enlightenment and clarification. This was something very different from the modern pedant, 'by some called the *Sieves* and *Boulters* of Learning', whose commonplace-book is more in evidence than their wisdom or taste. Their tools are 'large *Indexes*, and little *Compendiums*'; '*Systems* and *Abstracts*', a modern labour-saving device; and other short ways of becoming scholars or wits 'without the Fatigue of *Reading* or of *Thinking*'.

The famous eighth section of the *Tale* concerns 'the learned *Aeolists*'. The sect has predictably instituted 'certain refined Colleges'. There follows the most intensely debated section of the *Tale*, the Digression on Madness. At this time of day I would not wish to intervene in a discussion which often seems to leave the humdrum topic of Augustan satire far behind. My concern is with a particular literary genre in a given historical period, and the wider ranges of the debate surrounding this Digression are not germane to my purpose. But it should be noted that the central locale of the chapter is 'the *Academy* of *Modern Bedlam*'. A proposal is made for a group of high-flying Tory politiciams to act as Commissioners of Lunacy, and to inspect the merits and qualifications of 'every Student and Professor' in Bedlam. Guthkelch and Nichol Smith reproduce an illustration from the early editions which graphically underlines the immediacy and contemporanity of the satire. In the last section of this Digression, the author recommends a madman who feeds on his own ordure as a worthy 'Professor' for 'the Society of *Warwick-Lane*' – that College of Physicians whose scientific enterprises formed an exact equivalent of the literary mud-raking of Grub Street, and whose dissection of corrupt flesh so deeply perturbed Swift, a man of particularly marked sensitivity in this area of life.

Section X of the *Tale* spells out at its outset a primary meaning of the entire fiction. In accordance with established literary custom, thanks are liberally bestowed by the author. They go first of all to the sovereign and parliament, the Privy Council and every other body of remote eminence who could not possibly form any contact with so lowly a Dunce. 'But in a more especial manner' they go 'to my worthy Brethren and Friends at *Will's Coffee-House*, and *Gresham-College*, and *Warwick-Lane*, and *Moor-Fields*, and *Scotland-Yard*, and *Westminster-Hall*, and *Guild-Hall*; In short, to all Inhabitants and Retainers whatsoever, either in Court, or Church, or Camp, or City, or Country . . .' Why Scotland Yard is there is a bit of a mystery: the police, of course, had not yet claimed the locality. For the rest, however, we have the City, the law, coffee-house society, the new experimental science of the Royal Society, the College of Physicians and Bedlam all linked by one over-arching metaphor.[6] To be a resident of such a place was to be a retainer. The appeal to 'Brethren', with its aggressive mateyness, gives the game away. These are the new estates of the realm – if Westminster Hall was ancient, organised lawyers weren't to any degree. They are topographic sites, but more crucially interest-groups to which one belongs. One name is missing. Grub Street need not be thanked since its presence is everywhere. It presides over the conception of the book, it forms a good deal of the subject-matter, and its dictates govern the material throughout. The 'Republick of *dark* Authors', Wotton's 'Brother Modernists', will be placated by the very existence of the ill-made, garrulous, creaking carcase of a book. *Their* ready acceptance of the work can be taken for granted. One need no more thank them than one thanks a detergent firm for permitting its commercial to appear on television.

I said just now that Grub Street forms much of the subject-matter of the *Tale*. Some brief justification of this remark may be in place. No major work of English literature, excluding *The Dunciad*, contains more direct reference to contemporary writers and their situation. Apart from the individuals already mentioned, there is a comment on the 'faithful and painful Collection' of criminals' dying speeches, to be made in twelve folio volumes by 'that worthy Citizen and Bookseller, Mr *John Dunton*'. There is simulated rage at the activities of 'a certain paultry *Scribbler*' dealing in second parts, i.e. compiling continuation volumes to any popular book, a lucrative activity not uncommon at this time. It is interesting to note that in the *Miscellaneous Works* of 1720, where certain ancillary material appeared for the first time, the *Tale* is allotted a separate title-page on which the author is given as 'A Member of the Illustrious Fraternity of Grubstreet'. The Miscellanies that form the second part of this volume are attributed to 'a certain paultry Scribler, commonly called, The Author of the first'.[7]

As it happens, the authors named as having suffered from this pernicious habit are themselves the veriest Dunces imaginable: Blackmore, L'Estrange, and by implication Bentley. A few years later Swift might have mentioned Defoe, who suffered from this deceit at the hands of others, but who was also believed to have practised it on occasion.

The Conclusion of the shapeless *Tale*, of course, concludes nothing. The writer evinces some anxiety lest his 'treatise' should miss its due acclaim through appearing at the wrong moment. Luckily the bookseller who bought the copy is an expert in such matters; with the help of an almanac he is able to set the most propitious date for publication. The writer, '*considering* [his] *urgent Necessities*', is keen to have more immediate prospects of a good return. So that a characteristic expedient is devised:

> That when a Customer comes for one of these [copies of the *Tale*], and desires in Confidence to know the Author; he will tell him very privately, as a Friend, naming which ever of the Wits shall happen to be that Week in the Vogue; and if *Durfy*'s last Play should be in Course, I had as lieve he may be the Person as *Congreve*.

This is exactly the same stratagem as that dramatised by Pope, in which Dulness decks out 'Three wicked imps, of her own Grubstreet choir' like Congreve, Addison and Prior (B.II.123). Here the bookseller acts the part of Dulness, as one of her principal sublunary agents.

That is not the complete register of personal allusions (Dryden is brought in on several other occasions, for example as the great exponent of the puff by way of preface). The great line of critics, from Momus down to Rymer, Bentley and Dennis, figures prominently, too. But the constant play of literary comment is not wholly dependent on the introduction of individual names. 'The mutual Felicity of *Booksellers* and *Authors*' arises from their solemn league and convenant to defraud the public. The bargain is a crooked one on either side. As the scribbler complacently notes, books are produced for a variety of reasons, ranging from ill health, bad luck at the gaming table, and a long tailor's bill to 'Want of Books, and a just Contempt of Learning'. It is yet another way of expressing an idea central to the whole critique of Dulness – that the Moderns make books for extrinsic, casual or mercenary reasons, and not from the love of literature or wisdom.

In this gallimaufry of pedantry, insolence and plain stupidity, the character of the man of letters emerges in no very favourable light. The satire even infects portions of the religious allegory, which nominally concerns abuses in the Church. Thus Lord Peter is described as 'the Original Author of *Puppets* and *Raree-Shows*; the great Usefulness whereof being so generally known, I shall not enlarge further upon this Particular.' A footnote to the word 'Puppets' reads: 'I believe are the Monkeries and ridiculous Processions, *&c.* among the Papists.' In the light of what has been said earlier, the force of this passage should be 'generally known' enough to warrant no further particulars. The Smithfield muse is here conflated with the rites of the Catholic church, in a manner that Pope would not have countenanced. But for Swift as for Pope, puppet-shows were emblems of tawdry pseudo-drama. In modern terms, one might say that such shows are what the media make of literature; entertainments in which the display function quite overwhelms any serious inward purpose. Puppeteers are one more variety of the genus 'Smatterers', who have taken over the cultural lead in 'this Polite and Learned Age'. The freshest modern would be certain to pitch his stall at Bartholomew Fair every year.[8]

One other aspect of the work demands notice. It would be easy to get the impression from most of the extant criticism, that the *Tale* is set in some never-never land, closer to Lagado perhaps than

Illyria. In fact the narrative buzzes with direct allusion to contemporary London. There can be no doubt at all that the corruptions in learning anatomised have their headquarters in the metropolis. Swift employs, indeed, precisely the same moral gazetteer which we have seen in the case of Pope. I have already drawn attention to the use made of such conspicuous landmarks as Moorfields, the College of Physicians, Westminster Hall and Bedlam. To these we must add such lists as the author compiles to indicate the various styles of preaching, in Covent Garden, Whitehall, the Inns of Court and the City. Or the derivation of the word 'banter' from its currency among 'the Bullies in *White-Fryars*', that recurrent symbol of low-life London. Or Peter's indulgences towards 'any Rogue of *Newgate*', one of several indications that the religious narrative, too, is acted out in a sort of imaginatively recast version of the capital. Jack, one recalls from Section XI, was cured of a strange aversion to the sound of music, by 'taking two or three Turns in *Westminster-Hall*, or *Billingsgate* or in a *Boarding-School*, or the *Royal-Exchange*, or a *State Coffee-House*'. It must be confessed that the drift of this passage is not altogether clear. The point seems to be that the dissenters' hatred of church music was forgotten when they returned to their true religion of making money in the City, pleading casuistically in the courts, indulging in political intrigue, or setting up factious 'academies'. Incidentally, Westminster Hall crops up again at the beginning of *The Mechanical Operation of the Spirit*, where it is aligned with St Paul's churchyard and Fleet Street as a centre of the bookselling trade.[9]

As a portrait of the sordid fringe of the profession of letters, the *Tale* has never been excelled. Its vigour, raciness and wealth of comic absurdity remain unimpaired to this day. And while its range of allusion may to some extent confine its appeal to the modern reader, it survives as an achievement no less striking in its way than *Gulliver's Travels*. From our present vantage point, the *Tale* is particularly notable as combining so many of the satiric *topoi* of the age into an intelligible case against the scribbling fraternity. Unlike *The Battle of the Books*, the *Tale* is not explicitly set in London. But a mass of concrete references, supplemented by easily identifiable subject-matter in the illustrations (Bedlam; the Lord Mayor on his procession through the City; a mountebanks' stage set up against Tyburn), serve to fix the action in the metropolis. Swift, like Pope, was drawn towards mythological subjects in a good deal of his work; like Pope again, he drew on the classical store of timeless landscapes and sanctified dramatic locales. Yet these men, in the ultimate intensity of their vision, abjure, the bland remoteness of Olympus or Arcadia. In *The Dunciad*, the fall of Troy is a distant theatrical spectacle, which we observe through opera glasses at the instance of a superannuated City bard, whose spiritual home had been Smithfield and whose final home on earth had been in the Charterhouse. Just so Swift disposes his archetypal Peter, Jack and Martin about a modern Vanity Fair, with its sponging-houses, it raree-shows, its filthy kennels (or gutters), its shoplifters at the Exchange, its beaux and bawds. Only London would serve to catch up all the dispersed elements of a modern myth of Folly, since only London comprehended modern urban living in its developed form.[10] The supreme fiction requires the appropriate fictive venue: the great treatise on Grub Street learning can only bear a London imprint.

'Respublica Grubstreetaria'

With the metaphoric, uncapitalised 'grub street', Swift had much to do all his days. However, it was only around the time of his relatively brief stay in London, while he was in his middle forties, that he dabbled with Grub Street as such.[11] Four of the five references *eo nomine* which occur in his correspondence date from the years 1709 to 1712. The concentration is even more marked with the *Journal to Stella*. In the first half of the *Journal*, there are only two allusions, scattered through the major part of 1711. Between November of that year and December of the following year, Grub Street is mentioned no less than sixteen times. It should be noted that these occurrences run across the break in the text caused by the loss of those manuscripts which Deane Swift printed; 'Grub Street' is an authentic Swiftian phrase (as 'Presto', for instance, is not), and appears several times in the manuscript portion.

The concept, then, was most present to Swift's mind during his actual residence in London. You could be aware of the scribbling fraternity in Dublin or Letcombe Bassett – Swift obviously was. But it took direct contact with the everyday realities of the metropolis to slip, naturally and continuously, into the milieu of Grub Street, or into its idiom. Fielding was to argue that the extent of its dominions had been enlarged, and this is perhaps a proof that the term had lost symbolic identity when it shed topographical precision. The currency of the phrase in the first quarter of the century had preserved the London connection. After Pope's fantasy of Grub Street doings, blending so damagingly the *outré* and the down-to-earth, there was little room for fresh invention.

After his *Tale*, Swift seems to have left the idea dormant until March 1709. In that month he wrote from London to Robert Hunter, then a prisoner in French hands, and later Governor of New York: 'I could send you a great deal of news from the *Republica Grubstreetaria*, [*sic*] which was never in greater Altitude, though I have been of late but a small Contributor.' Swift, one observes, is thinking of himself as a citizen of the Grub Street realm. The language parodies the uninformative diplomatic intelligence of eighteenth-century newspapers. And once again the sphere of mercenary writing is allocated a posturing dignity, in this case a statehood of its own. In the following year Swift writes to his bookseller on the publication by Curll of *A Complete Key to the Tale of the Tub*: 'I believe it is so perfect a Grub-street-piece, it will be forgotten in a week.'[12] The locality is used here as an ordinary descriptive epithet, that is to characterise a shoddy and semi-piratical enterprise. In later years Swift would simply have written 'Curllian'. It did not take much in Scriblerian grammar to make a common noun from a proper.

As remarked, Swift appears to have grown more fond of the trope in 1711 and 1712. On 1 August 1712, or about then, he wrote to Vanessa, 'I will come as early on Monday as I can find Opportunity; and will take a little Grubstreet Lodging; pretty near where I did before; and dine with you thrice a week; and will tell You a thousand

Secrets provided You will have no Quarrells to me . . .' The letter is brisk, playful, relaxed. Its syntax tends to be staccato, conveying at once urgency and a certain determined orderliness. In the *Journal* he speaks of 'a hedge Lodging', address unknown, somewhere in the capital. Swift was obviously in no doubt that Vanessa would pick up the tone of his message. His accommodation will not be sumptuous, particularly after Windsor, but he will make do with it; it will be a reasonably convenient *pied-à-terre* from which to flirt with Vanessa, and anyway isn't it a suitable home for one who traffics in pamphlets and the public prints? A 'Grubstreet Lodging' is thus any old garret – you called it that because hacks infested such places and because there were plenty to let in the shacks of Cripplegate.[13]

In his very next surviving letter, Swift employs the expression twice in a couple of lines. He is writing to Jack Hill, soldier and *eminence grise*:

> Mrs Hill says, it was a very idle thing in you to send such a present to a man who can neither punish nor reward you, since Grub-street is no more: For the Parliament has killed all the Muses of Grub-street, who yet, in their last moments, cried out nothing but Dunkirk.

The allusion is to the imposition of stamp duty as from 1 August, a matter more fully dealt with in the *Journal*. One notes in passing that Swift cannot resist mythologising even in this perfunctory context. The mourning muses are a characteristic fancy by which he embellishes a piece of repressive legislation. After this date, Swift wrote several hundred more letters that have survived, not to speak of those which must have perished. But there is only one slight reference to 'the lowest Grub-street' in all these, and that relates to the Drapier's controversy in 1724. When Swift left London, he ceded Grub Street to his friends.[14]

It is the *Journal* which supplies most of the relevant material. Nor is that surprising. During the period of its composition, Swift was domiciled in London, deeply involved in public affairs, widely active in journalism. He moved amongst great men, but also among the underlings of the world of letters. As *Examiner* he combated stoutly with the Whig press, wielding their own chosen weapons in fierce and frontal assault. He was, some might say, himself an habitué of

Grub Street in these years.[15] Perhaps for that very reason, he eschews the phrase in his published works. He speaks regularly of '*Wit-starved* Writers, who have no other visible Support' (than attacking him). He adopts an air of mincing irony, recalling the *Tale*, when describing the 'Taste' of certain 'judicious Criticks'. He uses the terms 'Answerers', 'merciless Pens', 'malicious Papers', and the rest. But he abstains from the direct label 'Grub Street'.[16] Curiously, he was in this only reflecting all the more faithfully the manners of Grub Street itself.

On many of the occasions in which the trope occurs in the *Journal to Stella*, Swift makes little play with it. Often the term figures simply as a convenient shorthand. The first mention is on 31 January 1711; Swift had been to see St John, as he then was, the Secretary of State. 'They are here intending', he informs Stella, 'to tax all printed penny papers a half-penny every half-sheet, which will utterly ruin Grub-street, and I am endeavouring to prevent it.' If Swift is serious, and I think he is, his attitude is worthy of note. But the expression of his views looks careless enough. There is perhaps a more indulgent touch to the phrase than there would be later, but that is all. The metaphor might be as dead as it is today. So too with the heedless phrase 'Grubstreet paper' which turns up on 21 August of that year: 'We have only a Grubstreet paper of it, but I believe it is true.' Delicious *but*![17]

Towards the end of the year, Swift's imagination seems to have been caught in a more vivid and inward fashion by the possibilities of the conceit. Of course, we still hear of Grub-street papers, Grub-street accounts, and Grub-street speeches – though the latter (18 December) is noteworthy because Swift is protectively calling his own poem about the Earl of Nottingham by this deprecatory title, a trick he was to develop further.[18] Sometimes Swift hovers on the edge of half-hearted personification: 'Do you know, that Grub-street is dead and gone last Week,' he writes after the Stamp Act on 7 August 1712, 'No more Ghosts or Murders now for Love for Money.' Or on 17 January 1712, when the act was being considered, and Swift reported the Queen's desire to see 'some law to prevent libels against the government; so farewell to Grub-street.' At other times the phrase becomes one of straightforward opprobium: 'these devils of Grubstreet rogues . . . will not be quiet' (28 October 1712). In a more picturesque style, shortly afterwards: 'she [the Duchess of Hamilton] must have been tortured with the noise of the Grub-street Screamers, mention her Husbands murder to her Ears.' The elliptical syntax obscures neither the sense nor Swift's indignation. Another linguistic stratagem was to use a Grubstreet as a noun, mean-ing a hack effusion – a more or less kindly usage, depending on the origin of the paper. Thus, Stella is briskly addressed on 12 December 1712: 'So you read one of the Grubstreets about the Bandbox . . .' On one occasion this is truncated to 'Grub', and combined with a muted prosopoeic figure: 'To day there will be anothr Grub; a Letter from the Pretendr to a Whig Ld. Grubstreet has but ten days to live, then an Act of Parlmt takes place, that ruins it . . .' (19 July 1712).[19]

The most conspicuous of these references form a separate class. In these, Swift is using the term as an evaluative or defining expression rather than just as a statement of source. For instance, Swift com-ments on his friend Arbuthnot's satire (17 June 1712): 'Well but John Bull is not writt by the Person you imagine, as I hope – It is too good for anothr to own, had it been Grubstreet, I would have let People think as they please . . .' In a letter already quoted, and with reference to the alleged bandbox plot, Swift writes, 'There was a pure Grubstreet of it full of Lyes and Inconsistencyes.' The two best examples of this class occur at the end of the previous year. In one, Swift describes his making a ballad 'two degrees above Grub-street' (6 December 1711). The day before, he had written this significant sentence: 'I have got an under spur-leather [William Oldisworth] to write an *Examiner* again, and the secretary [St John] and I will now and then send hints; but we would have it a little upon the Grub-street, to be a match for their writers.' There is no clearer revelation of Swift's attitude than this. Grub Street is a fact of life, not something from which one averts one's eyes with horror. The battle has to be carried on, and if the terrain is Grub Street then the engines of war must be those fitted to such a mire-laden venue.[20]

On 17 July 1712 Swift told Stella, 'Since Dunkirk has been in our

Hands, Grubstreet has been very fruitfull: pdfr has writt 5 or 6 Grubstreet papers this last week.'[21] Swift himself was never so fruitful again, though he did not cease to turn out squibs, ballads, mock-petitions and anything else that topical events called for. With his departure from London and the full heat of publicist squabbles, he largely abandoned a concept which had been most prominent in his familiar writing around 1712. Of course, his *Journal* could not give added currency to the phrase, because it remained unpublished for over half a century. Yet Swift's reliance on the term is itself an indication of the part Grub Street played in early Scriblerian thinking. Moreover, Swift returned the expression to his vocabulary in his poems of the 1730's. On one momentous occasion, indeed, he capitalised on the situation which Pope had set up with *his* decisive mythmaking in the Grubean kind. And at least once he managed to turn one small plot of Irish land into a place that was forever Grub Street – a form of colonialism in fantasy that he must have relished more than the sterner forms it took in reality.

It may well be more than coincidence that Pope only draws on the expression twice in his extant correspondence, both in early years. In 1716 he writes to Caryll of 'a most ridiculous quarrel with a bookseller', that is the famous episode of Curll and the emetic, 'the history whereof has been transmitted to posterity by a late Grub-street author', namely Pope himself. At this stage of his career, Pope (like Swift in his *Journal*) unashamedly labels his polemical squibs in this fashion; later, he was to present himself as above the din of battle. Possibly his own removal to the then rural locality of Twickenham, distant from the clamorous suburbs of Dulness, helps to explain the change. Three years earlier, Pope had written to Gay a celebrated account of the new Scriblerian 'design', entered into by Swift, Parnell and himself:

> Dr *Swift* much approves what I proposed even to the very title, which I design shall be, *The Works of the Unlearned*, published monthly, in which whatever Book appears that deserves praise, shall be depreciated Ironically, and in the same manner that modern Critics take to undervalue Works of Value, and to commend the high Productions of *Grubstreet*.

The phrase recalls that earlier title promised in the *Tale*, namely 'A Dissertation upon the principal Productions of *Grub-street*', In the formative years of Scriblerian satire, it was Swift whose idiom and even phraseology dominated the club. Literary trash is imaged as 'high Productions' with obvious irony; it may also derive from the garret (as in the *Epistle to Arbuthnot*, where the rhymer dwells 'high in *Drury-lane*' (41)), and like a ramshackle Grub Street hovel its lofty port is no guarantee of security or permanence.[22]

I have just said that Swift took up the conceit again in his poetry of the 1730's. Actually there are a couple of brief mentions earlier. One comes in a broadside aimed against William Wood in the course of the Drapier's controversy, entitled 'Prometheus'. The author supplies an aptly turned version of the Prometheus myth, in which 'this *Thief* and *Black-Smith*' substitutes a chain of brass for 'that *Chain* of *Gold*, / Which links the *Subject* to the *King*'. Probably the real target of the satire is Walpole, for whom '*brass* and *brazen* had become the standard nicknames.' In a poem of 75 lines, the word 'brass' occurs four times, and 'brazen' no less than five. However, the official reading of the allegory is more politic:

> Ye Pow'rs of *Grub-street* make me able,
> Discreetly to apply this *Fable*.
> Say, who is to be understood,
> By that old Thief *Prometheus*? WOOD
> For *Jove*, it is not hard to guess him,
> I mean *His Majesty, God bless him*.

The muse who presides over ballads and broadsides has no name in the classical pantheon, but Swift knew where to find her. Similarly 'The Progress of Poetry' (1720) shows us the needy hack in his garret, 'while from below all *Grub-street* rings.'[23]

After *The Dunciad*, references crowd in. The splendidly vivacious poem 'To Doctor Delany, on the Libels writ against him' (1730) provides a good example. Early on, Swift advises Delany to compose panegyrics upon the Irish parliament – the public spirit and honesty of its members, especially. Then, he will find,

> Thus grown a Member of the Club,
> No longer dread the Rage of *Grub*.

Later in the poem comes a contemptuous vignette of the hack author's ambience:

> Yet, what avails it to complain:
> You try to take Revenge in vain.
> A Rat your utmost Rage defyes
> That safe behind the Wainscoat lyes.
> Say, did you ever know by Sight
> In Cheese an individual Mite?
> Shew me the same numerick Flea,
> That bit your Neck but Yesterday,
> You then may boldly go in Quest
> To find the Grub-Street Poet's Nest,
> What Spunging-House in dread of Jayl
> Receives them while they wait for Bayl?
> What Ally are they nestled in,
> To flourish o'er a Cup of Ginn?
> Find the last Garret where they lay,
> Or Cellar, where they starve to Day . . .

One notes how, consciously or unconsciously, Swift takes up the idea of a grub or bug, the form of insect life which might be encountered in a dirty garret and which (imaginatively, anyway) might serve as eponym for the hacks' quarter. In an early work Pope had noted the transmogrification of 'Grubs obscene' into 'wriggling Worms,/Then painted Butterflies.' The horror of Swift's vermin is that they lack even this life-history; they are indistinguishable, myriad, swarming and pullulating in their fetid hole. Moreover, Delany cannot even be sure that he *has* been libelled by this obnoxious brood. The print-seller may be lying in order to whip up sales:

> Whate'er the noisy Scoundrel says
> It might be something in your Praise:
> And, Praise bestow'd in Grub-Street Rimes,
> Would vex one more a thousand Times . . .
> On me, when Dunces are satyrick,
> I take it for a Panegyrick.

Thus a vehement poem moves to its breezily unworried close. The libellers of Delany have been made small in a number of ways. Imagery, open contumely, inserted fable, have played their part. Not the least telling section, however, is that in which the anonymous and waspish assailants are consigned to a wretched habitat, combining Gin Lane, the debtor's prison and abject living quarters. Is it too literal-minded to recall that Grub Street was 'scarred with pestilential slum dwellings', with mean 'Courts and Alleys'; that its alehouses and dramshops were legion; or that the district had its places of confinement even before the White Cross Street debtors' gaol opened?[24]

A year later Swift returned briefly to the theme in his best-known poem, 'Verses on the Death of Dr Swift'.[25] It is a casual usage:

> Now Grub-Street Wits are all employ'd;
> With Elegies, the Town is cloy'd:
> Some Paragraph in ev'ry Paper,
> To *curse* the *Dean*, or *bless* the *Drapier*.

But in his other great creation of these years, 'On Poetry: A Rapsody', the idea looms much more prominently. This work might be regarded as Swift's final review of the Grub Street cohorts, whose puny yet belligerent antics he had observed ever since the *Tale* and *The Battle of the Books*. Among the many miseries which Swift describes as incident to the scribbler's career, he notes the annexation of former hack territory by a licensed invader, the poet laureate:

> Your Portion, taking *Britain* round,
> Was just one annual Hundred Pound.
> Now not so much as in Remainder
> Since *Cibber* brought in an Attainder;
> For ever fixt by Right Divine,
> (A Monarch's Right) on *Grubstreet* Line.
> Poor starvling Bard, how small thy Gains!

Again one sees the emphasis on the hereditary succession of Dulness, in this case given the dynastic power of George II – a King among Dunces (as Pope depicted him) and kingmaker into the bargain. One stratagem which Swift recommends, to help the unfortunate scribbler out of this fix, is to make sure that his work comes out anonymously: for 'Criticks have no partial Views,/Except they know whom they abuse.' But if the hack reveals his identity:

You lose your Credit all at once;
The Town will mark you for a Dunce:
The vilest Doggrel *Grubstreet* sends,
Will pass for yours with Foes and Friends.

Finally, after the celebrated passage in which Swift images the literary world in terms of vermin, fleas preyed on by smaller fleas, comes a masterly change of key into pretended lament:

Thus ev'ry Poet in his Kind,
Is bit by him that comes behind;
Who, tho' too little to be seen,
Can teaze, and gall, and give the Spleen;
Call Dunces, Fools, and Sons of Whores,
Lay *Grubstreet* at each others Doors:
Extol the *Greek* and *Roman* Masters,
And curse our modern Poetasters.
Complain, as many an ancient Bard did,
How Genius is no more rewarded . . .
And all their Brother Dunces lash,
Who crowd the Press with hourly Trash.

O, *Grubstreet*! how do I bemoan thee,
Whose graceless Children scorn to own thee!
This filial Piety forgot,
Deny their Country like a SCOT:
Tho' by their Idiom and Grimace
They soon betray their native Place:
Yet *thou* hast greater Cause to be
Asham'd of them, than they of thee.
Degenerate from their ancient Brood,
Since first the Court allow'd them Food.

This is a climactic moment in the evolution of Grub Street mythology, characteristically handled (almost slurred over, indeed) by Swift, with his easy vernacular of scorn.[26]

In these lines a number of the principal elements in the myth are brought together. The image of parasitic insects carries with it the usual idea of internecine struggle, the relentless competitive urge of men on the make. Similarly, the scribblers emerge as ungrateful, groundlessly vain of their place in literary history, *arrivistes* whose low origins are only too clear. On this occasion, Grub Street is explicitly call a territory, in the comparison with Scotland. Elsewhere in the poem more is said of the 'Idiom', that is not just the argot but the whole life-style of hacks, and the 'Grimace', the unlovely postures they strike at the behest of any well-heeled patron. Like his friend Pope, Swift draws attention to the municipal organisation of the Dunces:

> But these are not a thousandth Part
> Of Jobbers in the Poets Art,
> Attending each his proper Station,
> And all in due Subordination;
> Thro' ev'ry Alley to be found,
> In Garrets high, or under Ground . . .

'Jobbers' because they are middlemen, ingrafters, men who profit out of warmongering. And Swift, too, has noticed the way in which urban civilisation mirrors the spread of Dulness:

> For Poets (you can never want 'em,
> Spread thro' *Augusta Trinobantum*)
> Computing by their Pecks of Coals,
> Amount to just Nine thousand Souls.
> These o'er their proper Districts govern,
> Of Wit and Humour, Judges sov'reign.
> In ev'ry Street a City-bard
> Rules, like an Alderman his Ward.
> His indisputed Rights extend
> Thro' all the Lane, from End to End.
> The Neighbours round admit his *Shrewdness*,
> For songs of *Loyalty* and *Lewdness*.

And further, the contention between 'two bordering Wits':

> Some famed for Numbers soft and smooth,
> By Lovers spoke in *Punch*'s Booth.
> And some as justly Fame extols
> For lofty Lines in *Smithfield* Drols.
> *Bavius* in *Wapping* gains Renown,
> And *Maevius* reigns o'er *Kentish-Town*:
> *Tigellius* plac'd in *Phoebus*' Car,
> From *Ludgate* shines to *Temple-bar*.

After Tigellius, the bard of Fleet Street, comes Cibber, court laureate. The point is exactly the same as Pope's – just as the civic hierarchy has broken down, with city men invading the West End, so
cultural order has been shattered. Dulness spills over from Drury
Lane to St James's.[27]

There could be no clearer demonstration of the impress of the
first *Dunciad* upon Swift's mind. He had been out of England for
almost twenty years, excluding two brief periods in the mid-
twenties. He lived in the comparatively un-metropolitan Dublin,
where city fathers counted for less and where the 'suburban muse'
had no chartered home. Yet he writes in the familiar 'idiom' of
Grub Street: the 'lofty Lines in *Smithfield* Drols' is a choice expression, holding much of *The Dunciad* in little. Elsewhere in the 'Rapsody', we encounter other ingredients of earlier Scriblerian satire.
There is the stress on duncely heritage, with the rollcall of bad poets
such as Flecknoe and Blackmore; the usual easy reference to topi-
calities, and to the passing London scene ('Sir *Bob*', 'A *Wills*', 'A
Statesman, or a South-Sea *Jobber*', and so on); the familiar quest for
the Bathos:

> For instance; When you rashly think,
> No Rhymer can like *Welsted* sink.
> His Merits ballanc'd you shall find,
> The Laureat leaves him far behind.
> *Concannen*, more aspiring Bard,
> Climbs downwards, deeper by a Yard:
> Smart JEMMY MOOR with Vigor drops,
> The Rest pursue as thick as Hope:
> With Heads to Points the Gulph they enter,
> Linkt perpendicular to the Centre:
> And as their Heels elated rise,
> Their Heads attempt the nether Skies.

There is the customary reference to a bookseller, here Lintot, whose
offences against Swift must have been marginal and second-hand.
There is a verse compounded of loathing, whose very utterance requires a sort of contemptuous expectoration: 'The Spawn of *Bridewell*, or the *Stews*'. Most striking of all, perhaps, following a reference
to 'A Duchess, or a Suburb-Wench', this bit of poetic townscaping:

Or oft when Epithets you link,
In gaping Lines to fill a Chink;
Like stepping Stones to save a Stride,
In Streets where Kennels are too wide:
Or like a Heel-piece to support
A Cripple with one Foot too short:
Or like a Bridge that joins a Marish
To Moorlands of a diff'rent Parish.

This is like some Hogarthian nightmare, with its crowd of infected, tumultuous, irrevocably *urban* visions. It would be fanciful to read into the lines a conscious reference to the marsh of Moorfields, abutting on the parish of Cripplegate. One need not even assert that Swift drew subliminally on such recollections of the London scene. It is quite enough to remark that, unfailingly, the topography and nomenclature of London's ghetto suburbs come to the aid of the poetry. When the Augustan satirists think of foul conditions, they never stray far from the map of London.[28]

I have not pointed out these elements in order to impugn the 'Rapsody' on the score of originality. On the contrary, it is full of the flavour and race of Swift. The interesting fact remains: it was written in 1733, the last of its author's major poems. (I exclude 'The Legion Club', where the undeniable power is in some degree a function of distortion or imbalance.) The 'Rapsody' is controlled, assured, precise in aim. If it lacks the dramatic conviction and engagement of the *Epistle to Arbuthnot*, the 'Rapsody' does exhibit abundant imaginative life. All in all, it constitutes Swift's most complete enquiry into the present state of Dulness, once the *Tale* was behind him. By contrast 'The Legion Club' offers sustained invective. Only the opening description of the 'large and lofty' building which houses Parliament can be seen to allude to the themes we have been considering.[29]

In the poems considered, a few references to the fraternity of 'Dunces' may have been observed. These also are concentrated in the later poems. Apart from the instances quoted, the expression is found in 'A Libel on Doctor Delany' (1730) and, in a less specialised sense than usual, in 'A Panegyric on Dr Swift' (1730). This is, of course, a further sign of the ways in which Swift's poetic vocabulary was modified after the appearance of *The Dunciad*.[30]

If Grub Street itself is not conspicuous in the correspondence of Swift, then the full panoply of ugliness which the term stood for is much more prominent. Both in letters to Swift and in his own communications to friends, the plagues of Dulness occupy a good deal of space. London correspondents, predictably, furnish apt examples. As remarked in Ch.I, the doughty City alderman, John Barber, wrote to Swift, in 1732 describing 'a raree-show (or pageant)' with a satirical poem 'thrown from the press to the mob, in public view'. This cavalcade had been briefly foreshadowed by Anthony Henley, in a letter of twenty years earlier. Swift himself writes to Barber of the riots occasioned by the Excise Crisis, with all the intense concern of an expatriate. The doings of the 'mob' and the 'rabble' figure largely in the letters of the Harley ministry era – as witness the index to Sir Harold Williams' edition, *sub voce* 'mob'. Events retailed to Swift in his isolation include a fire on Tower Hill, described by Charles Ford. Another time a correspondent mentions the sights of the town as they were then conceived: '[we] made the tour of the city: we saw *Bedlam*, the lions, and what not . . .' When Swift himself is in London, his topics range from the Mohocks to scurrilous 'Scribblers'. In short, the separate strands that went into the symbolic drama of Grub Street can be plucked from the journal of everyday doings that go into the correspondence. What was physically oppressive becomes no less painful when ritualised in art. The harsh lineaments of eighteenth-century London take on an aspect of grotesque comedy in the mask of satire; but the face still fits.[31]

The Road to Tyburn

It is hard to think of any major artist so possessed by one quarter of the town as was Swift by Newgate and its environs. Two aspects of the social character of this district were overlaid on one another to produce this striking impress. As outlined earlier, there came together in this quarter two potent currents of myth – Smithfield, with its tradition of fairs and boisterous showbiz junketings, and Newgate, the epicentre of crime and punishment. Thus geography locked in symbolic embrace the centre of the entertainment industry – a moddern, but not inappropiate, phrase – and the setting for that drama of guilt and retribution which acted out the same penal ethos as did Augustan satire. Clearly, physical proximity went with other bases of comparison. The Fleet ran across this tract of land, bringing in its sluggish wake the usual flotsam of squalor. In addition, since the procession to Tyburn set off from Newgate up Holborn, the abundant files of the malefactors' register supplied a ready-made Newgate literature, to match the productions of the Smithfield muse. When Pope wrote of 'hymning Tyburn's elegiac lay' (B.I.41), he was helping to forge this link. And when journalists of the time spoke of the court at Old Bailey as a 'scene' or 'theatre', they were likewise suggesting a parallel with the elaborately staged shows at Bartholomew Fair. Defoe, for example, relating the end of Jonathan Wild, speaks of 'the last scene of his Life at the Gallows' and adds 'the Scene was then short'. He refers to the 'Tragedy' enacted. Of course, the semantic facts follow the historical facts. Tyburn executions *were* staged as theatrical set-pieces.[32]

All this, every writer of the age inherited. Swift is unique in the pressure exerted on him, not in the nature of the influence. It was he who, in a suggestive aside, originally set out the idea of 'a Newgate pastoral, among the whores and thieves there', over a decade before *The Beggar's Opera*. Long before, in the *Journal*, he had spoken of 'a Smithfield bargain', the proverbial phrase for a sharp deal. He writes to Pope of 'deal[ing] in the Smithfield way.' His letters include references to Newgate and the Press Yard.[33] Throughout his life, he seems to have used Smithfield and Newgate as synonomous with quackery, crooked business and wrongdoing of every kind. It was he rather than Pope (or so the evidence suggests) who first seized the literary and lexical potentialities that were lurking beneath the London gazetteer with its offhand listing of familiar place-names. Swift, with his oddly literal-minded genius, leapt from the most commonplace reality to fancy.

In 1709-10 Swift wrote two famous poems for *The Tatler*. These comparatively short works have attracted a large amount of attention, perhaps because of a misleading 'realism' which causes them to be read as engaging travesties of classical originals, in which heroic idiom is risibly applied to squalid objects. That their effect is more complex than this, recent criticism has beugn to establish. Roger Savage, in a perceptive essay on 'A Description of the Morning', has shown some of the other contributory elements in the poem. He argues:

> The *Description of the Morning* has often been seen as a piece of un-complicated realism, vivid and assured or barren and pointless, accord-ing to the taste of the critic; but its realism is not simply the result of a walk through London at dawn with a camera. It is determined and moulded by what Swift has learned from the masters of the descriptive tradition and by the attitude to them he had come to adopt. The poem is basically mock-*descriptio*, a comic imitation of the classical ideal; and on this level it reads like a parody of the dawn-scene in Bysshe's *Parnassus* . . . The mythology is adapted daringly and wittily from the classical tradition, and the result is rich burlesque. . . . Swift here is not simply putting a moustache on the *Mona Lisa*, reducing outward tradition to mere grotesque. . . . [Whereas] his journalist contemporary, Tom Brown . . . has a journalist's camera: Swift is working on a canvas prepared for formal *descriptio*. . . . Where [other writers of burlesque see] realism as one device among many use-ful to the parodist, Swift seems to be using burlesque of the formal *descriptio* just so that he can draw attention to the real, to common city nature. There is no place in his strategy for conceits *or* whimsies.

After devoting some attention to the companion piece on 'A City Shower', Mr Savage concludes:

> traditional ideal art . . . is at once a yard-stick and a dead letter, while the crude actual is both a source of vitality and a target for neo-classic irony. . . . The classics embody a just and beautiful nature; the contemporary realities of a sordid Queen Anne London are no more than a travesty of true nature; so to copy these apparent realities . . . is to travesty the classics.

In the light of this clinching analysis, it would obviously be a mistake to regard these poems as simply rendering the 'crude actual' in a comically high-falutin' style. The high and the low interact on one another. They form (to adapt one of Mr Savage's expressions) a chemical compound.[34]

Some valuable insights are provided by another recent critic, Brendan O Hehir. In assessing the meaning of the 'Shower' poem, Mr O Hehir observes that 'the two named well springs of the Flood have each stronger associations with moral than with physical corruption.' He mentions such Smithfield attributes as the profligacy of Bartholomew Fair, and notes the attempts to suppress the fair around this time. Settle's presence there in 1707 is also brought into account. Mr O Hehir stresses the notorious connotations of Newgate, ranging from the Tyburn procession to the offal which was left near the meat emporium. His analysis neatly relates such phenomena as the Fleet Ditch, 'the notorious cloaca of eighteenth-century London', and the 'abuse of moral and civil laws' of which the indecorous, deliberately mangled conclusion is emblematic. In fact, though he makes no claim along these lines, Mr O Hehir's eassay could be viewed as a pioneering attempt to uncover the topographic strata in Augustan satiric vocabulary.[35]

With these studies behind us, it is possible to speak more briefly of Swift's two 'Description' poems. In particular, the 'Morning' assembles standard *topoi* of the critique of Dulness – dirt, shrill noise, the lascivious maid and the slipshod prentice, bailiffs crowding the doorstep, the ill-made road, and

> The Turnkey now his Flock returning sees,
> Duly let out a Nights to Steal for Fees.

Yet these elements are left as separate motifs in a posed landscape – what Mr Savage recognises as the *descriptio* framework. Later on, both Pope and Swift himself will energise this scene, and by dissolving physical squalor, poverty and crime in one supreme metaphor they will achieve a symbolic rather than an allegoric truth – a fictional rather than a scenic vividness – a mythic rather than a journalistic entity.

The 'City Shower' is more elaborate, but something of the same process can be discerned. Briefly Swift introduces a lay figure of the type Pope utilises in his Horatian poems:

> Sauntring in Coffee-house is *Dulman* seen;
> He damns the Climate, and complains of Spleen.

But the character is dropped straight away, and the kind of spectator through whom Gay focusses the London sights in *Trivia* is dismissed from the carefully managed tableau. The setting is representative rather than detailed; the method one of graphic portraiture instead of real dramatisation. In Mr Savage's terms, the poem displays 'the ludicrous attempt of an imperfect, trivial London to live up to classical dialects and situations.'[36] The first epithet is important. What would be sinister in other contexts – an offensive stink, spleen, the feuds of 'Triumphant Tories, and desponding Whigs', drunkards, bullies, 'frightful Din' – remain on the level of amiable vignettes. There is more than one reason for this state of affairs. It has a good deal to do with Swift's uninvolved, sharply dismissive tone. But another major factor is the absence of a controlling metaphor. In the 'Shower' there is a single momentary entrance by the 'needy Poet'. Not until the idea of Dulness, with its more than spiritual home in the suburbs, was developed, would the satirists manage to turn the impressionistic photomontage into a literary fiction embodying genuine understanding. The discovery of Grub Street opened a new imaginative continent. The satire moved from social, pictorial, emblematic observation towards poetic and cultural insight. Once the myth was evolved, the writers had a basis for imagery, an explanation along with a symbol, a story-line to go with a location.

Nevertheless, when we come to the famous closing passage, it does, I think, acquire a new reverberation in the light of the argument presented in this book:

> Now from all Parts the swelling Kennels flow,
> And bear their Trophies with them as they go:
> Filth of all Hues and Odours seem to tell
> What Streets they sail'd from, by the Sight and Smell.
> They, as each Torrent drives, with rapid Force
> From *Smithfield*, or St. *Pulchre*'s shape their Course,
> And in huge Confluent join at *Snow-Hill* Ridge,
> Fall from the *Conduit* prone to *Holborn*-Bridge.
> Sweepings from Butchers Stalls, Dung, Guts, and Blood,
> Drown'd Puppies, stinking Sprats, all drench'd in Mud,
> Dead Cats and Turnip-Tops come tumbling down the Flood.

Lengthy analysis would be redundant. The torrents of Dulness concentrate into the noisome 'Flood' (ironic, of course) which is the ditch. This confluence of all that is most physically oppressive and fetid reveals the modern capital in its full glory. Humanist lore had pictured the city as the repository of civilised values. Instead of this rounded, polished, refined nucleus of the best in communal living ('urbanity', in the old sense) there is the new urbanism. Mortality instead of the timeless perfection of the great city: 'Trophies' won not in heroic combat but dredged from the lowest haunts of men. Many commentators have argued that Swift, in *Gulliver* and else-where, achieves his almost unbearable power through a repeated con-trast he draws between the more-than-human aspirations of humanity and the sub-human physicality of life as it is actually lived. At the end of the 'Shower', he makes the same point; a vision of animalism as modern city experience make us live it. And all this in a single, precisely plotted corner of London.[37]

Swift reminds us that London was not only the great mart, but also a major productive centre. Yet, paradoxically, its landscape re-mained in part agrarian, with livestock commonplace in the streets. Nor was there anything paranoid or peculiar about Swift's view of Newgate. As noted, the *British Journal* compared 'the Droves that are carried to Tyburn' with those that are sent to Smithfield for the same purpose – thus linking the slaughter of beasts with that of criminals.[38] What was dubbed in *Bartholomew Fair* (II, iii) 'the heavy hill of Holborn' was ominous chiefly on account of the human carn-age; but this was also the route of the last journey for countless animals bound for the abattoir. The Augustans tended to be unsenti-mental about such things, but they were well aware of the atmosphere of sudden death which clung to Smithfield.

Nevertheless, the district was in the entertainment business. Apart from the fairground drolls, the executions were themselves among the biggest free shows in town. Rudé expresses it thus:

The greatest sport of all was to watch the hangings at 'Tyburn Fair' [note the expression] or to toast the victims in beer or gin as they were carried along Holborn, St Giles's and Oxford Street to the place of exe-cution. 'Within my recollection,' wrote [Francis] Place, 'a *hanging day* was to all intents and purposes a fair day. The streets from Newgate to

Tyburn were thronged with people, and all the windows were filled.'
The onlookers on such 'brutalizing occasions' were, added Place with
pardonable exaggeration, composed of 'the whole vagabond population
of London, all the thieves, and all the prostitutes, and all those who
were evil-minded, and some, comparatively few, curious people'.

This concourse of Dulness went on till public executions ceased in
1783, in the teeth of Samuel Johnson and others. At intervals of
about six weeks, the grisly charade would go on. It is worth recalling
that in the period 1688–1718 over fifty per cent of those convicted on capital charges actually went to the gallows. More rarely
burnings went on at Tyburn, generally for that inveterate Cripplegate practice, coining. Barbara Spencer, born in the parish and resident in a Moorfields alehouse, went to the stake at Tyburn in 1721.
Others such as Mary Berry, who lodged in Grub Street itself and
then in Moorfields, and who was found guilty of coining in 1732,
no doubt followed her. But more commonly the cart would halt before St Sepulchre's, the principal as likely as not dressed in his best
clothes, while the other supporting actors wore mourning, and the
cortege would wend its way to Tyburn.[39]

It was this performance which drove so deep into the eighteenth-
century mind. The literature of the time is full of allusions, bleak or
flippant, direct or indirect. Thus, Sir Sampson Legend – apposite
surname – of his son Valentine in Congreve's *Love for Love*:

> Sirrah, you'll be hanged; I shall live to see you go up Holborn Hill.
> Has he not a rogue's face? Speak, brother, you understand physio-
> gnomy; a hanging look to me – of all my boys the most unlike me. He
> has a damned Tyburn face, without the benefit of the clergy.

Naturally, literary men were not immune from the widespread interest in these regular displays. When Boswell first came up to London,
he succumbed to the popular feeling:

> My curiosity to see the melancholy spectacle of the executions was so
> strong that I could not resist it, although I was sensible that I would
> suffer much from it. In my younger years I had read in the *Lives of
> the Convicts* so much about Tyburn that I had a sort of horrid eagerness
> to be there. I also wished to see the last behaviour of Paul Lewis, the
> handsome fellow whom I had seen the day before [on a visit to New-
> gate]. Accordingly I took Captain Temple with me, and he and I got

upon a scaffold very near the fatal tree, so that we could clearly see all
the dismal scene. There was a most prodigious crowd of spectators.
I was most terribly shocked, and thrown into a very deep melancholy.

This dates from 1763, and it is filtered through Boswell's highly
idiosyncratic sensibility. Yet the passage comes close to the heart of
that fascinated disgust which permeates Augustan satire. Boswell's
'horrid eagerness' corresponds to the blend of emotions with which
society regarded glamorous criminals, and with which Pope ob-
sessively recorded the annals of a segment of the population whose
doings he held in abhorrence.[40] The 'grotesqueries sublimed into
loveliness' within his poems derive from this mixture of repulsion and
creative infatuation.

Undoubtedly the publication of a huge Newgate literature contributed to the state of affairs I have outlined. The 'Lives of the
Convicts' were important literary documents, if only on account of
their popularity. Moreover, the one Dunce of genius chances to have
forged a major imaginative vehicle (the novel) to no inconsiderable
degree out of the materials of rogues' tales. To this topic, I shall return in the next chapter. However, we may note at this point that
John Oldham had already noted how the suburban muse was active
in the composition of the malefactors' register. His lines 'Upon a
Printer' contain the following:

> May'st thou ne'er rise to History, but what
> Poor *Grubstreet* Penny Chronicles relate,
> Memoirs of *Tyburn* and the mournful State
> Of Cut-purses in *Holborn* Cavalcade . . .

On another occasion, Oldham had called up another local association:

> Till urg'd by Want, like broken Scriblers, thou
> Turn Poet to a Booth, a *Smithfield* Show,
> And write Heroick Verse for *Barthol'mew*.[41]

For most of his life Swift was unable to follow this 'cavalcade' himself, though he did take a close interest in a rather similar phenomenon, the anti-popery procession of 1711.[42] However, 'Memoirs of
Tyburn' were always in his line: witness a poem such as 'Clever *Tom
Clinch* going to be hanged' (1726). This opens,

As clever *Tom Clinch*, while the Rabble was bawling,
Rode stately through *Holbourn*, to die in his Calling;
He stopt at the *George* for a Bottle of Sack . . .

and passes on via reference to Jonathan Wild to a resolute conclusion: 'Then follow the Practice of clever *Tom Clinch*, | Who hung like a Hero, and never would flinch.'[43] Again, there is 'Blue-skin's Ballad', variously attributed to Swift and to Gay, a sort of *Beggar's Opera* writ small, with the ostensible setting named as Newgate gaol and the Old Bailey, but the animus obviously directed against Walpole, the Court and its placemen. ('Honest *Wild*' figures once more.)[44] These, and there are others like them, are not poems of high merit. Their interest derives from the fact that Swift, in exile, still turns to the criminal ecology of London to develop his moral and political critique of the age. There were criminals and desperados in Dublin; there was the full array of judicial pomp. But the authentic Tyburn imagery could not be translated to Ireland; it flourished only in its native soil, where the grisly 'tree' thrust its roots deep into the English imagination.

Swift's links with Bedlam and Bridewell have been noted in previous chapters. More interesting in some ways is his special involvement with the bookselling quarter of Little Britain. In fact the stretch of the road formerly known as Duck Lane, running out of Smithfield, was the part that interested him. In Stow's description, '*Duck-lane* cometh out of *Little Brittain*, and falls into *Smithfield*, a Place early inhabited by Booksellers, that sell second-hand Books.' According to some authorities Little Britain was already losing ground to the area about St Paul's; this is what John Macky, usually a reliable witness, implies in 1724. Certainly in the reports of Robert Harley's press spy around 1705, printers were still numerous in Little Britain: at least one leading music publisher set up there in the 1730's. A number of figures in the newspaper business were located there well into the century. The unfortunate John Matthews lived in the street, where the family printing works stood. According to the eminent antiquarian Sir Henry Ellis, the Ballards 'were the last of the old race of booksellers who inhabited Little Britain.' Probably the high point in the history of the area had been the late seventeenth

century. It was then that John Oldham wrote of the archetypal
Dunces Ogilby and Quarles,

> Who after shalt in *Duck-Lane* Shops be thrown,
> To mould with *Silvester*, and *Shirley* there,
> And truck for pots of Ale next *Stourbridg-Fair*.

Samuel Buckley, the printer turned Gazetteer and government
liaison man, lived in Little Britain in later years. It was through contacts such as these that Pope and Swift must have come to know the
place. For Moll Flanders it had been simply an avenue of escape; for
the Scriblerian group, it became a ready and affectionate topic. The
unusual name of the street occasioned some byplay. The author of *A
Trip through London* (1728) thinks it proper to remind the inhabitants
that 'the same is a Part of his Majesty's Dominions', although the
inhabitants act as if it weren't. And similarly Swift to Alderman
Barber in 1738: 'pox on the modern phrase *Great Britain*, which is
only to distinguish it from Little Britain, where old cloaths and books
are to be bought and sold'. In a pamphlet of five years earlier, Swift
makes mention of rummaging about in Duck Lane. If the 'Shower'
devises an *ur*-Grub Street in the Newgate area, Duck Lane formed a
sort of equivalent to Moorfields and Rag Fair – likewise the resting
place of the second-hand and the unwanted.[45]

Some of the associations trapped within the orbit of Smithfield
may be gauged from this passage of Andrew Marvell's *Rehearsal
Transpros'd*, the first satire to develop the Grub Street conceit
(Ch. VI).

> The Duke of Muscovy indeed declared war against Poland because he
> and his nation had been vilifyed by a Polish poet: but the author of the
> Ecclesiastical Politie [Samuel Parker] would, it seems, disturb the peace
> of Christendom for the good old cause of a superannuated chanter of
> Saffron-Hill and Pye-Corner. But though indeed he doth not write his
> books in the Smithfield metre, yet they are all blank ballad . . .[46]

Pope was equally to associate 'superannuated' bards like Settle with
Smithfield, on account both of the Fair and of his Charterhouse
lodging. Swift assuredly knew *The Rehearsal Transpros'd*.[47] Though
he never took this hint farther into a full-blown Smithfield myth, as
works like the 'Shower' seem to promise, he had two good excuses.

He was in close touch with Pope, and privileged to get advanced news of the progress of his friend's 'Dulness' during its composition. Secondly, and less happily, he was physically removed from the appointed shrine of Dulness.

Public Abuses

Swift often lamented his exile in Dublin. How genuine this often-expressed feeling was, we may find it hard to decide. Professor Ehrenpreis has suggested that 'there is always a first-handedness in his experience of his native country which the life in England lacked . . . Throughout his activities in Ireland one notices a zestfulness, a contact with reality, a depth of insight, which Swift often fails to exhibit in England . . .'[48] Whatever the truth on this point, it cannot be denied that Swift makes great rhetorical play with the fact of exile. A good example crops up in a splendid and too little considered poem, 'To Charles Ford Esqr on his Birth-day' (1723). Notable for rapid, well managed transitions, this work modulates at one juncture into a passionate outburst against London. Its swarm of 'bugs and Hanoverians', its oppressive police-state régime under Townshend 'threatning the Pillory and Jayl', are presented in lurid yet explicit terms, echoing for a moment those of Pope's 'Epilogue to the Satires' of fifteen years later. How can Ford, currently on a visit to Ireland, wish to return to such a place? Then Swift adopts a more confidential tone towards Ford; the style grows more intimate, if not chatty:

> I thought my very Spleen would burst
> When Fortune hither drove me first;
> Was full as hard to please as You,
> Nor Persons Names, nor Places knew;
> But now I act as other Folk,
> Like Pris'ners when their Gall is broke.
> If you have London still at heart
> We'll make a small one here by Art:
> The Diff'rence is not much between
> St James's Park and Stephen's Green;
> And Dawson street will serve as well
> To lead you thither, as Pell-mell . . .

And so on, for thirty sharply chiselled lines more.[49] It may look here like a desperate fiction, a wish-fulfilment perhaps. Yet there are indications that Swift may have been affected at a serious level by the notion of the mountain coming to Mahomet. At least, the goonish conceit of transplanting London 'by art' to the banks of the Liffey occurs more than once.

In this connection we must consider two works sometimes relegated to the Swiftian apocrypha. The first is the *Letter to a Young Poet*, well-known and often reprinted as Swift's. Some recent enquiries have cast doubt on this attribution and have disputed the validity of certain statististical findings. In my view the matter has not yet been established beyond doubt.[50] A fondness for certain syntactical forms is doubtless one important element in the profile of a given writer. It may be, however, that there are equally good tests, less amenable to statistical analysis. For example, the controls which an author brings into effect with relation to euphony deserve attention. It is possible to imagine, that is, the writer breaking a life-long habit and employing completely new syntactical patterns, for some particular end. Yet he might never permit a jarring hiatus – putting 'they amiably parted' for 'they parted amiably' – no matter what the overall structure of the sentence. It is also highly interesting, to return to the present case, to observe the use of Swift's favourite imagery in the *Letter to a Young Poet*. The rationale here is that critics were then largely unconscious of this element in style, or at least very little inclined to treat of it directly. Their terminology for discussing metaphoric activity of any kind was somewhat primitive, and they habitually take no account of such things as the sustained figures in Shakespeare or the controlling metaphors (as we should say today) in a work such as *Absalom and Achitophel*. One consequence of this state of affairs is that even an able parodist would be unlikely to attempt a close copy of his subject's figurative devices. When, therefore, we come on not merely the ideas of Swift, the language of Swift, and the humour of Swift in this *Letter*, but also – more tangibly – the metaphoric idiom of Swift, the case grows less easy to brush aside. I do not know if Swift did write the *Letter*, but I am sure that the evidence so far adduced against his authorship is less than conclusive.

Certain of the apparently Swiftian features might be explained as merely the product of a remarkably sedulous ape. There is a well-known section concerning the 'short and easy Method lately found out of Abstracts, Abridgments, Summaries, &c. which are admirable Expedients for being very learned with little or no Reading.' The hint for this might easily have been taken from the 'Digression in Praise of Digressions' in the *Tale*. Even here there is a surprising metaphysical wit in evidence: 'For authors are to be used like Lobsters, you must look for the best Meat in the Tails, and lay the Bodies back again in the Dish.' Perhaps a skilled paradist of Swift *could* have possessed his distinctly seventeenth-century character of mind, but one should not multiply such hypotheses beyond reason. At all events, the writer exhibits plenty of concrete life, with an easy recourse to homely analogy. Thanks to the modern editor, he says, 'every author . . . sweats under himself, being over-loaded with his own Index, and carries, like a North-Country Pedlar, all his Substance and Furniture upon his Back, and with as great Variety of Trifles'. It may not be Swift, but it really is quite magnificent.

The second half of the *Letter* is more directly relevant. The writer sets out his thoughts for the encouragement of poetry in the kingdom. Initially his topics are unmistakably Irish, with Hibernian politics and economics hovering in the background.

> . . . And withal of what great Benefit it may be to our Trade to en-
> courage that Science here, (for it is plain our Linen-Manufacture is
> advanced by the great Waste of Paper made by our present Sett of
> Poets, not to mention other necessary Uses of the same to Shop-
> keepers, especially Grocers, Apothecaries, and Pastry-Cooks; and I
> might add, but for our Writers, the Nation wou'd be in a little time be
> utterly destitute of Bum-Fodder, and must of Necessity import the
> same from England and Holland, where they have it in great abundance,
> by the indefatigable Labour of their own Wits . . .

Here are several familiar ingredients in the assault on Dulness. The patriotic projector, trumpeting his 'Birth-right as a Briton'; the sanitary allusions; the hypostasised present set of wits, unnaturally leagued together; the cosy intimacy with journeymen of the town.

No surprise, consequently, when the next paragraph makes this link explicit:

Seriously then, I have many Years lamented the want of a Grub-Street in this our large and polite City [Dublin], unless the whole may be called one. . . . Every one knows Grub-Street is a Market for Small-Ware in Wit, as necessary, considering the usual Purgings of the human Brain, as the Nose is upon a Man's Face: And for the same Reasons we have here a Court, a College, a Playhouse, and beautiful Ladies, and fine Gentlemen, and good Claret, and abundance of Pens, Ink, and Paper, (clear of Taxes) and every other Circumstance to provoke Wit; and yet those whose Province it is have not yet thought fit to appoint a place for Evacuations of it. . . .

This 'Defect' has not only prejudiced the commonwealth of letters, it has even impaired the citizens' health:

I believe our corrupted Air, and frequent thick Fogs, are in a great measure owing to the common exposal of our Wit, and that with good Management our poetical Vapours might be carry'd off in a common Drain, and fall into one Quarter of the Town, without infecting the whole, as the Case is at Present, to the great Offence of our Nobility and Gentry, and others of nice Noses. When Writers of all Sizes, like Freemen of the City, are at liberty to throw out their Filth and excrementious Productions in every Street as they please, what can the Consequence be, but that the Town must be poyson'd, and become such another Jakes, as by report of our great Travellers, Edinburgh is at Night, a thing well to be consider'd in these pestilential Times.[51]

For once, the projector is opposed to the effects of Dulness; but the diagnosis itself is the customary one. Likewise with the appeal which follows to the municipal authorities, asking them to serve two ends at once, 'both to keep the Town sweet, and encourage Poetry in it'. Nor is any exception to be made for satirical poets or writers of lampoons,

for though indeed their Business is to rake into Kennels, and gather up the Filth of Streets and Families, (in which respect they may be, for aught I know, as necessary to the Town as Scavengers or Chimney sweeps) yet I have observed they too have themselves at the same Time very foul cloathes, and, like dirty Persons, leave more Filth and Nastiness than they sweep away.

If this is simulated repugnance, a careful take-off of Swift's passion for cleanliness, it is notably well carried out.

At this juncture there appears the central thesis:

> In a Word, what I would be at . . . is, That some private Street, or
> blind Alley, of this Town may be fitted up at the Charge of Publick,
> as an apartment for the Muses, (like those at Rome and Amsterdam, for
> their Female Relations) and be wholly consigned to the Uses of our
> Wits, furnish'd compleatly with all Appurtenances, such as Authors,
> Supervisors, Presses, Printers, Hawkers, Shops, and Ware-Houses,
> abundance of Garrets, and every other Implement and Circumstance
> of Wit; the Benefit of which would obviously be this, viz. That we
> should then have a safe Repository for our best Productions, which at
> present are handed about in Single Sheets or Manuscripts, and may
> altogether be lost, (which were a Pity) or at the best are subject, in that
> loose Dress, like handsome Women, to great Abuses.

I hope that this far into my argument it will be unnecessary to specify
each commonplace of the Scriblerian satiric platform. Once again
hack writing is forced to find its accomodation in the worst part of the
town; its devotees go cheek by jowl with whores, its stock of 'every
. . . Implement and Circumstance of Wit' packed into crowded
commercial premises hedged about with garrets. The location of
Little Britain in relation to Smithfield, Saffron Hill and Holborn
comes quickly to mind.

The narrator then turns to the state of the playhouse, and moves to
a proposal that if the national bank is granted a charter, so then should
poetry be accorded this privilege. And he has another scheme, taken
directly from the *Tale*:

> I believe also, it might be proper to erect a Corporation of Poets in this
> City. I have been Idle enough in my Time, to make a Computation of
> Wits here, and do find we have three hundred performing Poets and
> upwards, in and about this Town, reckoning six Score to the Hundred,
> and allowing for Demi's, like Pint Bottles; including also the several
> Denominations of Imitators, Translators, and Familiar-Letter-Writers,
> &c.

These scribblers will easily 'furnish out' a corporation. Moreover,
there are abundant poetasters (if not one 'Masterly Poet') to supply
enough 'Wardens and Beadles' – the municipal image again. This
desire to see poetry made a lackey of the civic authorities is plainly
enunciated at one point:

I long to see the Day, when our Poets will be a regular and distinct Body, and wait upon our Lord-mayor on publick Days, like other good Citizens, in Gowns turn'd up with Green instead of lawrels; and when I myself, who make this Proposal, shall be free of their Company.

Pope was to go one better, and permit his regular troops of Dulness not only to parade on Lord Mayor's Day but to make sport and riot as they pleased.

At the end the writer brings us back to the comparison with the city where the true Grub Street lay.

What if our Government had a Poet-Laureat here, as in England? What if our University had a Professor of Poetry here as in England? What if our Lord-Mayor had a City Bard here, as in England? And, to refine upon England, What if every Corporation, Parish, and Ward in this Town, had a Poet in Fee, as they have not in England?

This is a beautiful piece of rhetoric, though distorted by its application to so silly an end. The repeated phrase 'as in England', followed by the splendidly anticlimactic 'as they have not in England' – even the cadence is bathetic. Not even England has yet sunk to that, despite their professors who are poetasters (Joseph Trapp, say) and their Elkanah Settles. The writer has in mind that domestic poets might be instituted, along the lines of a domestic chaplain, but he seems pessimistic about this plan.[52]

All in all, the *Letter* is a striking piece of writing. Its root ideas are ordinary enough – roughly, the establishment of what Pope, in his imitation of Donne's second satire, was to refer to as 'new tenements in Hell' (42). *The Dunciad*, needless to say, gives us a more comprehensive and integrated vision of these new quarters let out to the Dull. Yet the *Letter to a Young Poet* is itself executed with brilliant imaginative zest. The persona is deployed with finesse: he both embodies literary idiocy and exposes it in others. Moreover, the idea of blaming Dublin for lacking the horrors of Grub Street opens up splendid avenues for satire. Simultaneously the writer can draw attention to the real defects of the place, mostly shared with any modern city, and re-emphasise the still-unique nightmares of the London scene. There is an underlying political innuendo, as well. Ireland is subservient, dependent, even to the provision of a Grub

Street. Her deprivations extend to the public vices she is allowed to enjoy.

Several of the tracts Swift composed in his Irish years bear on the theme of this book, under one aspect or another. His interest in criminal biography appears in a characteristic hoax, *The Last Speech and Dying Words of Ebenezer Elliston* (1722). Similarly, another pamphlet full of the flavour of Swift, entitled *An Examination of Certain Abuses, Corruptions, and Enormities in the City of Dublin* (1732), displays the author's sharp awareness of the life of the streets. In this work he deals with the urban landscape that inspired Dickens to create a poetic symbolism of city living. But Swift for his part devises no elaborate imagery of dustheaps and rivers: he speaks with a flat finality of heaped-up human excrement, of raucous cries and bellows from the hawkers, of garrets and cellars. The tone is gaily ironic, indeed almost flippant, but these are the topics of the most intense Augustan vision. In a more glancing way, a curious piece called *On Barbarous Denominations in Ireland* exhibits the real Swift. Here the writer fulminates with mock-petulance against barbarous Hibernian place-names. He cites a number of English names, among them Farn-ham, Corn-bury, Barn-elms (thus printed), as a model of sensible nomenclature, against the 'hideous words' in the Irish brogue. He even proposes certain 'appelations, proper to express the talents of the owners' of various country seats. These include '*Dunce-hill*'. This analytic approach to language is as marked in Swift as in Joyce. One can hardly suppose that the implications of the phrase 'Grub Street' could have been lost on such a mind.[53]

Perhaps the most direct approach to our theme is found in *A Serious and Useful Scheme, to make an Hospital for Incurables* (1733). This was attributed by Scott and subsequent editors to Swift. It was, however, excluded from the eighteenth-century collections of the works, and Herbert Davis suggested Matthew Pilkington as a possible author.[54] As with the *Letter to a Young Poet*, the issue is largely academic. The *Scheme* is composed with assumed gravity, its manner that of a 'reasonable' advocate – a civil servant making a case, say – rather than a demented projector. It encapsulates much of the Grub Street legend as developed by the Scriblerian group.

The writer begins by pointing to the munificent provision of hospitals in London – for 'seamen worn out in the service of their country, and others for infirm soldiers', for those deprived of their reason, for widows and orphans, etc. Only one institution is lacking: a home for incurables of all kinds. With the usual confidence of the man who has an idea, he expects his innovation to be 'universally allowed necessary'. As a principal factor, he invokes the huge number of 'absolute incurables' in every walk of life:

> For instance; let any man seriously consider what numbers there are of incurable fools, incurable knaves, incurable scolds, incurable scribblers, (besides myself), incurable coxcombs, incurable infidels, incurable liars, incurable whores, in all places of public resort . . .

to which the writer adds such categories as the incurably vain. The process is a common one in Augustan satire: we move from a technical or neutral term (here the medical word 'incurable') to a loaded, moralising sense ('incurable' meaning 'inveterate' or 'obstinate'). To this list, there is further augmentation:

> Under the denomination of incurable fools, we may reasonably expect, that such an hospital would be furnished with considerable numbers of the growth of our universities; who, at present, appear in various professions in the world, under the venerable titles of physicians, barristers, and ecclesiastics.

The seminary of Dulness, in fact, by another name. And, predictably, the very next sentence uses the word – 'those ancient seminaries have been, for some years past, accounted little better than nurseries of such sort of incurables . . .'

The author goes on to analyse in detail the recruits to be expected, were such a foundation set up. (The last noun, incidentally, is employed more than once.) So many people will need 'accomodation', the inventor of the scheme concludes, that a strict rationing or quota system will be required. The legal profession would be denuded almost entirely; the Stock Exchange and the Palace of Westminster would likewise feel the pinch. A sort of nation-wide *anomie*, such as that envisaged in the *Argument against Abolishing Christianity*, is the likely outcome. A splendidly controlled hyperbole runs through the scheme:

> When I first determined to prepare this Scheme for the use and inspec-
> tion of the public, I intended to examine one whole ward in this city,
> that my computation of the number of incurable scolds might be more
> perfect and exact. But I found it impossible to finish my progress
> through more than one street.

None the less, this public-spirited enquirer carries out something of
a sample survey, starting with a wealthy Cornhill councillor. By a
statistical projection familiar to modern readers, the total number
of incurables in London, Westminster and Southwark is calculated.

At this point, the municipal interest shifts to the region of Cripplegate:

> As to the incurable scribblers, (of which society I have the honour to be
> a member), they probably are innumerable; and, of consequence, it
> will be absolutely impossible to provide for one-tenth part of their
> fraternity. However, as this set of incurables are generally more plagued
> with poverty than any other, it will be a double charity to admit them
> on the foundation; a charity to the world, to whom they are a common
> pest and nuisance; and a charity to themselves, to relieve them from
> want, contempt, kicking, and several other accidents of that nature, to
> which they are continually liable.
>
> Grub Street itself would then have reason to rejoice, to see so many
> of its half-starved manufacturers amply provided for; and the whole tribe
> of meagre incurables would probably shout for joy, at being delivered
> from the tyranny and garrets of printers, publishers, and booksellers.
>
> What a mixed multitude of ballad-writers, ode-makers, translators,
> farce-compunders, opera-mongers, biographers, pamphleteers, and
> journalists, would appear crowding to the hospital; not unlike the
> brutes resorting to the ark before the deluge! And what an universal
> satisfaction would such a sight afford to all, except pastry-cooks,
> grocers, chandlers, and tobacco-retailers, to whom alone the writings
> of those incurables were anyway profitable!

The ideas at the start are those of 'On Poetry: A Rapsody'; the idiom
generally that of Scriblerus. Pope, we recall, had thought fit to provide for 'the whole tribe of meagre incurables' by creating a Chelsea
Hospital for veteran hacks;[55] whilst the innuendo in the closing sentence is often paralleled in the satirists.

The author now moves on to Simon Wagstaff's territory, the
decayed beaux of St James's, here described as 'so many living
burlesques of human nature'. After this he turns to infidels and liars.

Then, recollecting his 'serious' intent, he produces a sort of costing exercise, headed 'A Computation of the Daily and Annual Expenses of an Hospital, to be erected for Incurables' (observe that last verb). In style this recalls the famous Bills of Gratitude drawn up by Swift in *Examiner* no. 17. This calculation does not reach quite the same delicious pitch of absurd-looking outrage; but it has its moments: as the item, 'Incurable coxcombs, are very numerous; and, considering what numbers are annually imported from France and Italy, we cannot admit fewer than ten thousand, which will be . . . £500.' At least forty thousand incurable scribblers are to be admitted, as they are amongst those 'in greatest distress for a daily maintenance'. Overall, this finicky and apparently literal weighing of the costs involved serves the writer's ends with conspicuous success: it reinforces our sense of his muddleheaded pertinacity, and bestows on his project a lunatic air of cogency. The same attention to detail emerges from a second calculation, the precise expense incurred in each category of inmate, as well as in the specific taxes which are to be levied to disburden society of these 'inconceivable plagues' in its midst.

After exculpating himself, very much in the style of Swift's projectors, from the charge of proposing 'an unjust or oppressive Scheme', the writer suggests a measure of self-help on the part of the incurables. Naturally the body of scribblers will have to be excused, as being 'found in very bad circumstances'. But other funds should be available for the 'endowment' from the estates of the other candidates for the hospital. Lotteries are another possible source of revenue. Finally, £6000 is to be obtained from the estate of Richard Norton, Esq, whose memory is to be fitly commemorated by a statue in the first apartment of the hospital. Now the footnote by the publisher (George Faulkner, Swift's main outlet) tells us that Norton was a man of fortune, who left his wealth to the poor of England. Now in fact Norton was a great crony of Anthony Henley, who had been a particularly good friend of Swift's over twenty years earlier. It is a little surprising that the much younger Pilkington should use this instance, although we know that he offered to the London bookseller Benjamin Motte a pamphlet on the subject, 'which he pretended came from an eminent hand' (doubtless Swift). According to Motte, another bookseller issued the book on his own refusal, but lost money on the venture. It is certain that Pope and Swift knew of the Norton affair; and the references in the *Scheme* are far from ruling out Swift's own participation.[56]

After this, the writer sets out certain features of the hospital as he envisages it. The governors should have '(if such a thing were possible) some appearance of religion, and belief in God' – a visionary expectation which would interest the arguer against abolition. Then comes the real *coup*:

> And I hope, in regard to the great pains I have taken, about this Scheme, that I shall be admitted upon the foundation, as one of the scribbling incurables. But, as an additional favour, I entreat, that I may not be placed in an apartment with a poet who hath employed his genius for the stage; because he will kill me with repeating his compositions: and I need not acquaint the world, that it is extremely painful to bear any nonsense – except our own.

Thus the scheme is commended to the legislature, in the hope that the endowment will duly be made. Again we find Nonsense given, not just institutional respectability, but a physical home – a place of its own. Not surprising, then, to find the dateline at the foot of the text: 'From my Garret in Moorfields, Aug. 20, 1733.' Whether the tract is by Pilkington or not, it is a characteristic development of garret mythology: one more lively survey of Grub Street properties.[57]

A work that comes into a slightly different category, and one undoubtedly from the hand of Swift, is *A Complete Collection of Genteel and Ingenious Conversation* (1738). The portion relevant to this study is not the 'conversation' itself, that curious anthology of worn-out cliché, but the Introduction. This is attributed to 'Simon Wagstaff, Esq.', a name possibly recalling Dr William Wagstaffe. The use of this persona involves something of a departure for Swift. In the *Tale of a Tub* he had likewise adopted the manner of a conceited, incompetent scribbler. And in his party writing during the Harley ministry he had taken over the accents of the hack journalist. What is new about Simon Wagstaff may be summed up under two headings – his social pretensions, and his technical concern.

Where the standard figure of myth is the garreteer, Wagstaff has spent his life in pursuing the great. And, whatever the rebuffs, he has to some degree made it – his address is not Moorfields or Hounsditch, but lodgings 'next door to the Gloucester-head in St James's-street'. This was a West End location, appropriate to one bent on instructing the public in the *ton* and manners of polite society. It was also a region familiar to Swift. He himself had lodged in King Street, St James's, and friends such as Sir Andrew Fountaine resided there at various times.[58] Possibly this in itself represents a dry comment by Swift. By the end of his life, that is, the scribbler has quit his former humble quarters in the slums, and set up house in the fashionable area. Grub Street has crossed the city into Westminster – the very removal allegorised in *The Dunciad*.

A large proportion of Wagstaff's energy is devoted to presenting himself as 'of good reputation in the world, and well acquainted with the best families in town'. He is, of course, one more in the grisly line of projectors compassed by Swift's imagination: his life has been spent 'improving and polishing all parts of conversation between persons of quality'. To this end he has 'laboured' in the usual misapplied fashion, having concocted a fixed routine by which the greater part of his days are nights are given to 'polite' company. With the methodical habits that the Scriblerian group always attach to pedantry, Wagstaff transcribes the choicest expressions he has overheard as soon as he returns home. Naturally, this Boswellian enterprise needs time – 'this I found was a work of infinite labour, and what required the nicest judgment, and consequently could not be brought to any degree of perfection in less than sixteen years more' than the twelve he had previously spent. With the usual complacence, he describes his resolution to defer publication until he could 'present a complete system to the world'. We are back with the threats of the author of the *Tale*. This recollection is driven home further when Wagstaff passes on to congratulate his native country on having 'outdone all the nations of Europe, in advancing the whole art of conversation to the greatest heighth it is capable of reaching'. Predictably, he believes that 'the whole genius, humour, politeness, and eloquence of England are summed up' in his system. Like the earlier Grubean spokesman, he makes a virtue out of every literary necessity. He boasts of the antiquity of his collection, that is its lack of originality. He delights in its amenability to rote-learning.

The place Wagstaff holds in the pantheon of Dulness comes out most clearly when the argument passes to the cultivation of this 'science'. He fulfils every Scriblerian demand by offering a 'proposal for erecting publick schools, provided with the best and ablest masters and mistresses, at the charge of the nation' to promote the subject. As often where the satirists are envisaging the 'selling' of a project by pressure-group methods, the verb *to erect* receives a special emphasis. It is as though Pope and Swift were not content merely to dramatise the founding or establishment of a college of unreason: they had to carry the idea as far as physical building. Another reason, of course, why Grub Street served their turn.

The prefacer goes on to display his gentility, by scornful asides on 'mean and vulgar people' (luckily, 'A footman can swear, but he cannot swear like a lord') as well as by easy references to the nobility in most cases, though, to an obscure baronet or a frumpish lady. But in reality the company he keeps is different. His 'intimate friend' is Tom Brown; he has been 'particularly acquainted, with Mr Charles Gildon, Mr [Ned] Ward, Mr Dennis, that admirable critic and poet, and several others'. His habitat, obviously, is the cell of the Dunces. He boasts of the 'great assistance' he has received from the 'illustrious' translators, John Ozell and Captain Stevens. His ambition is openly declared: to imitate these 'great refiners of our language'. And the last two of his ingenious friends to earn a mention are the King Dunces themselves, Cibber and Theobald. In the light of the foolish charade to follow, we cannot mistake the drift of the satire. Swift is showing Dulness no longer as pure ignorance, illiteracy, the literature of the ghetto. Its vices are now those of brisk confidence, shallow jauntiness, or vulgar familiarity. The faults apparent in the productions of the Dull have grown to be the faults of a *parvenu* culture, which has succeeded in lifting itself out of the slum but has not achieved true gentility. Its style will be (in a favourite term of Augustan criticism) 'pert'. Its general manner will be that of the pushing social climbers in Fanny Burney or Jane Austen.[59] The new Grub Street has given itself airs.

In conformity with this milieu, Wagstaff has learnt to parrot brightly of his methods as a writer. Here we see the second main point of distinction from the earlier scribblers I have mentioned in this chapter. Wagstaff introduces a note of the self-satisfied technician; he is the would-be craftsman as well as the would-be gentleman. Contemptuous as he is of 'one Isaac Newton, an instrument-maker, formerly living near Leicester Fields, and afterwards a work-man in the mint at the Tower', proud of his 'polite' orthography (which has *in sickly pay-day* for *encyclopedia*), his boorish approach undermines the intended civility of his undertaking. At times there is almost a trade-union flavour to his proposal: his conviction, for instance, that his public spirit ought to find due reward from the state, and also his unconscious xenophobia. At times he recalls rather the scientist, in the abstract perfection he commends in his useless scheme (cf. the Academy of Lagado). But mostly it is the upstart 'educator', embattled in his johnny-come-lately London mentality:

> I have rejected all provincial or country turns of wit and fancy, because I am acquainted with very few; but indeed chiefly, because I found them so much inferior to those at court, especially among the gentlemen-ushers, the ladies of the bedchamber, and the maids of honour; I must also add the hither end of our noble metropolis.

and incurably optimistic in his visionary dreams:

> I have determined next session to deliver a petition to the House of Lords, for an act of parliament to establish my book as the standard grammar in all the principal cities of the kingdom, where this art is to be taught by able masters, who are to be approved and recommended by me. . . . Neither shall I be so far wanting to myself as not to desire a patent, granted, of course, to all useful projectors; I mean, that I may have the sole profit of giving a licence to every school to read my grammar for fourteen years.

Such refined idiocy could not be bettered. It is, as the nineteenth century would say, the quintessence of solemn pretension.[60]

Swift's concern with the separate strands that went into the Grub Street structure of ideas was lifelong. He maintained, as all the world knows, an obsessive interest in physical corruption, and he was pre-ternaturally sensitive to the blots on the urban landscape. He was alive to the doings of those who occupied lower slopes on Parnassus, even if he lacked Pope's comprehensive service of information retrieval. He hated rascally booksellers as cordially as his friend, though with rather less cause. And he developed, in the *Tale* particularly, a resonant mode of satiric placing, whereby contemporary culture could be superimposed on the map of London, and its running sores subjected to the bright light of demonstration.

Yet he never quite attained the complex symbolism of *The Dunciad*, and never found so apt a vehicle for an integral survey of Grub Street. There are many reasons for this. Pope got in first; Swift was less effective in devising (as opposed to transforming) mythology to his purpose. Finally, Swift's use of disagreeable physical detail is not the same as Pope's. Swift tends either to be seeking a deflating, contrived coarseness; or else to find his outrage subverted by a kind of affection – unwilling, ungenial, but powerfully antiseptic in the presence of that revulsion which the satirist must always profess. Pope could make beauty out of squalor. If Swift was less consistently successful in his treatment of Grub Street, that may be because he couldn't help seeing some beauty *in* squalor.[61]

Epigraph.   Quoted from Trevelyan, II, 430 (the work dates from 1709).
 1. Maynard Mack has recently argued that 'the England of Pope's satires, like (Johnson's) . . . London in his poem *London*, is not wholly to be discovered on any of John Rocque's maps.' – *The Garden and the City* (Toronto, 1969), p. 231. There is only an apparent contradiction here with my contention. The *Tale* clearly embraces themes remote from contemporary London, and its effective geography is by no means limited to the capital under Queen Anne. My point is that it *starts* from the data offered up by topical reality; the facts of London life (Bedlam, Grub Street, etc.) are employed not just as setting but as symbols of the author's satiric vision.
 2. In this section I do not supply detailed page references to the *Tale*, since these are abundant and largely follow in a consecutive fashion the order of the text itself.
 3. See for instance Webb, IV, 367–9.
 4. Cf my article, 'Sir Henry Furnese, Matthew Prior and the Kit Cat Club,' *Notes & Queries* xviii (1971), 46–9.
 5. John Cleland, *Memoirs of a Woman of Pleasure* (London, ed. 1970), pp. 116,

146; Arbuthnot, pp. 231, 277, 289: cf. p. 300, where Arbuthnot mentions a project to unite 'several small corporations of liars into one society'. For the idea of an academy, as well as Swift's letter to the Lord Treasurer, see *Tatler* no. 18. Cowley had described his prophets' college as a 'university', caricatured by Dryden in *MacFlecknoe* as the 'Nursery' (cf Ch.I). Horace Walpole was later to describe bear-gardens as universities: letter to Dalrymple, June 1760, quoted by P. A. Scholes, *The Life and Activities of Sir John Hawkins* (London, 1953), p. 65. The pejorative use of 'seminary' is very common in the eighteenth century. See for instance Trevelyan, I, 27, where the open commons are described by a contemporary as 'seminaries of a lazy, thieving sort of people'. Smollett is another to use the expression, with special reference to the suburbs as 'seminaries of drunkenness': Radzinowicz, I, 400.

6. For Locke's juxtaposition of Westminster Hall, the Exchange, almshouses and Bedlam, see his *Essay concerning Humane Understanding*, ed. A. C. Fraser (New York, 1959), IV, xx, 5.

7. *Tale*, p. lxx.

8. See my article, 'Swift, Walpole and the Rope-Dancers,' *Papers on Language & Literature*, forthcoming.

9. *Tale*, p. 262.

10. Cf. Webb, IV, 407-8: 'the overgrown and unorganised conglomeration of houses of the Metropolis was, from the beginning to the end of the eighteenth century, pre-eminent in criminality. We despair of conveying any adequate picture of the lawless violence, the barbarous licentiousness, and the almost unlimited opportunities for pilfering and robbery offered by the unpoliced London streets of that century.'

11. There are a couple of brief and unimportant references in the Partridge pamphlets. They are not by Swift himself but they do confirm the availability of the trope. See Partridge's *Account of the Proceedings of Isaac Bickerstaff, Esq*: 'There is one John Partridge can smell a Knave as far as Grubstreet.'

12. Swift, *Correspondence*, I, 133, 165.

13. Swift, *Correspondence*, I, 305; *Journal*, II, 553.

14. Swift, *Correspondence*, I, 306; III, 44.

15. See for example Trevelyan, II, 120.

16. Swift, *Prose Works*, III, passim, esp. 35-6.

17. *Journal*, I, 178, 337.

18. *Journal*, II, 416, 426, 441, 468, 511.

19. *Journal*, II, 466, 551, 553, 568, 572, 579.

20. *Journal*, II, 430, 431, 539, 573.

21. *Journal*, II, 548.

22. Pope, *Correspondence*, I, 195, 339.

23. Swift, *Poems*, pp. 179, 279; Mack, *The Garden and the City*, pp. 131-2, 157.

The motifs of the garret, ragged poets and their master Curll reappear in 'Advice to the Grub-street Verse Writers' (1726), *Poems*, p. 309. However, the expression does not occur within the text of the verses themselves.

24. Swift, pp. 438, 440-1; Butt, p. 15. For the allusions to the Cripplegate quarter, see Ch.I.

25. Swift, *Poems*, p. 501.

26. Swift, *Poems*, pp. 571, 573, 578-9.

27. Swift, *Poems*, pp. 577-8.

28. Swift, *Poems*, pp. 570, 574, 580.

29. Swift, *Poems*, p. 601.

30. Swift, *Poems*, pp. 418, 420, 434.

31. Swift, *Correspondence*, I, 148; II, 65; III, 320; IV, 62, 143, 396 and passim.

32. *Romances and Narratives*, XVI, 277-8. 'All the way from *Newgate* to *Tyburn* is one continu'd Fair', says the writer of *A Trip through the Town* (1735), quoted by Ralph Straus, *Eighteenth Century Diversions: Tricks of the Town* (London, 1927), p. 145. 'Fairground droll', one might amend the phrase.

33. Swift, *Correspondence*, I, 215; II, 215; III, 253.

34. Savage, 'Swift's Fallen City', *The World of Jonathan Swift*, ed. B. Vickers (Oxford, 1968), pp. 176-9, 180, 190.

35. O Hehir, 'The Meaning of Swift's "Description of a City Shower"', *ELH*, XXVII (1960), 204-5.

36. Vickers, p. 187.

37. Swift, *Poems*, p. 93. For a similar account of 'real' London, see Webb, IV, 236, quoted by Holdsworth, X, 214-5.

38. Radzinowicz, II, 36.

39. Information chiefly from George Rudé, *Wilkes and Liberty* (Oxford, 1962), pp. 11-12; Radzinowicz, I, 210; II, 155-6; Dorothy George in Turberville, I, 175; Marshall, pp. 250-2. For the criminals mentioned, see especially *The Proceedings at the Sessions of the Peace, and Oyer and Terminer, for the City of London, and County of Middlesex* (London, 1732-3), pp. 222-5; and *Select Trials at the Old Bailey* (London, 1742), I, 40-4.

40. Congreve, *Love for Love*, ed. E. L. Avery (London, 1967), p. 47; Boswell, *London Journal 1762-3*, ed. F. A. Pottle (London, 1950), pp. 251-2.

41. *The Works of Mr John Oldham* (London, 6th ed., 1703), pp. 261, 426: cf. Irving, pp. 33, 35.

42. *Journal*, II, 415: a typical blend of the fire/rabble/carnival cluster of ideas.

43. Swift, *Poems*, pp. 312-3.

44. Swift, *Poems*, pp. 661-3.

45. Strype, III, 284; F. A. Mumby, *Publishing and Bookselling* (London, 1949), p. 141; H. L. Snyder, 'New Bibliographical Data for the Reign of Queen Anne', *The Library*, XXII (1967), 336-7; Stanley Morison, *The English Newspaper* (Cambridge, 1932), pp. 121-3; *State Trials*, XV, 1341; Sir Henry

Ellis (ed.), *The Obituary of Richard Smyth* ([London],) 1849), p. viin; Oldham, *Works*, p. 417; Pope, *Correspondence*, III, 70; *A Trip through London* (London, 8th ed., 1928), p. 51; Swift, *Correspondence*, V, 118; Swift, *Prose Works*, XII, 264. Campkin (p. 7) speaks of the street as 'the great emporium for booksellers and publishers'. Smithfield itself was the great emporium for flesh.

46. *The Works of Andrew Marvell, Esq*, ed. Edward Thompson (London, 1776), II, 280.

47. See *Tale*, pp. lix, 10, etc.

48. Ehrenpreis, II, 93.

49. Swift, *Poems*, pp. 236–9.

50. See (for the affirmative case), Paul Fussel, 'Speaker and Style', *RES*, X (1959), 63–7, and Louis T. Milic, *A Quantitative Approach to the Style of Jonathan Swift* (The Hague, 1967), and see for the sceptical view, C. S. Matlack and W. F. Matlack, 'A Statistical Approach to Problems of Attribution: *A Letter of Advice to a Young Poet*', *College English* XXIX (1968), 627–32. See Teerinck, § 621–2, for doubts about its authenticity; as well as *Prose Works*, IX, xxiv–xxvii.

51. On Edinburgh at this time, cf. Trevelyan, II, 218–20.

52. Swift, *Prose Works*, IX, 225–45.

53. Swift, *Prose Works*, IX, 35–41; XII, 215–32; IV, 280–4.

54. See Teerinck, § 730–3, and *Prose Works*, XII, 345. My discussion is based on the edition by Temple Scott of the *Prose Works* (London, 1905), VII, 287–303.

55. *Correspondence*, II, 3.

56. Scott, (ed.), *Prose Works*, VII, 301n. Cf. Swift, *Correspondence*, IV, 254; Pope, *Correspondence*, III, 390; E/C, VII, 324.

57. It is worth noting that Motte uses the very same verb as that stressed in the *Scheme*, to erect, when writing to Swift of his 'noble . . . design' to 'erect an Hospital for Lunaticks and Idiots' (Swift, *Correspondence*, IV, 373). Of course Swift himself used an analogous expression: 'He gave the little Wealth he had, / To build a House for Fools and Mad' (*Poems*, p. 512).

58. See for example *Journal*, II, 617. The Vanhomrighs lived in Bury Street at one time: *Journal*, I, 64.

59. A representative figure in the 'pert' tradition was Sir Roger L'Estrange, hack pamphleteer turned government official and censor. His literary style is often so described: it was the idiom of upstarts.

60. Swift, *Prose Works*, IV, 97–124.

61. Relevant here is Ehrenpreis's judgement (II, 386) that the stenches and vomitings of the 'City Shower' add up not to an indictment but to a cheerful acceptance of the urban scene.' He speaks, too, of 'a humorous comprehension.'

V

Life Studies

Are you not the beggarly Brood of fumbling Journey-men; born in Garrets, among Lice and Cobwebs, nurs'd upon Grey Peas, Bullocks Livers, and Porter's Ale? – Was not the first Light you saw, the Farthing Candle I paid for? Did you not come before your Time into dirty Sheets of brown Paper?

> Pope, '*A Further Account of the most Deplorable Condition of Mr Edmund Curll, Bookseller*'

Me wrangling courts, and stubborn law,
To smoke, and crowds, and cities draw;
There selfish Faction rules the day,
And Pride and Av'rice throng the way:
Diseases taint the murky air,
And midnight conflagrations glare:
Loose Revelry and Riot bold
In frighted streets their orgies hold;
Or, when in silence all is drown'd,
Fell Murder walks her lonely round:
No room for Peace, no room for you,
Adieu, celestial nymph, adieu!

> Sir William Blackstone, '*The Lawyer's Farewell to his Muse: Written in the Year 1744*'

The scribbler today springs to his most vivid life in the rarefied atmosphere of satire. But that is not to say that he never had any other home. Swift's 'Grubaean Sages', Pope's 'Dunces', were polemical extensions of a real class of men and women. The category of 'author to be let' is as authentic an occupational description as that of linkboy or milkmaid.[1] (Indeed it was perfectly possible for a writer to take up these means of livelihood, either as a preparation for the *Peine forte et dure* of authorship, or, more likely, as a job of the last

276

resort when the muses proved unrewarding.) There certainly was a large body of full-time professional authors in Augustan England. An exact numerical estimate would be hard to arrive at; but it would perhaps not be incautious to surmise that around 1725 there were up to a hundred men and women whose main (or only) source of livelihood was the pen. (I include printers such as Mist who were in effect newspaper editors, even if they were directly responsible for little of the copy in terms of the actual words on the page.)[2] In addition there might be several hundred others for whom literary labours furnished a supplementary income: whether the occasional translation or the timely political tract. We must exclude, of course, the authentic 'gentleman amateur' writer, though he may have reaped indirect financial benefits. It may be that Benjamin Hoadly received no fee for his Bangorian pamphlets, but it is certain that his standing as a controversialist and Church politician went up dramatically as a result of his writing. He was thus able to leap several rungs in the ladder of promotion, and lift himself from the indifferent see of Bangor via Hereford and Salisbury to the ultimate grandeur of Winchester, with all the aplomb of the pyramid climber in a modern corporation. Still, Hoadly was not a hack, even if his productions are often hard to distinguish on internal grounds from those of the meanest of Curll's day-labourers.

The question arises, how closely knit were the brotherhood of Scriblerus? Were they conscious of their duncely status before Pope unkindly reminded them of it? Did they have, in other words, a recognisable identity or community of interest other than the fact that they were leagued against the party of Swift? In the *Tale* and in *John Bull*, as we have seen, there are constant references to the 'Society of Writers', the 'Commonwealth of [Grubean] Learning', the 'Corporation of *Poets*', the 'Academy' of wits, and so on. Was this trade union spirit genuinely felt by the scribblers, and if so how was it achieved and nurtured?

I think the broad answer is that the hacks did see themselves as a group. True, they were constantly at loggerheads with one another, and if there is one thing which instantly identifies the Dunce it is his fondness for labelling his fellows 'dull prostituted Scribbler' or 'insolent and scandalous Libeller'. Nevertheless, this is basically an index of a partisan climate; and in my view the fact that the hack so often chose to address an 'answer' to his colleagues serves to confirm that this was a game for insiders which only hacks *could* play. A Dunce like Abel Boyer actually put together a belletristic collection of *Letters of Wit, Politicks and Morality* in which another Dunce is both a contributor and the object of a harsh attack in a letter from yet a third minor author to Boyer. The scribblers did, of course, provide retorts to the great, and inevitably it is these works which (if any) preserve their name as polemicists today. But it is notable, firstly that they produced a much greater volume of internecine retorts, within the brotherhood, which are now forgotten; and secondly that their usual controversial tactic was to claim, or pretend, that Pope or Swift was simply another member of the gang, unfairly privileged by fortune. Defoe's critics invariably claim him as a born Grub-streeter. The essence of the duncely comeback is the *tu quoque*.

It has recently been argued by Professor Zev Barbu that in France the new intelligentsia of the eighteenth-century formed a self-conscious class, socially as well as ideologically. He writes:

> There is little doubt that French intellectuals in the eighteenth century were aware of the specific nature of their occupational roles and often identified themselves with these roles. Cases such as those of Diderot and Rousseau, who had no other stable profession, can easily be multiplied. And there was social awareness, too, for the manner in which the men of letters perceived and referred to themselves as an occupational group was to a considerable extent accepted by other members of society. Indeed, the most remarkable thing about them was that their emergence as a socially differentiated group was almost a matter of consensus.[3]

It would not be so surprising to find that the hacks' social differentiation was readily accepted. Virtually none of the Dunces had any standing in society, or any clearly marked role at all apart from that afforded by his activity as a writer. It might be urged that such cases as Roger L'Estrange, the official licenser for the press, and Colley Cibber, poet laureate and Drury Lane manager, provide an exception. But it was precisely the activities mentioned which called down on the back of these men the lash of satire – it was as snooping government censor or as bumbling composer of birthday odes that they earned their ticket to the cave of Dulness. I exclude, of course, such men as Lord Hervey, whose position was that of fringe-Dunces: they are not *actors* in the drama like Curll or Settle. Finally, it should be remembered that the academic profession enjoyed much less by way of social recognition than is the case today.[4] It would be an exaggeration to say that the Master of Trinity had no status; but for Pope such doubtful eminence was totally eroded by Richard Bentley's major 'literary' avocation as pedant and wordchopper.

Professor Barbu provides little by way of direct sociological documentation of the men he has under review. In the case of the scribbling profession we may hope to be more specific. It has already been shown (Ch.III) that there was a definite life-cycle which many hacks experienced in common. Family origin, education, even marital status, monetary fortunes, all come into this picture. Secondly, we can point to a great deal of intercommunion amongst the lower class of writer, both personal and within their media of expression. Thirdly, we have not only explicit signs of the manner in which society regarded the hack (the coinage, and currency, of that very term is symptom enough): we have the range of evidence presented in this book to show that the satirists did everything in their artistic power to align their victims with low life.[5] The fundamental technique of Augustan polemic is forcibly to enrol one's opponent in the lowest segment of society. One branded his literary effusions as criminal, as prostituted, as pestiferous; and if possible one showed that his actual living quarters (as they might be) were set in a district whose social character partook of the same qualities. One placed him, that is, within the precincts of Grub Street.

Culture and Subculture

The term 'subculture' began to figure in anthropological and sociological writing around 1945. A widely accepted definition is that of Gordon:

A subdivision of a national culture, composed of a combination of factorable social situations such as class status, ethnic background, regional and rural or urban residence, and religious affiliation, but forming in their combination a functional unity which has an integrated impact on the participating individual.

The concept has been most generally adopted by students of delinquency, and it may therefore be more proper to attempt to apply it to that form of literary delinquency which was practised in Grub Street. Commonly, a subculture is seen as becoming apparent in an area of 'culture-conflict', that is when competing systems of thought and behaviour or competing allegiances overlap. It marks a point of tension within the culture of which it forms a part, and so characteristically makes itself felt through violence or some infraction of social norms.[6]

It is generally agreed that 'a subculture is only partly different from [its] parent culture.' In the words of the authors of a recent book on *The Subculture of Violence*, 'subcultural variants may partially accept, sometimes deny, and even construct antitheses of, elements of the central, wider, or dominant values, yet remain within that cultural system.' Further, it is not normally in dispute that 'a subculture may exist, widely distributed spatially and without interpersonal contact among individuals or whole groups of individuals.' An interesting review of the subject is that by Albert K. Cohen, whose tentative 'General Theory of Subcultures' appeared in his book *Delinquent Boys*. Cohen sees cultural innovation as a matter of adjustment to particular problems of living; and he points out that 'each age[-group], sex, racial . . . category, each occupation, economic stratum and social class' faces a different set of problems, and each is differently equipped for the process of adjustment. In Cohen's view, subcultural activity involves 'the interaction of a number of actors with similar problems of adjustment.' I do not wish to lose myself in a welter of dubiously relevant sociological jargon, but I believe that Cohen's analysis offers pertinent leads.[7]

The dilemma of the Dunces, as I see it, arose from a fairly simple set of circumstances. They were manufacturing to order a product – literature – which in the past had largely been the preserve of the learned, the leisured and the secure. On the other hand, they were in general less well educated, more hardpressed by life and occupied a far more ambiguous social position. They were playing a game whose Queensbury rules had been drafted by others in a different cultural climate. Their human and social deficiencies might actually debar them from practising a given literary genre; their artistic innovations were confined to 'lower' genres. Within these limits they were, as a matter of fact, quite inventive. It might be held that Mrs Haywood's romances, though new to England (they are a far cry from Aphra Behn) were but the naturalisation of a continental form. But, to take another female Dunce, it would seem that the vein of political allegory initiated by Mrs Manley's *Court of Atalantis* was essentially a new kind. For the rest, we have whole areas of literary expression, widely practised in the age, given over to the hacks *en bloc*. No polite writer, so far as I am aware, ever wrote a Secret History. Few can have put together a deathbed biography; the instant *Memoirs* of Thomas Wharton, sometimes attributed to Richard Steele, are by an *echt* scribbler, born and bred. (A common title-page device has fooled bibliographers.)[8] There was in fact a broad field of annals-compilation which was the special preserve of Dunces.

Now in terms of the basic definition, it is readily apparent that the scribbling profession did make up an eligible grouping. They were largely men, and the few exceptions – on whom more in a moment – are never allowed to forget their unwomanly incursion into a masculine territory. One or two were Huguenot refugees, but most were ordinary English stock. Some again were religious deviants, either Catholic or (worse) a member of some canting puritan sect. But the religious factor was not an important one in marking them off. It would be broadly true to say that by origin the hacks were not outsiders – that came later. Their background was often unexceptional middle-class parentage: the WASPs, as it were, of that era. Their origin was often provincial but they were overwhelmingly metropolitan in their base.[9]

Yet, on a subjective existential plane, they must have thought of themselves as outsiders. Insecurity bred, as it usually does, defensive techniques of abuse and exclusion. Their notorious and fatal jealousy

sprang immediately from their sense of not belonging, of imperma-
nence, of vulnerability. In particular, their sensitivity to the charge
of scurrility deserves more attention than it has received. The basic
fact here is that the law of libel was, as Holdsworth points out, the
'sole controller of the liberty of the press', following the decision not
to renew the Licensing Act in 1694/5.[10] Libel consequently represented the most direct threat to a writer's livelihood.

This can be clearly observed in Fielding's *Charge to the Grand
Jury* [of Westminster] (1749). After devoting some consideration to
offences such as blasphemy, contempt of the royal prerogative, keeping of bawdy-houses and gaming ('those articles which seem to be
most worthy of your inquiry at this time'), Fielding takes as his culminating example the offence of libelling. Several paragraphs are
occupied by a review of this crime, as it is 'of a very high nature
indeed'. In general, Fielding's approach is historical, his tone near-
legalistic. But finally his prose alters to one charged with emotion,
the tense emphatically present:

> I have mentioned these laws to you, gentlemen, to show you the sense
> of our ancestors of a crime, which, I believe, they never saw carried to
> so flagitious a height as it is at present; when, to the shame of the age
> be it spoken, there are men who make a livelihood of scandal. Most of
> these are persons of the lowest rank and education, men, who lazily
> declining the labour to which they were born and bred, save the sweat
> of their brows at the expense of their consciences; and in order to get a
> little better livelihood, are content to get it, perhaps, in a less painful,
> but in a baser way than the merest mechanic.
>   Of these, gentlemen, it is your business to inquire; of the devisers,
> of the writers, of the printers, and of the publishers of all such libels...[11]

We should possibly make allowances for the fact that Fielding had a
professional interest in upholding the existing law. Yet it remains
obvious that a hired author on (say) political affairs must have been
conscious of this depressing public image. His trade was stigma-
tised as banausic and venal; his 'livelihood of scandal' regarded as an
easy way out from respectable semi-poverty.

Throughout the century the law of libel continued to engage the
attention of the best minds of the age. Mansfield, Camden, Wedder-

burn and Burke had all considered the subject before Fox's Libel Act of 1792 introduced important changes in the law. The main innovation of the measure (32 Geo.III c.60) was that juries were given the power to give a 'general verdict' upon the whole matter at issue: i.e., they were enabled to adjudicate whether the alleged libel did or did not fit the law as that was laid down. Previously, the jury had been permitted only to decide whether the *fact* of publication had been established and whether the sense of the alleged libel were as it had been presented. Under the previous dispensation, it had been the practice for the judge to direct the jury to find the defendant guilty if the fact of publication and the tenor of the 'paper' had been demonstrated. It was the construction of the old law which precipitated more than one famous legal wrangle in the century. Laurence Hanson cites the cases of John Tutchin in 1704, and Richard Francklin, of the *Craftsman*, in 1729; other instances, such as those of Almon and Woodfall, could be added from later in the century.[12]

A special instance of libel is seditious libel: and it is not surprising that 'sedition' and its derivatives are prominent in the duncely lexicon. Quite closely allied is the offence of publishing an obscene libel; no less a Dunce than Curll was the principal figure in what amounted almost to a show-trial.[13] It is hardly necessary to add that terms like 'lewd' and 'scurrilous' besprinkle the pages of the hacks' works; they come with an iterative and mechanical rhythm, as though they were rubric signs or marginal asterisks to identify textual beauties. This group of offences stood near the centre of the scribbler's consciousness. The threat of prosecution was directly connected with the performance of the literary task.[14] In these circumstances the most vulnerable was the writer who made his living by political pamphleteering (and this was the commonest avocation of most miscellaneous authors). Such a hack would feel himself not so much underprivileged as actively unprivileged.

The scribbling profession, then, was united by a common fear of the law. Actual physical violence does not seem to have been a threat of any magnitude, after the celebrated cases of Dryden and Tutchin. It did, in passing, remain a literary *topos* of some potency for a time, as the bouts between Pope and Curll illustrate. The pillory, too, gradually became more of buggaboo – with the case of Defoe a story to scare cub authors – than a realistic hazard. But imprisonment remained a likely enough fate. It so happens that the most famous literary hacks, in Fielding and in Smollett, inhabit the debtors' prison. In reality, the hack author might just as well reach Newgate as the Fleet: as we shall see, Defoe again provides living testimony. This, of course, is all quite apart from the consideration that many hacks lived in such squalid circumstances that they were likely to feel the arm of the law for offences totally unconnected with literature.[15] There are far less spectacular, and therefore more typical, instances than that of the reprieved murderer Richard Savage, one who escaped the cave of Dulness by a special grace. But Savage will do. Authors lived in social circles where crimes against public decency or public order were a matter of common occurrence. At least one Dunce, got into trouble for taking part in a real-life affray; when Pope cast him in the fictive drama of tumult and insurrection which is *The Dunciad*, the poet was merely letting art pilfer from history.

Here was a great boon to the satirists. Duncely society was like criminal society, on an abstract plane. But it actually overlapped with criminal society, literally so. The hacks, I have suggested, were most conscious of their own corporate identity in terms of the risks they jointly ran. This was the sort of gift which Swift never disdained. He was always prompt to observe solemn leagues and covenants: witness *Examiner* no. 30:

> If we examine what Societies of Men are in closest Union among themselves; we shall find them either to be those who are engaged in some evil Design, or who labour under one common Misfortune: Thus the Troops of *Banditti* in several Countries abroad; the Knots of *Highwaymen* in our own Nation; the several Tribes of *Sharpers, Thieves and Pick-pockets*, with many others, are so firmly knit together, that nothing is more difficult than to break or dissolve their several *Gangs*. So likewise, those who are Fellow-Sufferers under any Misfortune, whether it be in Reality or Opinion, are usually contracted into a very strict Union; as we may observe in the *Papists* . . . and in the several Schisms of *Presbyterians*, and other Sects, under that grievous Persecution of the modern kind, called *Want of Power*.[16]

As with the Grand Whiggery, so with the Dunces. 'Fellow-Sufferers' under the misfortune, real or imagined, of persecution, these paltry men provide a threat because of their numbers and because of their common sense of grievance. Hence the anxiety of the Scriblerians to fit out their opponents with a sinister club or cabal, variously called the Grubean academy, the party of Dulness, the society of Grub Street, and so on. Much rhetorical and dramatic craft goes into rendering this idea. The works of the unlearned might mean a collection of heterogeneous nonsense. By the time Pope and Swift have finished, we recognise 'the unlearned' for a solid, locatable estate in the realm.[17] Such a feat was only possible because the satirists had more than their artistry to aid them: they had, too, cultural history on their side.

A few detailed instances will show the standing of a hack writer. As everybody knows, Richard Savage, the hero of Johnson's most arresting 'Life', found himself in Newgate for a murder committed during a brawl; fifteen years later Savage died in jail in Bristol, where his debts had brought him. But Savage became Pope's informant on hack circles, and escaped the role of Dunce.[18] Less fortunate was Charles Gildon, who in 1706 was fined £100 for publishing an inopportune pamphlet. The source of this information is another scribbler, John Oldmixon; he too achieved a prominent place in *The Dunciad*. Then there is George Ridpath, publisher and newspaper editor, who in 1712 was arrested at the instance of the Secretary of State, Henry St John (later Lord Bolingbroke). The charge was that Ridpath as a 'seditious Person, and a notorious Inventer and Framer of Libels', had published in the *Flying Post* a libellous attack on the negotiations leading to the Peace of Utrecht. He had been committed to Newgate, although (according to Oldmixon) he gave five pounds for a single night's lodging to avoid the Common Side of the prison where the ordinary felons lay. Ultimately Ridpath escaped to Holland via Scotland. Oldmixon says that the government's intention had been to 'put him in the Pillory, and there to expose him to the Rage of their Mobs'; he was saved by a gift from an unnamed gentleman who was at the same time prosecuting Defoe, William Pittis and 'other Libellers'. Pittis, an Oxford man turned Tory mercenary scribbler, had previously been pilloried – as of course had Defoe.[19] Curll fell foul of the law for publishing an obscene work,

The Nun in her Smock; two women members of the trade, Sarah Popping and Anne Dodd, likewise aroused official indignation. Nathaniel Mist even had to flee to France when his *Weekly Journal* offended the Walpole regime; on several earlier occasions he had been called before the Secretary of State, brought to the bar of the Commons and sent to the King's Bench. The attempts to tone down Mist's paper (or the *Craftsman*, for that matter) had little observable effect. Some years earlier, John Tutchin had suffered more than one prosecution, before he died, victim of a brutal assault, in 1707. Another printer to undergo a savage attack in the street – actually in Smithfield – was William Wilkins. This event took place in the same year that Pope cast Wilkins for a minor role in the Grub Street olympiad (A.II.117).[20]

Booksellers and printers were peculiarly accessible to the law, if only because they carried out a regular business at a distinct address. Consequently, when a warrant was issued by the Secretary of State for the royal messengers to apprehend the author, publisher and printer of a seditious work, it was the writer who was likeliest to escape. Sir Charles Hedges' 'greyhounds' were supplemented by the local magistracy in seizing one suspected person in 1704, namely the printer of a broadside who had taken refuge in Northamptonshire. The man they really wanted was Defoe, who almost certainly wrote *Legion's Humble Address to the Lords*. But he eluded the ministry: it was the printer who could be nailed on the concrete evidence of letterpress and copy.[21] So we find men like Curll and Mist constantly hauled in before the Secretary, usually as principals, occasionally as witnesses, now and then (surprisingly) as sureties for their writers. Baker, Morphew, Mrs Popping, Mrs Baldwin, Hurt and others crop up in the 'Criminal' files of the Secretary of State's office with wearisome regularity, like hopeless alcoholics in the magistrates' courts.[22] They were never put away for long, but they were never left alone for long either. The book trade accepted these things as a part of life, as prostitutes have generally taken occasional harrassment without complaint; but they cannot have enjoyed the experience.

And so one could go on. There is abundant evidence that writers, publishers and printers ran a very severe risk in the exercise of their trade. In 1721 there had even been a proposal to set up a 'general Libell-Committee', but the Lord Chamberlain, Newcastle, had dismissed the plan as unworkable.[23] Few literary men suffered such a desperate fate as the young printer, John Matthews, who was convicted of high treason in 1719 and hanged at Tyburn. This was a special case: Matthews 'was indicated under the Act of Anne's reign which made it a capital offence to maintain that the Queen was not the rightful heir to the throne'.[24] A similar prosecution was envisaged but not brought in 1729. In general, however, the offences for which these men would be charged were not quite so heinous as treason. (The oddest was that which faced Orator Henley: 'endeavouring to alienate the minds of his Majesty's subjects from their allegiance.') And as for the punishment, usually this took the form, as far as libellers were concerned, of pillory, imprisonment and fine, 'all three at the absolute discretion of the judge'. Men like Curll experienced each mode of penance. Prison was probably the most feared of these punishments: Hanson quotes the case of the non-juror Bedford who died in prison, as well as that of a certain Jacob Ilive who was impoverished by his 'long and grievous imprisonment among the common felons of Newgate . . .'[25] It is hard to escape the conclusion that the scribbling profession *was* a criminal class, quite simply. Hence the efforts from the satirists to portray their opponents as social delinquents – men who inhabited the underworld of letters and the underworld of London.[26]

There is a curious side-issue here. A surprising number of Dunces were connected with the law in another capacity, that is as members of the legal profession. That they did not necessarily stand on the other side on that account was no surprising implication for a satirist to make. From the time of its Roman origins, satire has found the shyster or the failed attorney an easy target. It was a favourite tactic of the *Grub-street Journal* to align Grub Street with Lincoln's Inn or Gray's Inn; and not without reason. Among prominent scribblers there were Thomas Burnet, who finally reached the bench: William Arnall, once an attorney's drudge; Matthew Concanen, Attorney-General and Advocate-General in Jamaica; Thomas Gordon, a Scottish advocate originally; Philip Horneck, Solicitor to the

Treasury; William Popple, an unsuccessful dramatist but a good organisation man who ended up Governor of Jamaica; Lewis Theobald; Stephen Whatley of Gray's Inn; and many others. Thomas Durfey was bred up to the trade, but quickly passed on to less mundane things. The usual charge against these men, however, is not that they were pettifoggers; rather, that they demeaned a profession that was, if not exactly noble, a necessary one graced by many eminent men.

Among these cases, that of Giles Jacob is peculiarly interesting. He enters *The Dunciad* briefly:

> Jacob, the Scourge of Grammar, mark with awe,
> Nor less revere him, Blunderbuss of Law. (A.III.149)

There follows the usual detailed note concerning the victim's career, supplemented by a malicious addendum in the revised version. On this couplet the Twickenham editor observes, 'There seems to be no good reason for calling Jacob's style ungrammatical. When Pope substituted him for 'Woolston, the scourge of Scripture' . . . he had to find an equivalent charge, and 'grammar' was, no doubt, an easy way out.'[27] But Pope does not always take the easy way: and there may be more to it than that. It is noteworthy that we have another proleptic label here, for Jacob became famous as the author of *A Law Grammar* (1744), subtitled 'Rudiments of the Law'. But by the time of *The Dunciad* he was already famous for his legal compilations. In particular, he entered the poem in 1729 at a significant moment in his career. Sir William Holdsworth explains the background:

> A new departure in law dictionaries was made by Giles Jacob, who began his law dictionary in 1720 and published it in 1729. It is a fine piece of work, and much superior to his other books . . . Jacob's dictionary is a new departure because it attempted . . . to combine in one work a dictionary and an Abridgement. . . . [Indeed] Jacob's dictionary comprised three things in one – a dictionary, an Abridgement, and a vocabulary. The dictionary was very successful.[28]

Here, surely, we have a clue to Pope's intention. Jacob boasts of his researches into the 'derivations and definitions of words and terms used in the law . . .' So he was not only a compiler, an abridger, but also a legal wordchopper – the equivalent of the classical pedants satirised in Book IV. As Bentley was the scourge of ancient usage, Jacob was for the modern cant language of the law.

Add to this, of course, Jacob's diverse productions: his porno-graphic *Tractatus de hermaphroditis* (1718), his *City Liberties* (1732) on the customs of London, his books with the self-satirising titles *The Modern Justice* (1720), *The Common Law Common-placed*, *The Compleat Attorney's Practice* (1730) and *Every Man his own Lawyer* (1736) – Dr Arbuthnot could not have bettered the last.[29] Add to this his foolish parody *The Rape of the Smock* (1717) and, most pertinent, of all his attack in the form of 'The Legal TRYAL and Conviction of Mr *Alex Pope* of Dulness & Scandal . . .'[30] Throughout Jacob convicts himself by misapplying the law.

We could take this a little further still. A litigious nature is apparent in more than one Dunce. Moore-Smythe's propensity to go to law was noted by the *Grub-street Journal*, incorporating a sneer at 'Attorney Theobald' in passing.[31] The *Journal* itself showed some-thing of a propensity to figure in lawsuits, a fact which may have hastened Pope's determination to separate himself from the paper. A more striking case was another barrister of the Inner Temple, Eus-tace Budgell, who displayed throughout his life an extraordinary capacity for imbroiling himself in litigation. The difficulties which arose from the deist Tindal's will, naming Budgell as his legatee, illustrate the point. Budgell was a notoriously unbalanced man, and in 1737 he drowned himself in the Thames.[32] For the Tory satirists, such ready recourse to the law would itself suggest mental abbera-tion. The civilised and mature man, *beatus ille*, would shun such in-trusions into his privacy. To go to the law at every opportunity was ungentlemanly; moreover, it showed that the individual concerned had no other way of defending himself – no authentic justification by the tone and tenor of his ordinary life. No one received more public insults than Pope and Swift; but it is difficult to imagine either of them seeking redress for a personal affront in the courts.[33]

The mention of Budgell brings up the question of suicide. Henry Carey, whose 'capacity in the Grubean way' was hailed in the 1730's, is believed to have put an end to his own life at his house in Clerkenwell. Another case is recorded by the *Grub-street Journal* in 1730: a 'hackney-writer, for some years disorder'd in his senses', who hanged himself in his garters near Lincoln's Inn. The *Journal* labels this unfortunate man a 'Grubean'. The paper delighted in noting such events; it recorded the coroner's verdict of lunacy upon Budgell, and often mentioned the seamier side of the hack environment. A malicious comment on the death of Duncan Campbell remarked on the recent departure of another of Curll's authors – at Tyburn. Again, in 1732, the *Journal* notes that a hack from Chancery Lane 'in this dearth of business' had gone to Bath on a thieving expedition, and duly received a sentence of whipping at Salisbury assizes. 'This Hackney Writer from Chancery-lane', says the *Journal*, 'had better have stayed here, and turned Political Writer.'[34] Such comments incorporate a sneer at poverty, imply venality, and align political writing with the pettier forms of crime. A few years earlier, it had been no 'Daniel Croker' but the well-known Charles Gildon who had striven for his pittance from a garret in Chancery Lane. Hacks were people whose condition in life separated them scarcely, if at all, from the ordinary riffraff of the Newgate calendar.

This leads on to a final point. One major branch of the scribbling industry, as we have seen, was the deathbed confession or the condemned malefactor's memoirs. In a sense, then, one could regard men such as Defoe, Paul Lorrain or Thomas Purney as being on the wrong side of the law. They stood to gain from the glamour attaching to celebrated rogues. More than that, they often chose actually to impersonate the criminal, that is to write in the first person. It is true that Swift once adopted such a persona, in the case of Ebenezer Elliston; but he did so with the direct aim of aiding the efforts of the law to convict Elliston's associates. Nobody could imagine that the Newgate ordinary wished his supply of articulate 'clients' to dry up. As far as the satirists were concerned, such writing was properly a division of Grub Street enterprise. Who better to chronicle the doings of malefactors than their literary embodiment, the Grubean sage?

Let us summarise these observations. The hacks were vulnerable to the law, especially the law of libel, as often as they set pen to paper.

Their uncertain way of life, with its irregular payment and lack of security, bred other evils in its wake: not least the fact that many scribblers were compelled to live in the lower quarters of the city, where ordinary crime was rife. Then again, literary taste was such that they, accused of piracy, were forced to write the lives of pirates: dubbed 'hackney', i.e. prostitute, they could live only by selling their services to any buyer, and often had to write of bordellos and pimps.[35] It was this feeling of being on the wrong side of the law which united the hacks. The particular set of problems which determined their cultural adjustment arose from this shared vulnerability. In other words, the subculture of Grub Street merged elements of criminal London (deriving partly from the actual surroundings in which the writers worked, partly from the nature of their work) with elements of the 'literary' subculture of coffee-houses, booksellers' shops and theatres which Pope himself knew. Grub Street was in this respect a point of tension, such as the sociologists have described. Its quiddity and its notoriety are alike symptoms of its anomalous condition. To be a resident of Grub Street was to frequent the disreputable suburb of a reputable metropolis. A profound social insight is built into the locative symbolism of this term. The phrase articulates the dilemma of the author by trade or profession: his condition is peripheral, uneasy, ill-defined. On the borders of social and literary respectability – Parnassus, Westminster – are set down the ramshackle mansions of Grub Street.

Private Lives

The tragic frontiers of Dulness, then, were marked off by the law. And this is not in any way surprising. Just as London was a more brutal place outwardly in the eighteenth century, so the visible symbols of authority stood out more clearly on the skyline. If crime surrounded the Londoner, so did punishment. It was an age when the leering skulls of Jacobites were left on Temple Bar for years as a political *memento mori*. Pillories and whipping posts were standard items of street furniture, if not constantly in use. So Defoe's '*Hi r'-glyphick* State *Machin*', which witnesses all and judges all:

> How have thy opening Vacancy receiv'd,
> In every Age the Criminals of State?

'Thou hast been the Satyr of the Age', the poet writes, and further:

> What need of *Satyr* to Reform the Town?
>   Or Laws to keep our Vices down?
>   Let 'em *to Thee* due Homage pay,
> This will reform us all *the Shortest Way*.
> Let 'em *to thee* bring all the Knaves and Fools,
>   Vertue will guide the rest by Rules . . .[36]

Similarly, in the introduction to *A Tale of a Tub*, Swift bestows ironic praise on the admirable English institution of the gallows:

> On *Ladders* I need say nothing: 'Tis observed by Foreigners themselves, to the Honor of our Country, that we excel all Nations in our Practice and Understanding of this Machine. The ascending Orators do not only oblige their Audience in the agreeable Delivery, but the whole World in their *early* Publication of these Speeches; which I look upon as the Choicest Treasury of our *British* Eloquence and whereof I am informed, that worthy Citizen and Bookseller, Mr. *John Dunton*, hath made a faithful and a painful Collection, which he shortly designs to publish in Twelve Volumes in Folio . . . A Work highly useful and curious, and altogether worthy such a Hand.[37]

A few years later, it would have been Defoe instead of Dunton (of whom, more in a moment). We note here the characteristic ambiguity of *painful*, and the bitter joke prompted by the nation's act in executing its ruler in 1649. More widely, we can see that the city, from Tyburn to Execution Dock, was a kind of standing penal colony; and that it was thus aptly the home of punitive satire.

Throughout *The Dunciad*, there is a terrible familiarity with confinement, torture, punishment in every form. Pope handles the topic with such casual ease that we tend to miss the allusions. When the scene is set up at Bedlam, we forget that this was a place of forcible incarceration as well as a spectacle. We overlook the irony by which Bridewell witnesses silly Dunces about their silly sport:

This labour past, by Bridewell all descend,
(As morning prayer and flagellation end) . . . (B.II.269)

We slip unthinkingly over references to the magistrate, the round-house and the Fleet, as ready to receive the scribblers (B.II.423–8). We fail to observe glancing allusion to other parts of the legal ma-chinery – the 'humorous allegor[y]' by which Chancery delays were satirised, over a century before *Bleak House* (B.II.263 and note); the vapour of Dulness spreading over the Temple (B.II.345); the mention of judges and sergeants (B.IV.591) and of templars (B.II. 379), along with the revelation that at the head of the supplicants for the degree in Duncehood are

Her children first of more distinguish'd sort,
Who study Shakespeare at the Inns of Court . . . (B.IV.567)

We may not even notice that 'our Midas' (Cibber) is made 'Lord Chancellor of Plays' (B.III.324), or that the yawn of Dulness over-takes 'the Hall', *sc*.Westminster (B.IV.609). We forget that 'May'rs and Shrieves' (B.I.91, 263) were first and foremost *legal* officers, active in court at the Goddess's 'own Guild-hall' (B.I.270). Cibber, in fact, at the start of Book II, sits enthroned like a Lord Mayor, surrounded by the bench of aldermen trying a case.

However, these topographic and specific references are backed up by a whole chain of imagery, which any sensitive reading of the poem ought to bring out. We learn of 'the Pains and Penalties of Idleness' (B.IV. 344). Two lines before comes the phrase 'stretched on the rack of a too easy chair', a metaphor used elsewhere: e.g. 'the Muses, on their racks' (B.III.159), screaming like Bedlamites.[38] Slaves are 'pinion'd' (B.IV.134), Jacob is the 'scourge of Grammar' (B.III.149), and Henley is fated 'Meek modern faith to murder, hack and mawl' (B.III.210) – the last a verb Swift likes to use of satire.[39] In the panoply surrounding Queen Dulness, next to 'Poetic Justice, with her lifted scale' is 'Prudence, whose glass presents th' approaching jayl' (B.I.51). Grub Street is hemmed in by penal institutions.

Two passages in particular stand out. The first is simpler both in content and in poetic working; it concerns a gift from the Goddess to her votary Curll.

> A shaggy Tap'stry, worthy to be spread
> On Codrus' old, or Dunton's modern bed;
> Instructive work! whose wry-mouth'd portraiture
> Display'd the fates her confessors endure.
> Earless on high, stood unabash'd De Foe,
> And Tutchin flagrant from the scourge below.
> There Ridpath, Roper, cudgell'd might ye view,
> The very worsted still look'd black and blue.
> Himself among the storey'd chiefs he spies,
> As from the blanket high in air he flies,
> 'And oh! (he cry'd) what street, what lane but knows,
> Our purgings, pumpings, blankettings and blows?
> In ev'ry loom our labours shall be seen,
> And the fresh vomit run for ever green!' (B.II.143)

This moves from a hint of Christian martyrology ('confessors'), which points up the sham ideals and real sufferings of the Dunce, through a heraldic vision of the scribblers to a direct reference to Curll's indignity at Westminster School. It was an odd punishment, but the slightly grotesque description (the buffeting alliteration of 'purgings, pumpings . . .') does not detract from its actuality. Hacks really did undergo this sort of humiliation, and everyone knew it.[40]

So much for Dulness on the receiving end. A more complex passage enlists the same body of imagery to depict the triumph of the goddess.

> Beneath her foot-stool, *Science* groans in Chains,
> And *Wit* dreads Exile, Penalties and Pains.
> There foam'd rebellious *Logic*, gagg'd and bound,
> There, stript, fair *Rhet'ric* languish'd on the ground;
> His blunted Arms by *Sophistry* are born,
> And shameless *Billingsgate* her Robes adorn.
> *Morality*, by her false Guardians drawn,
> *Chicane* in Furs, and *Casuistry* in Lawn,
> Gasps, as they straighten at each end the cord,
> And dies, when Dulness gives her Page the word.
> Mad *Mathesis* alone was unconfin'd,
> Too mad for mere material chains to bind . . .

But held in ten-fold bonds the *Muses* lie,
Watch'd both by Envy's and by Flatt'ry's eye . . . (B.IV.21)

This is superb writing. It is another cod version of the allegorical
setpiece, with the familiar personified abstractions suddenly invaded by homely Billingsgate. The pogrom of Dulness has an extraordinary immediacy, for all its largely formal phrasing. Partly this is
generated by the hints of sexual ravishment, with Billingsgate as a
whore and fair Rhetoric subjected to indecent assault, like a drug-
softened Clarissa. Unlike Richardson, though, Pope is aware how
far his own feelings are invested: the language prettifies the scene,
but leaves the horror still plainly visible. (The pause after the word
'gasps', prior to the unstressed syllables 'as they', produces a physical
gulp in reading this line.) Moreover, actuality is once more called
up with a bold punning reference to the hanging judge, Page. Add to
this such phrases as '*Chicane* in Furs', a marvellously resourceful
way of saying chicanery on the bench, and 'Penalties and Pains' (a
transposition of the legal phrase invoked in the attainder of Pope's
great friend Atterbury)[41] – add these, and it is clear that judicial
punishment hovers over the entire passage.

Why should this be so? First of all, no doubt, because the threat
of the statute book was greater at that time. It is true that the notorious game laws did not normally reach very high up the social scale
in their operation: Pope was unlikely to have been transported for
robbing a hen-roost. But political and religious toleration was still
embryonic. Pope himself had been brought up in Berkshire because
of the ten-mile clause; his friends Bolingbroke and Atterbury were
exiled, Oxford impeached, Prior grilled and imprisoned for months.
The charged quality of the language owes a good deal to the fact that
severe sentences awaited dissidents at any time. (After all, Walpole
himself had been in the Tower, thirty years previously.)

But there is another factor. Images of confinement and torture are
especially common in one branch of Augustan writing, satire. And
indeed there are numerous parallels between satiric ideas and penal
theory in this age. Satire was looked upon as a corrective activity;[42]
judicial sentencing, as Fielding and others testify, was held to serve
both deterrent and reformatory ends – generally in that order. In

both cases punishment had to fit the criminal; you hanged Earl Ferrers with a silk rope (having tried him before his peers), just as you adapted your satiric style according to the victim: one technique for Achitophel, another for Og; one for Addison, another for Curll. Again, in each case it was held aesthetically pleasing if you despatched your victim cleanly and gracefully, a mode of thinking made familiar by Dryden's memorable comparison with Jack Ketch, on the subject of making a malefactor die sweetly.[43] Last, satire was supposed (ideally) to be above persons: to deal impartially with wrongdoers, as (ideally) the law marked off the guilty from the innocent. Satire was detective and reformatory – so in theory the criminal code.

It is accountable, then, that *Absalom and Achitophel* should be constructed as a sort of state trial, with a prosecution case, statements by the defendants, and finally a judicial summary (and sentence) from Charles. That the *Epistle to Arbuthnot* should be explicitly labelled at the outset 'a Sort of Bill of Complaint', the technical term for a suit in the higher courts.[44] That critics should find in the most unlikely-looking Augustan works, e.g. *Pamela*, sustained use of the metaphor of a trial.[45] That Addison should couch his major satiric offering in the form of a trial scene, with Defoe well to the fore. And that Pope's opponents (such as Jacob) should attempt to bring him to the bar of justice. It is an obvious motif with a society so ready to believe in the curative power of the law – the sword having recently failed them – in constitutional as well as private disputes;[46] and in a culture which acted out its dissent, not in the staged television 'confrontation', but within the fictions of satire.

So we find Westminster Hall constantly hovering in the prose of Swift's *Tale*; and Pope's imagery returning with heavy iterative force to punitive sanctions:

> We ply the Memory, we load the brain,
> Bind rebel Wit, and double chain on chain,
> Confine the thought, to exercise the breath;
> And keep them in the pale of Words till death.
> Whate'er the talents, or howe'er design'd,
> We hang one jingling padlock on the mind . . . (B.IV.157)

Thus modern education. But death was not only the ultimate sanc-

tion, it was a proximate resource. The closeness of the remedy shines
through almost all Augustan prose.

> . . . When by the Errors of a Man's Youth he has reduc'd himself to
> such a degree of Distress, as to be absolutely without Three things,
> *Money*, *Friends*, and *Health*, he Dies in a Ditch, or in some worse
> place, an *Hospital*.
>
> Ten thousand ways there are to bring a Man to this, and but very
> few to bring him out again.
>
> Death is the universal Deliverer, and therefore some who want
> Courage to bear what they see before 'em, *Hang themselves for fear*; for
> certainly Self-destruction is the effect of Cowardice in the highest
> extream.
>
> Others break the Bounds of Laws to satisfy that general Law of
> Nature, and turn open Thieves, House-breakers, Highway-men, Clip-
> pers, Coiners, &c. till they run the length of the Gallows, and get a
> Deliverance the nearest way at St. *Tyburn*.
>
> Others being masters of more Cunning than their Neighbours, turn
> their Thoughts to private Methods of Trick and Cheat, a Modern way
> of Thieveing, every jot as Criminal, and in some degree worse than the
> other, by which honest men are gull'd with fair pretences to part from
> their Money, and then left to take their Course with the Author, who
> skulks behind the curtain of a Protection, or in the *Mint* or *Friars*, and
> bids defiance as well to Honesty as the Law.[47]

This is Defoe in a bitter mood. His language is filled with places of
incarceration: hospitals to die in, like Charterhouse or Bedlam; the
grimly canonised Tyburn; the refuges like Whitefriars and the Mint.
Suicide was not unknown among Dunces as we have noted (Budgell
plunged literally into the Thames, as the mud-divers leapt into the
Fleet Ditch near its outlet), or even among hacks too obscure to gain
admittance. For that matter, the 'casualties' section in Mist's
Weekly Journal for 25 June 1720 includes a wretch who 'hanged himself (being Lunatick)' in St Giles', Cripplegate Without. Of course,
there were suicides everywhere: but the parish seems to have had
more than its fair share of mischance. Coiners and clippers we have
met there before.

The lunatic was a fugitive from Bedlam, as likely as not. And that
reminds us that the venues of *The Dunciad* strike a grisly contrast
with the merrymaking scenes played out there. The Dunces trip

gaily past Bridewell and its flagellation rites (A.II.257), all agog over their next jolly enterprise. They troop down Ludgate, without a thought of the debtors huddled miserably together; they go through Temple Bar to the pillory in the Strand for the opening events in their sports; their final contests take place in the shadow of 'the neighbouring Fleet' (A.II.395). There is a harsh irony obtruding – the grimmer the associations, the more levity we witness.

This is especially so in respect of the Cave of Dulness. Pope makes it clear in both versions that a savage bacchanalian spirit rules here: a sort of 'wild creation' (A.I.80), pullulating with uncontrolled life, dancing crazily and breeding stupendously. This goes on in the vicinity of Rag Fair and of Bedlam. The second hardly requires comment. As for Rag Fair, we must recall Pope's succinct note, 'a place near the *Tower of London*, where old cloaths and frippery are sold.' Those words appeared in 1728. Ten years before, we read in Mist's *Journal* of an old cow-keeper near Rag Fair, who had built a house from timber taken from the scaffold on Tower Hill – a Grub Street lodging if ever there was one. The roof had blown off and the place was ruined.[48] A few years before that, the dominant image of punishment had surfaced here, too:

> Near a famed Tower, of old built to oppose
> Rude insurrections of Augusta's foes,
> Where ancient Thames, with crooked winding glides,
> Repletes and ebbs, with her alternate tides,
> A forlorn spot, called Execution Dock
> Appears to view; on it, of timber-stock
> A gibbet stands, a dire memento made,
> To frighten those that use the thieving trade,
> Poor common slaves, unskill'd in great affairs,
> That purloin sheep, and sometimes cows and mares,
> And now and then some pirates that have shares
> In robberies at sea; and such like deeds . . .[49]

Of course, I am not saying that Pope knew these passages, although he was certainly well aware of Mist's paper. The point is that London was full of such 'dire mementos', and consciously or not, Pope allocated his literary thieves and pirates a home well-fitted to their crimes, yet horribly ill-fitted to their frivolous highjinks. London embodied a submerged pagan mythology; it took comic genius to utilise this towards ends at once diverting and disturbing.

In one sense, then, *The Dunciad* is a retaliation by art, where the law offers no direct recourse: just as W. S. Gilbert took on those who had infringed his copyright and (having no legal redress) made *The Pirates of Penzance* his next subject. Pope uses satire to give people a chastening they can usually escape in real life. Curll may have been tossed in a blanket, Defoe sent to the pillory, Ridpath committed to Newgate. But their symbolic punishment was longer-lasting and carried out under conditions of higher security. Mist could flee to France to get away from the recurrent calls of the King's Bench, but *The Dunciad* has never loosened its grip.

Just how many hacks and booksellers actually spent time in custody or otherwise suffered judicial penalties, has never been ascertained. As regards the Dunces proper, Sutherland's 'Biographical Appendix' mentions only Chetwood in the King's Bench, presumably for debt; Curll at the bar of the Lords; Mrs Dodd's trouble with the authorities; Mist's indiscretions, for which he 'was more than once fined and imprisoned'; Ridpath; Tutchin, 'more than once prosecuted'; and Woolston, tried for blasphemy.[50] To this list it is possible to add some cases of great interest. I confine myself to writers excluded from the *DNB*, or to events not mentioned there or in published biographies.

For example, existing sources on John Dunton fail to observe this item from the Middlesex Session Books, dating from April 1708. It relates to an order 'fining John Denton, *alias* Dunton, the sum of 6d., and sentencing him to a whipping at a cart's tail from the Bell alehouse in Whitecross Street, St Giles', to the post and chain in the same street, for speaking seditious words, and profanely cursing the Queen's Majesty.' In view of the facts (1) that Dunton was living hard-by in Jewen Street, (2) that such punishments were inflicted more or less *in situ* as regards the crime, and (3) that Dunton was notorious for his unshackled free speech, it can hardly be doubted that this was the celebrated quack and pseudo-prophet.[51]

We can pass over such small fry as Stephen Whatley, who was threatened with prosecution in 1724 and convicted in 1726 for publishing a political libel on the Chevalier St George,[52] and Benjamin Norton Defoe, who was committed to Newgate in 1720 for a similar reason.[53] As for Theophilus Cibber, apart from the Chancery suits over theatrical management which were endemic to the family,[54] he was scarcely out of the courts at one period of his life immediately prior to the revised *Dunciad*. He brought his famous suit for criminal correspondence against William Sloper in 1738–9, a case which yielded him sixpence in damages. Meanwhile his marital troubles had led him to get his wife's brothers committed to Bridewell, had caused her to obtain an order against him not to molest her, and had seen him cited for incontinence in the spiritual courts, presumably as part of an attempt at divorce.[55] Cibber's own complicity in his wife's misconduct with Sloper is beyond doubt: Dunces were ready to incur any amount of public exposure and obloquy if they thought it would bring them £10,000. The self-display and theatricality of the breed, of course, are imaged throughout *The Dunciad*, as they are in Fielding's plays. Theophilus Cibber was worse than most; his private shames more publicly and shamelessly revealed in court on more occasions – that is the difference; *and* he was in and out of the Fleet at the same period.

More central figures are men like Gildon and Oldmixon. As already noted, the Dunces were notorious for their civil broils, but Gildon seems to have been outstanding even in this company:

> Ah Dennis! Gildon ah! what ill-starr'd rage
> Divides a friendship, long confirm'd by age?
> Blockheads with reason wicked wits abhor,
> But fool with fool is barb'rous civil war.
> Embrace, embrace my Sons! be foes no more! (A.III.167)

Settle's advice is timely: the Dunces are strongest when united in their corporation. The threat, once again, is 'barbarous civil war'. If Gildon, then, enjoyed this reputation, one can understand the relish with which Oldmixon describes his troubles. Briefly, Gildon was accused of publishing a scandalous libel with regard to the Electress of Hanover. When the complaint was made to the Commons, Gildon (a minor agent) was sacrificed, and

the Ministry order'd him to be prosecuted with the utmost Severity;
insomuch, that had it not been for Mr. [Arthur] *Maynwaring's* Inter-
position, he had certainly stood in the Pillory. He was fin'd above 100
times as much as he was worth, no less than 100*l.* Sterling, which was
also remitted by the good Offices of the same worthy Gentleman.[56]

At the end of his life, like Oldmixon, Gildon received a small royal
bounty – there were occasional ha'pence to set against the regular
governmental kicks.[57]

As for Oldmixon himself, a hitherto unknown Chancery suit shows
that he had lost an action at Taunton assizes around the end of Anne's
reign, and was seeking to reverse an order saddling him with family
debts.[58] Then, in 1716, he went to Bridgwater as customs collector
and quickly ran into all kinds of bother.[59] In March 1718 a warrant
was issued to the borough constables, with an order that Oldmixon
and others should appear before the Mayor to give an account of
certain riotous and seditious behaviour in the streets. The episode
concerned the Duke of Ormonde and his threatened renewal of the
Jacobite invasion plans. In July of the same year, information was
lodged that he was among the townspeople who had been frequenting
Presbyterian and Anabaptist conventicles. Named with him were a
number of prominent dissenters and at least one survivor of the
Monmouth Rebellion (which Oldmixon had witnessed as a boy) –
Roger Hoar[e] who had been led as far as the gallows and finally
escaped with a fine of £1000. Thereafter, Oldmixon's years in Bridgwater were marked by further upsets: a riot in the town in 1721,
when the local highflying Tories insulted the military (dutifully reported by Oldmixon to the office of the Secretary of State) and invasion scares, mysterious Swedish spies, etc.[60] Events of this kind
provoked alarmist accounts from Oldmixon, privately to the ministry,
publicly to the *Flying Post*.[61] They also excited a satire in Mist's
Journal, almost certainly from the hand of Defoe, in which a number
of future works to be expected from Oldmixon are listed. Most
appositely, they include a letter of advice to J[osep]h F[are]w[el]l in
Ludgate, on the theory and practice of begging; 'Observations upon
the Difference between lying in Gaol or Garret, and being in an
Office'; and a compendious method of carrying causes in the courts

at Westminster. Here, Oldmixon will receive help from one R[ober]t M[e]th[we]n, a Bridgwater attorney of most unsalubrious reputation.[62] And so on. Here are all the sad appurtenances of Dulness: street brawls, debtors' gaols, shuckster lawyers, the court order and the official summons.

It seems likewise to have escaped notice that Thomas Cooke, a Dunce of some prominence, found himself a prisoner for debt 'in the rules of the King's Bench'. From here he wrote two begging letters in 1737 to an unidentified peer, which are now in the Public Record Office.[63] Cooke wanted a subscription for his translation of Plautus, and again this is apt. Hacks were beggars and vagabonds: they beard inoffensive strangers from their debtor's sanctuary. One recalls that devastating opening to the *Epistle to Arbuthnot*:

> What Walls can guard me, or what Shades can hide ?
> They pierce my Thickets, thro' my Grot they glide . . .
> Ev'n *Sunday* shines no *Sabbath-day* to me:
> Then from the *Mint* walks forth the Man of Ryme,
> Happy! to catch me, just at Dinner-time.

And later in the poem:

> Is there, who lock'd from Ink and Paper, scrawls
> With desp'rate Charcoal round his darken'd walls ?[64]

The Mint and Bedlam are interchangeable. It is characteristic of the debtor, as of the madman, to badger shamelessly. And both kinds of supplicant, 'Oblig'd by hunger and Request of friends', are deaf to propriety, tact, good manners. They solicit in the manner of a street-walker. I do not know whether Cooke can have been in Pope's mind – he had been committed in 1731, and working on his translation for roughly the same period. But the symbolic application is neat enough.

This raises the question of how widespread real poverty was among the Dunces. There is comparatively little firm evidence. We know that Dennis was in distress in his later years, and that Pope indeed made some effort to relieve him. Gildon appealed to Prior in his declining days, and Oldmixon to the Duke of Newcastle from (very likely) a sponging-house.[65] Beyond that, one occasionally comes across a reference to the penury of a specified hack. Thus, John

Stevens, who had been the object of Swift's satire in *Polite Conversation* (Ch.IV), provoked something of a homily from the *Flying Post* in February 1729. The death of 'Captain' Stevens is recorded, with assets put at less than £20. Then: 'We hope this will be a Warning to others, how they fool away their time, in scribbling for the modern Goths.'[66] It is not very much but it is more concrete than anything we have on Samuel Boyse, who was to become the great exemplar of Grub Street miseries.

Fortunately, the Corporation of London Records Office does preserve registers of insolvent debtors which cover large portions of the period.[67] Few scribblers can be located with certainty. It is notable that the population of the debtors' gaols rose sharply between 1719 and 1724, and thereafter more gradually. No doubt this has something to do with the Bubble, though we might expect that this would be reflected by the bankruptcies of substantial men rather than the imprisonment of small debtors (as they mostly were). The comparative figures are as follows: Newgate 6 in 1719 (13 in 1724); Poultry Compter 37 (89); Wood Street Compter 56 (115); Ludgate 30 (253); Fleet 73 (125). The latter figures were not greatly increased in years to come, except the Fleet which grew steadily in future census years among the records, viz. 1728, 1737, 1739, 1742, 1748 and 1755. Individuals listed include Joseph Mitchell (1737), who may well be the Dunce of that name;[68] Anthony Hammond (1737), undoubtedly the minor author; [69] Samuel Johnson (1728), who may be the comic dramatist; and Elizabeth Thomas (? Curll's Corinna). There is a John Moore, printer, in 1724, along with William Hurt, likely to be the printer and informer.[70] Dryden Leach (1728) must be Swift's cousin, another printer.[71] In addition, a number of petitions for discharge under the Insolvent Debtors' Acts are preserved; in 1696 one John Dennis is found in this group.

In 1712 the name of Dennis turns up again, this time among the prisoners discharged from the Fleet. Here we can be confident that this is indeed the critic. It is known that 'from 1711 to 1715 Dennis lived, for a part of the time at least, within the verges of the royal court, where he was safe from arrest for debt. For a time he lived at Jack Richardson's Tower Den.' The source of the information is published material, notably Dennis's *Original Letters* (1721). For the previous decade, his biographer admits, the record is thin: 'Regarding the purely personal affairs of his life during this period [from 1710], we possess scanty information . . . [Dennis's] correspondence . . . contains but little concerning his private affairs during the earlier years of the second decade of the century beyond an occasional allusion to his 'great misfortunes'.[72] In these circumstances it appears certain that the John Dennis who applied for discharge in January 1712 must have been our man. It is also likely that William Bond,[73] who summoned the creditors, and who was himself discharged from the Fleet gaol in March, was the Dunce of that name: one of the 'inoffensive offenders against our poet; persons unknown, but for being mention'd by Mr. *Curl*':

> Lo Bond and Foxton, ev'ry nameless name . . . (A.III.151)

Bond is supposed to have collapsed and died whilst acting in a play by Aaron Hill, a true duncely end. The same passage alludes to 'Horneck's fierce . . . face' (A.III.146). Remarkably pat comes the discovery that in September 1721 one Philip Horneck was committed to the King's Bench for various debts. It seems surprising that a Solicitor to the Treasury should fall into such a plight, but it is not impossible in that age. Horneck is far from a common name. Incidentally, the following September there was committed 'Henricus Curle', who can only be Edmund's son and partner, mentioned at A.II.160.[74] Henry Curll absconded from the custody of the Keeper of the Fleet in 1735.

But we can go further. In the lines just quoted, the putative speaker is the ghost of Settle. Now, for the first time, it appears that Settle was himself confined in the Fleet for a number of years. In February 1704 he applied for discharge. It emerges that he had been committed at the suit of Robert Austen, as far back as 5 Wm & Mary (1692–3). Robert Barnham, citizen and haberdasher, summoned the creditors, including Mrs Katherine Austen, executrix of Robert Austen. The Recorder, Sir Salathiel Lovell, ordered the plea to be heard at the next quarter sessions, on 28 February. From a different archive we learn that Settle was discharged, and that he listed with

Captain Lloyd in Colonel [Prize?]'s Regiment – a common expedient for those bent on release from a debtor's gaol. At about the same time, John Partridge – the name of a visionary and satiric butt of another kind – applied for discharge.[75] Appositely does Pope call the Fleet 'Haunt of the Muses' (A.II.396).

The significance of this fact should not be overlooked. The great prophecy of Dulness (which included, in the first version, the culminating vision of universal Darkness) is uttered by the shade of a Fleeter: a man who had spent ten years as a prisoner for debt. Fielding called the debtor's gaol 'a prototype of hell': Settle's grisly vision reflects his experience. Of course, he may have been allowed the liberty of the Rules;[76] but that meant confinement to a mere square mile. Most of the less salubrious quarters of London were permitted such a prisoner, from Smithfield and Grub Street itself to Whitefriars and Temple Bar. You could, indeed, have taken part in the Dunces' procession without straining your permit; all the sports of Book II would have been open to you. But you could not have ventured very far in the direction of Twickenham.

It is worth noting, too, that Settle's vision culminates in 'a new world, to Nature's laws unknown':

> All sudden, Gorgons hiss, and Dragons glare,
> And ten-horn'd fiends and Giants rush to war.
> Hell rises, Heav'n descends, and dance on Earth,
> Gods, imps and monsters, music, rage and mirth,
> A fire, a jig, a battle, and a ball,
> Till one wide Conflagration swallows all. (A.III.231)

This is an almost literal description of Settle's most famous Smithfield show: that is, the transmogrified opera *The Virgin Prophetess: or the Fate of Troy*. This had been performed at Drury Lane, where Cibber now reigned, in 1701; it was converted into a fairground droll under the title of *The Siege of Troy* within a few years. This was performed regularly at Bartholomew Fair throughout the second decade of the century. But Pope would not have needed a very long memory: the droll was reprinted in 1728 as 'a Tragi-Comedy, as it has been often Acted with Great Applause. Containing a Description of all the Scenes, Machines; and Movements, with the whole Decoration of the Play . . .' Both versions, indeed, were full of sudden transformation scenes ('immediately, in a moment, all the Golden Statues of the Goddesses are chang'd from Head to Foot into Black . . .') The piece ends with a spectacular fire in which Troy is utterly consumed. This was a new emblem for the destructive power of Dulness; a further backhanded allusion to Virgil; but also a marvellously deft introduction of Settle's own dramatic career. Again we find the right Dunce in the right textual place.[77]

The difficulty of making identifications with complete certainty prompts some caution in interpreting these results. But it looks as if imprisonment for debt was a real hazard of authorship. Among the blacksmiths, lightermen, watchmakers and victuallers who appear in some lists, the designation 'hack' of course does not appear. But it could be said that the difficulties of these years were caused not just by the Bubble but by the particularly bad harvests of 1727–8 and 1739–40 – just before the two versions of *The Dunciad* – which sent prices rising steeply. In a predominantly agricultural economy, this caused widespread financial dislocation; but the scribblers were in a comparatively insulated position. They sold only to people who could read, and in that sense were not dependent on the mass market. Authenticated cases of hacks in Ludgate, indeed, are only a little more numerous than those of beatings in the street, such as Tutchin endured, or in a tavern, like the printer Wilkins. More extreme fates include that of Peter Motteux, who was brutally murdered and briefly enriched the language: the mistress of a coffee-house in Holborn was committed to Newgate in 1721, so Mist informs us, on suspicion of having 'Motteux't' a man.[78] Outside the Dunces proper, there was the sentence imposed on the writer for Read's *Journal*, Richard Burridge, after he had been found guilty of blasphemy in 1718. He was ordered to be whipped from the New Church in the Strand (where the Dunces assemble, A.II.26) to Charing Cross, as well as gaoled for a month in Newgate.[79] It is a slightly *outré* crime but the punishment is familiar-looking.

Duncehood, one might have thought, was its own punishment. But it is evident that Pope took pains to make satiric reproof condign in its effects. The first important rescension of the act dealing with

rogues, beggars and vagabonds since Elizabethan times was passed in
1713 (13 Anne, c.26). It was superseded by measures of 1740 and
1744. Among the other things, the act 'enlarged the list of persons
who fell under the description of rogues and vagabonds'; it defined
the procedure to be followed in punishing them; and it provided
more severe punishment for dangerous and incorrigible rogues.[80] If,
as I have argued, the Scriblerians constituted a society against the
propagation of literary vice; and if 'each Songster, Riddler, ev'ry
nameless name' (B.III.157) can be read as Pope's definition of
vagabondage, then it is appropriate that the hacks should be 'lashed'
like their real-life counterparts. As Settle himself observes,

> The needy Poet sticks to all he meets,
> Coach'd, carted, trod upin, now loose, now fast,
> And carry'd off in some Dog's tail at last. (B. III. 290)

This is very much the fate of the eighteenth-century vagrant. It was
not in fact until 1744 that the justices were given power (17 Geo.II,
c.5) to enlist male vagabonds and rogues in the army or navy; but it
was by no means unknown for such pressing to occur in earlier
years. Settle had joined the army on one occasion, as noted, under a
similar kind of compulsion. Again, the point is not that Pope is saying the Dunces *are* beggars and vagrants – close as they often come
to it. The poetry conveys the idea that they are *like* vagabonds. The
artistic context is such that the hacks stand exposed to comedy, as
real-life criminals stood exposed to penal provisions. Satire has become an imaginative common law.

So it is that Scriblerian writing often comes to resemble a rather
skewed abstract of the legal manuals. One has only to think of Burn's
Justices of the Peace, whose various editions take us into the heart of
the eighteenth century, almost more quickly than any other book.[81]
The longest entry is that headed 'Poor'; other compendious sections
are 'Game', 'Highways', 'Militia', each suggestive of the brawls and
hue-and-cry of the satirists. Some other headings are 'Affray', 'Alehouses', 'Assault and Battery', 'Bankrupt', 'Bastards', 'Blasphemy',
'Bribery', 'Buggery', 'Cheat', 'Coin', 'Debtors', 'Dissenters', 'Fire in
London', 'Fireworks', 'Forgery', 'Gaming', 'Gaol and Gaoler',
'Hawkers and Pedlars', 'Homicide', 'House of Correction', 'Hue and

Cry', 'Larceny', 'Lewdness', 'Libel', 'London', 'Lunaticks', 'Maim', 'Nuisance', 'Peers', 'Perjury and Subornation', 'Physicians', 'Pillory and Tumbrel', 'Plague', 'Players', 'Popery', 'Presentment', 'Prison breaking', 'Prophecies', 'Quakers', 'Rape', 'Restitution of Stolen Goods', 'Riot, Rout and Unlawful Assembly', 'Robbery', 'Sanctuary', 'Scavengers', 'Slander', 'Soldiers', 'Swearing', 'Thames', 'Transportation', 'Treason', 'Vagrants', 'Wine', 'Witchcraft', 'Women', 'Wreck'. This will do as a contents list for Augustan satire. It would require no fantastic attributes of scholarship or insight to discover the relevance of any of these terms to Pope, Swift and Fielding.

This is, I think, enough to explain why Pope should have chosen to surround his victims with an environment of crime and poverty. A rather different account has been given by Mr Emrys Jones, in his splendid lecture on 'Pope and Dulness'. It is a subtle argument, which needs to be rehearsed with some care. Hence what may appear excessive quotation.

> One of the aspects of the Grub-street setting which they [Oldham, Pope *et al.*] give marked attention to is that of ludicrous physical discomfort: the material conditions of life press with a harsh and unwelcome force on the hack writer's consciousness; the unlovely objects which furnish his garret loom large in his vision of the world – and the fact that they do so is given mirthful emphasis for us because the Grub-street hack is, after all, attempting to write *poetry* in this setting: he is 'Lull'd by soft Zephyrs thro' the broken Pane' . . .

Mr Jones goes on to argue that this disjunction between clumsy body and ethereal mind 'seems to make the writing of poetry . . . absurd'. The poet exists 'in a world of unsympathetic *objects*, an environment totally hostile to and unsuggestive of mental and literary activity'. In the Restoration, says Mr Jones, 'the reduced condition of the Grub-street poet' may have served as 'a grotesque reflection of the impoverishment' of poets at large, with the rise of rationalism and science. The hack aroused at once 'an intense curiosity . . . intense mirth, and perhaps a vague feeling of alarm'.

But this is not all. For Mr Jones,

> poverty reduced the hack poet to a man struggling for survival amidst unfriendly objects; and one way in which Pope and his predecessors

exploit the Grub-street theme is to insist on the gross materiality of *poems*, to focus on the poem not as mental artefact but as so many pages of solid paper, something that can be eaten by mice, burnt for fuel, used for 'wrapping Drugs and Wares' (Oldham), lining trunks (Pope),

and so on. Further,

> this aspect of the Grub-street setting has to do with the hack poet's physical need, his uncomfortable awareness of his physical environment . . . Images such as these of the sordid and grossly material are as exciting to Pope as they are repulsive. The deprived social underworld of Grub-street presented a challenge and a stimulus to a poet who was placed in a position of social comfort . . . The poet of consciousness and wit can be said to be contemplating a form of the mindless.[82]

There is a good deal in this. Nevertheless, the analysis seems to me tender-minded and a little far from contemporary realities. One might interpose, for example, the banal but pertinent fact that Grub Street wares actually *were* more likely to serve a number of domestic offices because (apart from being dispensable) they were not put out as finely textured objects of art. William King, the Jacobite author who knew most of the Scriblerian group well, wrote on one occasion, 'I printed the whole catalogue on a large sheet of coarse paper, such as Grub-street ballads are printed on . . .'[83] There was something lumpish and un-valuable about the very physical identity of the scribblers' works. And secondly, one branch of the scribbling profession genuinely was characterised by its production of 'learned lumber' (A.I.116) – the compilers who were responsible for massive folio collections, the garbage heaps piled up from other men's flowers. Pope is not saying that such hack products are more physical than any others; there's simply more of them, and their bulk it is (rather than their mere physicality) which belies their literary pretensions.

Beyond this, it is important to remember that the squalid material environment stands for a world 'deprived' – to misapply Mr Jones's word – of serious cultural ambition. It is possible to see the ideals of Augustan society embodied in a dignified Georgian townscape. A terrace of quietly elegant and imposing houses will stand in reassuring proportion. There is nothing of Mont Saint-Michel or Chartres;

no aspiring Gothic spires or turrets. If there is a skylight it will be hidden. On the other hand, the fenestration is regular, formalised, straightforwardly gazing out at the world of here and now. The material will be 'cheerful' red brick or, later, a decent stuccoed surface. Overall the aim is to achieve a pleasing harmony abjuring outlandish effects or distracting eccentricities. The Grub Street tenements embodied a directly contrary state of things. Jumbled in medieval or Tudor profusion, throwing out odd angles towards the sky and frequently leading the eye in a jerky trajectory, their graceless lines violate physical decorum as hack poems violate literary rules; and their crazy interiors are as bad as their ill-assembled exteriors. Finally, as we have seen, to site Dunces in such a habitat was to go some way to put them outside the law. It was an environment for rogues and vagabonds. And the Scriblerians, having set themselves up rhetorically as stewards of excellence, needed social validation for their imaginative flights. A beleaguered minority does well to impugn the legality of its oppressors.

Modernism has enshrined the figure of the poet-outcast. On the whole, the Scriblerian group found it possible to accommodate their vision within the social forms of the day. Yet increasingly they, too, came to see themselves as an embattled minority. The desperate stratagem they adopted was that of presenting their satiric opponents as outside the pale of society. If they could not altogether be sure of their own orthodoxy, they could at least impugn their victims' credentials. The expedient they used was to incriminate folly by means of the Grub Street metaphor. It is an outflanking manoeuvre. Like Sir William Blackstone, Pope and his friends turned from pastoral idyll to 'wrangling courts . . . to smoke, and crowds, and cities', from an Arcadian world to 'diseases . . . midnight conflagrations . . . loose revelry and riot bold'. Unlike Blackstone, they did not foresake their muse in order to do so.

Defoe as a Dunce

Swift has left us a barbed allusion to Defoe: 'one of these authors
(the fellow that was pilloried I have forgot his name) . . .' Pope did
not match this unkind parenthesis. His comment to Spence was
measured and thoughtful. 'The first part of *Robinson Crusoe*, good,'
he said. 'DeFoe wrote a vast many things, and none bad, though
none excellent. There's something good in all he has writ.'[84] Moreover, he admitted in a *Dunciad* note (A.I.101) that '*Daniel de Foe* had
parts', though his son lacked any. Slightly less charitable is the
innuendo when Norton's name again occurs (A.II.383): '*Norton de
Foe*, said to be the natural offspring of the famous *Daniel. Fortes
creantur fortibus.*' This ironic borrowing from a Horatian ode, IV.iv.
29, might be rendered 'a chip off the old block' – literally, 'the strong
are begotten by the strong.' Again it is the son who comes off worse.
Such careful discrimination might lead us to expect that Defoe would
have been spared Pope's lash. Instead, we find a number of unflattering references. Pope seems not to have objected to Wycherley's
contrast between '*De Foe*'s Burlesque' and '*Dryden*'s *Satyr*'.[85] Then
there is the unmistakable 'D.F.' who figures among the ostriches in
Chapter VI of *Peri Bathous*: that is, the writers 'whose heaviness
rarely permits them to raise themselves from the ground . . . their
motion is between flying and walking; but then they run very fast'.
In both cases, the author probably has the early poems of Defoe in
mind, especially *The True-Born Englishman* and *Jure Divino*. Chapter
IX of *Peri Bathous* explicitly acknowledges the fact – 'Who sees not
that De F— was the poetical son of Withers . . .'[86] Yet Pope was
content to publish these words after Defoe had found his true role as
a novelist. And his most severe thrust was reserved for *The Dunciad*
itself:

> Earless on high, stood un-bash'd Defoe . . . (A. II. 139)

The epithet had originally been 'pillory'd'. As the Twickenham
editor notes, 'Pope must have known that Defoe did not lose his
ears.'[87] Yet he permitted the reference to stand in the revised version.

And this, of course, in spite of his declared respect for much of Defoe's writing. How did this come about?

The question might be put more broadly. What is at stake is not just the particular set of credentials which earned Defoe admission to the poem: it involves some consideration of the status of the 'secondary' Dunces within the work, and also of the process by which Dulness is transmitted to the reader. Defoe is not among the principal actors in *The Dunciad*, as he is in Gildon's (?) *Battle of the Authors*.[88] Apart from the reference just quoted, he is mentioned twice; as 'restless Daniel' in the vision by Queen Dulness of a blessed futurity (A.I.101), and as father of Benjamin Norton Defoe (A.II.383). (Norton himself occurs in one other place.) Clearly Pope had no vital structural role for Defoe in his drama. This being so, it is apparent that Defoe's *reputation at large* entered into the reckoning when his name was grafted into the text.

Defoe in fact is a lay Dunce. His chief advantage from the point of view of Pope's satiric economy was the widespread recognition of his hack status. Whether his books were good or bad, was for the moment irrelevant. It is not the same case as with Cibber or Settle, important figures in the comic action whose personal histories are imaged and distorted in the role Pope allots to them. Defoe was useful initially not because of what he had done but because of what he stood for – what people thought he had done. In Professor Sutherland's words,

> As one of the most frequently abused authors of his generation, Defoe takes his place naturally in a satirical portrait gallery; it would have been surprising if Pope had left him out, or failed to mention the pillory. . . . Defoe . . . joins the dunces as a notorious political writer – his connection with *Mist's Journal* was common knowledge – and also as the type of popular author who wrote for 'porters and oyster wenches'.[89]

Defoe assuredly was an unpopular and controversial writer, even in a contentious age.[90] His opponents, again, certainly loved to bring up his past – he was portrayed as Judas and as Proteus,[91] and reviled as a turncoat as well as a hack: '*Daniel Foe*, who tack'd *de* to his Name, after he had stood in the Pillory . . . which he richly deserv'd after-

wards, when he scribbled for the People that put him there.'⁹² But
Pope does a little more. In both *Peri Bathous* and *The Dunciad* he
presents Defoe as one of a line of bad writers, founded alternatively
by Withers or Prynne.⁹³ This is the *MacFlecknoe* technique over
again. Defoe is the more culpable because he prolongs the great
tradition of Dulness. Secondly, he is the father of yet another scribbling generation:

> Norton, from Daniel and Ostroea sprung,
> Blest with his father's front, and mother's tongue,
> Hung down his never-blushing head. (A.II.383)

The grammar of the first verse enacts that commerce between the
real and the mythical which *The Dunciad* sets in motion. Pope har-
nesses in a single copulative form the local and the remote, the timeless and the temporary. There is a kind of linguistic miscegenation in
thus combining 'Daniel' and 'Ostroea', and that makes a fit emblem
for the illicit union described. That young Norton was to turn out
such a dreadful son is the bonus which Pope seems constantly to earn
by his methods. Benjamin Norton Defoe had all his father's defects
without any of his qualities.

These factors were enough for Pope, given the minor role he was
to accord Defoe. It is therefore beside the point to consult the verdict
of posterity, and label the inclusion of Defoe and Bentley as 'mistakes',
simply because they 'have not been laughed into oblivion'.⁹⁴ The
artistic texture of *The Dunciad* would not have been seriously damaged by a couple of random allusions to Defoe even if he had been
no sort of Dunce. The interesting thing is that this proviso cannot
be met. Defoe, for all his undoubted talent – recognised by Pope –
was a suitable case for satiric treatment. He might indeed have played
a much more central role in the proceedings without any impropriety.
He was, in a word, a born Dunce who happened to have literary
genius.

This is a large claim in a perverse-looking way. I shall therefore
take some pains to justify it, even though the point is academic in so
far as Pope chose not to take hold of all the levers which Defoe's
career afforded him. My excuse is that no one can understand the

genus classified by the satirists under the name Scribbler unless it is grasped that the first great English novelist was all-but-representative of the breed. Nor is that an accident of literary history.

The relevant attributes in Defoe may be ranged under three heads. First, his background and general experiences. Second, the nature of his literary output, along with the circumstances of its production. Third, his cultural situation at large. By this I mean his relations with other professional writers, his standing with the public, and so on. I shall take these groups in turn.

(1) As regards Defoe's background, it is almost too neat a symbolism that he should have begun and ended his days within the very purlieu of Grub Street. His father, a tallow chandler and member of the Butchers' Company, was living in Fore Street in 1688, and had certainly resided in the parish of St Giles', Cripplegate, around the time of Daniel's birth. Thus we have, in Moore's words, 'the first modern man born within the medieval walls [not strictly so] of Old London'; we also have the first hack to have entered the world at a Grub Street address – not quite strictly so. Seventy years later back came Defoe, like some nomadic animal creeping to its home to die. His final clandestine lodgings in Ropemaker's Alley stood a few yards from Grub Street, just as his literary career had lain a degree or two off pure hack writing.[95]

To quote Moore again, 'Defoe's native city had an incalculable influence on his mind. . . . [He] learned the life of the city as a fearless and inquiring child.'[96] In later years Defoe retained vivid memories of the Tower zoo, the Royal Mint, Tyburn, press-gangs in the streets, Billingsgate, dead-carts in the Minories, maypoles and bear-gardens. The teeming life of the city was nowhere more vigorous than in Cripplegate, a fact Paul Dottin brings out in his picturesque account of Defoe's final sojourn there:

Il retourna dans le quartier où il était né, celui de Saint-Gilles en Cripplegate, quartier pauvre et populeux, fouillis inextricable de ruelles tortueuses, de culs-de-sac et de cours inférieures, où il était mieux caché qu'au centre du grand désert africain ou dans une île déserte à l'embouchure du grand fleuve Orénoque. . . . De Foe loua un appartement convenable dans Ropemaker's Alley.[97]

The time when it mattered, however, was in Defoe's youth in the 1660's. It was then that he must have become aware of the unceasing impact of *place* upon men and women, and of the peculiar tensions of city living.[98] Defoe is truly the first great urban writer, in books such as *Colonel Jack*, *Moll Flanders* and the *Journal of the Plague Year*.

But his father brought him links with the City as well as with cities. He himself was to reject the church as a career and turn to trade, as a liveryman's son might well do. As luck would have it, he became not a hosier (as his enemies dubbed him) but a hosefactor: a distributor, a middleman, that archetypal figure of the new commercial England. He was thus leagued with the City of London long before Pope made the imaginative equation of Dulness with the trading and financial world. Worse, Defoe was an unsuccessful trader. We have not only his first bankruptcy, but also a series of aggrieved Chancery litigants, to witness the fact that he was not always regular in his business practices. He dabbled in the newfangled and precarious world of insurance, and that did not work either.[99]

So it was in Defoe's formative years. When he married, it was to the daughter of a wine-cooper, in the church of St Botolph, Aldgate. It must have been like hundreds of weddings contracted by young businessmen: but this time the bridegroom was to found no dynasty (except in Dulness). He was in fact to squander the substantial dowry Mary Tuffley brought with her, and to leave behind him a literary legacy rather than a commercial empire. Yet his work was always money-oriented; he wrote many economic tracts, and even his fiction displays something of this bent. We may reasonably discount the more extreme statements of this tendency: as has been pointed out, the attempt to make of Crusoe a great capitalist and exemplar of 'economic man' founders on the absence of anyone with whom he could trade or engage in any mode of economic activity.[100] None the less, it is certain that Defoe never completely erased the impression of these early years. According to Rachel Trickett, 'Pope was obliged to associate Grub Street and the City in order to make good his allusions to that ready-made mythology of City hacks – Ogilby, Settle and Blackmore – already immortalized by Dryden.'[101] But this is too determinist an account. You did not have to be City Poet as such to be representative of City thinking. And Defoe in the *Review* became very much the mouthpiece of mercantile London. He was as ready as Swift to attack the villainy of stock-jobbers, but he never doubted that Britain's greatness depended on the flow of trade. This inevitably meant some sort of money-market, some kind of central banking, some kind of speculative machinery: and even after the South Sea Bubble, Defoe retained a faith in the City (witness Letter 5 of his *Tour*)[102] which would have seemed pitiable to the Tory satirists.

Another family legacy was Defoe's puritan upbringing. This brought him into contact with the ejected minister of St Giles, Samuel Annesley, whose memory he later celebrated 'by way of elegy' (1697).[103] This in turn meant a link with the hack John Dunton and with Samuel Wesley (father of John and Charles), the two sons-in-law of Annesley. More widely, it meant an early inclination towards the ministry, and after that had passed a lasting taste for moralism, for self-inquiry and spiritual stocktaking. It may have contributed to the immediacy of his confessional writing, such as *A True Relation of the Apparition of Mrs Veal* (1705). And it must have helped him acquire that spare, concrete, colloquial prose. Incidentally, there is some chance that Defoe actually served as a dissenting preacher in his early twenties. However, his didactic treatises, such as *The Family Instructor* (1715–18), serve to demonstrate his earnest brand of nonconformist piety – something that Pope must have regarded as dangerously close to enthusiasm.

Whether the satirists were aware of all these facts is doubtful. Defoe took no great pains to conceal his origins or experience; and his adversaries in print delighted in ramming down his throat any biographic titbit he might not relish. There is at least one suggestion that Swift knew his man, as the very laziness of his dismissive contempt for Defoe might have warned us. At the start of *Gulliver's Travels*, among several apparent echoes of Crusoe, we find a brief allusion seemingly to his creator:

> I took Part of a small House in the *Old Jury*; and being advised to alter my Condition, I married Mrs. *Mary Burton*, second Daughter to Mr. *Edmond Burton*, Hosier, in *Newgate-street*, with whom I received four Hundred Pounds for a Portion.

There are some adjustments here (Defoe's own establishment lay some two hundred yards east of Gulliver's, and the dowry which Mary Tuffley brought with her was much larger). But the hint remains.[104]

We must turn from these early years to the period of Defoe's maturity to see Defoe's slow descent by 'due gradations' into the condition of Dulness. Here the turning point was his ill-judged exercise in irony, *The Shortest Way with the Dissenters* (1701), and his consequent spell in the pillory, which took place in July 1703. It is true that Defoe managed to turn his punishment into a personal triumph and, through his *Hymn to the Pillory*, into a literary success. (One could say of this work, as Mr Emrys Jones says of *The Dunciad*, that it is 'a historical event' as well as a literary opus.)[105] True also, as Professor Moore has said, that 'No man in England ever stood in the pillory and later rose to eminence among his fellow men.'[106] The difficulty is that Defoe's eminence was almost an extension of his 'criminal' activities; that is, he was put in the pillory *because of* (rather than despite) his bold literary enterprise. The qualities which made Defoe a denizen of Grub Street were precisely those that qualified him to pioneer the new bastard form of the novel, and at the same time aroused the ministry to their anxious suppressive measures.

This event was the most striking instance of Defoe in trouble. But it was far from the only occasion that he found himself on the wrong side of the law. His two bankruptcies, in 1692 and 1706, may have had an element of ill luck in them, though perhaps most bankrupts could claim as much. However, records hitherto overlooked survive to show that Defoe was sent to the Fleet (and thence the Queen's Bench gaol) in 1692 and 1702.[107] And we are left with the fact that Defoe was so often in gaol that he must almost have risked becoming institutionalised, as criminologists term it today. To quote Moore once again:

> At least seven times he was confined in Newgate, the Queen Bench's Prison, some debtors' prison, or the house of a Queen's messenger – once for a continuous period of four months. In 1706 he was meeting his creditors in Robert Davis' chamber in the Temple. He had secret

lodgings in the Old Bailey and near Greenwich . . . When he was arrested in May, 1703, he was concealed at the home of a French weaver in Spittlefields. He was in lodgings in Ropemaker's Alley, Cripplegate, when he died [hiding from a creditor].

To this tally must be added further brushes with the law overlooked by Moore;[108] the possibility (though the story may be apocryphal) that he fled once to Bristol, and another time sheltered in the Mint; the occasion when Dr Sacheverell's counsel adduced several passages from the *Review* as examples of scurrilous writing then current; his recurrent appearances as a defendant in Chancery suits; his admitted acquaintance with 'Alsatia-men'; his incarceration in the Fleet; and a good deal else. When Defoe comes to list the London gaols in his *Tour*,[109] one almost expects an asterisk and a marginal note to indicate the prisons of which the writer had first-hand experience. It is true that many of these scrapes were the result of literary and not social offences. His misdemeanours would not have incurred the interest of the authorities in an age less sensitive on the score of seditious publication. All the same, one can only assess a man's standing with his contemporaries according to a yardstick they would understand. One can make a judgment of the character or the abilities of a historical figure by 'timeless' standards. But it does violence to the meaning of words if one claims, by some private semantic fiat, to have made a new estimate of his reputation. That is open to a man's contemporaries alone. On this showing, it is undeniable that in his own day there were few who would have given Defoe a good reference.[110] As we have seen, writers as a profession were peculiarly vulnerable to certain operations of the law. Within this broad pattern of habitual delinquence, Daniel Defoe stands out as a persistent recidivist.

There were even people who thought that Defoe would, or should, end on the gallows. He was told as much at regular intervals, and must have grown accustomed to the warnings, like another scapegrace, Tom Jones. To give a single example, his fellow Dunce Oldmixon invoked a judicial opinion:

The Court [Queen's Bench] was unanimous, that the Books for which he was bound over were *scandalous*, *wicked*, and *treasonable Libels*; but

D. Foe endeavouring to excuse himself, by saying the Books were writ Ironically, he was told by Judge *Powis*, after several learned Arguments to prove the Absurdity of the Pretence, that he might be hang'd, drawn and quarter'd for those Books: But *Daniel Foe* had the good Luck to escape the Gallows, in the manner as has been mentioned.[111]

How often D. Foe received such adjurations from the Bench, we cannot now be sure. Nor does it appear what special critical acuity was vouchsafed to judges of the time, by which they could so confidently pronounce on the rhetorical intentions of a satirical writer. However, it is plain as day that Defoe lived a life of constant threat. It may have been this exposure which gave him the insight into men and women under pressure which irradiates his novels: the psychological states he is able to convey most vividly are those of individuals existing on their nerves, minds stretched taut but not quite to the end of their tether, sensibilities not paralysed but quickened by danger.[112]

As indicated, there was a short step from lawbreaker to law enforcement officer in the eighteenth century. Defoe may never have become Warden of the Fleet, but he was amanuensis to its chaplain.[113] And he was government spy, informer, *agent provocateur* in a sense when he was on the staff of Mist's *Journal*. He was a double agent before the term was invented. His readiness to serve the Hanoverian régime is explicable, in that he would not have known of Harley's flirtations with Saint-Germains. Equally, it requires little imagination to see that many would have found the use made of Defoe by the Under-Secretary of State (who was in effect head of the secret service) as confirming Defoe's knavishness.[114] This was the age of men like William Fuller; even Titus Oates was not long in his grave. Pope could have known only a limited amount concerning Defoe's work on behalf of successive ministries, but what he knew he doubtless held in contempt. Swift, too, spoke of informers with striking bitterness – even for Swift – and when he got into trouble with Delafaye's office in 1715 it cannot have mended matters.[115]

(II) Defoe's life-style, then, shows a number of characteristics. It was insecure, urban, competitive. His literary career might be seen as an extension of this mode of living into the realm of art. In the first place, the content of his work is marked by a similar range of preoccupations – crime, controversy, the problems of money. He was a specialist on the Plague, so severe in Cripplegate. Secondly, the genres he attempted and the rhetorical forms he adopted are expressive of attitudes towards his material violently different from those of Pope, Swift or Gay.

Consider the nature of his oeuvre. Modern scholarship attributes some five hundred separate works with fair confidence to Defoe. Of these items, at least two-thirds deal with contemporary issues; mostly, that is, political issues and often party-political issues. A large number constitute in effect reprints of material written for the periodical press; others are expansions of work so produced. Defoe's long association with newspapers is itself significant. His prolific journalism symbolises the absorption with day-to-day temporalities which the humanist camp found limiting and unworthy. Another considerable group of books is formed by sensationalist works, often on the theme of 'visions', parapsychology, wonders such as the dumb philosopher (if Defoe did indeed write *Duncan Campbell*). Other books represent spurious versions of that revered humanist form, historiography: there are secret histories (private scandal, arcane allegories and the like), and the sort of instant history adequately illustrated by the title *The History of the Reign of King George, from the Death of her late Majesty Queen Anne, to the first of August 1718* (1718). At other times Defoe sprang on to the world letters from a Turkish spy, a letter from the Jesuits, a brief answer to a long libel, a vindication of the press, secret intrigues of the Chevalier de Saint George, an account of the abolishing of duels in France, the case of the poor keel-men of Newcastle, the Jacobites detected, and scores of diverse pamphlets. The miscellaneous character of these productions must bespeak a certain opportunism: a quality we admire in Defoe today, but one which his contemporaries looked on with suspicion. There were numerous essays in religious controversy, many straight economic tracts, and instructive manuals on every topic imaginable. Defoe may not have been strictly an autodidact, but he was practically the inventor of Teach Yourself books. He wrote Answers as readily as the supposed author of Swift's *Tale*, and when nobody took any notice of his reply he issued a further rejoinder.[116]

From his comment to Spence, it appears that Pope knew the bibliography fairly well. By the time of *The Dunciad Variorum* he might have come across *Augusta Triumphans: or the way to make London the most flourishing City in the Universe* (published March 1728). Both Swift and Gay used the equation of Augusta with London in a sharply ironic sense: it had been the favourite, unironic, usage of Elkanah Settle in his City pageants and funeral elegies for defunct aldermen.[117] For one so sensitive to the comic ambiguities behind the 'Augustan' motif, Defoe's title must strike a note of shallow optimism. Around the same time, having got out of his *System of Magick*, having considered the *History and Reality of Apparitions*, and having compiled a less visionary *Plan of the English Commerce*, Defoe turned his hand to the iniquities of imprisonment for debt. He added an *Atlas Maritimus & Commercialis* to his highly imaginative *New Voyage round the World* – a compilation from published sources largely, blending a certain amount of Jules Verne with it all – and his *Tour* of Great Britain. He proclaimed himself the authority on *The Complete English Tradesman*, exposed *Conjugal Lewdness*, and wrote an *Essay upon Literature* which has more to do with hieroglyphics than Homer. He compiled a public relations handout for the distilling industry, and a *General History of Discoveries and Improvements*. This last came appropriately from one who had taken out a share in a project for a diving engine, which proved abortive, and who would certainly have been busy in a land so hospitable to inventors and speculators as Laputa. All these in the mid-1720's, among the usual flow of controversial pamphlets.[118]

I have left out what is perhaps the most important class in fixing Defoe's reputation. He had long been associated with the literature of crime.[119] It was not until the last decade of his life, particularly after his connection with John Applebee, that this element came to predominate. But it is visible years before, with his *Hymn to the Pillory* (1703). His regular concern with dying speeches, manifest during the Applebee period, had turned up in *Remarks* on the speech of the Earl of Derwentwater, after the Earl's execution on Tower Hill as one of the Jacobite rebels. When Defoe became a specialist in 'hymning Tyburn's elegiac lay' (A.I.39), he was drawing on years of experience with criminals great and small. He had been qualified for half his lifetime to do what was only now required: to capitalise on the sudden vogue for sensational criminal lives, occasioned by largely non-literary factors, and apparent in the huge public interest in the exploits of Jack Sheppard and in the downfall of Jonathan Wild.[120] Defoe wrote five books on the pair in the space of a few months.[121] Simultaneously he was developing for Applebee another paying line: the stories of notable pirates such as Captain Gow. The trial of a sadistic sea-captain who had murdered his cabin boy occasioned a short pamphlet in 1726. The same year saw *Some Considerations upon Street-walkers*. This title might suggest a partly sociological approach in Fielding's manner, but in fact the pamphlet is mainly an excuse to insert a letter allegedly written by a prostitute. Also in 1726 there appeared *A Brief Historical Account of the Lives of the Six Notorious Street-Robbers*, at least one of whom, Edward Burnworth, had strong Cripplegate connections. Other private adventures came out at this period, and in 1728 came the more or less definitive two-volume *General History of the most notorious Pyrates*, by a Captain Charles Johnson who grows less and less distinguishable from Defoe as scholarly research proceeds. Then, in the last year or two of Defoe's life, came a number of essays on the theme of preventing street robberies, one 'written by a converted thief'. The last item in the whole bibliography, at any rate as regards books published in Defoe's lifetime, is *An Effectual Scheme for the Immediate Preventing of Street Robberies*, which came out in December 1730. To these books should be added a constant recurrence to criminal matters in Defoe's periodical work: e.g. his interest in the thwarted Bury St Edmunds murder (Applebee's *Weekly Journal*, 21 April 1722).[122]

All this is quite apart from the fictional treatment of analogous topics. There has been a good deal of argument, not very conclusive, regarding the place of the rogue-biography in the genesis of Defoe's novels. It is enough here to observe that much of his creative writing – the sort of thing Pope might have found more palatable than the run of Defoe's output – deals with low characters on the fringe of respectable society, who yet have some ambition towards gentility.[123] And however convincing or otherwise in artistic terms the reforma-

tion of a Singleton or a Colonel Jack may be, the fact remains that
the subject-matter of the book as a whole is irremediably tainted by
eighteenth-century standards. As for Moll Flanders, we know that
Defoe composed in 1720 a letter from a pickpocket called Moll of
Rag Fair – a haunt of Dulness indeed.[124]

But the fiction (even *Robinson Crusoe*, otherwise safer from criticism on socio-moral grounds) raises another difficulty. This relates to
Defoe's habit of blending truth with invention. Traditional theory
could justify the seeming 'lying' of an invented fable. The trouble
with Defoe's fables is that they are often based on historical fact, bent
and if need be distorted. The procedures seen most clearly in the
Memoirs of a Cavalier and *Memoirs of an English Officer* apply in a less
sustained fashion to all Defoe's imaginative writing. His art is inextricably linked with *pretence* in a way unique to himself. Other
novelists, such as Sterne, Joyce or Nabokov, occasionally blur the
line between fact and fiction by allowing the 'real' to invade the
'invented'. The difference is that all Defoe's richest artistic effects
depend on mixing recorded fact with lies, the authentic with the
spurious, genuine history with pseudo-history.[125]

This comes out especially in Defoe's use of an assumed narrative
voice. Swift, of course, regularly uses an authorial mouthpiece. And,
fatigued as the term is, one can fairly call Gulliver or the *Tale*-teller
or the Modest Proposer a 'persona'. The reason is that there is some
consciously achieved distance (usually, but not necessarily ironic)
between the supposed speaker and the real author. Only Irish bishops
are tempted to speak of lies in connection with *Gulliver*. With Defoe
it is less easy. His use of a contrived narrator is far more casual: in *A
New Voyage round the World*, ostensibly factual, he got himself in a
terrible tangle.

The reader is told (p. 6) that the narrator speaks for the Captain, and
that the Captain's name will be given although the name of the actual
author remains concealed: '. . . I shall for the present conceal my
Name . . . the Captain in whose Name I write this, gives me leave to
make use of his Name, and conceal my own.' But the Captain's name
is never mentioned, and the supposed narrator is forgotten so completely that the Captain seems to speak throughout in his own person.[126]

Elsewhere, too, Defoe seems uncertain whether he expects us to believe in his narrator's identity or not. There is none of the transparence of Swift's rhetorical pose. It is as though Defoe wished to hunt with the fictional hounds and flee with the factual hare. He will insert a certificate of authenticity at the head of a book which is the least authentic thing in it; and he will suppress the genuine credentials he has. His seventeenth-century military history is made up of authentic accounts, but so tessellated and interwoven as to be ultimately a species of fantasy. With Defoe, it follows, to speak of 'lying' is not of necessity a childish or inappropriate act. One responds to his art not, as with Swift, by recognising pretence but by failing to do so.

Now Pope knew as well as any man the shifts to which the practice of writing might impel one. He is unlikely to have been outraged by Defoe's rejection of one *Collection* (authentic though it now appears to have been) and its substitution by another *True Collection*.[127] On the other hand, the perpetual blurring of truth and invention in Defoe may have disturbed him. It is rather as with the secret histories – Defoe even produced a secret history of a secret history on one occasion[128] – and with scandalous allegories such as *The Court of Atalantis*. Defoe could fairly be aligned with Mrs Haywood as a writer who neither reported the true facts about the world, or created an imagined world with its own autonomous criteria of reality. Instead, both authors described arabesques around the truth, and left the reader to sort out what he could. It goes without saying that the artistic effect of *Memoirs of a Cavalier* is of a different order from that of *Memoirs of the Kingdom of Utopia*. But it is not clear that the authors can be so easily separated in respect of literary integrity or of insight into their own purposes.

Defoe, in any case, was fishing in deep waters. The novel was not only new, which was bad enough; it was also born out of accepted literary wedlock. It had some pretensions in the direction of such forms as epic and romance; but it had stooped to borrow from journalism, biography, picaresque tales and popular theology amongst other things. Its miscellany was part of its novelty and its appeal. There is something deeply suitable in the contribution of a man who had written books called *Armageddon*, *An Apology for the Army*, *A Hymn to the Mob, A Letter from the Man in the Moon, The Second-sighted Highlander, Wise as Serpents* and *Mere Nature Delineated* to this upstart genre. Pope must have found it all very suspicious. Even the one acknowledged achievement – *Robinson Crusoe*, part one – had no home to go to in the Augustan pantheon. Socially, Defoe was an outsider.[129] Sad that his best work should wear the same air of forwardness and bounce. There was nothing more pert than a Dunce.

(III) Finally, there is the matter of Defoe's general standing. He had in truth allied himself with the duncely party some time before he tangled directly with Pope. According to Professor Moore, 'Defoe's strictures on Pope's *Homer* probably helped him to win the place in *The Dunciad* which was otherwise so uncalled for.'[130] Help it must have done, though Defoe's admission is not the simple issue of literary merit here implied. The more important point is that Defoe had all along breathed the air of controversy; he was a polemicist in and out of season, with or without a cause. There was, as we have seen, guilt by association; and Defoe's noisy encounters with men of the calibre of Abel Boyer, Joseph Browne, John Tutchin, Charles Leslie, John Oldmixon, Ned Ward and so on gave him anything but a good start. (All were Dunces or too obscure to rank as such.) By 1705 Defoe had effectively signalised himself as a popular writer, intent on stirring up public interest on one pretext or another.

There is, however, no evidence that the popularity of Defoe – or of anyone else – counted against him. Not all the hacks who figure in *The Dunciad* wrote books that were popular in intention: their productions range from law manuals, rhetorics and metaphysical treatises to editions of Sallust and translations of Tacitus. And *a fortiori* not all the Dunces were popular writers in the sense of achieving general acclaim. It is therefore doubtful if Professor Kramnick's statement can be accepted as it stands: '[The] brothers of the Scriblerus Club thought Defoe's work socially and intellectually inferior, a fact indicated by its success with the new bourgeois reading public.'[131] All the signs are that the reception accorded to Defoe's work had little to do with his treatment by Pope and his circle. It is true, as Paul Dottin remarked, that 'the poor hack-writers of Grub Street' were filled with envy by the success of *Robinson Crusoe*, and Gildon in his retort must have spoken for many of them.[132] But Defoe had long been at odds with Grub Street – that was part of being a resident of the place. Pope was not in direct competition in the same way. If anything, he reserved his most waspish attacks for those who dared to rival him in translating Homer, in pastoral or in verse satire. The truth is that Defoe was little of an immediate threat to the Tory group; he roused no personal amimus, and earned his Duncehood for other works than the successful *Crusoe*.

In this context, it was probably Defoe's association with Nathaniel Mist which sealed his fate. The notorious printer was in trouble with the authorities even more often than Curll (for whom Defoe actually wrote little). Sedition, rather than obscenity, was Mist's usual line. When Defoe became a colleague of Mist around 1717, even if it was as a government agent (a story the least credulous are strangely anxious to swallow), he was injuring his reputation with most thinking people, let alone the observant Pope. Contemporary journalists could now align Defoe with the obscurest of hacks: '. . . his [Mist's] nonsensical Scriblers, Foe, Seddon, and the debauch'd author of the Entertainer, a poor unbenefic'd Parson . . .'[133] Defoe had allowed himself to appear as the hireling of a disreputable printer, in the company of scribblers too little known to risk Duncehood.

A second factor was pure ill luck. Benjamin Norton Defoe may or may not have been legitimate, but he was certainly as bad a son as even the eighteenth century knew, Chesterfield and the Hanoverian kings included. He was in trouble with the ministry as early as 1721, and thereafter he experienced all the ills of Grub Street, poverty and prosecution hovering over his head all his days. Near the end of the century his grandson was hanged at Tyburn, the fate which had been popularly anticipated for Daniel. Hereditary Dulness could scarcely go further.[134]

The fairest summary of Defoe's all-round standing is that of his best biographer, James Sutherland:

The contempt with which writers like Pope allude to Defoe is instructive; they sneer because they are secretly uneasy. Here was this fellow, throwing off book after book, and he had no business to be writing at all. He was outside the 'ring'; he had not graduated from the recognised school of authorship. His Latin was contemptible, he paid far too little attention to polite diction – he actually wrote more or less as he spoke – and he was full of vulgar sentiments that appealed to the lower orders. And yet Pope *felt* that he was a remarkable writer.[135]

I should not quarrel with most of this, although it seems doubtful whether Pope would envy Defoe's prolific output or look on *that* as mitigation of his Duncehood. I wish to leave a slightly different emphasis: granted that Pope recognised special qualities in Defoe, they were special for a writer in his position, special for one relatively so disadvantaged, special for a Dunce. The satirist knew he was dealing with a man of peculiar abilities. But you did not escape *The Dunciad* by fitful good works, if your career as a whole placed you among the elect.

The Genuine Grub-Street Opera

Fielding's career mirrors the history of Grub Street in little. He was the last legatee of the Tory satirists' tradition, and the first populariser of a new standard version. He thus marks the transition between two orders of Grubean existence: the critical concept and the human-interest story. Although the process is not fully developed in Fielding, we can see the beginnings of a slide from the Dunce as wrongdoer to the hack as victim.

It is well known that Fielding began as a playwright. As early as *The Tragedy of Tragedies*, we find the adoption of a persona – H. Scriblerus Secundus – immediately deriving from the Tory satirists. The entire joke which underlies the play is a straight crib from the Pope circle, more particularly from *Peri Bathous*, whose vocabulary, ideas and satiric stratagems are borrowed wholesale. The usual *topoi* of London life are present: Fleet Ditch, Monmouth Street, Bridewell. Fielding carries the absurdity a little further, so that the mock-solemnity of Scriblerian farce is toppled over into a sort of freakish nonsense. Instead of learned tomfoolery, we have the scholarly grotesque. All the same, the debt is clear. With plays such as *The Historical Register* (1737), *Euyrdice Hissed* (1737) and *Pasquin* (1736), we encounter the 'rehearsal' form in one variant or another, with poets or dramatists in the leading role, and incidental satire on theatrical or literary types to give edge to the primary political theme. It is demonstrable that these plays influenced Pope when he came to write the last book of *The Dunciad*,[136] but (apart from the slightly earlier *Author's Farce*, considered in a moment) they lie outside the mainstream of Grub Street tradition.

So, despite its title, does *The Grub-Street Opera* (1731).[137] This was originally *The Welsh Opera*, the aptest title it bore, and then *The Genuine Grub-Street Opera*. We can see why the work was renamed – even if the reasons are not particularly good – and why the play served to blunt the efficacy of Grub Street, if we look at the introductory scene added by Fielding. Enter Scriblerus (once more!) and a Player:

> *Player.* I very much approve the alteration of your title from the *Welsh* to the *Grub-Street Opera*.
>
> *Scriblerus.* I hope, sir, it will recommend me to that learned society, for they like nothing but what is most indisputably their own.
>
> *Player.* I assure you it recommends you to me, and will, I hope, to the town.
>
> *Scriblerus.* It would be impolite in you, who are a young beginner, to oppose that society, which the established theatres so professedly favour. Besides, you see the town are ever on its side, for I would not have you think, sir, all the members of that august body confined to the street they take their name from. No, no, the rules of Grub Street are as extensive as the rules of the King's Bench. We have them of all orders and degrees, and it is no more a wonder to see our members in ribbands than in rags.

The continuity of idiom with earlier Scriblerian humour strikes the reader. But the energy is starting to drain from this particular mode of comedy, as a following exchange shows:

> *Player.* You have made additions indeed to the alternative scenes, as you are pleased to call them.
>
> *Scriblerus.* Oh, sir, they cannot be heightened; too much altercation is

> the particular property of Grub Street. . . . Ah, ah, the
> whole wit of Grub Street consists in these two little words –
> *you lie.*

Then comes the play itself, a kind of allegorical pastoral farce. What,
then, of the ostensible subject? The position has been well put by a
recent editor:

> *The Grub-Street Opera* . . . is only secondarily a literary attack. . . .
> In [the] larger sense, the play attributes such [Grub Street] witlessness
> not only to politicians but to society at all levels . . . Grub-Street wit
> is all-pervasive and destructive in society.

This is perhaps to exaggerate a little the play's unity of purpose and
seriousness of design; but it is right to say that 'the title . . . serves
by analogy to connect the play's action with much of human life.'[138]
In other words, the title might be paraphrased along the lines of
'The Present-Day Charade', 'The Way We Live Now', *'Cosi fan
Tutte'* – Grub Street being an emblem of acceptance, what everyone takes for granted. Fielding presents contemporary life as a show
('opera') whose popularity reflects the ubiquity of Grubean standards. This was a less subtle and potent device than that of Pope,
who had let the Dunces have their shows but had related these entertainments to a whole pattern of Grub Street living. Pope's opera
was played not just at Drury Lane or Smithfield, but also at Bedlam,
Fleet Ditch and Tyburn.

Much more important, however, was *The Author's Farce* (1730).
Although this was Fielding's great success, it held the stage for a
comparatively short time, and was rarely acted in the second half of
the century.[139] Nor was it ever precisely famous, as some unacted
plays were and are. Yet this comedy did much to set the pattern of
the Grub Street myth; the mythologists often quote snatches of the
play (see Ch. VI), and subliminally the legend assimilated Fielding
as it did Hogarth's 'Distressed Poet'.

It may not be immediately obvious why this should have been so.
On the surface, *The Author's Farce* is a rumbustious, fast-moving
piece of dramatic writing, with clear debts to Pope. There are paltry
hacks and rascally booksellers, vain actors and a lustful landlady.
Above all, there is a puppet-play within the play, whose *dramatis*

personae include the Goddess of Nonsense along with Signior Opera, Don Tragedio, Mrs Novel and Monsieur Pantomime. There are jokes about Orator Henley, Durfey and translators who have been sent to Newgate for shoplifting. Is this not simply an extension of *The Dunciad* into the terms of stage comedy, with a prescient hint of Book IV?

In fact, no. The crucial difference is that the hero, Luckless, author of the puppet-show, is himself a scribbler. It is as though we should have been invited to see the events of *The Dunciad* through the eyes of Settle. When there is at the outset a confrontation with Mrs Moneywood, his landlady, our sympathy remains with the hack, despite the damage he has done.

> *Moneywood.* Well, I am resolved, when you are gone away (which I
> heartily hope will be very soon) I'll hang over my door in
> great red letters, *No Lodgings for Poets.* Sure, never was
> such a guest as you have been. My floor is all spoiled with
> ink, my windows with verses, and my door has been
> almost beat down with duns.[140]

The hero's name, Luckless, gives the game away. Here is the beginning of the Unfortunate Poet. Of course, Fielding presents these calamities of authorship with an amused, rather than a maudlin, tone of voice. The 'most abominable distemper', poverty, of which Luckless complains, is treated as a mildly embarrassing form of indisposition. Yet there is a critical shift. In the puppet-show Luckless is threatened with arrest for abusing Nonsense; in other words the scribbler is now leagued against Dulness. The bedraggled poet has changed sides.

Moreover, there is a marked innovation as regards the hacks. Dash, Blotpage, Scarecrow and Index are silly and ignorant, to be sure. But they elicit a measure of sympathy as the victim of Book-weight's tyranny:

> Fie upon it, gentlemen! What, not at your pens? Do you consider, Mr
> Quibble, that it is above a fortnight since your Letter from a Friend in
> the Country was published? Is it not high time for an Answer to come
> out? At this rate, before your Answer is printed your Letter will be
> forgot. I love to keep a controversy up warm. I have had authors who

have writ a pamphlet in the morning, answered it in the afternoon, and compromised the matter at night.[141]

Absurd as this is, it is giving the scribblers a moral escape route. Likewise when Scarecrow brings a translation of the *Aeneid* to the bookseller.

> *Bookweight.* . . . To oblige a young beginner, I don't care if I print it at my own expense.
> *Scarecrow.* But pray, sir, at whose expense shall I eat?
> *Bookweight.* That's an empty question.
> *Scarecrow.* It comes from an empty stomach, I'm sure.
> *Bookweight.* From an empty head, I'm afraid. Are there not a thousand ways for a man to get his bread by?[142]

And so on. Bookweight goes on to reveal secrets of his trade, including the use of assumed names on the title-page. The style is quibbling, short-winded, blandly evading any trace of real human intensity. Yet there is a change in vantage-point. We see the baneful effects of Bookweight on the hacks, not as with Pope the pollution by Curll of civilised standards. When Curll is made to call his hirelings together, in Pope's short prose squib, we are reminded of the insult done to the memory of the departed and to surviving members of the family by a scandalous biography.[143] Here, it is just the hack who suffers.

It follows that *The Author's Farce* embodies less particular criticism of Grub Street as a whole. To call your bookseller Bookweight (or Curry, the name employed in the puppet-show), instead of Curll, is to set him at one remove. To call your hacks Quibble and Scarecrow, instead of Ozell or Gildon, is to allow them to hide behind allegory, or to engage in a gentle comedy of humours. Moreover, where Dulness is imperious, Nonsense is a typical burlesque goddess, reduced to mortal size, anxious to marry Opera, as puny a threat as any single scribbler.

If Fielding takes much from Pope, then his departures are quite as striking. In the puppet-play, Luckless is cast into the Thames and escapes by swimming into Billingsgate. 'I was taken up half-dead by a waterman and conveyed to his wife, who sold oysters, by whose assistance I recovered. But the waters of the Thames, like those of

Lethe . . . caused an entire oblivion of my former fortune.' All the symbolic potential which Pope would have realised goes to waste. Fielding takes over the form but little more. So with Grub Street itself. The puppet-show has a poet telling the dead bookseller of the present state of London.

> Why, affairs go much in the same road there as when you were alive; authors starve and booksellers grow fat, Grub Street harbours as many pirates as ever Algiers did, they have more theatres than are at Paris, and just as much wit as there is at Amsterdam, they have ransacked all Italy for singers and all France for dancers.

Grub Street is the home of cheating booksellers, with Italian opera as the new threat. The links with the criminal ecology of the city have been lost. Later in the play, there are references to 'The scribbler in a pamphlet war, / Or Grub Street bard composing', and in its closing lines:

> *Luckless.* Taught by my fate, let never bard despair,
> Though long he drudge and feed on Grub Street air,
> Since him, at last, 'tis possible to see
> As happy and as great a king as me.[144]

At last the bard has come into his own. Luckless is found to be the rightful heir of the King of Bantam. There is a good deal of burlesque tragedy (Fielding's fatal Cleopatra, as a comic dramatist) surrounding this discovery; and the whole sequence might be regarded as a wish-fulfilment, with Luckless acting out his fantasies within the harlequinade he has devised. The fact remains that the poet (not the Goddess Nonsense) triumphs; that the ending is comic, not apocryphal or tragic; and that we are invited to celebrate with the victor, mere puppet as he is, rather than to consider the state of things his reign will usher in. In *The Dunciad* it had been a different story.

This split has something to do with the change from mock-epic to stage farce. It may relate to Fielding's position as an outsider, hustling hard to make his way, as against Pope's established position at the top of the heap. What is undeniable is that *The Author's Farce* heralds the breakdown of an incisive critique and its replacement by a cosier idiom.

When Fielding turned to the novel, he lost touch to a great extent with the Scriblerian tradition. *Jonathan Wild* starts from the moral-cum-topographic picture of criminal London used by the satirists, but its overall design is one of broader ironic effects allied to mock-heroic. Some of the introductory chapters of *Tom Jones* bear a passing relation to Grub Street: see, for example, the opening sections of Books 4, 5, 9 and 12. Pope and Swift are often invoked, and Dunces such as James Moore-Smythe and Oldmixon briefly put in their place. Fielding, to put it crudely, was still on the side of the angels; he had not shifted his sympathy to the Dunces, as the Victorians were largely to do. Nevertheless, his methods as a novelist have less and less to do with formal satire: his concerns have less and less to do with men like Curll, Orator Henley and Colley Cibber. Nor is *Amelia* an exception. It is true that the hero, Booth, spends much of Book 8 in the custody of a bailiff, with a typical hack as his companion. Fielding derives some incidental fun from this situation. The hack shows his ignorance and venality; he confuses Lucian and Lucan, he writes parliamentary reports from the sponging-house, he solicits subscriptions for a translation of the *Metamorphoses*, and generally reveals himself a vain coxcomb. That is the trouble. Unlike the Dunces, he is never plausible, and he resembles a seedy modern confidence trickster in the Graham Greene mould rather than the true enthusiastic breed of hack: his self-deluded fantasies are rich enough almost to persuade us that they have a worthy cause. Moreover, the hack is himself a purveyor of the Grub Street myth ('There is no encouragement to merit, no patrons'), a form of self-pity that further robs him of Duncely independence. And again the booksellers are to blame, as far as the bailiff is concerned.

'He hath been here these five weeks at the suit of a bookseller for eleven pound odd money; but he expects to be discharged in a day or two, for he hath writ out the debt. He is now writing for five or six booksellers, and he will get you sometimes, when he sits to it, a matter of fifteen shillings a day. For he is a very good pen, they say, but is apt to be idle. Some days he won't write above five hours; but at other times I have known him at it above sixteen.' 'Ay!' cries Booth; 'pray, what are his productions? What does he write?' 'Why, sometimes,' answered Bondum, 'he writes your history books for your numbers, and sometimes your verses, your poems, what do you call them? and then again he writes news for your newspapers.' 'Ay, indeed! he is a most extraordinary man, truly! – How doth he get his news here?' 'Why he makes it, as he doth your parliament speeches for your magazines. He reads them sometimes to us over a bowl of punch. To be sure it is all one as if one was in the parliament-house – it is about liberty and freedom, and about the constitution of England . . .'[145]

We have slid over into a kind of half-indulgent and whimsical social comedy. The hack has no name – he is just a lay figure, put to opportunistic use. Grub Street itself was to experience a similar fate.

In his last years, Fielding was chiefly occupied by his work on criminal and reformatory topics. Perhaps his *Proposal for Making an Effectual Provision for the Poor* (1753) could be seen as parallel to the satirists' joking provision for a 'hospital' for the Dunces. I have argued that the Scriblerians saw themselves as a Society for the Suppression of Vice (that characteristic product of the age), in so far as the 'corrective' function of their satire was achieved by giving the culprits symbolically appropriate lodgings. Again, the *Inquiry into the Causes of the late Increase of Robbers* (1751) has its pertinence for Grub Street. The causes listed include 'too frequent and expensive diversions among the lower kind of people' – Fielding has in mind 'temples of idleness' such as the masquerades, but what could be more expressive of Book II of *The Dunciad*? – as well as drunkenness, 'almost inseparably annexed to the pleasures of such people', and gaming. Fielding also examines the law relating to vagabonds, with this significant observation :

> Whoever indeed considers the cities of London and Westminster, with the late vast addition of suburbs, the great irregularity of their buildings, the immense number of lanes, alleys, courts, and bye-places; must think, that, had they been intended for the very purpose of concealment, they could scarce have been better contrived.

This aptly describes the home of the suburban muse, and might remind us that the press had originally come to Cripplegate to avoid official surveillance. Grub Street was a settlement of fugitives. Fielding later describes Tyburn executions as set up 'to make a holiday for, and entertain, the mob'. He praises Swift, describes the night-houses of St Giles' in the Fields, and reviews the punishments available.[146] All this seems to me loosely analogical to what *The Dunciad* had offered, by way of its enquiry into the increase in Dulness. The parallel must not be stretched too far, but it is suggestive as far as it goes.

One other branch of Fielding's work deserves mention. In the *Covent-Garden Journal* (1752) he kept up a regular fire on the approved targets of the Scriblerus party. In the first issue the terms are laid out for a paper war between Sir Alexander Drawcansir (Fielding's persona) and the army of Grub Street. This body of scribblers is said 'to threaten the republic of letters with no less devastation than that which their ancestors the Goths, Huns, Vandals, &c. formerly poured in on the Roman Empire' – a limp paraphrase of *The Dunciad*. However, an uneasy truce is soon established: and despite token allusions to 'the records of Grub Street', 'the whole race of Grub Street', 'the genuine anonymous productions of Grub Street', and so on, most of the spirit has gone out of the joke. We get one or two hints of how the critique could have been extended:

> By the 14th article of the Treaty of Covent Garden, the importation of French words and phrases in English writings is declared to be the sole right of Grub Street.

More interesting are references to Savage:

> . . . the case of one Mr Richard Savage, an author whose manufactures had long laid uncalled for in the warehouse, till he happened, very fortunately for his bookseller, to be found guilty of a capital crime at the Old Bailey . . .

to the gallows and the whipping post as each 'a great friend of the press', and to *The Dunciad*:

> He [Pope] employed a whole work for the purpose of recording such writers as no one without his pains, except he had lived at the same time and in the same street, would ever have heard of. He may indeed be said to have raked many out of the kennels to immortality, which, though a somewhat stinking condition, is to an ambitious mind preferable to utter obscurity and oblivion; many, I presume, having, with the wretch who burnt the Temple of Ephesus, such a love for fame, that they are willing even to creep into her common sewer.[147]

It would be otiose to point out how many standard components of Grub Street satire are brought together here. Fielding understood his *Dunciad*, of that we can be sure.

The relation, then, of Fielding to his predecessors is a complex one. He was the last writer of genius to whom live meaning inhered in this particular trope. He was the first to dilute it, and to portray the hack as sinned against as well as sinning. Only in *The Author's Farce* does he achieve a wholly successful recreation of the world of the scribbler: and he does this by inverting the perspective of Grub Street – Luckless, Mr Average Nobody among the hacks, triumphs and not the great Goddess of Nonsense. Of course, Fielding knew quite as much about scribblers, about poverty, about crime, about low-life London, as did Pope or Swift or Gay.[148] But though these elements of the fiction went on (as did the historic Grub Street), the literary truth it asserted through metaphor was ebbing. *The Author's Farce* is energetic and observant comedy: it is hardly satire. Not because Fielding was a more benevolent man than the Scriblerians – though he may have been – but because he inherited their forms without their cultural situation. He did not hate Grub Street because he could not quite believe in it as they had done.

Epigraphs. (*i*) Pope, *Prose Works*, I, 284:
　　　　　(*ii*) *The Shorter Poems of the Eighteenth Century*, ed. I. A. Williams (London, 1923), p. 352.

　1. George Rudé adopts Defoe's classification of social status of 1709, and places among the 'professional' classes doctors, artists, poets and lawyers, although 'Defoe and other contemporary writers paid little or no attention' to this group. One wonders how much attention Professor Rudé has given the poets. Few professional writers achieved social status as a result of their literary work, although a poet who was by vocation a doctor was not degraded by his secondary calling. Men such as Cibber achieved some prominence at Court for their theatrical enterprises, but it is hard to think of a case, apart from Pope, where literary distinction by itself gave social esteem. And even Pope owed much of his independence to his unprecedented financial success, which made it possible for him to resist most of the difficulties of professional authorship – and to keep out of the hurlyburly in Twickenham. For Rudé's comments, see *Paris and London in the Eighteenth*

Century (London, 1970), p. 44. My own view is that an absolute majority of poets, if we exclude peerage of the realm, belonged to grades below Defoe's 'middle sort, who live well'.

2. The calculation is based quite simply on adding up recorded cases and making an allowance for possible oversights. Naïve as the method is, it can hardly be improved on in the absence of anything like a census. W. A. Speck does record the instance of a poet so designated in a Norwich poll-book. But this was obviously an exceptional circumstance; and one could not, for instance, deduce from it that the absence of such entries elsewhere means that no poets ever had votes. See Speck's *Tory and Whig* (London, 1970), p. 120.

3. Barbu, 'The New Intelligentsia', *French Literature and its Background: The Eighteenth Century* (London, 1968), p. 80.

4. There is evidence that scholars came from a perceptibly lower segment of society, on average, than the run of university entrants. There are some relevant comments in Nicholas Hans, *New Trends in Education in the Eighteenth Century* (London, 1951), pp. 41–54, though Hans' methodology and his judgement appear suspect in places.

5. In fact, even the most spectacular worldly failures among the Dunces (Gildon or Dennis, say) did not occupy a permanent position in Defoe's bottom group – 'the miserable, that really pinch and suffer want.' The worst that could happen in general to a hack, who could after all read and write, was to experience something like these conditions for intermittent spells. But that may have made it worse.

6. M. E. Wolfgang, F. Ferracuti, *The Subculture of Violence* (London, ed. 1967), p. 97. See pp. 95–113 throughout. Following quotations from pp. 100, 102. On culture-conflict, see T. C. N. Gibbon, R. H. Ahrenfeldt (eds.), *Cultural Factors in Delinquency* (London, 1966), pp. 52–71, esp. p. 55.

7. Albert K. Cohen, *Delinquent Boys: The Culture of the Gang* (London, 1956), pp. 49–72.

8. The book is by John Oldmixon. See my article, 'The Memoirs of Wharton and Somers', *Bulletin of the New York Public Library*, forthcoming. Other Dunces who practised this kind include Giles Jacob, who subjected Addison to the treatment; Defoe; Budgell; and later Theophilus Cibber, who gave his name to *The Lives of the Poets* (1753). Theobald's intended life of Buckingham was suppressed (TE, V, 456; Sherburn, p. 222); but we know that Pope kept a careful eye open for such events. Cf. my article, 'The Conduct of the Earl of Nottingham', *RES*, XXI, (1970), 175–81.

9. A hack might leave town for one reason or another. He might be fleeing his creditors: in the case of Mist and Ridpath, this meant escaping to the continent. Or perhaps sent on dubious government business: in such a case the Dunce was liable to pine for the metropolis, as with Oldmixon in

Bridgwater. Very few Dunces were based permanently outside London, and they tended to be men of slightly higher standing such as Barnham Goode, a master at Eton, and George Duckett, a Wiltshire squire who spent much time in London. Neither of these men was a full-time scribbler.

10. Holdsworth, X, 673.

11. Fielding, XIII, 218.

12. See Holdsworth, X, 672–96; Laurence Hanson, *Government and the Press 1695–1763* (Oxford, 1936), pp. 16–25.

13. For the famous case of *R. v. Curll*, in which it was laid down that even an offence *contra bonos mores* fell under the jurisdiction of the temporal courts, see *State Trials*, XVII, 153–60; as well as the report by Curll's counsel, Sir John Strange, in his *Reports of Adjudged Cases in the Courts of Chancery King's Bench, Common Pleas and Exchequer* (London, 1755), II, 788–92. Straus, pp. 98–120, gives a somewhat jaunty version. The original indictment survives in the PRO, KB 10/19 (?Lent, 1725). Judgment was finally given in the King's Bench in the Michaelmas Term of 1 Geo.II (1727).

   Curll's troubles went back much earlier, to such episodes as the trial of the Earl of Winton in 1715, when he was called to the bar of the House of Lords and reprimanded on his knees. See *State Trials*, XV, 805–98, as well as Straus, pp. 65–7. It is hardly possible to list here all Curll's brushes with the law. Straus records about half a dozen instances; there are certainly far more. Nor does Straus allude to the significant suit in Chancery, *Pope v. Curll*. Similarly, the only existing account of Nathaniel Mist (that by G. A. Aitken, in *DNB*) mentions about ten occasions on which Mist was bought up before the authorities. Further cases can be identified or surmised from PRO, KB 10/17; SP 44/79A, 80, 81, 289; SP 35/14, 21, 43, 55; SP 36/151. A thorough enquiry would be needed to disclose the full extent of Mist's legal difficulties.

14. The suggestion was made from time to time that it was advantageous to a bookseller financially if he was arrested and prosecuted. See for example Ralph Straus, *The Tricks of the Town* (London, 1927), p. 245.

15. One who was a relatively uncontroversial writer, even in his Grub Street days – Christopher Smart – wrote in a letter, 'After being *six* times arrested; *nine* times in a spunging house: and *three* times in the Fleet-Prison, I am at last happily arrived at the King's Bench. . .' Quoted by Arthur Sherbo, *Christopher Smart, Scholar of the University* (East Lansing, Mich., 1967), p. 256.

16. Swift, *Prose Works*, III, 96–7.

17. Or, more precisely, an estate in London. Apart from factors mentioned elsewhere in this book, it should be noted that the 'process of occupational and social differentiation among (London's) internal divisions – a process accelerated by the Great Fire' was further developed in the capital than

elsewhere. See Max Beloff, *Public Order and Popular Disturbances 1660–1714* (Oxford, 1938), p. 28. The same author refers to the 'chaotic array of local authorities' in London as an obstacle to effective control of disturbances: it was likewise a symptom of the medieval huddle in which local administration found itself, based to some extent on fierce parochial loyalties which no longer answered to genuine social interests. Much the same is true of Grub Street as an organisation of mutual protection within the republic of letters. See also Holdsworth, XI, 138.

18. Savage had been arrested as early as November 1715 for possessing a treasonable pamphlet: there may also have been a suspicion that he had been its author and/or publisher. See Clarence Tracy, *The Artificial Bastard* (Toronto, 1953), p. 30; for Savage in Newgate, see p. 83; for his arrest by the bailiffs for a debt of £8, and spell in a sponging house, see p. 148.

19. Oldmixon, pp. 525–7, 510. For Gildon, see also PRO, SP 44/77/36. Oldmixon describes how evidence was given at Ridpath's trial, by a printer's devil, on behalf of the prosecution. 'But the *Devil* was committed to Hard Labour at *Bridewell* in about a Month after, by a Warrant from Sir *William Withers*, for stealing some Plate . . .' (p. 526). This is an interesting example of the way specifically literary offences overlapped with the common pattern of everyday crime. For Pittis, see also PRO, SP 44/77/132, 159; SP 44/80, unfoliated.

20. Hanson, p. 105. *State Trials*, XIV, 1095–200, reports Tutchin's trial in 1704. For his own reactions, see Hanson, p. 57. See also David H. Stevens, *Party Politics and English Journalism 1702–1742* (Menasha, Wisc., 1916), p. 10. For Wilkins, see TE, V, 459.

21. PRO, SP 34/4/45–6; SP 44/105/152. Two duncely authors who were caught were Boyer and Burnet: SP 44/77/139, 152.

22. See especially the 'criminal' letterbooks, PRO, SP 44/77–80. For Curll as a surety for Pittis, SP 44/77/159. For Thomas Warner, allotted a role in *The Dunciad* at A.II.117, see SP 44/81/55.

23. Stevens, p. 129.

24. Hanson, pp. 57–8. The best account of the Matthews affair is that of James Sutherland, 'Young Matthews', *Background for Queen Anne* (London, 1939), pp. 182–200. See also *State Trials*, XV, 1323–403.

25. Hanson, pp. 58–9. Ilive later became involved in a dispute with Pope which led to a Chancery suit: Pope, *Correspondence*, IV, 425; later still he was in the Fleet gaol – PRO, Pris. 10/89. For Henley's troubles, see TE, V, 174.

26. In the case of a man like William Fuller, instanced by Hanson on p. 59, it is doubtful how far his troubles can be ascribed directly to literary crimes. His seditious offences were but the extension of a lifetime career as confidence trickster and informer. Fuller certainly underwent many of the misfortunes of Duncehood: a pamphlet called *The Scribler's Doom*, relating to

Fuller and 'Defooe' (1704), sums up the position. He was forced to hide in Whitefriars; he was pilloried at Charing Cross and Temple Bar, and sent to Bridewell. He was summoned before the House of Lords with the bookseller Anne Baldwin. His contacts included men like Ridpath and Settle. As Hanson notes, he spent many years in the King's Bench prison. And from the Corporation of London records of debtors, preserved at the Guildhall, it appears that he was in the Fleet in 1712. Yet Fuller would probably have suffered a very similar fate if he had never written a line. He was a malefactor who happened to write, rather than an *echt* Dunce. Pope seems not to have troubled himself with men like Fuller. One curious sidelight, however, is provided by the fact that Fuller once committed a fraud on a victualler of Grub Street in order to obtain a post at the Tower. See George Campbell, *Impostor at the Bar* (London, 1961), passim. There are additional details in PRO, Pris. 10/157, where the pamphleteer Bevill Higgens also figures.

27. TE, V, 469.
28. Holdsworth, XII, 176.
29. Other items in Jacob's laborious oeuvre include *Lex Mercatoria or the Merchant's Companion*, published by Curll in 1718; works on the law of murder and taxation; *The Law Military* (1719); *The Compleat Sportsman* (1718); *The Compleat Gentleman's Vade Mecum* (1717), a handbook for parvenus; and *The Land-Purchaser's Companion*. Jacob prints a paeon on London, oddly, in his *Vade Mecum*, p. 120; and following this a 'Poem in Praise of a Country Life' (pp. 130–2).
30. *The Mirrour: in Letters Satyrical, Panegyrical, Serious and Humorous on the Present Times* (London, 1733), p. 76 ff. The recipients of these letters include Barnham Goode, Lewis Theobald, John Dennis and James Moore-Smythe, Dunces all. As well as Pope, Gay is attacked for his 'low *Newgate Opera*' (p. 14).
31. *Society*, II, 58 and passim.
32. 'His later life was one long litigation' says the Twickenham editor with trenchant accuracy (TE, V, 432.) Cogent evidence is provided by PRO, Pris. 10/88/19, 23, 28, 79.
33. Pope's suits against Curll, Lintot and Ilive were all entered in the last period of his life. Earlier there are few signs of entanglement with the law, other than family transactions and real estate wrangles. It should be noted, however, that Pope was compelled to testify in the Atterbury prosecution; and that there was a rumour he had been taken in custody as a result of his edition of the works of the Duke of Buckingham: see *London Journal*, 2 February 1723. Cf. Sherburn, pp. 224–9; and *Correspondence*, III, 494, IV, 343.
34. *Society*, passim.

35. For relevant comments on the hack as 'a relatively new species . . . the man who accrues his own profit by peddling the products of other people,' see Ronald Paulson, *The Fictions of Satire* (Baltimore, 1967), p. 148.

36. Quoted from *Daniel Defoe*, ed. J. T. Boulton (London, 1965), pp. 101, 107.

37. Swift, *Tale*, pp. 58–9.

38. There are references also to eggs flying at [Ned] Ward in Pillory (B.III.34), to the 'tingling' schoolboy holding on to his breeches in the expectation of chastisement (B.IV.147), and a passage on the power of Dulness to 'bind' all mental faculties (B.IV.267). Incidentally, there were stronger criminal overtones in some words than survives today: 'poach' for 'unlicensed Greek', for example (B.IV.228), which the Game Laws must have animated more than appears today. 'Whip and spur' (B.IV.197) refers to the management of horses, but it offers a subliminal hint of cruelty and punishment – the 'fierce' riders were bent on expelling Locke.

39. See for example Swift, *Tale*, p. 48; *Poems*, pp. 398, 465. 'Lash', of course, is a common term in Swift with respect to satire.

40. There is another instance of the way in which Pope's fiction borrows from historic fact. Within the poem, Curll is made to engage in a crude physical contest with another bookseller, in the environs of the Fleet Ditch. In 1718 Nathaniel Mist was alleged to have challenged Curll to a duel, by sword or pistol, as a result of the quarrel ensuing from (Defoe's?) 'Curlicism Displayed', which had recently been printed by Mist in his *Journal*. The story goes that the men were to meet on the Fleet Bridge, i.e. in the vicinity of modern Ludgate Circus, but that Mist decided to go to the Chapter coffee-house instead, where he fell asleep. See Read's *Weekly Journal* for 14 June 1718. No doubt Read embellished the story to embarrass his great rival Mist; but probably there was some fire to go with this smoke.

41. See TE, V, 342.

42. 'The End of Satyr is Reformation', says Defoe baldly (Boulton, p. 53).

43. John Dryden, *An Essay on Dramatic Poesy and other Essays*, ed. G. Watson (London, 1962), II, 137.

44. Butt, p. 597. It does not seem that sufficient attention has been paid to the dangerous prevalence of legal forms and ideas in Pope's imagination at this time. It may be an accident that Horation imitations are addressed to Fortescue, later Master of the Rolls (see Holdsworth, XII, 245–6), as well as to Murray, the future Lord Mansfield. But Fortescue's friendship may have resulted in more than periodic recourse to equity in Pope's last years: the imitation in question (*Sat.ii.i*) is full of legal jargon, precedents, case law; it takes the form indeed of a sort of counsel's opinion. (Besides equating Bedlam and the Mint once more.) And the *Epistle to Arbuthnot* is itself pervaded by terms such as *information, counsel, term, libel, commission, judge, engross, theft, templars, slander, jail, knight of the post, pillory, suits, oath,*

courts, pilfer. The arm of the law was long enough to reach into satiric idiom; only in the more reflective passages, as at the close of the *Epistle*, is it likely to be absent.

45. See Albert M. Lyles, 'Pamela's Trials', *Twentieth Century Interpretations of Pamela*, ed. Rosemary Cowler (Englewood Cliffs, 1969), pp. 103–5.

46. 'A spirit of legalism pervaded the English government both central and local, and was reflected in the attitude of all Englishmen, from the highest to the lowest, towards their rulers.' Thus Holdsworth, XI, 35. It was reflected in a good many other aspects of the national consciousness.

47. Boulton, p. 24.

48. *Mist's Weekly Journal*, 8 March 1718.

49. Quoted by Philip Pinkus, *Grub Street Laid Bare* (London, 1968), p. 239; taken from a reply to Defoe's 'True-Born Englishman'.

50. TE, V, 433–59.

51. *Middlesex County Records: Calendar of the Sessions Books 1689–1709*, ed. W. J. Hardy (London, 1905), p. 327. Dunton wrote two begging letters to James Stanhope in 1717, complaining ,'I can't now go abroad without Great Hazard of being Arrested,' and asking that a debt of 'ye small sum' of £1000 might be paid. His mind was clearly deranged by this time. See PRO, SP 35/8/37, 45a.

52. Stevens, pp. 28–9; PRO, Treasury Solicitor's Papers, Calendar for 1726–30. Whatley remains obscure: Hanson, p. 114, supplies a little information, as do Oldmixon, p. 525, and Dunton in *The Life and Errors of John Dunton*, ed. J. Nichols (London, 1818), p. 735.

53. PRO, SP 35/28/11. For Norton Defoe's later troubles, see TE, V, 437.

54. See R. H. Barker, *Mr Cibber of Drury Lane* (New York, 1939), passim.

55. Several sources consulted, but see esp. *The Comforts of Matrimony* (London, 6th ed. 1739), and *The Tryals of Two Causes* (London, 1740). For Theophilus Cibber in the Fleet, see PRO, Pris 1/8 /300; Pris.10/89. Another name listed is that of Thomas Arne (Pris.10/88/70): this is probably the same man who acted as surety for Curll in 1725 (SP 44/81/399), and very likely the father of the composer – which would make him Theophilus Cibber's father-in-law.

56. Oldmixon, pp. 368–9.

57. PRO, T 38/225, mentioned in TE, V, 441. For Oldmixon's bounty, see PRO, T 11/15/165.

58. PRO, C 11/2619/5. I have not been able to find the result of this suit in the registers of court orders and decrees.

59. The episodes described in the text are printed in HMC 3rd Report (London 1872), App. pp. 318–19, and briefly alluded to in G. A. Aitken's article on Oldmixon in *DNB*. But they have not been fully explained or the individuals concerned identified.

60. See for example PRO, SP 35/15/119, 129; SP 35/16/16 (1); SP 35/27/23, 59; and compare Oldmixon, p. 618.

61. The account of Bridgwater affairs in the issue for 5 July 1718 manifestly proceeds from Oldmixon.

62. Mist's *Weekly Journal*, 26 July 1718, quoted in part and misdated '1716' by Pinkus, pp. 78–9. The satire is explained and Defoe's responsibility argued in my article, 'Defoe in Mist's *Weekly Journal*,' forthcoming.

63. PRO, SP 36/44/5, 15; letters of 7 and 5 November 1737, respectively. There are other letters by Cooke in the BM, Bodleian and Houghton (Cholmondley) MSS, now on deposit at Cambridge University Library. These confirm the observation of Dr Johnson that Cooke spent many years soliciting subscriptions for his Plautus, and endeavoured perhaps to live off these; but obviously not too successfully. See Boswell's *Life of Johnson*, ed. G. B. Hill, L. F. Powell (Oxford, 1950), V, 37.

64. Butt, p. 598.

65. HMC 58 (London, 1908), III, 506–7; BM, Add. MS 32697, f. 308.

66. Quoted by A. D. McKillop (ed.), *James Thomson (1700–1748): Letters and Documents* (Lawrence, Kansas, 1958), p. 66.

67. Various books and files consulted, chiefly shelfs 228–9. Manuscripts in other classes (e.g. Prisons) have been used, but the records of Insolvent Debtors have proved the most valuable.

68. On Mitchell see TE, V, 448. The article in *DNB* is exiguous as regards relevant information: it appears to be based chiefly on Theophilus Cibber (or Robert Shiels), *The Lives of the Poets* (London, 1753), IV, 347–51. Cibber provides an early piece of Grub Street mythologising: 'Mr Mitchel, who was a slave to his pleasures and governed by every gust of irregular appetite, had many opportunities of experiencing the dangerous folly of extravagance. . . . Notwithstanding this, his conduct was never corrected, even when the means of doing it were in his power. At a time when Mr Mitchel laboured under severe necessities, by the death of his wife's uncle several thousand pounds devolved to him, of which he had no sooner got possession, than he planned schemes of spending it, in place of discharging the many debts he had contracted. This behaviour, as it conveyed to his creditors no high idea of his honesty, so it obliged him to be perpetually skulking, and must consequently have embittered even those hours which he falsely dedicated to pleasure: for they who live under a perpetual dread of losing their liberty, can enjoy no great comfort even in their most careless moments.' Joseph Mitchell is also listed in the Fleet records at the PRO, Pris. 10/88/180: this dates from 1734.

69. For Hammond see *DNB*. He died in the Fleet in 1738; see also *London Gazette*, 6 December 1737.

70. On Hurt see H. R. Plomer et al., *A Dictionary of the Printers and Booksellers . . . 1668 to 1725* (Oxford, 1922), p. 148 (under 'Hart'), where it is recorded that Hurt was fined and pilloried in 1713 for printing a libellous pamphlet. For Hurt as informer with respect to another printer in 1715, see Stevens, pp. 104–5. For another bookseller, William Warner, in gaol for debt in 1740, see PRO, Pris, 10/89.

71. See Plomer, p. 185. The PRO files show that John Cleland, author of *Fanny Hill* and son of the putative editor of *The Dunciad*, was in the Fleet in 1747: Pris. 1/10/394.

72. H. G. Paul, *John Dennis: His Life and Criticism* (New York, 1911), pp. 57–9. Further information is provided by a letter from James Stanhope to the Earl of Carlisle on 8 July 1715, regarding 'poor Dennis the poet': PRO SP 44/117/197. Dennis was seeking to sell his customs post.

73. On Bond, see TE, V, 430, and *DNB*. It is interesting that at almost exactly the same moment as these literary malefactors were applying for discharge from the Fleet, the great criminal Jonathan Wild was seeking discharge from the Wood Street Compter (Corporation of London Records Office, shelf 228B.) Since I came on the material relating to Wild, it has been printed by Gerald Howson, *Thief-Taker General* (London, 1970), pp. 303–5. Mr Howson, however, fails to note William Wood among Wild's creditors. This is almost certainly Swift's great adversary of the Drapier's controversy, the ironmaster of Wolverhampton – whence Wild had come to London, and where many of his debts may have originated. Wood had a finger in many disreputable but more-or-less legal business pies. Wild's application is listed in the *London Gazette* for 8 November 1712; I have not located entries for Dennis and Bond, but they should logically follow approximately a month later. Unfortunately Mr Howson's book appeared too late to be used in preparing the text of this work.

74. PRO, Pris/4/1, ff. 64, 93, King's Bench committals. Unfortunately the records for this period are very defective; this is the only archive in the series bearing on the gaols at this time. On Henry Curll, see TE, V, 436–7, and Straus, p. 135ff; for his absconding, see PRO, Pris. 10/88. An Elizabeth Curle, widow, was in the Fleet in 1742: Pris. 1/9/193.

75. Corporation of London R.O., Insolvent Debtors 1704/5. See also PRO, Pris. 1/1A/605.

76. He must have had a measure of liberty in 1702, when it was reported to Robert Harley that he was one of a group of men of uncertain loyalty (including George Ridpath and the notorious William Fuller) who met at the Feathers Tavern, Doctors Commons; this lay comfortably within the Rules of the Fleet. For this report, see Campbell, p. 239. For the Fielding quotation, see Cross, I, 278.

77. Settle's other offences included writing unironic Triumphs of London,

showy pageants dedicated to City magnates such as Sir Charles Duncombe or Sir Henry Furnese, none of them persona grata with the Tory satirists. I have in preparation a study of 'Pope, Settle and the Fall of Troy', setting out in more detail the credentials of the hack for such an important role in *The Dunciad*. See also the reference at A.I.187 ('Could Troy be sav'd by any single hand . . .') Settle had some time before been described as 'a lusty fellow . . . who has an indifferent Hand at making of Crackers, Serpents and Rockets, and the other Play-things, that are proper to the fifth of November': quoted by Sheila Williams, 'The Pope-Burning Processions of 1679, 1680 and 1681', *Journal of the Warburg and Courtauld Institutes*, XXI (1958), 106.

It is not surprising that he reached the Fleet, if his usual scale of re-muneration was adequately represented by the single guinea he got from William Nicolson for a poem on the House of Hanover. See F. G. James, *North Country Bishop* (New Haven, 1956), p. 225.

78. Mist's *Weekly Journal*, 22 April 1721.

79. Mist's *Weekly Journal*, 8 March 1718. See Read's *Journal* for the same date, and also James Sutherland, 'Burridge the Blasphemer', in *Background for Queen Anne*, p. 29.

80. Holdsworth, I, 178: see also Radzinowicz, II, 9–19; and Cross, I, 229, where it is pointed out that the famous Theatrical Licensing Act was in fact an amendment to the Vagrant Act of Queen Anne's time 'relative to common players of interludes.' An actor at the Haymarket Theatre was actually arrested during a performance on a charge of vagrancy, as late as 1735: Cross, I,149.

81. This paragraph is based on Holdsworth, XI, 161–2, collated with Burn's volume itself.

82. Emrys Jones, 'Pope and Dulness', *Proceedings of the British Academy*, LIV (1969), 246–9.

83. Quoted by David Greenwood, *William King, Tory and Jacobite* (Oxford, 1969), p. 209.

84. Swift, *Prose Works*, II, 113: Joseph Spence, *Anecdotes, Observations and Characters of Books and Men*, ed. J. M. Osborn (Oxford, 1966), I, 213.

85. Butt, p. 275.

86. Steeves, p. 24ff.

87. TE, V, 117.

88. On this work, see J. R. Moore, 'Gildon's Attack on Steele and Defoe in *The Battle of the Authors*', *PMLA* LXVI (1951), 534–8.

89. TE, V, 437.

90. This has been disputed by Maximilian E. Novak, in a review published in *PQ*, XLVIII (1969), 348–9; but the volume of abuse directed against Defoe

seems to me quite exceptional. My forthcoming book, *Defoe: The Critical Heritage*, will illustrate the range and ferocity of the attacks on Defoe.

91. See *Judas Discover'd, and Catch'd at last: or, Daniel de Foe in Lobs Pound* (London, 1713), p. 3.

92. Oldmixon, p. 301.

93. Prynne was likewise seen as 'one of the greatest ornaments of the society of *Grub-street*' by the authors of the *Grub-street Journal* (*Society*, II, 267.)

94. TE, V, lxii. The most earnest statement of this view is probably that of John Forster, in his *Daniel De Foe* (London, 1855), p. 137: 'The assailant lived to regret it more than the assailed, and to confess to his friend Spence, that out of all the countless works written by "restless Daniel", there was not one that did not contain some good – in other words – that did not brand reproach on the man who had stigmatized their author as a dunce.' Even more positive is John Dennis, in *The Age of Pope* (London, 1894), p. 48: 'His [Pope's] satire is often unjust, and he includes among the dunces men wholly undeserving of the name, who had had the misfortune to offend him. To place a great scholar like Bentley, an eloquent and earnest preacher like Whitefield, and a man of genius like Defoe among the dunces was to stultify himself . . .' Neither critic, of course, enquires into the name or nature of *dunce*. See also Pinkus, p. 237n.

95. Moore, *Citizen*, p. 2; pp. 1–27 are relevant to this paragraph, as are Sutherland, pp. 1–13, esp. 4–5, and Michael Shinagel, *Daniel Defoe and Middle-Class Gentility* (Cambridge, Mass., 1968), pp. 4–5.

96. Moore, *Citizen*, p. 2; cf. Sutherland, p. 5ff. See also Henry Campkin, *Grub Street* (London, priv. pr. 1868), pp. 3–4.

97. Paul Dottin, *Daniel Defoe et ses Romans* (Paris, 1924), I, 283. Shinagel, p. 4, states on insufficient authority that St Giles' was 'the city parish most densely populated by nonconformists'. For 'the Tower zoo . . .', etc., see Moore, *Citizen*, p. 21ff.

98. Moore, *Citizen*, pp. 2, 20–1, writes well on the specifically London background to the most exotic of Defoe's works.

99. See Moore, *Citizen*, pp. 82–8; Sutherland, pp. 26–47. Shinagel, p. 71, points out that Defoe was thirteen times rich and poor, and was arrested at least six times.

100. See Diana Spearman, *The Novel and Society* (London, 1966), pp. 166–8. Mrs Spearman's case seems to me well-founded.

101. Rachel Trickett, *The Honest Muse* (Oxford, 1967), p. 176.

102. See especially Defoe, *Tour*, I, 338–57.

103. On Annesley, see Sutherland, pp. 23–4, and Moore, *Citizen*, pp. 13–19.

104. See J. R. Moore, 'A Defoe Allusion in *Gulliver's Travels*', *Notes & Queries*, CLXXVII (1940), 79–80. Quotation from Swift, *Prose Works*, XI, 20.

105. Jones, p. 231.

106. Moore, *Citizen*, p. 104.

107. PRO, Pris. 1/1A/533; Pris. 10/157. Further details of this discovery appear in an article, 'Defoe in the Fleet Prison', *RES* (forthcoming).

108. Moore, *Citizen*, pp. 47–8. Defoe's other troubles are described in a note I have prepared for publication. For the stories about Bristol and the Mint, see Moore, *Citizen*, p. 102. Defoe's comments on the Mint and Whitefriars are quoted by Shinagel, pp. 45–6. For the Sacheverell trial, see *State Trials*, XV, cols. 339–43, 454.

109. Defoe, *Tour*, I, 355–6. References to Bridewell in Defoe are mentioned in Ch. II.

110. His appearance in Addison's *Trial of Count Tariff* presents him in the setting which men of the time considered most apt – in a lawcourt.

111. Oldmixon, *History*, p. 510. See also the *Review* of 10 July 1712, quoted by Richard I. Cook, *Jonathan Swift as Tory Pamphleteer* (Seattle, 1967), p. 111, on threats of Tyburn.

112. He is particularly good at rendering the feelings of a fugitive, a man perpetually on the run: *Colonel Jack* and *Memoirs of a Cavalier* furnish good examples.

113. For Bolingbroke's comments on Paul Lorrain, see Pope, *Correspondence*, II, 350 ('that great Historiographer').

114. See Defoe, *Letters*, pp. 450–61.

115. See Pope, *Correspondence*, II, 71; and Swift, *Correspondence*, V, 220–3. Fielding, XIII, 107, comments on the odium suffered by informers.

116. Moore, *Checklist*, is the major recourse here. Not all scholars have accepted Moore's list: e.g. Professor Rodney M. Baine has recently challenged the authenticity of *The Dumb Philosopher*. But Baine's own claims have not gone undisputed: and in general the *Checklist* can be taken as a reliable basis for the sort of generalised calculations I offer in this paragraph.

117. See for example (many others could be given) Settle's showpiece *The Triumphs of London* (London, 1708), p. 6.

118. Sutherland, p. 39; Moore, *Citizen*, pp. 284–5; *Checklist*, passim.

119. See F. W. Chandler, *The Literature of Roguery* (London, 1907), I, 155ff, II, 285–300.

120. It is interesting that Defoe later criticised *The Quaker's Opera*, based on Sheppard's life, and attributed its popularity to the bad example set by *The Beggar's Opera*! See Forster, p. 136 & n.

121. Moore, *Checklist*, pp. 193–7.

122. Lee, II, 512; cf. Defoe, *Tour*, I, 50–1.

123. Christopher Hill comments on 'the contemporary popularity of literature about criminals and social outcasts (*The Beggar's Opera*, *Jonathan Wild*, later *The Newgate Calendar*). . . . We contemplate the actions of men and women . . . in a social state which is not bound by the traditional inherited

conventions: and this criminal society is regularly used to satirize the conventions of existing society . . .': see 'Clarissa Harlowe and her Times', *Puritanism and Revolution* (London ed. 1968), p. 365. Hill also attempts to enlist *Robinson Crusoe* in a movement 'to cut the individual free from the inherited traditions, customs, and laws of society', to reach 'freedom' and 'individualism' instead of 'the corporate loyalties and customs of subordination' of feudalism. This is strange company in which to find the author of *The Great Law of Subordination Consider'd*: and it seems to me that Defoe's criminal writings were designed (consciously and unconsciously) to cement social ties rather than to question the validity of the law: the appeal to the reader is 'let us join in throwing vegetables at the shameful transgressor Wild', and not 'Wild is a villain, but aren't we all?' Fielding may satirise the body politic through the figure of Wild: Defoe seeks to bolster up society, to promote a feeling of security rather than anxiety, to assure himself and us that evil will not pay.

124. Moore, *Citizen*, p. 242. Shinagel, p. 152, is relevant.
125. A. W. Secord rightly points out, 'Defoe's invention begins where history leaves off, embroidering fiction around the facts': *Studies in the Narrative Method of Defoe* (Urbana, 1924), p. 236. It is true that 'the sources of Defoe are not literature; his best works are' (p. 239); but the process of transformation is often a slippery one.
126. Moore, *Checklist*, pp. 195–6.
127. Moore, *Checklist*, p. 23, sums up his earlier researches.
128. In 1715: see Moore, *Checklist*, p. 115.
129. Cf. Shinagel, p. 5.
130. Moore, *Citizen*, p. 240.
131. Isaac Kramnick, *Bolingbroke and his Circle* (Cambridge, Mass., 1968), p. 196; pp. 188–204 deal with 'Defoe and the literature of the new age.'
132. *Robinson Crusoe Examin'd and Criticis'd*, ed. P. Dottin (London/Paris, 1923), p. 55.
133. Read's *Weekly Journal*, 18 January 1718: cf. issues for 4 October, 8 November, 6 December of the same year.
134. Sutherland, p. 257; TE, V, 437; Brian Fitzgerald, *Daniel Defoe* (London, 1954), p. 215.
135. Sutherland, p. 228. For another account of the ways in which Defoe's practice was at odds with the views of the Tory group, see Paul Fussell, *The Rhetorical World of Augustan Humanism* (Oxford, 1965), p. 264.
136. See George Sherburn, 'The *Dunciad*, Book IV', *Texas Studies in Literature and Language*, XXIV (1944), 174–90.
137. I quote the edition by Edgar V. Roberts (London, 1969), pp. 3–4. The corresponding passages occur in Fielding, IX, 209–10. There are also one or two brief references to Grub Street papers, the *Grub-street Journal* and

so on, in *The Covent-Garden Tragedy* (1732); but these are chiefly side-thrusts in Fielding's battle with the editors of that newspaper. See Fielding, X, 107–113. The burlesque in this case is almost entirely theatrical: one might almost say that Grub Street has not just reached Covent Garden, it has *become* Covent Garden. The comments of Simon Trussler in his edition of *Burlesque Plays of the Eighteenth Century* (London, 1969), pp. 171–2, are interesting, but to my view somewhat inflated and over-indulgent towards Fielding's actual achievement.

138. Roberts (ed.), pp. xxiii–xxiv.
139. See the edition by C. B. Woods (London, 1967), pp. xvi–xix. This is the text I quote: it differs in some particulars from the 1734 version, Fielding, VIII, 197ff.
140. Woods (ed.), p. 9; cf. Fielding, VIII, 198–9.
141. Woods (ed.), p. 29; cf. Fielding, VIII, 218–9. The short scenes in this act, II.iii–vii, were of crucial importance in the iconography of the myth.
142. Woods (ed.), p. 31; Fielding, VIII, 221–2, supplies the later and less useful text.
143. Pope, *Prose Works*, I, 262–5, 280–5.
144. Woods (ed.), pp. 72–3, 48, 64, 77; cf Fielding, VIII, 259.
145. Fielding, VII, 69–70.
146. Fielding, XIII, 21ff, 73, 83, 91, 123.
147. Fielding, XII, 77, 88, 93, 133, 204, 225. For a reference in the earlier *Champion*, see Cross, I, 236.
148. It should not be forgotten that Fielding had felt the impress of the law long before he became a barrister and magistrate. He was brought up as a ward in Chancery (the eminent jurists in his ancestry not being able to settle family quarrels without recourse to the courts). Then, at the age of eighteen, Fielding planned an elopement in Lyme Regis. He was summoned before the mayor of the borough and bound over to keep the peace. Then, before the trouble over the Licensing Act, he became involved in the lawsuits constantly impending over the theatres. In 1742 he was forced to obtain an injunction against a bookseller who had pirated *Joseph Andrews*. More to the immediate point, he had been sued for debt in the Common Pleas in Trinity 1742; and in the same term was given judgment for debt against a certain Seagrim in the King's Bench. See Cross, I, 35ff, 51, 148ff, 355, 376 and passim.

VI

The Grub Street Myth

Grub street, renown'd in old and modern times,
The venerable seat of prose and rhimes . . .
The Grub-street Journal, 28 October 1731

Depressed authors are nothing new. The question arises, why did
the idea of Grub Street crystallise as it did around 1700, and why did
it develop in the particular form manifest later on? The psychological need for a Grub Street (if that could be described with any precision) ought to give us an important insight into the literary climate
over the past two and a half centuries.

The difficulty is that the nature of this need appears to have
changed with time. As used by the Augustan satirists, Grub Street
stood as a concrete image of folly and depravity. It was peopled chiefly
by scribblers, because the Pope circle identified cultural threat most
readily in the sphere of letters. And these hacks were generally poor:
because they were bad at their trade, unworthy in most cases to be
called journeymen; because they would have fared comparatively
ill in any walk of life, even without the supreme act of dulness which
caused them to take up a profession least suited to their mediocre
parts (all Dunces play on a *violon d'Ingres*); and because they exhibit
themselves most completely, most farcically, in that condition. (The
satirists chose their victims for comic effect, not socio-economic
spread.) The varied overtones of 'grub' – dirt, maggot or whimsy –
were all utilised. Above all, the particular connotations of this part
of London were quietly assimilated: crime, foolish entertainments,
fugitives, Bedlamites, etc. It is notable that pedantry, which made
up so large a part of the Scriblerus figure, is relatively subdued in the

Grub Street critique. To sum up: Grub Street is here a carefully particularised *comic* metaphor.

In later years there developed what I have termed the myth. Grub Street was now called on to serve a wholly different function. It was a vague expression, growing ever more remote from its original root in topography. Its principal associations were those of fecklessness, eccentricity and poverty. The idea of literary incompetence disappeared to a considerable extent, and crime was linked only to the degree that the lurid career of Richard Savage lay at the heart of the myth. (For the Scriblerians, 'crime' had portended not murder, private assault, but sedition, public disorder, obscenity.) The myth also had recourse to Grub Street for conjuring up a sympathetic, if not a sentimental, mood. It frequently enlisted the term in the office of deploring something else – miserly booksellers, cruel satirists, absent patrons.

The reason for this is clear. Hacks, however slight their artistic pretensions had been, became involved in the cult of artistic alienation. They were sufferers, victims of society. Hence the role allotted to such wildly atypical writers as Boyse and Savage, whose course of life could be charged with everything except bourgeois conformity. The existence of the lowly scribbler was seen as a standing rebuke to complacent middle-class taste. Romantic ideology gave an entry to such notions long before modernism sanctified them; by the time Macaulay wrote, there was something not quite decent in a writer as un-isolated as Pope. Of course, recent critics have made a desperate effort to fit Pope out with a tolerable alienation (as cripple, Papist, Patriot, *vir bonus*) to make him respectable and existentially credible. But the Victorians had not got around to that. So it is that many of the most picturesque and colourful accounts of Grub Street come as a by-product of attacks on Pope or Swift. The nineteenth century was to a large degree deaf to Pope's music, insensitive to the texture of his verse, occasionally shocked by his wit and confused by his rhetorical devices. Swift fared little better. More particularly, satire came to be thought of as a nasty and destructive activity. It followed naturally that to comfort the Dunces was to discountenance Pope. In pardoning the victim, you explained everything about the satirist.

The chief use of Grub Street, in fact, arose from its serviceability in arguments about the deplorable state of letters in the eighteenth century. It became an adjunct to a tendentious bit of cultural history.

With time, the crude version of the myth lost ground, owing to George Saintsbury as much as anyone. A slightly different Grub Street evolved: an image born perhaps of collective guilt. Gissing's appropriation of the term reflects the change: it now expresses an idea of semi-genteel poverty, the struggling (but scarcely dissolute) life led by men on the fringe of creative writing. A 'hack' was now most commonly a journalist, or perhaps a translator; rarely an epic poet. Grub Street had come almost full circle. Its existence, or invention, appeased the feeling that it was honourable not to succeed. The original phrase consigned to the comic area things that were frightening and disagreeable. The new Grub Street made things worse even for its inmates by suggesting they didn't belong there.

Legend and Legacy

The celebrated entry for Grub Street in Johnson's *Dictionary* dates from 1755. But, in remembering the topographic basis of the phrase, Johnson was, as so often, more conservative than the literary world at large. By the time of Fielding's death in 1754, the connotations of the term had developed in such a way that the link with a real street had become nominal. By the middle of the eighteenth century 'Grub Street' was well advanced towards its present disembodied lexical state. The associations with a live social geography, which Pope and Swift had evoked to such telling effect, had become contingencies that could safely be left out of account. The republic of Grub Street was removed from the precincts of London, almost as the empire of Christ had been removed from the face of the earth in Hoadly's Erastian theology. Up till now Grub Street had been an eponym (defined as 'real or mythical bearer of a name from which a clan, family, nation, or place derives its title'). Henceforth the usage was a dying metaphor; no semantic shock was registered when the place ceased to exist, officially, and became Milton Street.

The start of this process can be observed in two fields of literature above all. These are, firstly, the works of Henry Fielding; and secondly, the pages of the *Grub-street Journal* (1730–37). The two sources provide us with an especially clear view of the transformation by which the term was gradually blurred and enlarged. We have just seen how this process went on, as regards Fielding: what of the other case?[1]

Every one of the 418 issues of the *Journal*, together with the thirty of its successor *The Literary Courier of Grub Street* (1738), is relevant to this transformation. However, it is the 'Preface' to a reprint volume of 1737, called *Memoirs of the Society of Grub-Street*, which furnishes the most valuable evidence. The preface is a strange document: interesting but in the last analysis deeply ambiguous. The author was almost certainly Richard Russel, the principal editor of the *Journal*. At times Russel seems to be on the point of grasping the nettle, and resolving the difficulties posed by the Grub Street formula. He recognises, for instance, more openly than Swift, the embarrassment occasioned by a journalistic or polemical exposure of a 'Grub Street' whose vehicle is polemical journalism. But in the end the issue is confused, and the satiric point of the term blunted rather than sharpened.

Russel begins by referring to the pernicious effect exercised by writers without knowledge or integrity, who will lead their readers into 'a wrong, dark, dirty, and dangerous road'. The application comes pat:

Of [this] sort, for the most part, were those Literary Guides, who, for cheapness and obscurity of lodgings, resided in Grub-street, in the seditious times of King CHARLES I. and from their garrets and cellars dispersed those false reports and reasonings, which were very instrumental in stirring up the people at last to a rebellion. And tho' some of those original Grubeans made themselves most remarkably infamous for want of integrity, by wilfully publishing what they knew to be false; yet many of them shewed as great a deficiency in parts and learning, by writeing in a very low manner, adapted only to the taste of the vulgar. From these genuine productions of Grub-street the same appelation has been by degrees extended to all Pieces of the like nature, in which bad matter has been expressed in a bad manner, in what soil soever they have been produced. Insomuch that all false, confused Histories, weak Treatises on any subject, low, creeping Poetry, and groveling Prose, whether written in any other part of the City, in the Court, or in the Countrey, have been distinguished by the title of *Grub-street Perform-ances.*

The writer adds that authors who have chosen to remain anonymous, or who have adopted fancy titles such as 'Right Honourable' have alike been included under this head: 'the impartial world has ranged them all under one general title of *Grub-street Authors.*'[2] At the out-set several features of the critique are apparent. There is the signifi-cant correlation of Grub Street with puritan publicism at the time of the Civil War. There is the stress on low surroundings (garrets and cellars, the taste of the vulgar). Above all, there is the insistence that literary incompetence (*weak, creeping, grovelling,* are revealing epi-thets) qualifies a man as surely as does malicious intent: 'bad matter . . . expressed in a bad manner.'

The preface continues in its historical vein. 'When the Press was under the arbitrary restraint of Licensers, the genius of Grubean Authors was very much confined, and the increase of their number hindered.' Scurrilous or impious books could obtain no imprimatur. However, with the lapsing of the Act, all was changed. Many dul-lards 'have become very infamously eminent by composing or trans-lating false *Histories,* lewd or immoral *Treatises, Novels, Plays* or *Poems.* But none have been more ridiculously remarkable than some great pretenders to *Free-thinking* . . .'[3] This is a neat summary of Grub Street activity; we might notice, too, that Grub Street proper begins around the turn of the century. Irreligious writers head the list, in turpitude if not in number.

Another characteristic ingredient of the myth turns up in the next paragraph, where Russel blames the booksellers for their mer-cenary schemes to take in a gullible public. He mentions compendia of the sort Goldsmith was later to practise,

> either compiled from a great number of lesser books, and appearing under the title of *Histories, Dictionaries, Commentaries,* &c. or trans-

lated from voluminous French Authors. In such great undertakings several hands are necessarily employed, which work under the inspection of some superior Operator, with whose eminent name the whole is graced; tho' perhaps scarce a tenth part was really supervised by him.

An example would be the *Complete History* (1706), attributed to White Kennett but also incorporating many earlier chronicles with some specially compiled sections put together by a hack. There is again a literary undertow: apart from the dishonesty of the procedure, such books lack real authorial unity. They are also, Russel strongly suggests, too long. Then Russel mentions the great increase in the number of daily and weekly newspapers, together with monthly 'pamphlets' (i.e. monthly periodicals, such as the execrated *Gentleman's Magazine* and *London Magazine*).

> To furnish materials for the Dayly Papers, Collectors are sent all over the City, suburbs and neighbouring villages, to pick up articles of News; who being payed according to the length and number of them, it is no wonder that so few of them are true.

There follows a lively passage describing imaginary preferments, deaths and marriages. Domestic news is always unreliable: and

> as to the *Foreign*, there is good reason to think the case worse: so that the chief, if not the only articles, upon the truth of which we can safely depend, are those inserted in direct contradiction to some published before.[4]

Russel next relates this outline to the founding of the *Journal*.

> The affairs of Grub-street being in this disorderly situation, about seven years ago; it was thought necessary to endeavour to repress, in some degree at least, the exorbitances of Authors, Book-sellers, Printers, and Publishers.

To this end certain gentlemen 'formed themselves into an imaginary Society, as meeting once a week at the Pegasus, which is a real house in Grub-Street.'[5] At this point the meaning of the opprobious term comes into question. The preface notes that the description 'Grub Street' is often applied to unfortunate writers of merit whose work does not at first achieve popularity. In addition, there is a category of books which once enjoyed great esteem, but now owing to changes in fashion are read only by the learned. Thirdly there are disagreements about the standing of certain authors. Russel instances Dryden who had been aligned in Swift's *Tale* with such indisputable Grubeans as Rymer and Durfey; but who had been lauded by that other great authority, Pope, in the highest terms. Russel seems content to explain this contradiction between 'the two finest Writers of the age' by postulating a measure of prejudice on Swift's part. The real issue is dodged. One other case taken is that of the historian Rapin, whose numerous inaccuracies are said to qualify him for 'the appellation of a *Grub-street Author*.'[6] Historians were always leading candidates for that title, especially if they could be shown to have committed factual error – hence a great sensitivity on that point within the historiographical branch of the Dunces. But it cannot be said that the preface establishes any satisfactory principle when it uses Rapin as a means of correcting uninformed taste. A more instructive passage is that immediately following:

> But nothing is more diverting, than to see the Combatants in political and other Controversies, continually abusing each other with this title. All News-papers, as to their historical parts [i.e. in their function as reporters and chroniclers], may be justly looked upon as the productions of Grub-street; and even as to those which are moral, political or literary, they very frequently seem to come from the same place. So that these disputants are as often right in their reciprocal applications of this appelation; as the religious Controvertists are in applying the names of *Schismatic*, *Heretic*, *Reprobate*, *&c*.

Drily Russel adds:

> For the comfort of unsuccessful Authors, it may be observed, that Grub-street is more like Purgatory, than Hell; since good authors are sometimes put into it by their adversaries, and delivered from it by the interposition of their friends in the same, or the succeeding age.[7]

Grub Street has come to mean literary disrepute, however occasioned: a broader but weaker connotation.

In the light of these three factors, Russel can offer a definition, but not a very satisfactory one:

> Since therefore some Authors from a Grubean obscurity have risen to the fame of Parnassians, whilst others by a contrary motion from the

latter have sunk into the former; and since many have been suspended,
as it were, in a middle situation, for a long time, by the opposite characters conferred upon them by well and ill-qualified Judges; we thought
proper to assume the humble title of *Grubeans*, taken in the most extensive signification, as comprehending all kinds of authors, good, dubious,
and very bad; to all whom the appelation has been frequently applied.
We profess ourselves Members of the Society of Grub-street in general,
but have formed our-selves into a select company, in order to restrain
the enormities of our worst brethren . . .[8]

The phrase has indeed been allotted a most extensive signification;
its accustomed meaning has flown right out of the window. All the
same, this usage, applied consistently, might serve as the basis of a
rational critical practice, however unsatisfactory in theory. In the
event, the *Journal* (and even the preface) exhibits a variety of con-
tradictory applications. There is no doubt that on occasions 'Grub
Street' comes to mean bad writing, and the 'Parnassian' antithesis
plainly excludes 'Grubean' in a logical sense. At other times the
phrase seems to imply all regular, quasi-professional writers. Sometimes the editors kept up their ironic pose, as a sort of General
Council disciplining wayward members: but on other occasions they
simply burlesque duncely productions. This is basically a failure in
technique; the editors lacked the ironic skill of the original Scriblerian party. But it means in practice that the notion of a locatable
Grub Street is steadily eroded. The term becomes blunted – an
essential stage on its journey from descriptive allusion to vaguely
prescriptive myth.

Russel goes on to consider a number of difficulties raised by this
editorial decision. For example, he mentions the policy of printing
contributions of very different merit, 'either as the high or low productions of an imaginary or real Grub-street.' The last four words
are interesting: the preface had effectively cut away 'real' Grub
Street. He proceeds:

The distinction, it is true, into high and low, may be likewise used,
with respect solely to the productions of real Grub-street [i.e. *bad*
writing, as opposed to all writing?]: and then, as the latter denotes all
the creeping, groveling pieces in prose or verse; so the former com-
prehends all the bombast and fustian, all the false and unintelligible

Sublime. For as in the precincts of Parnassus there are valleys as well as mountains: so in those of Grub-street, strictly so called, there are *Hills*, as well as *Dales*. But we beg leave to extend the distinction much farther: to range all the meaner Pieces under the *Low Productions*; and to dignifie with the title of *High* all which are written so much above that standard, as to render it disputable, whether they ought to be ascribed to Grub-street, or not. Those smart Adversaries of ours, who, having nothing to say in particular, so frequently cast a general censure upon our Paper as being *true Grub-street*, on the account of some Pieces published in it, were intirely ignorant of its comprehensive nature and design, calculated on purpose to incourage the correspondence of all sorts of writers, and to contain something suteable to all sorts of readers.[9]

At the end there may be a measure of defensive irony. As a whole the argument is unconvincing, and the writer's almost atavistic dependence on the old category of 'bad' Grub Street is most apparent. Many of the ideas in the passage are derived from *Peri Bathous*: in particular, the valleys and hills, the opposition between the natives of Parnassus and those of Grub Street. But it cannot be said that the ideas are exploited with Pope's delicacy or with his comic power.

The Preface then moves off on to different issues. There is a long section attacking such journals as the *Gentleman's Magazine*. Apart from a reference to Edward Cave as the '*Chief Engineer of Grub-street*', which strangely foreshadows his literal activities on Turnmill Brook, this is of little direct interest. An occasional passage stands out; such as this, concerning literary pirates:

> For these Members of Grub-street have given great cause of offence, not only by the *quantity*, but by the *quality* of their pillage, in *compiling* which, they have indiscriminately packed up good and bad Pieces together, many weakly and wickedly written, which tend only to mislead their readers, corrupting their principles and practice, and propagating ignorance, immorality, and irreligion.

Moments of literary insight are rare, however. For the most part the Preface promises more than it delivers.[10]

Such a judgment would be too harsh for the *Journal* itself. It is not possible here to give a full account of its contents; in any case Hillhouse has provided an adequate summary. A few articles of special interest may be picked out for our attention. In the first number, for example, the parallel with the French Academy, rather *à la* Swift, is made early on; a volume of 'the Antiquities of Grub-street, with its History, continued down to the present time' is announced as imminent from the hand of 'a learned Member of our Academy'.[11] This project seems not to have been realised; and I must acknowledge that only with this present study is the promise fulfilled – my own qualifications for the Academy must be left for others to judge. This opening issue also hints that the members of the Society are already well represented among the works of the learned, as they are periodically abstracted. We are introduced to the historiographer of the Society, Giles Blunderbuss, Esq. The persona adopted is that of the Secretary, Bavius: a common pseudonym of Russel and Martyn. The fourth issue contains Curll's application for the post of bookseller by appointment to the Society; a wish due to be disappointed, since no. 15 contains an account of the election instead of 'captain L. Gulliver'.[12] The latter can be broadly identified with Lawton Gilliver, who was associated with the distribution of the *Journal* from that issue.

No. 5 of the *Journal* provides a full outline of the anti-Grubean case. As usual, the method is ironic. A letter to Bavius from an unknown correspondent in Duck Lane takes as its subject Miltonic verse. The genuine sublimity of the master poet is contrasted with the anticlimactic afflatus of Dennis, Ralph and (in the original issue) Thomson. The inspiration throughout is *Peri Bathous*, a fact which is obvious long before an express acknowledgement is made towards the end. The writer divides authors into two contrasting classes, the Parnassian and the Grubean. This typology, which the *Journal* often employs, probably derives from a passage in the first chapter of *Peri Bathous*. The Parnassians are virtually equated with the Ancients, and the Grubeans with the Moderns – a further blurring of the 'Grub Street' concept. The Grubeans excel in the new kind of 'imitation', that is to say plagiarism .

By this means, a poem of the Parnassian kind in one language may be translated into a Grubean one in another. By this means, a Parnassian

359

tragedy of CORNEILLE has been made to shine with true Grubean honour, on a British stage, by an eminent Dramatic writer of your Society.

Equally, Milton, 'altho' a most vehement Parnassian, may neverthe-less without difficulty, be imitated in the most profound Grubbism.' The writer goes on to illustrate how Grubean ornaments and figures may be substituted for Parnassian.[13]

The thirty-third issue has already been briefly mentioned as a picture of the Grub Street 'College' to which Pope and Swift often allude. At this point I refer principally to the opening, which indi-cates the desire to free Grub Street from its specialised associations:

> The street from which our Society derives its name has within these few years been so metamorphosed, that it is no longer fit for the recep-tion of authors. There is now not so much as one printer or book-seller left in it: nor any sign of literature remaining, beside this single house, which is appropriated to the weekly meetings of the Society, and the residence of two or three of its members. And this very house is become so crazy, that the residentiary members begin to be afraid of dwelling in it any longer: and they would long ago have removed, if they could have supported the expense of better accomodations.[14]

It is uncertain how literally we should take this information regard-ing the 'two or three' members. But the main point is literary, not documentary. The passage represents a wish to give Grub Street a more general and less mappable set of associations. Paradoxically, this was ultimately to weaken the impact and satiric energy of the term. To move Grub Street – even the short step to Moorfields – was in reality to destroy it.

Another pertinent section is found in no. 40. A letter on behalf of the Dunces is signed by their 'secretary', Leonard Welsted. This con-cludes:

> We perswade our selves, you will not be wanting in any respect, to preserve that brotherly love and natural alliance, which ought ever to subsist between the *gentlemen of the Dunciad* and the *gentlemen of Grubstreet.*

It is notable that the Dunces are not exactly coterminous with Grub

Street, although there is a clear overlap. To suggest a community of interest was, of course, to vindicate Pope's judgment in his choice of Dunces. The Dunces have branches outside Grub Street proper, but their nucleus is to be found there.

Much of the information sent to the Society, in their garret at the Pegasus in Grub Street, relates to the appointment of the new Poet Laureate. In no. 44 the suggestion is made that the office should be put into commission, with Theobald, Cibber, Dennis, Moore-Smythe and Stephen Duck making up the board. When subsequently the elevation of Colley Cibber was announced, the Society were quick to congratulate their son and to see the act as a mark of royal favour for their number. Around this time, in no. 47, a letter was published from 'Philo-Duncius', addressed to the Pegasus from that other home of cheap literature, Little Britain. This accuses the Pegasean club of fifth-column activities and of a 'wicked design of exposing the Grubean art to contempt'. The writer suspects that its members '[breathe] an air somewhat different from the climate of Grub-street'. He has detected many signs of irony which make him believe that the *Journal* is really run for anti-Grubean propaganda purposes 'under the protection of very powerful patrons'. He misses 'the essence of Grubism, and particularly of the political *bathos*, [which] consists in dullness and Billingsgate'. It is an interesting reflection that to define the literary manifestations of Grub Street, it was found necessary to use the name of another part of London. Philo-Duncius goes on to examine the technique of 'our modern political GRUBEANS'.[15]

Defoe's death occasioned a number of satiric comments in the *Journal*.[16] No. 74 contains a cautious response to a proposed peace treaty instigated by the *Craftsman* and the *British Journal*. The reply is made in the name of 'the States General of the united provinces of *Grub-street*'. No. 74 also includes a dispatch on the young Westminster scholars, who are said to be trained up as resolute opponents of the prolific Grubeans. No. 80 has a letter from Philo-Grubaea, who may either own himself a Grubean or else live in poverty – a hard choice. No. 84 carries further the question, how did the 'honourable appellation' of Grubean become a mark of disgrace? Research has shown that 'the title of *Grubean* is as reputable, as that of *Academician* in France, or of *Fellow* of any College or Society in Great Britain'. Not just as reputable: the same thing, for all practical purposes. The parallel with the Royal Society and the College of Physicians, standard since the *Tale*, is once more hinted in no. 90. Later on, in no. 112, a dissertation on the theatre, we are told that 'Players are a sort of inferior order of *Grubeans*.'17

However, in the first two years of the *Journal*, it is no. 95 which stands out. This issue contains 'a representation of the procession at the Lord Mayor's Show; with an account of the original of that honourable Office, and the manner of his election'. Maevius, i.e. probably Russel, contributes verses to the Lord Mayor elect, Francis Child, who was also to receive an ironic dedication in the second volume of the reprinted *Memoirs* of 1737. Child was a man of a different complexion from his immediate successor, John Barber, who was a close ally of both Pope and Swift (see p. 111). This poem, a *Dunciad in parvo*, appears as Appendix C. In evoking the depopulation of Grub Street, occasioned by the migration of 'manual' art to the fashionable theatres, it supplies an invaluable footnote to Pope's masterpiece. As we have seen, Pope and Barber hatched an idea for a Lord Mayor's pageant, including the public dissemination of a satiric poem. The verses in the *Journal* link the decline in City pageantry with the removal of the City poet and his dramatic 'machinery' (the word is loaded) to Drury Lane and Lincoln's Inn Fields. The primitive techniques of Grub Street have been appropriated by would-be 'polite' literature, and the original Grubeans left without a trade. The relevance of this idea to the central theme of *The Dunciad*, as expounded by Aubrey Williams, needs no emphasis.18

Throughout the remainder of its life the *Journal* continued to take up the same *topoi*. When that rather able Dunce, James Ralph, began publishing articles on London architecture in 1734 – these were to form the basis of his well-known *Critical Review* – he was dubbed the Grub Street architect, and burlesqued under the name of Vitruvius Grubeanus. But in general the Grubean trope became staler through usage, and the weapon less keen in the satirist's hand. Stanley Morison once argued that 'if [Samuel] Johnson could write a regular column for one of the journals, it is largely owing to the efforts of *The Grub-street Journal*'. But then Johnson is a topic in himself.[19]

Mournful Narratives

The rise of the Grub Street myth has much to do with Samuel Johnson. It was he who gave the first graphic prose description of the hack's lifestyle. And it was he who occasioned the most celebrated picture of the Dunces' milieu, when Macaulay came to review Croker's edition of Boswell. Johnson is not to be blamed for the fact that his own account of Richard Savage was put to bad purposes; that its narrative should have been turned into a reflexive construction, and that Macaulay in particular should have surrounded Johnson's career with a mass of semi-fictional detail. Nevertheless the myth can hardly be separated from the Johnson legend as that developed in the century after the writer's death.

Johnson first published his *Life of Savage* in February 1744. He was thirty-four and had still not emerged from his hard apprenticeship in obscurity. A few years earlier Pope had predicted, on the basis of *London*, that Johnson would 'soon be *déterré*', and had helped the younger man in his struggle for a secure livelihood. But the breakthrough to fame and success had not yet come. Pope himself would be dead within a few months, and his former good relations with Savage had been soured just prior to the latter's death in August 1743. The book therefore came out under no special auspices.[20] It is distinguished from an earlier anonymous life (1727) by the quality of its writing and the weight of its moral commentary, not by any formal attribute. In the press advertisements, the usual claims for authenticity and accuracy were made by the publisher Roberts (handmaiden to the Dunces on numerous occasions). They were as usual highly dubious. The truth is that the *Life of Savage* is not only the story of an archetypal Grub Street figure: in the manner in which it came before the public, in its fundamental authorial genetics, it is itself a Grub Street product. It might well have turned out one more 'terror of death', a hastily assembled compendium of anecdotes and literary remains like scores of other lives. It was only Johnson's genius which redeemed the work. The outcome was a biography flawed in detail as Grub Street books generally were, but with a most unGrubean drive, cohesion and unity of purpose. So we have what Professor Clifford calls 'a brilliant character study, but factually unreliable'.[21] Its merit was principally as a human document – and so Pope's teeming Grub Street was *personalised*. The lay-hero legend requires had been born.

This stress on the individual, Savage or Boyse, instead of the solid mass of Dulness, was to be extremely important in the genesis of the myth, and especially in aiding the process by which the scribblers came to be looked on with sympathy. A patronising affection for the hack as a lovable eccentric lay at the heart of Victorian attitudes towards Grub Street.[22] This was despite the fact that the *Life of Savage* was best known as an item in the *Lives of the Poets* (1779–81), and indeed came before the public for many generations only in that context. Today we are struck by the differences between the more or less straight Savage biography, and the highly wrought criticobiographic essays which make up the rest of the *Lives*. But at the time when the myth was growing up, such distinctions were not made. Accordingly, I will discuss the work as it was most influential: in the form of a contribution to the *Lives*.

Sir John Hawkins neatly sums up Johnson's aims:[23]

> The manner in which Johnson has written this life is very judicious: it afforded no great actions to celebrate, no improvements in science to record, nor any variety of events to remark on. It was a succession of disappointments, and a complication of miseries; and as it was an uniform contradiction to the axiom that human life is chequered with good and evil accidents, was alone singular. The virtues and vices which like flowers and weeds sprang up together, and perhaps with an equal degree of vigour, in the mind of this unfortunate man, afforded, it is true, a subject of speculation, and Johnson has not failed to avail himself of so extraordinary a moral phenomenon as that of a mind exalted to a high degree of improvement without the aid of culture.
>
> But if the events of Savage's life are few, the reflections thereon are many, so that the work may as well be deemed a series of economical precepts as a narrative of facts.

Hawkins grasped what the nineteenth century failed to see: that the 'complication of miseries' arises from particular failings in Savage. The interest is psychological, not sociological. And though evil 'accidents' attended Savage's career, as Johnson points out, their very accidental quality forbids generalisation. We are to be sorry for Savage the man, because ill-luck combined with his own defects to make his literary career a harsh and penurious one. But we are not to be sorry for literary candidates *per se*.[24]

Johnson begins with sounding commonplace ('It has been observed in all ages . . .') and moves to a reflection in Isaac D'Israeli's fashion, 'Volumes have been written only to enumerate the miseries of the learned, and relate their unhappy lives and untimely deaths.' Plangently he goes on:

> To these mournful narratives I am about to add the Life of RICHARD SAVAGE, a man whose writings entitle him to an eminent rank in the classes of learning, and whose misfortunes claim a degree of compassion, not always due to the unhappy, as they were often the consequences of the crimes of others, rather than his own.

Right away he is making exceptions. And already he is stressing Savage's learning and literary merit. Whether or not he overestimates Savage as a poet is not germane. Johnson is immediately presenting Savage as one who *could* have transcended Grub Street, had things been different. (Grub Street is represented by 'the heroes of literary . . . history . . . no less remarkable for what they have suffered, than for what they have achieved.')[25] The things which needed to be different were partly within Savage, partly external circumstances. But instantly we can see that Savage is not a representative Dunce. Our compassion is elicited by his failure to achieve what his talents made envisageable goals. Dunces excite contempt or pity – depending on the circumstances – because they *do* achieve what they set out to perform: produce scurrilous best-sellers, enflame party controversy, and so on.

Johnson recounts the story of Savage's alleged origins as illegitimate son of the Countess of Macclesfield and Earl Rivers. He describes the process of illegitimisation and how the putative mother disowned the boy. The various cruelties served on him as he grew up are quoted from Savage's own account, and then Johnson turns to the first attempts of the young man in the field of letters. The biographer sees the influence of the easygoing and improvident Steele as a bad example too readily followed. He discusses Savage's contacts with the theatre, and takes the story up to the fateful crime of 1727 without paying much detailed attention to Savage's fortunes or his promise as a writer. The effect of this method, with its orthodox chronological flow, is to dissociate Savage's deed from his literary identity. We are given a lengthy account of Savage's trial, and Johnson makes little effort to disguise his prejudice in favour of the defendant. He goes on to describe Savage's efforts to obtain a pardon, finally successful in spite of Lady Macclesfield's efforts. By the time this section has concluded, we have almost forgotten what Savage's avocation had been. The human interest of a murder story has effaced the first faint traces of a study in Dulness.[26]

Johnson can now pass to 'the golden part of Mr Savage's life'. In this phase Savage was courted by literary aspirants, and fêted by society. 'His presence was sufficient to make any place of publick entertainment popular; and his approbation and example constituted the fashion.' His expenditure ran high, and he enlarged his circle of acquaintance. At this time he produced his *Author to be lett*, one of the side-blasts to *The Dunciad* and *Peri Bathous*. This occasioned him the enmity of Grub Street; but, as Johnson puts it, 'Mr Savage . . . set all the malice of all the pigmy writers at defiance, and thought the friendship of Mr Pope cheaply purchased by being exposed to their censure and their hatred.' Less admirable was his act in writing panegyrics upon Walpole, despite a professed opposition. Johnson then describes how Savage lost the patronage of Lord Tyrconnel after a quarrel. For Macaulay this was a disease most incident to scribblers; but the reality is that many writers spent years cultivating their patrons with the utmost assiduity, and could scarcely be brought to criticise anyone who had ever supported their work.[27] Once again Savage's independent will removes him from Grub Street, rather than fixing him there.

On this episode Johnson builds some interesting reflections on fame and success. He devotes space to Savage's leading works of this period, *The Wanderer*, *The Bastard* and the series of *Volunteer Laureat* poems for Queen Caroline. The discussion is sometimes incisive, but it has nothing to do with the literary embodiment of Dulness (in the manner, say, of Swift's digs at L'Estrange). For a brief instant one sees how Savage's oeuvre could be invoked to such an end:

> As he was never celebrated for his prudence, he had no sooner taken his side, and informed himself of the chief topicks of the dispute, than he took all opportunities of asserting and propagating his principles, without much regard to his interest, or any other visible design than that of drawing upon himself the attention of mankind.

However, for the most part we see Savage merely as an imprudent individual, beset by calamities of living, who happened to write work exhibiting certain qualities. The case of Savage tells us a lot about the condition of man, little directly about the conditions of authorship.[28]

Johnson moves towards his climax with smooth gradations of intensity. As Savage's situation grows more desperate, so the prose becomes more inventive, more fanciful or more lapidary. It is here that the passages which helped to make the myth are concentrated:

> He lodged as much by accident as he dined, and passed the night sometimes in mean houses, which are set open at night to any casual wanderers, sometimes in cellars, among the riot and filth of the meanest and most profligate of the rabble; and sometimes, when he had not money to support even the expenses of these receptacles, walked about the streets till he was weary, and lay down in the summer upon the bulk, or in the winter, with his associates in poverty, among the ashes of a glass-house.
>
> In this manner were passed those days and those nights which nature had enabled him to have employed in elevated speculations, useful studies, or pleasing conversation. On a bulk, in a cellar, or in a glass-house, was to be found the author of The Wanderer, a man of exalted sentiments, extensive views, and curious observations; the man whose remarks on life might have assisted the statesman, whose ideas of virtue might have enlightened the moralist, whose eloquence might have influenced senates, and whose delicacy might have polished courts.[29]

But here we are light-years away from the original Grub Street trope. *That* was designed to assert the true association between hacks and paupers; to identify Dulness with riot and filth; to give literary low-life its proper home among the bulks, the cellars and the glass-houses. What price the exalted sentiments of a Curll? What would Swift have thought of the idea that Wotton should assist the states-man, or Ozell enlighten the moralist? And does not *The Dunciad*, Book II, enact the process by which the eloquence of Grub Street influences the sleeping senate? The point is that Savage is the Spoilt Poet, and Grub Street was not made of such. In this passage, the note is of irony, paradox, piquant contrast. We could not be further from the satirists' world, where the actions of each Dunce are ex-quisitely fitted to his mean surroundings. Johnson extracts pathos from contemplating the situation of Savage. The satirists extract comedy from *their* vision of Grub Street.

Johnson gradually accumulates detail, selecting telling instances to fill out his picture of the fraught life led by Savage. The hero seems increasingly detached, almost alienated. His sense of reality is palpably impaired, and again a bitter irony obtrudes, as when Savage leaves London for Swansea:

> As he was ready to entertain himself with future pleasures, he had planned out a scheme of life for the country, of which he had no know-ledge but from pastorals and songs. He imagined that he should be transported to scenes of flowery felicity, like those which one poet has reflected to another; and had projected a perpetual round of innocent pleasures, of which he suspected no interruption from pride, or ignor-ance, or brutality.[30]

This radical innocence belongs to a modern existentialist hero. Actu-ally, Savage is presented pretty well as the first Outsider. Here again he is far from the Dunce, who is never more at home than when consorting with his (true) 'associates in poverty', and who never feels alienated from the crude world of materiality. Savage makes a pastoral idyll out of the real-life landscape of Wales. The Dunces make a Fleet Ditch knees-up out of the materials of epic. In its deep-est sense, Grub Street is a low reification of the ideal: the translation into base physical terms of the spiritual potential of the art of letters.

From now on, the tragedy moves comparatively swiftly, and Johnson is too able a writer to interrupt its course for long. He relates how Savage was disappointed of his hopes in Bristol, how on his return to London he was arrested for debt, and how he spent the last months of his life in Newgate. When the close of Savage's career is reached, Johnson switches from narrative to reflection with a single economical sentence:

> Such were the life and death of Richard Savage, a man equally distinguished by his virtues and vices; and at once remarkable for his weaknesses and abilities.

There follow ten paragraphs, masterly in their lucidity and orderly progression, as stately as anything Johnson ever wrote, summing up Savage's complicated personality. After that comes a concluding paragraph, adjuring the reader to learn from Savage to cultivate patience and prudence. Johnson ends with a truism dignified into insight by the exact choice of words: 'Negligence and irregularity, long continued, will make knowledge useless, wit ridiculous, and genius contemptible.' A striking sentence on which to end, with its tardigrade movement and considered epithets. But it all has little to do with the Dunces, since their vices run another way. Most of them were only too industrious; and they stretched a tiny expanse of knowledge quite as far as it would go. One might say that this pardox was echoed on a wider scale. The Grub Street myth grew up around a man who (hard as his life was, with murder, debts, Newgate and the rest) scarcely inhabited Grub Street at all.[31]

In the years following the *Lives of the Poets*, the myth slowly accreted. A polite antiquarian interest in Grub Street is exemplified by Thomas Pennant's *Account of London* (1790), a popular work which reached a fifth edition by 1812. The street is glossed, 'Celebrated for the (supposed) residence of authors of the less fortunate tribe, and the trite and illiberal jest of the more favored.'[32] Already the connection is seen as arbitrary. Similar entries appear in topographical works throughout the nineteenth century. More important was Sir John Hawkins' *Life of Samuel Johnson* (1787), since its author was in closer touch with the origins of the expression. The material is tucked away in a footnote, where the older writers were wont to hide their best thoughts; but it constitutes the fullest account of the matter then available.

Mention is often made, in the Dunciad and other modern books, of Grub-street writers and Grub-street publications, but the terms are little understood: the following historical fact will explain them: During the usurpation, a prodigious number of seditious and libellous pamphlets and papers, tending to exasperate the people, and encrease the confusion in which the nation was involved, were from time to time published. The authors of these were, for the most part, men whose indigent circumstances compelled them to live in the suburbs and most obscure parts of the town; Grub Street then abounded with mean and old houses, which were let out in lodgings, at low rents, to persons of this description, whose occupation was the publishing of anonymous treason and slander.[33]

This was admirably concrete; and Hawkins went on to provide equally pertinent facts (also in footnotes) on various hacks. He mentions a number of contributors to the *Gentleman's Magazine*, mostly with connections in the St John's Street/Clerkenwell neighbourhood, describes the Moorfields academy run by John Eames – a prolific nursery of hacks – and gives some account of the *Grub-street Journal* editors, Martyn and Russel.

All this was very much to the good, though it did little to arrest the progress of the myth. Writers seldom followed Hawkins even when he was commendable, such was the ill repute this tetchy fellow had acquired. However, Hawkins devoted a section to Johnson's hard times in the later 1740's, and to it he prefaced some remarks that came to be misused just as the *Life of Savage* was. That the profession of writing was 'far from an eligible one', says Hawkins, Johnson had already discovered: whilst

his aversion to labour magnified the evils of it, by bringing to his recollection the examples of Amhurst, of Savage, of Boyse, and many others, from which he inferred, that slavery and indigence were its inseparable concomitants, and reflecting on the lives and conduct of these men, might fear that it had a necessary tendency to corrupt the mind, and render the followers of it, with respect to religion, to politics, and even to morality, altogether indifferent. Nor could he be ignorant of that mortifying dependence which the profession itself exposes men to, a profession that leads to no preferment, and for its most laborious exertions confers no greater a reward than a supply of natural wants. [James] Ralph, a writer of this class . . . in a pamphlet entitled *The*

Case of Authors by Profession, has enumerated all the evils that attend it, and shown it to be the last that a liberal mind would choose.

All this, according to Hawkins, 'Johnson knew and had duly weighed.' Yet he persisted, and showed the inference to be a false one.[34] Later writers behaved as though Johnson, in his adoption of a literary career, had demonstrated the truth of the theorem.

One decision of Hawkins encouraged this. He included notes on the three writers Nicholas Amhurst, Savage and Samuel Boyse.[35] For long they were to be regarded as the quintessential hacks, in their disordered manner of life and early death. In particular, the case of Boyse was used to vivid effect in every recital of Grub Street fortunes or misfortunes. Grub Street mythology for some time is bound up with Boyse martyrology. Even Professor Clifford, the greatest modern authority on Johnson, has kept up the tradition. 'Boyse was the typical improvident poet, often in trouble, always in debt. Gifted but erratic . . . he made use of the most disgraceful expedients to excite charity . . . complete irresponsibility . . . continual recourse to the pawnbroker . . . neither breeches nor waistcoat,' and so on.[36] For some of this we have Johnson's testimony, and a few letters of Boyse survive. But much is certainly exaggerated – the earliest accounts, in Cibber's *Lives of the Poets* and *Biographia Britannica* are unreliable – and there is little enough sign of special gifts in Boyse's extant works. More to the point, he was as far from being representative as was Johnson himself. The absurdities which grew up around his name indicate a desire to make the hack figure at once stranger and yet more lovable than he was in reality. That Boyse was buried at the expense of the parish, as Hawkins says, may well be true. That he died with his pen in his hand, or that he can be called 'this truly unfortunate child of genius', as two Victorian writers have it, we may take leave to doubt. Hawkins himself said that he had inserted narratives of men like Boyse, Ralph and Amhurst as 'beacons', in order to point out 'rocks and shoals' to 'ignorant and benighted persons',[37] In the event, these case-histories were used as proofs of society's indifference to genius (Chatterton, of course, became a tutelary figure here, but he is too late and too talented to be applicable). Further, these scribblers attained a sort of nobility as passive victims of wicked, well-off satirists. Pope and Swift did not attack Boyse or Amhurst in sober historical fact (though Ralph did make *The Dunciad*); but that was the symbolic contest proposed by the myth.

By 1800 the idea of 'the improvident, intemperate, hail-fellow-well-met Grub-Street hack'[38] – a modern formulation – was developing in a predictable way. The whole basis of Isaac D'Israeli's *Calamities of Authors* (1812), astringent as some of his judgments are, proceeds from the assumption that 'Most Authors close their lives in apathy or despair, and too many live by means which few of them would not blush to describe.' D'Israeli takes it for granted that the reader will be intrigued by the spectacle of disappointed genius.

> I have drawn the individual character and feelings of Authors from their own confessions, or deduced them from the prevailing events of their lives; and often discovered them in their secret history, as it floats on tradition, or lies in authentic and original documents. I would paint what has not been unhappily called the *psychological* character.

It is not plain exactly what D'Israeli means with his talk of secret histories floating on tradition. But evidently this is something more than the Romantic notion of the writer as the man who suffers. Writers like the obscure Dr Drake, who died 'raving against cruel persecutors, and patrons not much more human', reveal the corruptions of society as much as the alienation of the author. Grub Street is now an emblem of man's inhumanity to man. The examples chosen are significant: Guthrie and Amhurst, the new 'Authors by Profession' apparently swarming 'during the administration of Harley and Walpole' (?)[39] The instance of 'Disappointed Genius' is the absurd Orator Henley, whom D'Israeli regards as ill-served by *The Dunciad* but whom he seems to confuse with Anthony Henley.

> A scholar of great acquirements, and of no mean genius; hardy, and inventive; eloquent, and witty; he might have been an ornament to literature, which he made ridiculous; and the pride of the pulpit, which he so egregiously disgraced . . .[40]

Eccentricity spoils literary talent but is also a proof of it. As for 'The Despair of Young Poets', there is Henry Carey, author of 'Sally in our Alley':

372

Henry Carey was one of our most popular poets: he, indeed, has un-luckily met with only dictionary critics, or what is as fatal to genius, the cold undistinguished commendation of grave men on subjects of hum-our, wit, and the lighter poetry. . . . Yet Carey was a true son of the Muses, and the most successful writer in our language [*sic*].

D'Israeli's judgment must have been affected by his belief that Carey wrote both words and music of the national anthem; but his general attitude is reflected by the opposition of genius to 'dictionary critics'. A writer has difficulty making it, not *if* he is good, but *because* he is. And little as D'Israeli regards John Dennis, who stands for 'Bad Temper in Criticism', there is the same note of pity – 'in his last days, the blind and helpless Cacus in his den . . .'[41] For D'Israeli, the literary condition is to be examined through the fate meted out to its agents, not through the books they produced. The more piquant the contrast between apparent merit and unhappy life-style, the better. So both sides are exaggerated. Actually, Pope with his physi-cal maladies or Swift with his deafness and woman-trouble would have made an acceptable hero-figure for D'Israeli. Only they were unlucky enough to achieve and succeed. The Grub Street myth could not cope with such inadvertencies.

Now the stage was set for Macaulay. In 1831 he wrote an essay for the *Edinburgh Review*, ostensibly a notice of Croker's edition of Boswell, but like most contributions in this kind ranging freely on the subject of Johnson.[42] It is an extraordinary piece of work. Only a writer of the highest gifts, with a talent for comic effect and a mas-tery of language, could have carried it off. Only a student of the eighteenth century, long familiar with the byways of Hanoverian gossip, could have attempted it. And only a biographer with superb powers of observation could have produced a portrait so alive, so imaginatively convincing and sharp in focus. Yet the clarity is some-times won at the expense of depth of insight. Comprehensive vision is sacrificed for the immediately striking (but selective) detail. And in the end Macaulay gives us something less subtle, less accurate and less reliable than he could, with all his attainments, have compassed. The process by which Johnson and Boswell are simplified into near-comic stereotypes is familiar to all students of the eighteenth century.[43] Here I wish to single out another aspect of the essay which has received less notice. This is the creation of the definitive Grub Street stereotype.

As usual, Macaulay makes his case with admirable directness. Johnson came up to London in 1737, he tells us, *precisely* at the time 'when the condition of a man of letters was most miserable and degraded'.

> It was a dark night between two sunny days. The age of patronage had passed away. The age of general curiosity and intelligence had not arrived.

Nowadays, says Macaulay, the number of readers is sufficient to support a popular author 'in comfort and opulence'. Around 1700 even Congreve or Addison would not have been able to live like gentlemen on the sale of their works. But a remedy existed in the 'vast system of bounties and premiums' which obtained.

> There was, perhaps, never a time at which the rewards of literary merit were so splendid, at which men who could write well found such easy admittance into the most distinguished society, and to the highest honours of the State. The chiefs of both parties into which the kingdom was divided, patronised literature with emulous munificence.

Unfortunately, the instance Macaulay supplies hardly prove his case.[44] No-one attained 'the highest honours of the state', except Addison, whose Secretaryship of State was a worthy rather than truly eminent station. Modern research shows Addison to have been a hardworking administrator, and his elevation probably had more to do with a shortage of men of business in the Sunderland/Stanhope faction than any desire to appease the Muses. Rowe became an Under-Secretary (a post Macaulay strangely omits) but this as ordinary functionary in the Scottish office, not in a position of great political sensitivity, as with Charles Delafaye a few years later. Congreve's places were mostly of a modest order and no sinecures. Newton became Master of the Mint because of his mathematical distinction and for political reasons: literary merit did not enter into it. Macaulay cites the cases of Stepney and Prior, 'employed in embassies of high dignity and importance'. But each was a career diplomat:

Stepney more that than a poet, indeed, whilst Prior was regarded by each side in turn as a dependable party man. It is true that writers sometimes gained employment because of their *future* usefulness as publicists; thus Steele's entry into Parliament, quoted by Macaulay, was no doubt the easier because the Whigs expected services from him along the lines of *The Crisis*. But this is significantly different from 'patronising literature with emulous magnificence'. Arthur Maynwaring, again, was made a commissioner of the customs years before he wrote anything resembling Whig propaganda, or anything of note in any field. And so on. Almost all Macaulay's examples can be hedged with damaging qualifications.

This state of affairs, Macaulay states, arose from the liberal patronage of men like Dorset, Halifax, Harley and Bolingbroke. But soon after the Hanoverian accession a change took place.

> The supreme power passed to a man who cared little for poetry or eloquence . . . [Walpole] paid little attention to books, and felt little respect for authors . . . During the whole course of his administration, therefore, he scarcely befriended a single man of genius. The best writers of the age gave all their support to the Opposition . . . [but] the Opposition could reward its eulogists with little more than promises and caresses. St James's would give nothing: Leicester House had nothing to give.

This account obviously derives from Goldsmith and from the anti-Walpole writings of the Patriot faction in the 1730s. Macaulay is simply turning into the accents of nineteenth-century Whiggery the complaints of Ralph's *Case of Authors*, or those of Goldsmith in *The Bee* no. 8 (24 November 1759). These are nakedly *parti-pris* effusions, and beg many questions (even before 1714, had Swift done any better out of his intimacy with Harley than Edmund Gibson was to do from supporting Walpole?). The contrast between the 'rich harvest' of Anne's reign and the 'period of famine' later is unduly melo-dramatic. Moreover, Macaulay conveniently forgets the support of Hervey, Edward Young and (later on) Fielding for Walpole, whilst enrolling Ambrose Philips, John Hughes, Stepney and Edmund Smith to his corps of literary genius basking in the sunlight.[45]

There are, then, grounds for questioning this survey of the rise and fall of patronage. But, whatever its merits, this passage has no necessary logical connection with what follows. We proceed to a kind of extended hyperbole, vivid in its imagery but frequently reckless in its assertions.

> All that is squalid and miserable might now be summed up in the word Poet. That word denoted a creature dressed like a scarecrow, familiar with compters and spunging-houses, and perfectly qualified to decide on the comparative merits of the Common Side in the King's Bench prison and of Mount Scoundrel in the Fleet. . . . To lodge in a garret up four pair of stairs, to dine in a cellar among footmen out of place, to translate ten hours a day for the wages of a ditcher, to be haunted by bailiffs from one haunt of beggary and pestilence to another, from Grub Street to St George's Fields, and from St George's Fields to the alleys behind St Martin's church, to sleep on a bulk in June and amidst the ashes of a glass-house in December, to die in an hospital, and to be buried in a parish vault, was the fate of more than one writer who, if he had lived thirty years earlier, would have been admitted to the sittings of the Kitcat or the Scriblerus Club, would have sat in Parliament, and would have been intrusted with embassies to the High Allies; who, if he had lived in our time, would have found encouragement scarcely less munificent in Albemarle Street or in Paternoster Row.[46]

This is such splendid rhetoric that it is a shame to have to point out what rotten history it is. One does not find that Gildon, Oldmixon or Ridpath figured in the Kit-Cat, or Ned Ward earned admission to the Scriblerus circle. The Fleet and the King's Bench, as we have seen, were known to the favoured scribblers of Queen Anne's day; Elkanah Settle managed to die in a hospital despite being fortunate in his generation; and there is no indication that Boyse would have been spared a parish burial had he been a contemporary of Halifax rather than Speaker Onslow. Macaulay, in short, takes the imaginative assertions of satire as literal statements. It is as though one should attempt to use Hogarth's 'Distressed Poet' as a deposition in court.

At this point Macaulay explains the new hardships by reference to the special temptations now meted out to authors. 'All the vices of the gambler and the beggar were blended with those of the author' – the very identification with vagonbondage that Pope had striven to effect.

After months of starvation and despair, a full third night or a well-received dedication filled the pocket of the lean, ragged, unwashed poet with guineas. He hastened to enjoy those luxuries with the images of which his mind had been haunted while he was sleeping amidst the cinders and eating potatoes at the Irish ordinary in Shoe Lane. A week of taverns soon qualified him for another year of night-cellars. Such was the life of Savage, of Boyse, and of a crowd of others. Sometimes blazing in gold-laced hats and waistcoats; sometimes lying in bed because their coats had gone to pieces, or wearing paper cravats because their linen was in pawn; sometimes drinking Champagne and Tokay with Betty Careless; sometimes standing at the window of an eating-house in Porridge Island, to sniff up the scent of what they could not afford to taste; they knew luxury; they knew beggary; but they never knew comfort. They looked on a regular and frugal life with the same aversion which an old gipsy or a Mohawk hunter feels for a stationary abode, and for the restraints and securities of civilised communities. They were as untameable, as much wedded to their desolate freedom, as the wild ass . . .

And so on.[47] It is magnificent, but it is scarcely the warfare on earth that constituted the life of a wit (as Pope put it). Macaulay does go on to make a few minor reservations; but he allows this garish picture to stand in its main outline. Who the 'crowd' of hacks in the Savage mould were, does not appear. It is as though the satirists' comic projections of real life had been taken for reality. Macaulay adopts the manner of one who thinks that, because there was an historic Grub Street, historic hacks must have lived up to it. Pope, as we have seen, had extended certain elements in the Dunces' surroundings, and made them the basis for a symbolic drama. He had associated Dulness with the growing evils of urban life, and made the scribbler stand for a pattern of criminality, degradation, anti-social behaviour. Macaulay, far more simplistically, has the unfortunate poets *exhibit* these things directly. What was in Augustan satire a complex metaphoric fiction has become a picturesque story asserted as truth. The spurious particularity of Macaulay's references should not blind us to a sharp decline in localised insight. Grub Street has become a figment of colourful social history, and with it has lost its deeper cultural implication.

Macaulay's graphic account of literary miseries exercised a

profound influence on Victorian attitudes towards the eighteenth century. He repeated his views, more briefly, in the article on Johnson
he contributed to the *Encyclopedia Britannica* in 1856.[48] ('A porter
was likely to be as plentifully fed, and as comfortably lodged, as a
poet.') There was a new story of Fielding pawning his best coat, 'the
means of dining on tripe at a cookshop underground, where he could
wipe his hands, after his greasy meal, on the back of a Newfoundland
dog'. So the myth acquired its stock of anecdotes. Nor was its progress impeded by Carlyle's review of the same edition by Croker of
The Life of Johnson. This came out in *Fraser's Magazine* in 1832.
Fundamentally Carlyle is more moderate in his claims than Macaulay, and his appreciation of Boswell is saner: 'Boswell wrote a good
Book because he had a heart and an eye to discern Wisdom, and an
utterance to render it forth.' But his realisation that 'in these days,
ten ordinary Histories of Kings and Courtiers were well exchanged
against the tenth part of one good History of Booksellers' was not
matched by any detailed understanding of the problem here raised.[49]
Carlyle writes with comparative restraint: but his essay could not
undo what Macaulay had wrought, as regards either Johnson or
Grub Street.

Thackeray's lectures on *The English Humourists of the Eighteenth
Century* (1853) and *The Four Georges* (1861) were of some importance
in propagating the myth.[50] Thackeray enjoys phrases such as 'the
Grub Street Timon, old John Dennis',[51] but this is a mere conventional genteelism. However, one single section went beyond Macaulay in attributing the downfall of the literary profession to *The
Dunciad* by itself. At least, says Thackeray, the hacks had lived in
decent seclusion before Pope came along.

> Pope was more savage to Grub Street than Grub Street was to Pope
> [?] The thong with which he lashed them was dreadful; he fired upon
> that howling crew such shafts of flame and poison, he slew and wounded
> so fiercely, that in reading the 'Dunciad' and prose lampoons of Pope,
> one feels disposed to side against the ruthless little tyrant, at least to
> pity those wretched folk on whom he was so unmerciful. It was Pope,
> and Swift to aid him, who established among us the Grub Street tradi-
> tion. He revels in base descriptions of poor men's want; he gloats over
> poor Dennis's garret, and flannel nightcap and red stockings; he gives

instructions how to find Curll's author . . . It was Pope, I fear, who contributed, more than any man who ever lived, to depreciate the literary calling. It was not an unprosperous one before that time . . . at least there were great prizes in the profession which made Addison a Minister, and Prior an Ambassador, and Steele a Commissioner, and Swift all but a Bishop. The profession of letters was ruined by that libel of the 'Dunciad'.

Naturally a writer will 'side against' a man who has blown the gaffe so completely:

> If authors were wretched and poor before, if some of them lived in haylofts, of which their landladies kept the ladders, at least nobody came to disturb them in their straw; if three of them had but one coat between them, the two remained invisible in the garret, the third, at any rate, appeared decently at the coffee-house and paid his twopence like a gentleman. It was Pope that dragged into light all this poverty and meanness, and held up those wretched shifts and rags to public ridicule. It was Pope that made generations of the reading world (delighted with the mischief, as who would not be that reads it?) believe that author and wretch, author and rags, author, and dirt author and drink, gin, cowheel, tripe, poverty, duns, bailiffs, squalling children, and clamorous landladies, were always associated together. The conditions of authorship began to fall from the days of the 'Dunciad'; and I believe in my heart that much of that obloquoy which has since pursued our calling was occasioned by Pope's libels and wicked wit.[52]

Not even the Dunces themselves, not even James Ralph, laid quite so much at the satirist's door. The 'mischief' done by Pope is not to have left the scribbler 'invisible in the garret'. Had he done so, presumably the reputation of the calling would have been safe. But no doubt hacks would have gone on living in garrets, which does not seem very desirable. Thackeray is saying two things in the same breath – that Pope maliciously drew attention to the miseries of authorship, and that he created them. The confusion is symptomatic. The myth relies on persecution mania ('ruthless little tyrant'), yet it needs to present the hack as innately feckless. We are to feel indignation towards Pope, a patronising compassion for the scribbler. To portray Grub Street in all its vileness is 'to depreciate the literary calling', so it has to be vile. But the Grubeans themselves elude any such accusation.

In the middle of the nineteenth century, local historians and topo-graphers did a good deal to sustain the myth. John Timbs' *Curiosities of London* (1855) is a case in point, notable only for the flavour of its language.[53] Thus the entry for Grub Street:

> From this renowned and philosophic spot, celebrated as the Lyceum of the Academic Grove, issued many of the earliest of our English lyrics, and most of our miniature histories, and the flying sheets and volatile pages dispersed by such characters as Shakespeare's Autolycus.

It is a little like the earlier and over-facetious Dickens. Timbs men-tions the Grubaean sages, and gives the familiar description of seventeenth-century Grub Street, 'abounding with mean old houses let out in lodgings', full apparently of seditious ballad-mongers. More independently, he suggests, 'Possibly, from Grub-street being the booksellers' suburb of Aldersgate and Little Britain it became the abode of small authors.' As we have seen, Grub Street was never itself a book-trade centre on the scale of Little Britain: but it is an intelligent speculation. Timbs claims to recall a time when the Grub Street author was common, but this has passed away 'with the change in the social position of men of letters, who no longer resemble the literary hacks of the reign of George II.' This seems directly con-trary to the views of Thackeray, whom Timbs had just quoted. But it illustrates the increasing feeling of remoteness now present – essential to the genesis of a durable legend. Timbs adds that Milton Street is now 'noted for its great number of alleys, courts, and backways, and old inn-yards': Victorian respectability may have killed the name and the concept, but it still harboured the physical Grub Street near the heart of London.

More beguiling still is the mid-century topographer Walter Thornbury, whose lurid fantasy world almost outdoes Pope in comic invention:

> Here [Grub Street] poor hacks of weak will and mistaken ambition sat up in bed, with blankets skewered round them, and encouraged by gin, scribbled epics and lampoons, and fulsome dedications to purse-proud patrons. Here poor men of genius, misled by Pleasure's *ignis fatuus*, repented too late their misused hours, and by the flickering rush-light desperately endeavoured to retrieve the loss of opportunities by satires

on ministers, or ribald attacks on men more successful than themselves selves . . .

Pope, says Thornbury, 'degraded literature' by associating poor writers with ribaldry, an obvious crib from Thackeray.[54] It does not seem to occur to Thornbury that the 'poor hacks' (note the iteration of *poor* as, Thackeray had repeated *wretched*) might have done the same thing. In fact Thornbury was an antiquarian of some learning and great industry. The trouble was that Grub Street was by now a piece of antiquarian detritus.

Around this time there was written the only monograph, up till the present day, wholly devoted to the subject of Grub Street. It was basically an extended paper from a local history journal, privately printed for its author, Henry Campkin, F.S.A.[55] It is a pleasant compilation, bringing together most of the historical associations of the place in a readable (but over-seasoned) style. If there is a good deal about the hermit of Grub Street, Henry Welby, of Dick Whittington and the like, there is also useful information regarding recent changes in the district. Campkin tells us that owing to the coming of the Metropolitan railway, houses had been pulled down on both sides of the road. Hanover Court is still riddled by pickpockets, full of old courts; the formerly genteel Haberdashers Square is now a 'squalid quadrangle'. Campkin mentions Type Court and speculates on the propinquintity of typefounders. He adds that Little Britain was formerly 'the great emporium for booksellers and publishers', hinting that the writers chose or were forced to live within earshot.[56]

All this is excellent. Campkin was not immune, however, from adding the usual picturesque touches. In the street, he says, dwelt 'those unhappy writers whose lucubrations and whose lives have identified the epithet of Grub Street with every thing that is mean and degrading in English literature.' As London spread, and movement about the city became easier, most of the writers vacated the district, till 'few of their fraternity remained, save the impoverished, the self-indulgent, the dependent, and the unprincipled, and thus ultimately Grub Street became synonomous with all that was mean, scandalous, filthy and libellous in our literature, in a word with the dregs and scum of our literature . . .' There follows some account of 'The Distressed Poet', called a 'masterly tableau vivant' of the Dunces' habitat; along with a less sympathetic description of Pope and Swift on Grub Street. 'What writers were more unscrupulous than Pope and Swift, when it suited their purposes to be so?' They bandied the term about, yet 'no scribbler of their day was more amenable to the accusation of Grub Street, in its worst sense, than they themselves.' Like all the Victorians, Campkin spends half his time depicting the mean lives lived by the hacks and the rest of it blaming Pope and Swift for pointing these out. There is no inkling of the way in which grotesque fiction may be used to serious literary ends.[57] Finally, much of this monograph is taken up by a potted biography of Samuel Boyse, by now the scribbler *par excellence*.[58] Campkin stresses his idleness and dissipation, tells the story of his fraudulent subscription, and describes his writing wrapped in a blanket. The climax is a masterpiece of sentimental mythology: 'He is believed to have died with his pen in his hand, in obscure lodgings near Shoe Lane, and been buried at the expense of the parish.' Not even Pope dared to have Settle die pen in hand, an exquisite comic payoff if ever there was one.

Books and Characters

A convenient summary of late Victorian attitudes is provided by W. C. Sydney, in his *England and the English in the Eighteenth Century* (1891). The general picture of the profession of letters comes straight from Thackeray and Macaulay.[59] Men like Rowe and Congreve were 'comfortably provided for'. Places and appointments seemed to exist 'for no other reason than to be conferred upon the servants of the Nine, in order that they might take their ease, eat, drink and be merry.' This is a straight paraphrase from Thackeray:

> A lad composed a neat copy of verses at Christchurch or Trinity, in which the death of a great personage was bemoaned, the French king assailed, the Dutch or Prince Eugene complimented, or the reverse; and the party in power was presently to provide for the young poet; and a commissionership, or a post in the Stamps, or the secretaryship of an

Embassy, or a clerkship in the Treasury, came into the bard's possession . . . What have men of letters got in *our* time ?

Actually, Sydney is wilder than Thackeray. It would be interesting,
though laborious, to calculate what percentage of the huge ministerial
patronage-list was taken up by men with literary pretensions. At a
guess one might speculate that ninety-eight percent of all 'places and
appointments' went to party servants, reliable local agents, superannuated colonels, sharp-eyed attorneys and tidy accountants. Now
and then a ragged poet might be awarded a minor post in the customs, or a bohemian architect the rangership of some royal forest.
But these were just striking exceptions. The great industry of place-
seeking went on untroubled, regardless of the state of literature.

Sydney's portrait of the hack is built up with the familiar motifs.
Sooner or later, we are told, 'he found his way to the cockloft of
Drury Lane, or to Grub Street, near Moorfields, the classic grounds
of destitute authors, who there eked out an existence so miserable
that the very name of these localities passed into synonyms for
misery and hunger.' Dr Johnson has amply revealed the truth. We
hear of Nathaniel Lee, expiring on a bulk in Clare Market after orgies
at a Butcher Row alehouse. Another case cited is Samuel Derrick.
The scribbler has a shop-bulk for a dormitory, where he lies beside
homeless wanderers or belated wine-bibbers. And then – inevitably –
there is Boyse. 'Worn out with poverty and disease, this truly unfortunate child of genius died in May 1749 in a garret in Shoe Lane,
and was interred at the expense of the parish. Through a life similar
to this passed most of those who achieved fame in English literature
before the accession of George III' – a delightful absurdity! By now,
of course, the Grub Street myth could have spared Boyse as ill as
garrets, night-cellars or persecuting satirists. All the same, Sydney
also enlists a fictional case in the shape of Smollett's Marshalsea poet;
understandably, there is little sense of transition. What stands out
above all is the domestication of the unruly Dunce. Hacks are now
associated with misfortune: rarely with misconduct or folly. Grub
Street is the 'classic ground' of destitution; it has been swept clean
of dirt and crime. A satiric weapon has become sentimental defence.

This was the nadir in historical understanding. When the *Cam-*

bridge History of English Literature reached the later eighteenth century in 1914, H. G. Aldiss was more judicious in his section on 'Book Production and Distribution'.[60]

> The name of Curll is also closely associated with Grub street, a domain which is wont to be a temptation to indulge in the picturesque – and to figure as a literary hades, inhabited by poor, but worthy geniuses, with stony-hearted booksellers as exacting demons. Not that the existence of Grub street is to be doubted: it was, indeed, a grim actuality, and many a garreter realised by experience
>
> > How unhappy's the fate
> > To live by one's pate
> > And to be forced to write hackney for bread.
> > [*The Author's Farce*]
>
> But the iniquity was not all on the side of the bookseller, nor did the initiative come from him alone.

This improvement can be attributed almost solely to one man, George Saintsbury. There are signs in Saintsbury's early work of scepticism towards the received view. And when he writes in his *Dryden* (1881) that Pope transferred 'his own conception of Grub Street to the times when to be a poetical man certainly was no argument against gentility', we can see a less literal-minded, more historically aware spirit prevailing.[61] However, it is in Saintsbury's contribution to *Social England* (1896) and in *The Peace of the Augustans* that a serious attack on the myth was first attempted. I shall quote first from *Social England*, as it is earlier and more compact.

'A sketch of social history', writes Saintsbury, 'cannot afford to pass Grub Street.' Yet he regards Grub Street with a great deal of suspicion.

> A few of its houses may have been built on solid ground; but I think it went off into Cloudland. In other words, I regard the Macaulayan picture of the almost necessary and regular woes and hardships of mid-century men of letters with a great deal of scepticism. The stock instances, the awful examples, are open to very considerable demur. Savage, Boyse, and Chatterton are the usually quoted victims. Now Chatterton's case was so altogether exceptional that it might have happened at almost any time; Savage was, at best, a very minor poet who had the luck to have a man of genius for comrade and panegyrist, at the worst a Bohemian Mohock who must have come to grief in almost any

circumstances; Boyse was such a scoundrel that his own legend accuses him of sharing the profits of his wife's dishonour, and such a *fainéant* that he lost a good appointment because it rained on the morning when he was to have presented his letters of recommendation.

This, then, says Saintsbury, is the tally.

> You can draw no inferences from instances such as these – of persons who poison themselves as mere children after a huge piece of forgery, or of persons who would have starved, in the very paradise of the six-shilling novel, from sheer vicious folly.

That the myth was right in detecting a loss in private patronage between the age of Anne and that of George II, Saintsbury concedes; but he points out that by the end of the latter reign, hacks such as William Whitehead and Shebbeare were making a comfortable income from the booksellers. The outcome of this enquiry into 'the supposed existence of Grub Street' is one of cautious and moderate judgment. To Saintsbury, the case that a prudent and able writer had less chance of success in the middle of the eighteenth century is 'Not quite proven'.[62]

The case is extended and further illustrated in *The Peace of the Augustans* (1916). As for Savage and Boyse:

> . . . is there anybody who, having critically and dispassionately read the works and lives of these two persons, believes that 'Grub Street' had anything to do with their misfortunes? The real Grub Street was no doubt their proper place; but it was quite unnecessary for the ideal one to exercise its maleficent spells on them.

Savage is described as 'probably a measureless liar, certainly an unmitigated ruffian, and even more certainly a very indifferent poet.' His works are briefly set upon. Boyse is a 'lazy literary hack–industry being the only thing that makes acquiescence in hack-work pardonable.' Johnson, who lived with him 'in the partly fabulous regions', wisely left Boyse out of the British Poets. The works are characterised as 'ditch-water'. Saintsbury concludes:

> If Grub Street had really been responsible for quenching the ignoble race of gutter-scribblers like these, one might take a new view of the matter, and say, 'All honour to Grub Street!'

After the Victorian distressed-bardolatory, such trenchant common sense is refreshing.[63]

It might be argued that Saintsbury, in showing the atypical nature of Macaulay's instances (a case he must be allowed to have made), is doing little to counter the basic assertions of the myth. That is, it could still be true of the run of writers, even if it is not of such confessedly oddball examples as Savage and Boyse. Saintsbury goes some way to meet this point by examining the case of Dr John Campbell, 'who was merely a typical bookmaker of the better class', and prospered at least as well as more recent writers of his order. Saintsbury believed that 'Grub Street was not too stingy or hard, but a great deal too liberal to its supposed denizens.' He argues this without complete logical rigour, but with sharp intelligence, fluent articulacy, and more scholarship than he is usually credited with these days.[64] All these qualities are shown in a passage devoted to Johnson, and specifically to Macaulay's account of Johnson in Grub Street. Here the determinism of the myth is abridged by a realistic appraisal of the facts.

Saintsbury first observes that Johnson 'never came within very many miles of the shadow of Grub Street till he was twenty eight.' By this time, his character was fixed. All his life, Johnson had to contend with difficulties, but 'Grub Street had uncommonly little to do with it.' From his youth he had manifested the physical and nervous disabilities which were to mark his whole career. He had been forced to leave Oxford prematurely through lack of money, and had perhaps wasted his time there. He had 'dawdled at home without doing anything particular before he went, and, after he left, his bad luck, not quite unaided by injurious conduct, kept him dawdling for some years more before he went to London.' He quarrelled with his actual patrons and 'gave other possible ones the idea of an ill-conditioned and impossible person.' Then his marriage:

> He married at six-and twenty, without any assured income, a woman nearly twice his age, with hardly any fortune, and sank what money she had on a most unpromising adventure of a private school. And then he went to 'Grub Street' with twopence-halfpenny in his pocket.

And so to the triumphant forensic climax:

Even supposing that Grub Street was the malevolent and maleficent monster that it has been depicted as being, need it have exerted much of its fiendishness to prevent a man of this stamp from at once attaining affluence or even comfort?

This is a splendidly prepared conclusion. Saintsbury is as selective in his choice of evidence as Macaulay; but the facts are marshalled with a stricter regard for relevance, and they *are* facts rather than picturesque snatches of gossip. Saintsbury goes on to emphasise that he is not trying to blacken Johnson or depreciate his achievement. But 'I am bound to say that I see in these facts little of anything that throws special blame on the eighteenth century, or that supports the notion of Grub Street as a cause of Johnson's misfortunes.' Thus to excise the great doctor from the myth was to do more than to place question-marks against Savage or Boyse. It struck at the whole legend.[65]

It ought to have been definitive. Critics should now have been in a position to see Grub Street as a constructive fiction of satire, rather than a cant phrase for all literary misfortune. But the calamities of authors and unscrupulous booksellers continued to figure strongly. Paul Dottin wrote the following passage in 1923, but it might have been eighty years earlier. The Grub Street hack is one of the class 'which, in order to secure a good sale for their writings, sought noisy success obtained through slander and blackmail, lowered their talent to the coarse tastes of the vulgar, and, at the bidding of unscrupulous booksellers, embittered contemporary polemics by hastily-written pamphlets.' So they did (though blackmail would be hard to prove in all but a tiny handful of cases); but the booksellers' role is over-stated. Once more Pope's rhetorical projection has been taken *au pied de la lettre*. Dottin apologises for the company we must keep with him: 'We hope that those who will undertake this sort excursion into the world of the poor hack-writers of the Augustan Age, will not be repelled by the filth and the stench of the dark deep courts.'[66] At all events this is better than what E. B. Chancellor produced ten years later: 'the haunt of the miserable class of men called authors by profession whose remuneration so often fell far short of the labours to which their sordid and unhappy lives were given.' For Chancellor,

Nat Lee is a 'typical author by profession.' Grub Street was good enough for beggars and literary men, too bad for any more self-respecting class.[67] The term has relapsed into vagueness and whimsy.

It might be objected that Chancellor had few pretensions as a literary scholar. But *mutatis mutandis* there is not much more precision in the use of the term by Sir Sydney Roberts, where the same defence will not do. Roberts' essay 'Johnson in Grub Street' (1930) meanders around familiar material.[68] As noted elsewhere, Roberts observes that the topographic element in the expression is now dead. He quotes Goldsmith, Johnson and Fielding – *The Author's Farce* – and then moves on to *Pendennis* and *The New Grub Street*. As for *The Private Papers of Henry Ryecroft*, Roberts declares boldly, 'The Grub Street pictured in that book is the Grub Street Johnson knew.' If so, the phrase has certainly extended its range of application. Roberts next gives a potted history of *The Grub-street Journal*, before outlining Johnson's relations with the hacks of his time.

> . . . With that magnificent realism which is one of his greatest qualities he faced the prospect of Grub Street without illusion and without a whine. . . . It is more fitting . . . to admire Johnson's courage in Grub Street than to grow sentimental in pity for the drudgery which was his lot.

Roberts believed that 'Johnson went into Grub Street with his eyes open', and he went out of his way to praise the 'truly Johnsonian common sense' which Saintsbury had brought to this issue. Yet his final conclusions are oddly faint:

> The picture of Johnson in Grub Street, then, is not one of unmitigated gloom. Johnson, though he never ceased to regard poverty as anything but an evil, would have admitted that he owed much to Grub Street. It is true that it left a touch of bitterness. It left him coldly critical of men like Gray and Walpole and Lyttelton, men who had enjoyed the continuous comfort of domestic or academic bowers. But it was in Grub Street that he gained his immense knowledge of what ultimately interested him most – all sorts and conditions of men; it was in Grub Street that he learnt to practise his magnificent charity. Broken-down hacks, broken-down doctors, broken-down women – nothing mattered save that they were broken down. It was in Grub Street that Johnson became the apostle of the undeserving poor.

The term has become a feeble synonym for 'the hard school of life'. Grub Street had symbolised folly and iniquity; now it was the place where you learnt to practise charity.

A valuable supplement to Saintsbury's demolition work was the essay by R. W. Chapman in *Johnson's England* (1933) concerned with 'Authors and Booksellers'.[69] For the first time, due emphasis was laid on the *ex parte* nature of the authors' complaints about the booksellers. Chapman took a wider view.

> Publishers have at all times been a much abused class. We hear a great deal, both from contemporary writers and from modern commentators, of their monopolistic practices, of their inordinate wealth, of their oppression and contempt of genius, and of the worthless trash manufactured to their order in Grub Street, both by worthless scribblers and by men who deserved better work and better pay.

Chapman then presents the other side, and puts the booksellers' case. He concludes, 'On the whole we need not refuse to accept Johnson's verdict in favour of the booksellers, that they were "generous, liberal-minded men," and that their enterprise "raised the price of literature." ' This is more cautious in its phrasing than I would wish. The truth is that the oppression of authors by their publishers was a key part of the whole myth. It depended on feeling sorry for the hack (whatever his merits as an author); and it derived from the scribblers' own publicity campaign. Basically, like the rest of the myth, it originated in the Dunces' desire to clear themselves from the charges of the Pope/Swift circle. It was a sociological defence to an artistic attack. That being so, Chapman's examination of the alleged 'penury of Grub Street' is of special value. He observes that 'pure literature . . . has never afforded much more than competence to other than a very small proportion of writers by profession'. He rightly points out that most of Johnson's early writing, 'though much of it was drudgery, ought not to be called hack-work'. And so on. The myth was starting to dissolve.

The distinction Chapman draws between 'worthless scribblers and . . . men who deserved better' has been developed by recent commentators. James L. Clifford, for example, writes thus:

The precise difference between a literary hack and a writer of genius is sometimes difficult to define. The two, as in Goldsmith, may merge in the same man. Often there is no clear point where one begins and the other leaves off. It is true that the traditional Grub Street journalist was weak-willed, improvident, venal, and pathetic, his pen to be bought for any scheme, no matter how dishonest. With a limited capacity, he could never rise above a certain flat level of competence. Yet working with him were others who had superior ability and needed only a chance in order to produce genuine literature.

Johnson, says Clifford, for all his later eminence, 'in the early 1740s was a hack'.[70] Again it comes down to a question of definition. I would side with Chapman in assessing the work Johnson did at this time as something other than 'hack' writing in character. *The Dunciad* provided a working method of distinction. The Dunces were men of weak head and corrupted heart, and their doings show them to be so. This has nothing directly to do with their lack of monetary success or with their 'chances' in the world. You could be a practising author by profession and never arouse the satirist. It was specifically the factors Clifford alludes to – and not casually, as he seems to suggest – which marked out the true Grub Street inmate. To write muck-raking biographies or inane pantomimes, to sell your pen to each faction in turn: it was thus that you defined your status, and not by writing for payment. An author of genuine talent (as we have seen in the case of Defoe) could attain Duncehood. It was a matter of the options you took. The hack was marked off from the decent compiler, not by some Calvinistic predestination but by the life he led and the books he produced. It was a purpose of the myth, then and later, to shift the blame. To lump all professional writers together was to exculpate all.

One recent discussion of the patronage issue is that of Bertrand H. Bronson, who treads a delicate path between credulity and undue scepticism.[71]

The great Whig and Tory statesmen made it their business to look out for most of the abler writers in the days of Anne. The posts these writers found were supposed to leave them leisure to write; but on the other hand there were conditions and consequences. Their status as poets necessarily became more amateur, while they devoted time and energy to political activity, whether in office or by the pen . . .

Indeed the obligations of office could almost remove them from the sphere of *belles lettres*.

Bronson instances Steele, who 'became more interested in politics than in letters'; Addison; Swift, who 'never laid claim to being a literary man'; Prior, 'an able but reluctant diplomatist'; and Gay, who 'remained a frustrated poet.' He goes on:

> Goldsmith might look back with nostalgia to the days 'when the great Somers was at the helm' as the golden age of patronage, but it was only relatively so, and in fact Pope derived none but indirect benefits from the current posture of affairs. Poetry was not a dependable calling, even so early . . .

All this is well said, though I do not think there is much evidence that a writer given a post of any substance 'was supposed to [have] leisure to write.' A place was either an invitation to serve the government (Steele as gazetteer, Prior as plenipotentiary), or just a reward pure and simple. It was occasionally something like a pension, but never in the ordinary course of events a subsidy. Nevertheless, what Bronson says is of great pertinence. Mythology required that patronage should be an unmixed boon, given disinterestedly and accepted without reservation. Once more, the reality was different. To be unprovided for did not mean you were a writer of neglected genius who could have done great things. To be provided for did not mean you would now do great things. No doubt it was more pleasant, on the whole, to fritter away your time on the commission for the salt duty than to starve in a garret; but it is not self-evident which is the more appropriate fate to hold out to art.

Not all recent contributions to this area of study have been as successful. Leo Lowenthal's 'The Debate Over Art and Popular Culture: English Eighteenth Century as a Case Study' (1957) is marked by many of the old confusions, and in it the myth shows vestigial signs of life.[72] Lowenthal overestimates, in my judgment, the importance (and probably the volume) of middle-class readership in the period. That reading matter became 'less costly' during the course of the century, as he asserts, is a doubtful proposition, *tout court*. Some tendencies which Lowenthal imputes to the later part of the century, as part of its literary evolution – e.g. the interest in 'abstracts, abridgements, and anthologies' – were at least as prominent in 1700, as *A Tale of a Tub* might warn us. Moreover, his literary judgments are often very strange. After the splendours of the mid-century novel, we are told, came a period of imitation and shoddy work: 'it was not until the closing decades of the century, with the advent of the tremendously popular Gothic novel, that there was a return to more craftsmanlike work.' The study relies largely on secondary materials, and the only primary source for the book trade seems to be Lackington's familiar *Memoirs* of 1803.

These deficiencies show themselves particularly in the treatment of Pope. Much of it is trivial and gossipy:

> Pope . . . spent a great deal of time talking with fellow-writers in his favorite coffee-house, until he found that the consumption of wine was beginning to get the better of his health. Among the more notable literary coffee clubs . . . was the Kit-Cat Club . . . This club consisted mainly of Whigs, but it went out of its way to encourage young writers, presumably regardless of political persuasion, with financial prizes, particularly for comedies. Swift helped to found the Brothers' Club, whose members were mainly Tories, but whose interests were largely literary – and they, too, contributed to the support of promising younger writers.

For 'mainly' on each appearance here, read 'wholly'. The Brothers' Club, *eo nomine*, is a subsequent invention. And despite what Leslie Stephen (Lowenthal's source) wrote, neither club showed any desire to patronise literature on bipartisan lines. In any case, Lowenthal seems to misunderstand Stephen, whose words are, 'It [the Kit-Cat] not only brought Whigs together but showed its taste by giving a prize for good comedies. Swift . . . helped to form the Brothers' Club, which was especially intended to direct patronage towards promising writers of the Tory persuasion.' It probably wasn't, but Lowenthal crucially alters the statement beyond that. Stephen's observation that the Kit-Cat gave a prize on a single occasion, with the very good idea of the kind of merit it should reward, has been transformed into a general practice.

The detailed comments supplied by Lowenthal on Pope's relations with the world of the Dunces are no more reliable. In consonance with the run of mythologists, he always takes the hacks' word for it. For example:

> Pope, himself an author living from the sale of his works . . . was convinced that the literary genius would eventually win public support, and, conversely, that the writer who did not live well must also be dull. 'To prove them *poor*,' wrote an anonymous contributor to *Mist's Journal* in 1728, Pope 'asserts that they are *dull*; and to prove them *dull* he asserts they are *poor*.' His successors were not so sure; Johnson, Fielding, and Goldsmith were writing works that were certainly not 'dull' in Pope's meaning of the word for an audience which made it increasingly clear that it was not capable of rewarding the good writers with more popularity than the bad.

Luckily we are not required to accept everything an anonymous contributor to Mist's *Journal* tells us. The actual position is more complex, as we have seen. In any case, the basic assertion is false: Pope was quite as far from linking popularity with literary distinction as were the others named. Predictably, Lowenthal is vague and inaccurate on *The Dunciad* itself. He makes an obvious reference to Ambrose Philips apply 'presumably' to Milton's nephew John Phillips. He retails the old orthodoxy regarding the two *Dunciads*, which he seems to regard as separate entities:

> The second edition of *The Dunciad* (1743) was considerably less personal and at the same time broader in scope than the first, going beyond the realm of literature proper to address itself to the theater, the opera, and even to education and politics. The two editions together compose the major broadside against particular writers; and the popular 'little rogues' of literature whom Pope attacked . . . have all vindicated his judgment by sinking into oblivion.

Two chapters in particular of J. W. Saunders' survey of the literary profession are relevant. These are 'Prose, Print and the Profession' and 'The Profession Established', each a brisk account based almost entirely on secondary sources (and not always very good ones). Saunders' references to Grub Street are conventional enough – 'This was the Grub Street, successfully turning out rubbish to demand', applied to Arnall and company – a note to *The Dunciad* is, as usual, the source. However, his treatment is largely vitiated by errors of fact and emphasis. His hold on the political affiliation of writers is extremely shaky. He speaks of 'Anti-Whig writers like Henry Fielding in his *Historical Register, or the Life and Death of Tom Thumb* (1731)': not only has Saunders coalesced two utterly dissimilar plays, he has quite misconceived the nature of the Patriot opposition. (Another dramatic invention on the same page is Lillo's *The London Tragedy*, i.e. *London Merchant*.)[73] Saunders includes a very dubious paragraph on Defoe, which asserts that 'keeping in favour with the Tories had led him to co-operate not only with Harley but also with more extreme politicians like Godolphin and even the Jacobite Bolingbroke' – a view which altogether distorts Godolphin's position at the head of the Whig coalition, not to mention Harley's own readiness to intrigue with the Pretender.[74] Saunders thinks Defoe was 'essentially a non-party radical'; similarly he asserts that Prior had 'few political beliefs beyond a loyalty to William III'. Here Saunders is inaccurate in the very commercial matters he is professedly discussing. The statement that Prior 'because he needed the extra income . . . had never been averse to selling poems to a publisher, either to journals like *The Examiner*, or to professional editors like Charles Gildon or Jacob Tonson for publication in their Miscellanies . . .' contains a series of odd assumptions. Prior helped to found the *Examiner*, contributed (prose) to early numbers, but is very unlikely to have received any direct payment. Gildon was an editor in the modern sense, Tonson a publisher who may or may not have employed editors on a given occasion. What remuneration Prior would get we do not know. Saunders goes on to describe Prior's subscription volume of poems. He says that the income 'was enough to enable [Prior] to buy Down Hall in Essex, reserve the services of the leading architect, James Gibbs, to redesign it on an Augustan scale, and to begin to lead the life of a self-made squire'. Alas for such hopes! It is well attested that the second Earl of Oxford (Pope's friend Lord Harley) presented the house in effect to Prior; it was on a modest scale anyway.[75]

Nor does Saunders give a reliable picture of patronage at work. His comment, 'The Earl of Halifax patronized Prior and Addison, but expected them to help him not only as poets and diplomats, but also as propagandists,' begs several questions; Saunders in any case believes that Addison's appointment as 'Secretary for Ireland' [*sic*] was his ultimate advancement. The account proceeds:

> To the Earl of Oxford, Defoe and Swift were primarily useful as propagandists, while Walpole's only act of purely literary patronage was a pension to Edward Young: his other protégés were all journalists. The Court itself seems gradually to have lost interest in poetry: Queen Anne seems to have read nothing but books of piety and official documents, while George II is reported as saying, in an appropriately guttural accent, 'I hate bainting and boetry . . .'

One can only say, in an appropriately gruff accent, that this is not the whole story. It is doubtful how far Oxford was Swift's patron at all, in any ordinary sense (he received neither money nor real promotion, only a little cheap prestige and some half-disinterested friendship). Moreover, it now appears that Anne herself – the presiding Maecenas in the noontide of patronage, according to myth – was no reader herself, and spent far too much time scribbling to her favourites and reading devotional manuals. The final story, like all anecdotes of the early Hanoverians, is a bit of second-hand gossip. Besides, the courtiers of the 1730's – men of the generation of Hervey, Bubb Dodington, Sir William Yonge – were at least as interested in poetry as those of the 1690's; Caroline, with all her limitations, had more literary taste than Mary II. (The Queen actually dispensed quite a lot of patronage through James Johnston.) What had changed was not the literary inclination of the royal family and its entourage, but the system of awarding prizes and the kind of loyalty and dependence a ministry needed or could recompense. The story has more to do with the twittings of the Duke of Newcastle than George II's Teutonic prejudices. The answer has to be sought in constitutional and administrative history, not in coffee-house chat.[76]

With the background so vague, it is not surprising that Saunders' view of individual works is often highly idiosyncratic, that he misstates fact, or that the judgments should be hasty, Thus, Saunders asserts that 'Swift made [*Gulliver*] look as much like a novel as he could'; he calls Defoe's *Augusta Triumphans* 'a paean of joy for the new Augustan commercial society he saw springing up round him' (it is really a preservative, an incantation masquerading as a project –

the foundling's hospital is to prevent murders, there is a scheme to cut down street robberies, an idea to save youth from destruction and the lower class from utter ruin – *this* was a paean for contemporary London?). As to fact, it is not on record that Jacob Tonson 'founded' the Kit-Cat Club. Saunders twice refers to Pope's collaborator William Broome as 'Browne', and otherwise telescopes dates. And though he is rightly sceptical about the part played by 'a rising middle class', his final summary is tinged with mythic accretions:

> The dividing line between Pope and Johnson, on the one hand, and Grub Street on the other, is not a social distinction, one of degree and class: it is a difference which only becomes clear when one considers the quality of what each side has to say about human nature. An honest observer may live in a garret, while the literary prostitute (the term is exact and far from melodramatic) may live in a palace. One can only tell the difference between the true professional and the fake, in all his manifold varieties, by the quality of the work done.[77]

Maybe: but Grub Street (the term is exact and far from well-understood) imaged this qualitative distinction in social terms. As men and women of the eighteenth century saw it, the scribbler *belonged* in a garret – whether, like Gildon, he ended up there, or, like Theobald, he escaped to Bloomsbury. No doubt there can be such a thing as a high-class hack, or even a classless hack. But the Grub Street critique did enact a social judgment, for the purposes of satiric clarity and comic bite; and Saunders' picture of the Romantic dilemma is beside the point. Grub Street lay at the other end of town from the castles of fancy. It was a legend that died when Romantic mythology pre-empted the poetic imagination.

This, in outline, is the progress of a single metaphor. I have had to leave out a number of side-skirmishes, e.g. those set up by Beljame's *Men of Letters and the English Public*.[78] But the evidence ought to be enough to show that to trace the history of an idea can often be a circuitous business. People go on using phrases long after they have forgotten how the term came into being, and what it was meant to convey. Ordinary literary currency has its stock images, its subconscious word clusters, and even its archetypal patterns – a bad habit to copy from high art.

A Lexical History

The acceptation of the phrase 'Grub Street' has described a course of steadily increasing generality. The earliest usage recorded in *NED* is that of John Taylor, the Water Poet; but it is in the later seventeenth century that the expression acquired full identity. In the first part of *The Rehearsal Transpros'd* (1672), Andrew Marvell says of Bishop Usher, 'He, honest man, was deep gone in Grub-street and polemical divinity', indicating that the phrase already connoted eristic zeal.[79] This was a work Swift admired, though there have been few to do so since. In 1689, the prologue to Thomas Shadwell's *Bury Fair* relates this phrase immediately to the shabby side of London life:

> With viler, coarser jests than Great Bear-Garden
> And silly Grubstreet songs worse than Tom Farthing . . .[80]

It is an accident that disreputable literature came to be associated with Cripplegate rather than Southwark, in so far as there were other districts almost equally fitted to the semantic and symbolic role allotted to this quarter. In the Restoration, Grub Street was just one of a number of opprobious terms. Billingsgate, Smithfield, Saffron Hill, Tyburn – all were as recognisable and as full of metaphoric potential. It took the alchemy of major art to give Grub Street its peculiar immortality.

Among the Scriblerian group, it was Arbuthnot who made the simplest use of the term. His influential *Law is a Bottomless Pit*, otherwise *John Bull* (1712), developed one lasting archetype for posterity: the contrast between blunt John Bull and scheming Nich. Frog. But it also helped to lend specificity to the Grub Street trope. Arbuthnot speaks of the 'University of Grub Street', 'the learned Society of Grub Street', the 'Bretheren' of the place and the 'Education' there to be met with, the 'Meridian of Grub Street' and the 'Literati' of the district. Here we have a link between Swift's casual innuendo in the *Tale* and Pope's more finished dramatisation of the College of Dulness. In another work, *The Art of Political Lying*, the projector wishes to unite 'several small corporations of liars into one society' on the model of the hospitals at Greenwich and Chelsea. Elsewhere Arbuthnot alludes to 'the enemies of good living, the starve-gutted authors of Grub Street' – poverty rather than puritanism was now the hallmark. As we should expect, Arbuthnot's work is full of the concrete imagery of London found in the other satirists: Hockley, pesthouses in St Giles', Wapping and the rest.[81]

But this is commonplace in writing of the day, in Ned Ward as much as Pope. What strikes one is the comparative reluctance of the hacks to throw 'Grub Street' at one another. The expression is very rarely found in controversial exchanges, where the Scriblerians or the friends were not involved. On one occasion Read's *Weekly Journal* spoke of its rival Mist as 'the Printer of that infamous, Grub-street Paper . . .'[82] But more commonly, one encounters the term in the pages of established writers of known standing. Thus, Congreve writes in a private letter of a paper 'too like Grub Street to send . . . to you.'[83] Addison employed the term in his opening *Freeholder* in 1715,[84] and again in the *Old Whig* for 2 April 1719 – with his erstwhile friend Richard Steele the target:

> The author of the Plebeian, to show himself a perfect master in the vocation of Grub Street, with declaring the great esteem he has for himself, and the contempt he entertains for the scribblers of the age.

Such contempt was, indeed, a common element in duncely productions. But, strangely perhaps, the denizens of Grub Street were shy of carrying their 'vocation' to the point of employing that very term. If Defoe is to be regarded as one such resident, he scarcely affords an exception. In the introduction to his *True and Genuine Account* of Jonathan Wild (1725), Defoe does fall into the idiom, in speaking of tricks used by 'our Hackney *Grub-street* Writers, upon the old Pickpocket Principle of Publishing any Thing to get a Penny . . .'[85] But in the millions of words Defoe set down on paper, the incidence of the term is negligible. And he assuredly never made any effort to body forth the full Grub Street conceit in the manner of *The Dunciad*. He was too near the game to be able to afford that.

The currency of the expression in general discourse nevertheless showed a steady, if slow, growth. By 1720 Allan Ramsay was heading a poem 'Grubstreet nae satyre'. An extended use came to the common noun 'grub', meaning either a duncely composition (as Swift had used it) or else a Dunce himself. A defence of Fielding, written possibly by Thomas Cooke in 1732, has the line:

When *Grubs*, and *Grublings*, censure *Fielding's* Scenes . . .[86]

Christopher Smart introduces into *Jubilate Agno*, a 'Song from Bedlam' written c. 1760, the figure of 'Mr Grub'. Horace Walpole writes to his friend Mann about this time of a 'Grub ballad' on criminal themes. Clearly the root sense of 'maggot' is reasserting itself here. It is part of the process of blurring, the loss of specific density, which the expression underwent over time. This is the period of Johnson's famous definition, and the rival dictionary based on Nathaniel Bailey also kept alive the topographic basis: '*Grubstreet*, the Name of a Street in *London*, once inhabited by Persons who wrote for Hire, hence used for a paltry Composition.'[87] But the memory was fainter as the century wore on, and before the literal Grub Street was turned into Milton Street around 1830, the idea it had stood for had become wholly bereft of sharp or living significance. What had been a potent symbol for Pope was now little more than a slack cliché of belletrist prose.

The history of the term in the Victorian era is largely the history of the wider myth, considered elsewhere in this chapter. It is at the end of the century that 'Grub Street' came into fairly general usage, now for the first time liberated from its primary Augustan context. It came to be applied to the miseries of authorship at large: a vaguer, slightly pitying note attached to it. Here the important event was the appearance of George Gissing's novel *The New Grub Street* in 1892. Of this work it has been said, 'Half-starved geniuses in attics are, of course, the real connecting-link between Gissing's New Grub Street and the original Grub Street of the *Dunciad*, the *Epistle to Arbuthnot*, and the early Dr Johnson.'[88] For *real* one might substitute *only*. The calamities of authorship have become a matter for sorrow rather than outrage; the writer is on the side of the new hacks, embodied particularly by the hero Reardon. Vulgarity is now represented by success rather than failure; the sentimentalised Myth has replaced vigorous comic exposure. Whatever the merits of the novel as an artistic creation (and they are considerable), it must be said that Gissing helped to make Grub Street a less precise and evocative notion. From now on, the troubles of struggling authors will be the fault of society, rather than an emblem of faults in society. The complex symbolism of Augustan satire has been overturned: to lodge in Grub Street is no longer to be associated with shameful crimes, it is to be the victim of such a crime. In short, Grub Street is no longer available to satire.

A selection of quotations will illustrate the progress of ideas in this phase of taste. In 1897 John Ashton has this, in his *Social Life in the Reign of Queen Anne*: 'Literary men had their money troubles then as now – probably not more so – as many a melancholy tale of modern Grub Street could tell.'[89] The component of poverty has come to dominate all others, so that penury by itself is seen as sufficient qualification for admission to Grub Street – a radical shift from Pope's viewpoint.[90] The semi-technical sense survived in historical contexts; thus in 1905 Harvey Cushing wrote of 'a paper warfare, emanating from Grub Street', which attended the controversy regarding the free dispensary scheme at the end of the seventeenth century.[91] But through the Edwardian era such examples of fairly strict application become thinner on the ground. George Saintsbury's *Peace of the Augustans* did much to arrest the myth at large, but little to halt the degeneration of the phrase itself. Saintsbury in fact spoke of the 'Grub Street time', a mode of historical placing that was increasingly rejected. Usually indulgence is shown towards the hacks: in *The Age of Pope*, a widely read manual by a John Dennis scarcely less sympathetic to Dulness than the first, the implication is that 'the Grub Street side' was about as culpable and about as admirable as Pope himself.[92] The epithet 'poor' is often prefixed to a locution 'Grub Street hacks' (as by Paul Dottin in 1923);[93] and generally the reader senses a measure of gentle regret in the epithet.

In the 1920's the phrase took on a new lease of life. A. St John Adcock produced two books, each undated but obviously early in the decade, which show the ways things were moving: *Gods of Modern Grub Street*[94] was followed by *The Glory that was Grub Street*. Nothing prepares us for the contents: a chatty review of writers such as Shaw, Belloc, Bennett, Kipling and Hardy. Plainly for Adcock, Grub Street = the literary profession. This had simply not been the case up till then, but oddly Adcock seems unaware of the fact. Success is the main common factor of the writers discussed. After this strange lexical reversal, it is not too surprising to find Ronald Knox naming a book *Caliban in Grub Street* (1930): an entertaining book with little reference to anything the term had hitherto connoted.

Parallel with this process (represented also by J. C. Squire's *The Grub Street Nights*, 'entertainments' also undated) came a tendency to apply the expression to almost any quarter of Augustan literary life. To take a single example, G. M. Trevelyan used it with careless liberality in his great history of Anne's reign. Always ready to identify the true 'voice of Grub Street', he speaks of Defoe as 'an obscure inhabitant of Grub Street' at the time of *The Shortest Way*. This is perhaps justifiable – though *The True-Born Englishman* was hardly an obscure production – but Trevelyan speaks too of Addison being 'lifted out of Grub Street' and of Swift in 1710–11 as 'a denizen of Grub Street'.[95] This usage has not quite died out. As recently as 1968 Isaac Kramnick wrote of 'Addison, Steele, Defoe, Swift and lesser luminaries of Grub Street', and from time to time similar formulas are encountered. T. H. White's list seems to include Pope and Swift! To stretch the term to cover any professional writer is to blunt its meaning and to lose a valuable shade of thought.[96]

More individual than most was Ralph Straus, in 1927, with his 'grubbiest of Grub Street hacks'. A few years later, the coinage 'Grub-Streeteers' was made by E. M. Gagey, along with the less novel phrase 'devotees of the Grub Street muse'. The former expression was taken over by J. W. Johnson in 1967.[97] Meanwhile, S. C. Roberts had asserted that 'Grub Street is one of that group of place-names which remain in literary currency long after their topographical significance has vanished. . . . For the modern reader the associations of the words "Grub Street" are purely literary.' These associations apparently range from Goldsmith and Fielding (*The Author's Farce*) to *Pendennis* – 'a Grub Street softened and sweetened with essence of early Victorian sentiment.' Roberts moves on to the wider myth, but it is evident that he regards the original identity of the place as a piece of extrinsic antiquarian lumber. Still on related issues, we find A. D. McKillop writing in 1936 that Johnson 'was never a dweller in Grub Street'[98] – equally the view of E. A. Bloom twenty years later. Despite Bloom's title, *Samuel Johnson in Grub Street*, he insists that Johnson was 'not a Grubean'. The distinction may be finer than he knows.[99]

Roberts, too, had used as the title of an essay 'Johnson in Grub Street'. Other authors employed a similar formulation. H. W. Troyer's *Ned Ward of Grub Street* came out in 1946. Benjamin Boyce had headed a section 'History and Literature in Grub Street' as part of his study of Tom Brown (1939). Michael Foot has a chapter called 'Grub Street' in his book *The Pen and the Sword* (1957). So does Oscar Sherwin, in a popular life of Goldsmith published in 1962. Here Sherwin was following a more eminent biographer, John Forster, who devoted the sixth chapter of his *Life and Times of Goldsmith* (1854) to 'Peckham School and Grub Street', a nicely Augustan blend of fact and legend. All these indicate that the expression is regarded as a convenient shorthand form which makes a good title but which carries no very precise meaning. Certainly the more specialised implication of Grub Street is quite lost in these instances.[100]

In recent years the term has cropped up most frequently as a kind of attributive epithet. Commonly it precedes words such as 'poverty', as with A. R. Humphreys (1954); the same writer has 'garret-and-Grub-Street pattern' and 'Grub-street misery', this last with reference to *The Dunciad*. One element of this turns up in a phrase of E. J. Oliver (1958), the 'garrets of Grub Street' of which Gibbon was no inhabitant.[101] More picturesquely, O. H. K. Spate speaks of the 'ugly offstage chatter of London gutter-sparrows in Grub Street'.[102] Arthur Sherbo (1967) has 'the Grub-Street industry', and remarks that Christopher Smart 'was not unacquainted with Grub Street, if only at second or third remove': a slightly puzzling contention. J. M. Stedmond alludes to 'Grub Street productions' and 'Grub-Street formlessness'. For Stedmond, incidentally, Tristram Shandy is a 'self-conscious Dunce': an interesting but imprecise extension of the word.[103] However, by far the commonest adjunct in modern usage is 'hack'. This tendency was no doubt given impetus by Ronald Paulson, who actually went so far as to designate the supposed narrator of *A Tale of a Tub* 'the' Grub Street hack. But Paulson was developing the idea of W. B. Ewald (1954), who had used the identical phrase. Since then, writers as different as Sherbo and Sir Harold Nicolson (1960) have employed it, along with other academic critics: Richard I. Cook (1967), Stedmond (1967) and Kramnick (1968) among them. The last named also has 'Walpole's Grub Street stable'.[104] Plainly for most of these writers, the term has lost all particularity and force. A Grub Street hack is a hack is a hack. Some commentators have deplored the vagueness with which the epithet 'Augustan' is invoked. But that was always an aspiring, ahistorical, portentous word and known to be so. Grub Street is marvellously apt and definite in Pope; it has grown cloudy through carelessness or pretension.[105]

It follows that no deep social or psychological need is met any longer by the existence (or invention) of a Grub Street. For the Augustan satirists, there had been important levels of meaning which had been trapped by the metaphor. They had wanted to show that folly was on the move; that the corruption and enfeeblement of letters were aided by the very group who should uphold its probity; and that there was a new kind of self-interest among the purveyors of bad literature. They had intuited that the city had reached a critical stage in its development, and that the seething, unpoliced conditions of modern urbanism brought a new sort of social violence with it – a tendency towards riot and upheaval, to match the physical dangers (plague, fire) which were specially incident in the large towns.[106] All these factors gave a particular aptness to the idea of the league of Dunces, against whom the tiny Scriblerian party defiantly waged their symbolic contest. One might apply to the riotous mob of *The Dunciad*, bent on fire and destruction, what Matthew Hodgart has so well said on a more general basis: 'The literary satirist will not permit his victim the psychic space to assert himself as an individual; when he sins, he sins with the mob.'[107] The Dunces are more than the sum of their parts. Earlier satire had usually been directed against particular figures, Labeo or Sir Epicure Mammon. The Augustans learnt to portray folly as a collectivity.

But the provision of a well-stocked Grub Street helped the writers more directly. Works such as *A Tale of a Tub*, *The Dunciad* and *The Author's Farce*, more briefly *Trivia*, the *Epistle to Arbuthnot*, 'On Poetry: A Rapsody' – these constitute a standing rebuke to Dulness. In their exuberant invention, their glittering texture, their comic *brio* and literary resource, they serve in themselves to point up the dreary pretension and solemn vacuity of the hacks. Grub Street was a drab and joyless part of town. The cutting irony is that it was made the vehicle of farce. Its shabby purlieus are irradiated by the gaiety of vision that belongs to Pope, Swift and their friends. The verve and glitter of their art bring to intense life a London that is gone and a circle of men and women otherwise lost in the mists of time.

Epigraph. Reprinted in *Society*, II, 155.

1. I quote from the reprint volume (*Society*), but have collated all references with the original issue. There is an excellent study by James T. Hillhouse, *The Grub-Street Journal* (Durham, N.C., 1928), on which I have relied for background information.
2. *Society*, I, i–ii.
3. *Society*, I, ii–iii.
4. *Society*, I, iii.
5. *Society*, I, iv–v.
6. *Society*, I, vi–vii.
7. *Society*, I, viii.
8. *Society*, I, viii–ix.
9. *Society*, I, x–xi.
10. *Society*, I, xii, xxii.
11. *Society*, I, 2.
12. *Society*, I, 70.
13. *Society*, I, 7.
14. *Society*, I, 163–4.
15. *Society*, I, 199, 233–4. Political scribblers are said to be 'possess'd of the largest as well as the most fruitfull province in the whole extended dominions of Grub-Street'. Note *extended*.
16. See, for example, no. 90 (23 September 1731), a letter from the Elysian Fields, in which Defoe is welcomed on account of his extensive knowledge

of the intrigues carried out by both hacks and booksellers. The idiom of this paper is borrowed directly from *Peri Bathous*: '. . . We have here established in these lower [regions] a regular Grubean Society. We are situated at the foot of the Elysian Parnassus: and as we are so near our enemies, several of our members are continually endeavouring to desert us, by climbing up towards them; but are soon brought back again by their own specific gravity' (*Society*, II, 139). When a Grubean Society could be set up in Elizium, the concept had indeed been disembodied.

17. *Society*, II, 107, 239. Another notable inclusion is a series of attacks on Fielding as a dramatist, in nos. 130, 136 and 138 – once in the unenviable company of Theophilus Cibber. No. 78 satirises N.M., that is the exiled Nathaniel Mist.

18. *Society*, II, 154–5.

19. Stanley Morison, *The English Newspaper* (Cambridge, 1932), p. 115. According to Morison, 'By bringing a critical public into existence, the paper prepared the way for the ably conducted weeklies of the next generation.' This seems to me to overrate the critical pretensions of the journal, and to underrate its partisan functions. None the less, it is true that the editors did place the Grubean conceit in a wider context of literary discussion, perhaps at the cost of some precision and aptitude in its meaning.

20. On the circumstances of the book's appearance, see Clifford, pp. 262–6 ('To the public Johnson remained just an anonymous compiler').

21. Clifford, p. 264.

22. As Clifford says (p. 265), in Johnson's hands 'Savage became both a symbol of injustice and an example of weakness.' The myth stressed the former at the expense of the latter.

23. Here I quote the abridged edition of Hawkins' *Life of Samuel Johnson*, ed. B. H. Davis (London, 1962), p. 68. Cited as 'Davis'.

24. The life of Savage is quoted from *The Works of Samuel Johnson, Ll.D.*, ed. A. Murphy (London, 1824). Professor Clarence Tracy's forthcoming edition will provide a more authoritative text than is at present available.

25. Johnson, *Works*, X, 283–4.

26. *Works*, X, 284–315.

27. John Oldmixon's courtship of the Duchess of Marlborough over some forty-five years, through all the changing circumstances of political life, is exceptional but not misleading as regards Duncely habits.

28. *Works*, X, 321–66; quotation from p. 354.

29. *Works*, X, 367.

30. *Works*, X, 381.

31. *Works*, X, 381–410; quotations from pp. 404, 410.

32. Quoted from the third edition, *Some Account of London* (1793), p. 261.

33. Omitted by Davis, and therefore quoted from the second edition (1787) of

Hawkins' *Life*, p. 31n. For the hacks, see pp. 46–9n; for the *Grub-street Journal*, pp. 31–2.

34. Cited from Davis, pp. 68–9.

35. Omitted by Davis: see Hawkins, pp. 58–60n.

36. Clifford, p. 228.

37. Hawkins, p. 157n.

38. Arthur Sherbo, *Christopher Smart Scholar of the University* (Lansing, Mich., 1967), p. 131.

39. Isaac D'Israeli, *Calamities of Authors* (London, 1812), I, ix, x, xv, 9.

40. D'Israeli, I, 183–4 (cf. p. 158, for the apparent confusion.)

41. D'Israeli, I, 282–3, 150. See also I, 274–81, on William Pattison, 'a young Poet who perished in his twentieth year . . . one more child of that family of genius, whose passions, like the torch, kindle but to consume themselves.' Pope, of course, scorns the youthful genius. His career prompts the reflection, 'Such was the complete misery which Savage, Boyse, Chatterton and more innocent spirits devoted to literature, have endured – but not long – for they must perish in their youth!' One can only say, '!' indeed. For myth and reality concerning Pattison, see my article 'A Cambridge Chatterton', *Cambridge Review*, LXXXV (1964), 311–3.

42. I quote from *Critical and Historical Essays by Thomas Babington Macaulay* (London, 1907), II, 523–62, there titled 'Samuel Johnson'.

43. See for example Bertrand H. Bronson, 'The Double Tradition of Dr Johnson', *Johnson Agonistes and Other Essays* (Berkeley, 1965), pp. 158–9 and ff. For Boswell, see pp. 54–5.

44. Macaulay, II, 543–4.

45. Macaulay, II, 545. Later on, there is a brief reference to Young (II, 547), but he does not retrace the quoted statement, concerning 'the best writers'. It is likely that Macaulay did not know of Fielding's shift to the support of Walpole.

46. Macaulay, II, 545–6.

47. Macaulay, II, 546–7.

48. Reprinted in *The Miscellaneous Writings of Lord Macaulay* (London, 1865), 307–27. The relevant passage occurs at p. 310.

49. Thomas Carlyle, *Critical and Miscellaneous Essays* (London, 1899), III, 76, 81. For Carlyle's aim to 'offset' Macaulay, and his substitution of his own mythical abstraction, see Bronson's essay, 'The Double Tradition', p. 160.

50. I cite the Everyman edition, which combines these two works in one volume (London, 1912).

51. Thackeray, p. 53.

52. Thackeray, pp. 178–9.

53. John Timbs, *Curiosities of London* (1855). I cite the edition of 1868, where

the entry occurs on pp. 383–5. In the 1855 edition the passage is at pp. 335–7.

54. Thornbury, II, 240–1.
55. Henry Campkin, *Grub Street* (*Now Milton Street*) (London, priv. pr., 1868). There is no copy in the British Museum but the Guildhall Library holds one.
56. Campkin, pp. 4–7. The writer quotes *The Weekly Oracle* (1755), posing the question, 'Why is a bad author commonly called a Grub Street author?' The usual answer follows, with Foxe and puritan connections stressed. Evidently the meaning of the trope was not self-evident by this date.
57. Campkin, pp. 3, 8, 9, 12–13, 14. Johnson, says Campkin (p. 9), knew Grub Street well, but allowed no sneer against its habitués 'to escape from his pen' in the *Dictionary*.
58. Campkin, pp. 16–22, a *locus classicus* of the myth.
59. W. C. Sydney, *England and the English in the Eighteenth Century* (London, 1891), II, 114–9. The quotation from *The English Humourists* is taken from Thackeray, p. 48.
60. H. G. Aldiss, in *The Cambridge History of English Literature*, ed. A. W. Ward, A. R. Waller (Cambridge, 1914), XI, 311–42. Quotation from p. 329.
61. George Saintsbury, *Dryden* (London, ed., 1916), p. 181.
62. Saintsbury, in *Social England*, ed. H. D. Traill (London, 1896), V, 251–3.
63. Saintsbury, *The Peace of the Augustans* (London, ed. 1948), pp. 97–9. The writer refers to Grub Street with studied generality (pp. 92–3): 'the supposed time and place of poverty, persecution, and contempt which fell upon literature . . . between the golden age of preferment under Anne and the very late openings for profit by periodicals and public buying and so forth.' He speaks of the 'charm' of the expression: 'The eighteenth century caught up "Grub Street"; it might even be said that Grub Street itself caught itself up' (p. 95). The argument is that people take you at your own valuation, and that the scribblers were too ready to throw the nickname at one another – the mud stuck. Saintsbury effects this act of realignment, despite a normal enough Vicwardian attitude to Pope: 'Pope's poisonous and self-torturing spite was not satisfied . . . he must needs represent the whole corporation of letters, with hardly any exceptions beyond the narrow circle of his own friends and associates, as a mere College of Dulness, and, not content with this, must exult and triumph in its supposed degradation, suffering and contempt' (p. 94). This is very strange – has Saintsbury forgotten the plot? It is the College which exults and triumphs, 'old England' which suffers degradation and oblivion. Saintsbury was much better at identifying Grub Street than most of his contemporaries: unfortunately, he does not seem to follow the rhetoric of Pope's satire so well, and has the victors vanquished.
64. Saintsbury, *The Peace of the Augustans*, pp. 100–1.

65. *The Peace of the Augustans*, pp. 186–9.

66. [Charles Gildon], *Robinson Crusoe Criticis'd and Examin'd*, ed. Paul Dottin (London/Paris, 1923), pp. 9, 62, etc.

67. E. B. Chancellor, *The Literary Ghosts of London* (London, 1933), pp. 57, 106.

68. S. C. Roberts, *An Eighteenth-Century Gentleman and Other Essays* (Cambridge, 1933), pp. 27–45.

69. R. W. Chapman, 'Authors and Booksellers' in Turberville, II, 310–30. Quotations from pp. 317–18, 319, 323. Dorothy George's phrase in Turberville, I, 177, 'the squalor of Grub Street', mitigated by the amenities of the coffee-house, represents the older usage.

70. Clifford, p. 254.

71. Bronson, 'The Writer', *Man versus Society in Eighteenth-Century Britain* (Cambridge, 1968), pp. 109–10.

72. Reprinted in Lowenthal's *Literature, Popular Culture and Society*: I cite the Palo Alto ed., 1968, pp. 52–108. Marjorie Fiske is named as co-author. Quotations from pp. 52, 53, 56, 74, 92n, 93. Lowenthal's judgment on Jacob Tonson – 'He commanded the admiration of most of his authors, to whom he was generous in his commercial dealings and stimulating in his intellectual contacts' (p. 59) – is hardly borne out by Tonson correspondence which survives or by the run of contemporary allusions. Tonson was a good and dignified man of business, but he was no more a philanthropist than Curll.

73. J. W. Saunders, *The Profession of English Letters* (London, 1964), pp. 123, 112. Other references to Grub Street occur at pp. 115, 138 and 147.

74. Saunders, p. 126. The source here appears to be a work listed in the bibliography, B. Fitzgerald's *Daniel Defoe*, a strained and inaccurate Marxist reading of Defoe's career. Similarly, Saunders' authority for Fielding is Homes Dudden, not Cross; for Pope, Root rather than Sherburn; for Johnson, Krutch rather than Clifford; for Dryden, Young rather than Ward. To use these books when the standard lives are available is a curious decision – even supposing Saunders had accurately summarised their contents, which he often does not.

75. Saunders, pp. 126, 131–2, 135. For Lord Harley's gift of money to enable Prior to buy Down Hall (on condition that Harley obtained the reversion, as he did within a short space of time), see James Lees-Milne, *Earls of Creation* (London, 1962), pp. 196–203.

76. Saunders, pp. 113–14.

77. Saunders, pp. 103, 127, 121, 137, 119, 147. An example of telescoping events is the statement that Defoe secretly doctored Mist's *Journal* and Dormer's *News Letter* for eleven years (p. 126) – almost twice the period authenticated.

78. A. O. Beljame, *Le Public et les Hommes de Lettres en Angleterre au dix-*

huitième Siècle 1660–1744 (Paris, 1897), belatedly translated as *Men of Letters and the English Public*, ed. B. Dobrée (London, 1948). Beljame's work has some interest as a synthesis of the sources then available, but in the light of later research a great many of his conclusions will not stand up. The book is really a monument to nineteenth-century research methods: though intelligently put together, its wholesale reliance on dubious sources (literary, printed, secondary) and ready acceptance of Macaulayan dogma make it a study to be approached with caution. Beljame's lack of detailed grasp is instanced by his treatment of Arthur Maynwaring (whom he calls Maynwairing). This Kit-Cat socialite and Whig publicist, the secretary and confidant of the Duchess of Marlborough, is listed among those whom Walpole 'salarait brutalement' . . . Beljame sees Maynwaring as one of 'des alliés peu utiles . . . à la Chambre des communs'. But Maynwaring began his serious literary endeavours for the Whigs *after* he entered Parliament; he was dead by 1712; his intended usefulness for the Whigs lay in checking the efforts of Auditor Harley (the chief minister's brother) to smear the outgoing Whigs with a public debt scare; and finally, he was a colleague rather than a servant of Walpole. See Bejame, pp. 366, 358. As Dobrée points out in his edition (p. 219), Maynwaring would have held his post if he had never written a line. Many similar examples could be given. Beljame's view that the hacks were '*ex abrupto* laissés à leurs propres forces', on the advent of Walpole to power, and his stories of Savage and Boyse (pp. 367–71) came straight from Macaulay. They are myth virtually unadulterated.

79. *The Works of Andrew Marvell, Esq,* ed. Captain Edward Thompson (London, 1776), II, 21. Marvell also speaks of 'the Puritans in Grub Street'. The best source for these early usages is *London Past & Present*, II, 166–9, where Charles Cotton, Thomas Randolph and others are cited.

80. Quoted from *Types of English Drama 1660–1780*, ed. D. H. Stevens (Boston, 1923), p. 226.

81. Arbuthnot, pp. 231, 277, 289, 300: *London Past & Present*, loc. cit.

82. Read's *Weekly Journal*, 26 July 1718. For another example, involving 'the Fraternity of *Grub-Street*', see *Plain Dealer*, 17 May 1712.

83. *William Congreve: Letters and Documents*, ed. J. C. Hodges (London, 1963), p. 47. The term is occasionally used by the Earl of Shaftesbury around 1712; see his *Second Characters*, ed. B. Rand (Cambridge, 1914), pp. xiv, xvi.

84. *The Free-Holder* (London, 1716), p. 1 – the 'Grub Street patriot' well acquainted with gaol.

85. *Romances and Narratives* does not include this work. Quoted from *Selected Poetry and Prose of Daniel Defoe*, ed. M. Shugrue (New York, 1968), p. 272.

86. Quoted by Ronald Paulson, Thomas Lockwood (eds.), *Henry Fielding: The Critical Heritage* (London, 1969), p. 40.

87. Quoted from the 1782 edition, revised by E. Harwood, sig. Ccc 1r. In the 1731 edition there is no entry for Grub Street: *grub* is defined as a maggot or dwarf. An early nineteenth-century dictionary, *Walker Remodelled* (by B. H. Smart) (London, 1836), p. 262, has 'the accredited abode of scribblers for the press.'

88. R. C. Churchill, 'Three Autobiographical Novelists', *From Dickens to Hardy*, ed. B. Ford (Harmondsworth, 1958), p. 343.

89. See Ashton, *Social Life in the Reign of Queen Anne* (London, 1897), pp. 294–5.

90. On the nineteenth century application of the term, see also James Hepburn, *The Author's Empty Purse* . . . (London, 1968), p. 17 and passim.

91. Harvey Cushing, M.D., *Dr Garth the Kit-Kat Poet 1661–1718* (Baltimore, 1906), p. 9. Garth actually died in 1719.

92. John Dennis, *The Age of Pope* (London, 1894), p. 47. The term is extensively used by Cross, I., ix, 74–5, etc.

93. *Robinson Crusoe Criticis'd*, ed. Dottin, p. 3.

94. Published c. 1923?

95. Trevelyan, I, 203, 290; III, 120. For the 'authentic, unhappy voice of Grub Street', see I, 99.

96. Isaac Kramnick, *Bolingbroke and his Circle* (Cambridge, Mass., 1968), p. 11; T. H. White, *The Age of Scandal* (Harmondsworth, 1966), p. 14.

97. Ralph Straus (ed.), *The Tricks of the Town* (London, 1927), p. x; E. M. Gagey, *Ballad Opera* (New York, 1937), pp. 55, 66; J. W. Johnson, *The Formation of English Neo-Classical Thought* (Princeton, 1967), p. 100. 'Grub-Streeter' also occurs in Melvyn New, *Laurence Sterne as Satirist* (Gainesville, Fla. 1969), p. 190.

98. Roberts, pp. 27–31; McKillop, *Samuel Richardson, Printer and Novelist* (Chapel Hill, 1936), p. 16.

99. E. A. Bloom, *Samuel Johnson in Grub Street* (Providence, R. I., 1957), p. 6.

100. H. W. Troyer, *Ned Ward in Grub Street* (Cambridge, Mass., 1946); Benjamin Boyce, *Tom Brown of Facetious Memory* (Cambridge, Mass., 1939), pp. 46–68; Michael Foot, *The Pen and the Sword* (London, 1957), pp. 73–91; Oscar Sherwin, *The Life and Times of Oliver Goldsmith* (New York, 1962), pp. 111–24; John Forster, *The Life and Times of Oliver Goldsmith* (London, ed. 1877), I, 73–93. See also I. M. Williams, *The Criticism of Henry Fielding* (London, 1970), p. 77ff. The section of A. S. Turberville's *English Men and Manners in the Eighteenth Century* (New York, ed. 1957), pp. 337–55, is almost wholly devoted to Defoe and Johnson despite its title 'Grub Street'.

101. A. R. Humphreys, *The Augustan World* (London, 1954), pp. 9, 45, 92; E. J. Oliver, *Gibbon and Rome* (London, 1958), p. 65.

102. O. H. K. Spate, 'The Muse of Mercantilism', *Studies in the Eighteenth Century*, ed. R. F. Brissenden (Canberra, 1968), p. 120.

103. Sherbo, pp. 58, 90; J. M. Stedmond, *The Comic Art of Laurence Sterne* (Toronto, 1967), pp. 17, 64.

104. Ronald Paulson, *Theme and Structure in Swift's Tale of a Tub* (New Haven, 1960), passim; W. B. Ewald, *The Masks of Jonathan Swift* (Oxford, 1954), p. 23; Sherbo, p. 131; Nicolson, *The Age of Reason* (London, ed. 1968), p. 360, and cf. p. 265; R. I. Cook, *Jonathan Swift as Tory Pamphleteer* (Seattle, 1967), p. 93; Stedmond, p. 64; Kramnick, p. 18, and cf. p. 243. See also New, p. 91.

105. Other casual modern usages are found in Geoffrey Holmes, *British Politics in the Age of Anne* (London, 1967), p. 30; W. A. Speck, *Tory and Whig* (London, 1970), p. 92. Untypical in his precision is W. K. Wimsatt (ed.), *Alexander Pope: Selected Poetry and Prose* (New York, 1950), p. xx. See also C. H. S. Fifoot, *Lord Mansfield* (Oxford, 1936), p. 226. For an interesting discussion of Grub Street as 'a trope of the printing press', see Denis Donoghue, *Jonathan Swift: A Critical Introduction* (Cambridge 1969), pp. 10–11.

106. S. T. Bindoff points out that in the sixteenth century, 'The physical antithesis between town and country was certainly much less marked than today. The average Tudor town . . . was simply an overgrown village.' (*Tudor England*, Harmondsworth, 1950, p. 39.) It was the growth of Stuart London which brought a completely new kind of urbanism by 1700. Bindoff also points out that the plague had at first ravaged town and country alike. After about 1400, it had affected chiefly London and provincial towns. 'After 1500 London, and towns infected from London, alone were touched' (p. 15). It could be shown that other 'plagues' – organised crime, say – became localised in the city at roughly the same period.

107. Matthew Hodgart, *Satire* (London, 1969), p. 129.

Appendix A
Evidence from the Rate-Books

The Corporation of London Records Office possesses a limited number of rate-books and polltax returns for Cripplegate Without at this period. The ratebooks, of course, do not supply any indication of the residents' occupation. Nor are there any recognisable names to be encountered, unless 'Mr Fay' assessed in the Fore Street Precinct can be Defoe's father or (less probably) 'Edward Ward' could be associated with the Dunce of that name. See Assessment Box 19, MS 9, ff. 15, 31; Assessment Box 27, MS 8, f. 49. It is noticeable how many houses are recorded as empty, particularly in the Grub Street precinct (the others are Fore Street, Red Cross Street, White Cross Street). In 1689 the courts off Grub Street were particularly lowly rated: Honeysuckle Court, Flying Horse Court and Hartshorne Alley among them. Many houses on Grub Street itself were assessed at only 2d, 4d or 6d: the minimum rates. By far the most highly rated property in 1689 was that of Sir Gilbert Barrington, assessed at 12/- (inhabitants' tax) and 12/6 (landlords'). The polltax returns for April 1692 (Assessment Box 41, MS 2) show that few residents had maidservants; among those listed are several weavers and the city sawyer. In Whites Alley a substantial property was occupied by Daniel Williams, presumably the dissenting minister of that name who founded Dr Williams' Library on a site further west within the parish. The polltax for 1698 provide evidence of a number of occupations among the residents of Grub Street: professions listed include baker, stablekeeper, chymist, victualler, refiner, tayler, porter, founder, pipemaker, plasterer, turner, twister [?], and sawyer. The commonest ascription is 'laborer', with occasional entries such as sugar baker and officer of the excise (a larger property). A number of foreign names, possibly Huguenot, are evident, as are Irish names.

(Assessment Box 18, MS 1.) Various members of the Leake family, probably that of the printers into whom Samuel Richardson married, appear in these books. John Leake, for instance, is entered as having a lodger in June 1683 (Misc. MS. 87.4). Rather later material includes a tax return for 1718. Hanover Court and Haberdashers Square are notably more substantial than the run of the precinct; the stable rates of the latter are a good deal higher than those for the residential property in Sugar Loaf Court. One 'John ffoe' is listed as a tenant in or about Butlers Alley. In Petty France, on the other side of Moorfields, is listed Samuel Humphreys, possibly the associate of Handel.

In general more information is to be found in the parish records of St Giles, kept in the Guildhall Library. Defoe's death from a 'lethargy' in April 1731 is a familiar entry: more representative than this is the laconic 'Woman found in ye street'. The cause of death most frequently met with is either 'Fever' or 'aged'; other common ailments are 'convulsion', 'fisick', 'looseness', 'dropsy', 'smallpox', 'teeth' – a strange and horrific concatenation.

Few names connected with the bookselling trade can be found. In a sample of burials and marriages for four years, comprising several thousand entries, the only relevant instances were those of Elizabeth, daughter of Henry Harriott and his wife Mary, christened on 31 March 1728, the father being a letter-founder; and David Coulthorp, a printer, buried on 21 January 1732/3. The commoner trades encountered are those of smith, weaver, baker, mason, carter, draper, clogmaker, mariner, lighterman, buttonmaker, vintner, shoemaker and watchmaker – artisan occupations now and then interspersed with 'gentleman' or, most frequently of all, 'labourer'. Watchmaker and lapidary are other professions found. 'French Protestant' occurs with some regularity. This is of course to disregard the harrowing repetition of 'child' in the burial records.

The Guildhall Library also possesses some poor-rate books, which make instructive reading. Those for 1710 (MS 6104/1) show Red Cross Street precinct as the highly rated part of the parish. Around Grub Street itself Haberdashers Square again stands out as the most substantial area. Honeysuckle Court is notably poor, with no property assessed above the 1d rate. Bullhead Court, off Jewen Street, where

Charles Gildon came in his blind and pauperous old age, is moderately assessed, indicating something of a fall from its earlier status. The meeting house near Paul's Alley, in Red Cross Street precinct, is rated at 6d – 'but a Collection is promised to be made in November next' to clear arrears. A similar entry appears in the 1714 books (MS 6104/2). This was the Anabaptist chapel which, as Leslie Hotson has argued, probably stood on the site of the theatrical nursery that figures as the chief venue of *Mac Flecknoe* (see p. 68). The 1718 books (MS 6104/3, 4) have little of fresh interest, except that Hanover Court, as its title might lead us to guess, has appeared for the first time. Tenter Alley is notably low on assessments, with a large number of 'poor' recorded in the parish. A certain Thomas Gordon appears in the books, but this is unlikely to be the hack of that name. By 1721 (MS 6104/8) Hanover Court has become Hanover Square. Further records are preserved for 1723 and 1726, but they merely confirm previous findings.

All in all, these documents show Cripplegate Without to have been a district of no very high social tone. Towards the end of the period covered, in 1725–30, it was probably a more salubrious quarter than St Giles in the Fields, or than some parts of Southwark: the building of Hanover Court, eastward off Grub Street, made some temporary improvement to the immediate locality. But the area remained one consigned largely to the poorer artisans and labouring people, with a high density of population, a large foreign intake, and a depressingly level mortality rate. The forest of small alleys and courts running into Grub Street – Maidenhead Alley, Hartshorne Court, Butlers Alley, Bell Alley, and the rest – can have done nothing to brighten this prospect.

Incidentally, it is noteworthy that Pope does refer to 'Grubstreet alleys' (A.I.256). The literal, topographic basis to the metaphor is again apparent. One can speak easily enough of Wardour Street writing, or of Bloomsbury culture: but one does not so readily extend the trope and mention terraces of Wardour Street prose or squares of Bloomsbury thinking. That one *could* think in terms of Grub Street alleys, connoting cells of duncely industry, suggests the kind of physical presence which the image carried with it.

There are other indications in criminal records of the character of the district. For example, a yeoman of Grub Street, John Rich, was among those indicted in 1682 at Middlesex Sessions, having been taken at an unlawful conventicle (an offence of which Dunces like Oldmixon were suspected). He was fined 13s 4d. See *Middlesex County Records*, ed. J. C. Jeaffreson (London, 1892), IV, 192. Many other parishioners of St Giles' (labourers, weavers, stocking-makers) were indicted on similar grounds (pp. 171–2, 192, 264, 301–2). In 1682 Richard Francklyn, clerk, was convicted and fined for preaching at a meeting house in Blue Anchor Alley (p. 172). For coining and fraudulent offences, and other misdemeanours committed by residents of Moorfields and Grub Street, see *The Proceedings at the Sessions of the Peace, and Oyer and Terminer, for the City of London, and County of Middlesex* (London, 1732–3), passim. For instance, Alderman John Barber sat on the bench when two forgers, lodging in Grub Street, were convicted and sentenced to death in October 1733 (pp. 222–5).

Appendix B
The Trades of Grub Street

Despite a vaguely held impression that Grub Street was the centre of surreptitious book production, no evidence has ever been brought to support this view. An encyclopedia entry furnishes the information that a printer of Grub Street was bound over in the sum of three thousand pounds, with two sureties each of £200, 'not to print any seditious or unlicensed books or pictures'.[1] This was in 1649, and legend has it that Cripplegate was particularly infested at that period. But unlicensed printers leave few traces, fugitive authors none at all. The few things that can be said for certain are these: (1) Thomas Fawcett was engaged as a printer from 1621; although there is no reason to suspect that his trade was other than respectable.[2] (2) Smyth's *Obituary*, besides revealing the heavy impact of the Great Plague, lists a number of residents of Grub Street with their occupation. They include Mistress Franklyn, 'a woman very free of her tongue'; another resident of the same street, called simply 'a poore man'; a hatband maker in White's Alley; a vintner of Grub Street; a poulterer of Fore Street (long reputed for its butchers); a glazier of Red Cross Street; and the sexton of Cripplegate, who himself died of the plague. But though the book trade is well represented in entries naming Little Britain, no such connection can be traced for Grub Street itself.[3] (3) Francis Kyte, the engraver and mezzotint artist who is best known for his portrait of Handel, lived in the parish, as his will of 1734 discloses. In 1725 Kyte had been arrested in Southwark and, following his conviction for a banknote forgery, he was put in the pillory on Little Tower Hill. He seems also to have been a highwayman, with that profligate and promiscuous energy which marked out so many eighteenth-century artists.[4]

Amongst famous criminals, as noted, Barbara Spencer belonged to the parish. She was hanged and then burnt at Tyburn for the misleading offence of 'high treason':[5] but this was no romantic episode on Mata Hari lines. She was a counterfeiter, and this was one calling which can be positively linked with Cripplegate. It would be tedious to multiply instances; one case may serve for all. In 1672 Magdalen Price, alias Rogers, was 'burnt in Smithfield for clipping coin in Tenter Alley, in the Moorfields.'[6] Tenter Alley ran off Moor Lane, the very next thoroughfare parallel to Grub Street. For the rest, we can be sure only that the ward had more than its share of alehouse-keepers. Radzinowicz cites the almost unbelievable figure of twenty-three public houses dotted along the short extent of White Cross Street.[7] Besant names some sixteen taverns in the parish amongst those culled from Ned Ward's *Vade Mecum*, but only one lies in White Cross Street – four are located in the even shorter Moor Lane.[8] If these ratios were maintained, there must have been two to three hundred inns within St Giles' bounds. But how many publicans were, like '*Ward* of *Bunhill*', writers by secondary profession, we have no means of telling.

1. William Kent, *An Encyclopedia of London* (London, 1937), p. 306. Bernard Alsop, a seventeenth-century printer in Grub Street, is mentioned in *London Past & Present*, II, 166–9. For the popular impression, cf. E/C, IV, 29–30.
2. H. R. Plomer (ed.), *A Dictionary of the Booksellers and Printers 1641–1667* (London, 1907), p. 72.
3. *The Obituary of Richard Smyth*, ed. H. Ellis ([London,] 1849), passim. Smyth lived in little Moorfields (Denton, p. 180).
4. W. C. Smith, *Concerning Handel* (London, 1948), pp. 121–2. Denton (p. 68) refers to the 'secret printing presses off Red Cross Street and Golding Lane pour[ing] off seditious pamphlets exhorting the Saints again to draw the sword for the "good old cause".' This would suit Dulness, which also has its old cause; but Denton cites no authority. Valerie Pearl quotes an apposite remark, to the effect that St Giles' was 'crowded with artisans of the weaving, printing and paper-making trades': *London at the Outbreak of the Puritan Revolution* (Oxford, 1961), p. 16. But this is not to locate specific printers.
5. *Calendar*, I, 44.
6. Denton, p. 15n.
7. Radzinowicz, II, 288.
8. Besant, pp. 639–40.

Appendix C
A Grub Street Ode

The Grub-street Journal, 28 October 1731:

This number contains a representation of the procession at the Lord Mayor's Show; with an account of the original of that honourable Officer, and of the manner of his election.

To FRANCIS CHILD, Esq; Lord Mayor Elect.

> Since Pageants ceas'd with curious figures wrought,
> And tuneful verse to tell the painter's thought;
> Your annual pomps with glory less have shin'd,
> And Grub-street's ancient honour much declin'd:
> But what most fatal to this Province prov'd,
> Our Laureat Prince his residence remov'd.
>   The Muses then forsook their ancient seat,
> To nobler domes invited by the Great.
> The Tragic Muse with Comic chang'd her part;
> Both Nature scorn'd, and both apply'd to Art:
> To manual Art; which drew more glorious Scenes,
> And turn'd fine Pageants into grand Machines.
> Here RICH in clouds descending shone a God;
> There BOOTH and CIBBER fiery dragons rode:
> Grub-street resounded with th'united din,
> That rose from Drury-lane and Lincoln's-inn.
>   To make their court, much higher place in view,
> From their high lodgings numerous Bards withdrew:
> Success soon swell'd their vain, impostum'd mind;
> They scorn'd their brethren, who remain'd behind:
> To turn whose greatest glory into shame,
> They made GRUBEAN an opprobious name;

And strove with all the rage of mortal foes,
To sink the Seminary whence they rose.
　But when their thoughts, as thirst of lucre burn'd,
From Poetry to Politics were turn'd;
Their works, now written not for fame, but pay,
Unsold, were weekly giv'n in reams away.
In vain: – for most with repetition tir'd,
Would not e'en read those learned gifts, unhir'd.
　Grub Street, renown'd in old and modern times,
The venerable seat of prose and rhimes,
Unpeopled lay: no tuneful voice was heard:
Their silent heads our antique garrets rear'd,
Like those of authors, empty, crack'd, and odd;
And seem'd, like readers of their works, to nod.
　Ambitious to retrieve its former fame,
Or keep alive a while its dying name,
As house most ancient of this ancient Street,
Some choice Grubean Wits resolv'd to meet;
Where of sound native beer, not foreign wine,
A long-wing'd Pegasus hangs out, the sign
Auspicious Fortune seem'd our aims to bless,
And prove their goodness by their great success;
To our young, weekly, old, reviv'd, new Club,
Each wednesday added some illustrious GRUB.
　From hence our *Journals* take their weekly flights,
And far out-soar all other paper kites:
Mounted on pinions pluck'd from grey-goose wing,
Like geese, in various figures flying, sing;
Now high, now low, they rove from place to place,
And lead pursuers a long wild-goose chace.
Borne on these wings, to every countrey town
The whole Transactions of the world are shown:
And whilst by us such numbers famous grow,
We grow more fam'd ourselves, who make them so.
　But since no diet is so thin as fame,
Your City Poet's once illustrious name
In me revive; with pension by the year;
And perquisite a pipe of PARSON's Beer
With this inspir'd, and scorning nauseous wine,

419

APPENDIX C

In annual pomp your Bard shall crowned shine,
Attending in the train of New Lord Mayor,
Bright as on New-year's day the Laureat Player.

Grub-street,   MAEVIUS.
Oct. 27, 1731.

Index

The index aims to be useful and selective, rather than daunting and exhaustive. This has meant imposing these limitations: (1) References to Grub Street are not entered, since they occur on virtually every page. (2) References in the notes are ignored. (3) Ordinarily, figures mentioned in passing on a single occasion are omitted. (4) Streets and districts have been gathered together in the entry on 'London' and only those with an important literary bearing have been included.